MW01639787

This volume is dedicated with deep affection to the memory of Franz Boas, a beloved and loving grandfather who was a lifetime inspiration for me.

Oil painting of Franz Boas by Maxwell N. Boas (2002) after a photograph by Wilhelm Fechner.

# FRANZ BOAS
## 1858-1942
## AN ILLUSTRATED BIOGRAPHY

Norman Francis Boas, M. D.

Mystic, Connecticut
2004

FIRST EDITION

Library of Congress Control number: 2004096865

ISBN 0-9672626-2-3

This book is printed on acid-free paper.

SEAPORT AUTOGRAPHS PRESS
6 Brandon Lane
Mystic, Connecticut 06355
www.seaportautographs.com

# CONTENTS


| Chapter | | Pages |
|---|---|---|
| FOREWORD | | vi |
| PREFACE | | viii |
| I. | Days of Youth in Germany. | 1 |
| II. | University Days – Plans for the Future. | 20 |
| III. | Expedition to Baffin Island – 1883-1884. | 41 |
| IV. | Immigration and Early Days in America. | 72 |
| V. | Clark University and the Museum Years. | 98 |
| VI. | Vacations at Lake George, New York. | 139 |
| VII. | Columbia University – The Early Years. Professor of Anthropology. | 163 |
| VIII. | Columbia University – Later Years. Ordeals of the 1920s. | 203 |
| IX. | Political Activism and Retirement. | 232 |
| X. | The Legacy of Franz Boas. | 262 |
| EPILOGUE | | 271 |
| GENEALOGY | | 289 |
| INDEX | | 297 |

# FOREWORD

Dr. Norman Boas is to be congratulated for undertaking to write a biography of his famous grandfather Franz Boas. Others have written about Franz Boas the pioneering anthropologist and scientist, who was born in Germany in 1858, moved to the United States in 1886, taught for nearly forty years at Columbia University, published 650 books and articles, and died in 1942. Norman Boas adds a new dimension. While he discusses Franz Boas's academic and scholarly career in considerable detail, he places prime focus upon Franz Boas the devoted family man and public citizen who "dedicated his life to the welfare of mankind." Norman Boas was twenty years old when Franz Boas died more than sixty years ago, and he knew his grandfather intimately. He thus brings a very valuable personal touch to his subject. This personal touch is especially helpful to readers in the twenty-first century, since almost all of Franz Boas's colleagues and students have now died. Furthermore, Norman Boas has profusely illustrated his biography with over 150 photographs and prints, which greatly add to the depth and variety of his narrative.

Dr. Norman Boas has drawn upon a wide variety of archival sources, and has also made interesting use of Boas papers and photograph albums preserved by various members of his family, in writing his biography. But his chief source is the massive collection of Franz Boas papers housed at the American Philosophical Society, the oldest learned society in America. This magnificent collection was given to the APS Library in 1946 by Franz Boas's children, Helene Boas Yampolsky, Ernst P. Boas, and Franziska Boas. It is very appropriate that the Boas papers are housed at the American Philosophical Society, because Franz Boas was an active participant in the intellectual life of the APS for fifty-five years. He presented his first paper at a Society meeting (his topic was the ethnology of British Columbia) in November 1887 when he was twenty-nine years old—only a year after his immigration to the United States. He was elected to membership in the Society in 1903 at the age of forty-five. And he read his last paper at a Society meeting (his topic was Individual, Family, Population and Race) in November 1942 when he was eighty-four years old—only a month before his death.

The legacy of Franz Boas lives on at the APS, where we have assembled important manuscript collections documenting the careers of a number of his students and colleagues. Every year scholars come to our Library to study the Boas Papers and to gain new insights into the history of anthropology in the early twentieth century. And now, thanks to Dr. Norman Boas, we have yet another fresh perspective on the life and work of this fascinating man.

Mary Maples Dunn Richard S. Dunn
Co-Executive Officers
American Philosophical Society

# PREFACE

Recollections of Franz Boas, who died sixty-two years ago, must be culled primarily from his writings and from the writings and anecdotes passed on from his students to other generations. There are few of his students, friends, and associates now alive. The most poignant and loving memories of Franz Boas now exist only with his three surviving grandchildren.

In 1992 Barnard College held a one-day symposium on anthropology at which many papers were presented to honor the $50^{th}$ anniversary of the death of Franz Boas – a German tradition. Chaired by Professor of Anthropology Paula Rubell, of Barnard College, it encompassed many phases of his professional life. The Boas descendants were invited, as were one or two of his surviving students. Anthropologists from all over the country participated. The pioneering career and achievements of Boas were clearly acknowledged, but at the same time, there were a few unfriendly assaults on his professional judgments, methodologies, failures to study certain ethnic groups – self-promoting derogatory comments, common to many academic gatherings. These were particularly disturbing to the family. It was apparent that none of the participants knew Franz Boas as a man and thus were unable to appreciate his life and works with a full perspective.

I was honored when Professor Rubell asked me to give the after-dinner speech at a gathering of all of the participants of the daylong session. I spoke of the kind, loving man that I had grown up with and whom I had known for twenty years. I spoke of the joys and tragedies in his life, the lessons he gave us as grandchildren, his stories of life with the Eskimos in the Arctic, with the Indians in the Pacific Northwest, the weekly visits to his home in Grantwood, New Jersey, our summers with him in Connecticut and even some Franz Boas jokes. It was a simple accounting of a cherished relationship. This little talk generated more response than had any of the speeches earlier in the day. It told me that I was one of a very few left who was able to bring the humanitarian Franz Boas back to life – an experience that the audience seemed to appreciate. It was for this reason, more than any other, that I was prompted to write this book. Although this is a biography, it is in part a photographic record of his life, beginning with the early days of photography with carte de visite photographs of the 1860s. We claim no expertise in anthropology, but have given a sketch of his life in a chronological manner with some commentary, annotated with references to the illustrations. We hope that you will come to know Franz Boas better, not only as a pioneer scientist in his field, but as a compassionate human being, a devoted family man, a man who dedicated his life to the welfare of mankind, and who with scientific precision destroyed the myth of racism.

Very few biographies have been written about Boas. Shortly following his death in 1942, Melville Herskovits[a] wrote a brief biography as did George Stocking, Jr.[b] Others have written of Boas through letters and letter-diaries to his family, translated from German, covering his experiences in the Arctic[cd] and Pacific Northwest.[ef] One of the difficulties for most Americans doing biographical work on Boas has been the fact that many of his early personal papers were written (scribbled) in German script and very difficult to transcribe. The most definitive biography to date was written by Professor Douglas Cole.[g] In spite of a labor of over ten years, Cole was only able to complete one volume covering the years, 1858 through 1906. This detailed interpretive biography, is based largely on many unpublished family letters and extensive field research. Cole's tragic death in 1998 has deprived us of his contemplated second volume.

---

[a] Herskovits, Melville J. *Franz Boas -The Science of Man in the Making*, Charles Scribner's Sons, New York & London, 1953

[b] Stocking, George W., Jr.,. Editor, *The Shaping of American Anthropology, 1883-1911.* Basic Books, Inc. New York, 1974.

[c] Müller-Wille, Ludger. Editor. *FRANZ BOAS Among the Eskimos of Baffin Island, 1883-1884.* University of Toronto Press, Toronto, Buffalo, London, 1998

[d] Cole, Douglas & Ludger Müller-Wille. *Franz Boas" Expedition to Baffin Island, 1883-1884. Études / Inuit / Studies 8,* No. 1:37-63, 1984.

[e] Rohner, Ronald P. Editor. *The Ethnography of Franz Boas,* University of Chicago Press, Chicago & London, 1969.

[f] Codere, Helen. Editor. *Kwakiutl Ethnography*, University of Chicago Press, Chicago & London, 1966.

[g] Cole, Douglas - *Franz Boas - The Early Years 1858-1906*, Douglas & McIntyre, Vancouver & Toronto and University of Washington Press, Seattle & London, 1999.

This volume encompasses a chronology of Boas's entire life, highlighting the most significant events in his career and personal life. We have also included brief biographical sketches of many individuals who played an influential role in his life. This of course includes his parents, siblings, children, and in-laws. Special emphasis is placed on the influence that Abraham and Mary Putnam Jacobi, Ernst Krackowizer and Carl Schurz had on Boas. Also included in this category are George Hunt and others in the Pacific Northwest with whom he worked for so many years. Presented are backgrounds of his professional mentors, from Rudolph Virchow to Frederick Ward Putnam, his associates at the Smithsonian Institution, American Museum of Natural History and Columbia University. Many of his outstanding students are also cited.

His thirty summers vacationing at Lake George, New York are detailed from extensive family records.[h] It was a gathering place for the Boas, Krackowizer, Jacobi, Schurz, Theodore Meyer and Willy Meyer families. Included are family photographs, many of which have never been published. The Boas tragedies of the 1920s and the medical history of Franz are expanded on for the first time, as are profiles and interrelationships of his children and grandchildren.

When Franz Boas died, his professional library was sold by his surviving children, Helene Yampolsky, Ernst Boas and Franziska Boas, to Northwestern University, where a special collection was established in his honor. Boas's children gave virtually all of his professional papers, correspondence, artwork and photographs to the American Philosophical Society (A.P.S.) of which Franz Boas had been a member. There are well over one hundred photographs in this A.P.S. collection, some of which are unpublished. Many are presented here. We are grateful to Murphy Smith, Stephen Catlett, and Beth Carroll-Horrocks, former manuscript librarians at the A.P.S.; and to Scott de Haven, assistant manuscript librarian, for their assistance in reviewing the Boas papers and for preparing copies of these photographs for our use. We also wish to thank Robert Cox, Keeper of Manuscripts of the A.P.S., for his great help in completing our studies at the Library of the A.P.S. We would especially like to thank Mary Maples Dunn and Richard S. Dunn, Co-Executive Officers of the American Philosophical Society for preparing the Foreword to this volume. A number of photographs were

---

[h] Boas, Norman F. & Barbara L. Meyer. *ALMA FARM, An Adirondack Meeting Place.* Published by Boas & Meyer, Mystic, Connecticut and Bolton Landing, New York, 1999.

obtained from the Smithsonian Institution through the courtesy of Paula Richardson Fleming, Photograph Archivist, National Anthropological Archives. Some were reproduced from glass negatives. We have also included photographs from the Esther Goldfrank collection in the Smithsonian anthropology collection. She was a student and friend of Franz Boas. Barbara Mathé, Museum Archivist and Head of Library Special Collections at the American Museum of Natural History, kindly furnished us with all the known photographs of Franz Boas in their collection, for which we are very grateful. We also wish to express our gratitude to members of Clark University: Thomas M. Dolan, Senior Vice President; William A. Koelsch, Professor of English, and Dorothy E. Mosakowski, Coordinator of Archives and Special Collections, for their cooperation in supplying us with photos and pertinent literature on Franz Boas. Theta Curri of the Historical Society of Bolton, New York kindly furnished us with photographs of Abraham Jacobi.

Many of the family photographs came from Helene Yampolsky's album, later passed on to her sister Franziska Boas and now in the possession of Franziska's daughter, Gertrud (Trudel) Michelson. Some came from the collection of Barbara L. Meyer, granddaughter of Helene Krackowizer Meyer, sister and sister-in-law of Marie and Franz Boas, respectively. We are especially grateful to Trudel and Barbara for supplying photographs and family letters used in this volume. Dr. Valerie Pinsky, daughter of Trudel, and former research assistant at the Smithsonian Institution and the American Museum of Natural History, kindly directed us to archival resources at these institutions. This author as well as his family took a number of photographs presented here; most are unpublished. The late Donald P. Boas, Barbara Boas Crutchley, and the late Philip Yampolsky, other grandchildren of Franz Boas, and Judith O'Brien, granddaughter of Emil Krackowizer, were also very helpful with their recollections, letters, and photographs that have been included here. Raymond Boas was particularly helpful with his literary expertise and advice in the preparation of this volume.

My grandson, Maxwell Norman Boas, recently completed a large oil painting of my grandfather, Franz Boas. We agreed that it should represent a period of his life when he was most productive as a scientist. It is based in part on a photograph taken by Wilhelm Fechner in Berlin between 1900 and 1910. Max has produced a fine likeness, which I am delighted to include with this volume.

Professor Rita Terris of Connecticut College and Professor Thomas Huber of Middlebury College contributed greatly to this narrative by translating the Boas articles in the *Berliner Tageblatt* and family letters. Dr. Hans Nordsiek, former archivist and Dr. Monika M. Schulte, present archivist of the Town of Minden, have been very helpful in supplying us with references and photographs for this work.

In writing this volume I have been inspired by relationships that have evolved from this project. These were the outcomes of meetings and conversations with the late Professor of History, Douglas Cole, of Simon Fraser University, Professors of Anthropology Helen Codere of Brandeis University, Paula Rubell of Barnard College, Herbert Lewis of the University of Wisconsin and Professor of Geography, Ludger Müller-Wille of McGill University. I also wish to acknowledge friendships that further encouraged me in this project, including those with Gloria Webster, her late mother, Agnes Cranmer, granddaughter of George Hunt, and their family of Alert Bay as well as Hunt descendants in Fort Rupert, British Columbia. Aldona Jonaitis, Professor of Anthropology at the University of Alaska, has been another inspiration with her excellent publications on the art and artifacts of the Indians of the Pacific Northwest. Her magnificent orchestration of "Chiefly Feasts," a traveling exhibit of the Boas-Hunt collection of the American Museum of Natural History in New York, is deeply appreciated.

Barbara Johnson Boas, my daughter, was a valued editor of this manuscript. She corrected missed ambiguities and style and offered many other valuable suggestions. My wife, Doris W. Boas, served as my research associate in expeditions to various archival collections and spent countless hours in proofreading and making needed revisions and corrections in the text. I am most grateful and indebted to both for their help.

Norman F. Boas, M.D.

# CHAPTER I

## DAYS OF YOUTH IN GERMANY

Franz Boas was born in the walled city of Minden, Westphalia, an enclave with some fortresses dating to the 13th century. The recorded history of Westphalia (western plain) began about the time of Charlemagne (ca.800 A.D.). In the 11th century this geographical area was a portion of the early duchy of Saxony. Westphalia was separated from Saxony in 1180, adopted its own constitution, and was governed, under the church, by a marshal who was also a municipal officer. This system continued until 1803 when the church lands were secularized and the duchy of Westphalia was given to Hesse-Darmstadt. It was during the latter part of this period that records of the early ancestors of Franz Boas began to appear. In 1814, after its seizure by Napoleon and the after the brief rule of King Jerome, Westphalia became a Prussian province. In 1815 the Prussians built a wall around the city of Minden for protection against the Hanover and the French armies.

At the time of the birth of Franz Boas, on July 9, 1858, Minden was a small industrial city. It lies 45 miles west northwest of Hanover on the west side of the Weser River and has been an important trading center since the eighth century or earlier. In the 19th century, Minden was a center for shipbuilding, the manufacture of linens, glass, other industrial products, and had several breweries.

In the opening of Franz Boas's curriculum vitæ, written at the completion of his Gymnasium (high school) education in Minden, he wrote, "My name is Franz Boas and I am the son of the merchant M. Boas and his wife Sophie Boas nee Meyer of Hebrew religion."[1]

This document is lengthy, somewhat disorganized, but an invaluable autobiographical account of his life to that time. In later years, Boas rarely reflected on his youth. Additional detailed accounts of this period may be found in letters, particularly the correspondence written by Franz, his parents and sister Antonie (Toni) to one another.[1,2]

Franz Boas's earliest known forebear, on his father's side, was Heineman (ca.1650-ca.1710), who lived in Werther in the Rhineland. Franz's grandfather, Feibes Boas (1798-1836), was born in Lübbecke where he apprenticed in business with his father. Feibes married Caroline Frank of Minden and moved there in 1821, establishing the Boas line in Minden. Here he became the proprietor of a general store that had belonged to his father-in-law, Joseph Meyer Frank, specializing in textiles and catering primarily to farmers and the working class. Feibes died of tuberculosis in 1836 at the age of 38. Following his death, his family continued to operate the business for a number of years. Feibes and Caroline had eight children including Meier, the father of Franz Boas.[3] All of their sons entered business, Max in Paris, Salomon in Berlin; Meier and Aron remained in Minden.

On his mother's side, the first authenticated ancestor of Franz Boas was Jonas Meyer (1723-1784) of Petershagen. His grandson, Jonas Meyer (1787-1851) and his wife, Jette (Henriette) Menke, the grandparents of Franz Boas, moved to Minden early in the 19th century where they raised eleven children, including Sophie, the mother of Franz Boas.[4]

Minden had a central marketplace (Marktplatz), which was the focal point of commerce and community activities in the 19$^{th}$ century. Most of the Boas and Meyer homes and shops were located on or within a few paces of the Marketplace. The Feibes Boas building was on Kleiner Domhof (Figure 1), just east of the town hall and diagonally across the street from the cathedral (Dom).[5] Many years later, with obvious nostalgia for his home town, Franz Boas had a bookplate designed by his daughter, Franziska, that showed the Minden Cathedral as seen through an archway of the town hall (built ca.1280) (Figure 2).

The birthplace of Franz Boas was a building on the east side of Die Scharnstrasse, which was one of two parallel streets running north from the market-place to the Poos. Scharnstrasse ran past the west side of the town hall (Figure 3).[a] Prior to that time the Meier Boas family lived on Ritterstrasse "in the upper city."[5] The second home of Franz was on Kampstrasse, a block to the west of the Marketplace, where his family shared the first floor with Meier's brother, Aron. At the age of three, Franz and his family moved to his third home, Number 166/167 "on the market," located in the middle of the west side of the Marketplace (Figure 4). It had been the home of Jonas and Jette Meyer, the parents of Sophie Boas. When they both died in 1851, ownership of the house was passed on to their six children who eventually quitclaimed their interest in the property to Abraham, the only son to remain in Minden. It was here that the Meier

---

[a] The house, which was the birthplace of Franz Boas, was bombed and destroyed by the Allies during World War II, as was the building to the west that had been the home of Franz's paternal aunt, Emelie Löwenbaum. The town hall and the Minden cathedral were damaged but restored. After the war, the remains of the narrow Löwenbaum building and the buildings to the north were demolished to make Scharnstrasse a wider thoroughfare.

Boas family lived for the next 17 years, paying rent to Abraham. This large rambling four-story building was shared with Abraham (Onkel Hamster) and Bertha Meyer and their children, Willy, Theodor, Julius, and Adele.[5]

Figure 1. Minden home and store of Feibes Boas, with a steep tiled roof, is on the left. Note the high-hipped roof of the Town Hall behind the store. Photographer: T. Hülsenbach, Minden, ca.1900 (American Philosophical Society).

Willy, born the same year as Franz, was his constant playmate. A large family surrounded Franz, including more distant relatives, the Menkes and Maasses. In later years, all of these Meyer children immigrated to America, where they maintained close family ties. Franz wrote in his curriculum vitae, "My early childhood I spent happily with my sisters in my parents' house..."[1,5]

Figure 2. Bookplate of Franz Boas designed by his daughter, Franziska, in 1923. A View of the Minden Cathedral through an archway of the Town Hall (NFB).

Their last home, a mansion by comparison, was referred to as "Villa Boas." Between 1874 and 1875 the Prussian wall that surrounded Minden was torn down. Most of the site of the wall was preserved as open space, but the elimination of the wall opened up the surrounding countryside for residential development. In 1878 Meier Boas built a house at Marianstrasse 19 on a lot he had acquired, which straddled a portion of the site of the old wall. When the house was completed, Franz had barely moved in before he had to leave for Heidelberg (Figure 5).[6] The only time that he actually lived in the house was during his army service when he was stationed in Minden for one year.[a]

Figure 3. Birthplace of Franz Boas on Die Scharnstrassse. The building in the right foreground is the Town Hall. The Boas home is fourth on the right, the one with the lowest roofline. Lithographer: Ernst Höfer (Kommunalarchive, Minden).

[a] The Boas house on Marianstrasse was torn down in 1980, despite protests of local citizens. An apartment complex now covers the site.

Figure 4. The Marketplace in Minden, ca.1840. The house on the extreme left was the home of the Boas family from 1861 until shortly before Franz left home for Heidelberg. Lithograph by Sickert (Kommunalarchiv, Minden, A I 62a).

The sister of Meier Boas, Emelie Boas Löwenbaum, lived in the upper stories of a narrow four-story building at the north end of the Marketplace, across the street from the town hall (Figure 4). The cigar store of Herrn Stratmann was on the first floor. After Feibes Boas died, Emelie helped her mother, Caroline, manage the store. Thus, there was a strong presence of the Boas and Meyer families in downtown Minden for many years.

The oldest known Jewish congregation of Westphalia was formed in about 1550 in an overwhelmingly Protestant and Roman Catholic community. By the end of the 18th century, there were no more than a few dozen Jewish families in the Minden area and very few in Westphalia. In 1714, a charter issued for the Jews of the Prince-Diocese of Minden listed only twelve Jewish families, nine of them in Petershagen. During the 18th century and probably earlier, it was necessary for Jews to register, obtain permission to settle in towns, marry and procure special permits to buy a house in a residential area.[3] In 1859, shortly after the birth of Franz Boas, there were about 200 Jews in Minden out of a total population of 12,252. Most were merchants; a few were bankers and others tradesmen – most were successful businessmen.[5]

Figure 5. The home of Meier and Sophie Boas in Minden as seen in 1881 (NFB).

Upon the signing of the peace treaty between France, Germany and Russia on August 18, 1807, the kingdom of Westphalia was created by Napoleon I. He installed his brother, Jerome, as king. One of the first actions taken by the new order was to grant Jews full rights of citizenship and require that they adopt surnames. Prior to that time they were referred to by their given names only. Responding to this new edict, Franz Boas's great grandfather, Bendix Feibes Aron of Lübbecke assumed the surname Boas for his wife, himself and seven children. It was presumably chosen from the biblical name in the Book of Ruth.[4]

Franz Boas's father, Meier (or Meyer) Boas (1823-1899), was a successful merchant in Minden (Figures 6). During his early mercantile career, from the time of his marriage to Sophie Meyer in 1851, he owned a dry goods and clothing establishment. It was considered one of the finest shops in town.[5] When Franz was about six years old, his father discontinued his retail business and became an exporter of fine goods to his brother-in-law, Jacob Meyer, in New York. During his years at home, the Franz Boas family lived in comfortable circumstances.

Whereas Franz's father was a successful breadwinner, he left no record of intellectual pursuits. According to Franz, his father was a "liberal," but left active participation in liberal causes to his wife, Sophie (1828-1918). Sophie Boas, on the other hand, was very accomplished, a liberal activist, and a scholarly woman (Figures 7). Franz was reared in a home in which, "the ideals of the Revolution of 1848 were a living force..."[5-7]

Figures 6 & 7. Carte de visite photographs of Meier Boas, ca.1865 and Sophie Boas, ca.1860-65 (American Philosophical Society).

The liberal activism that supported the Revolution of 1848 was a motivating force in the Boas household, even years after the birth of Franz Boas. His mother Sophie, as well as Fanny Meyer, sister of Sophie, were close friends and supporters of leading Prussian participants in the Revolution, Abraham Jacobi, Carl Schurz and Gottfried Kinkel (Figure 15).[8]

The names of Jacobi, Schurz and Krackowizer (Franz Boas's future father-in-law) will appear again and again in this narrative. The three escaped to America where they became inseparable friends for the rest of their lives. They had shared similar experiences during the Revolution, were all liberal activists, humanitarians and powerfully motivated to participate in American democracy. They set standards that Franz Boas followed for the rest of his life.

Abraham Jacobi (1830-1919), Franz's uncle by marriage, became the first pediatric specialist in America and held the first university chair of pediatrics in his adopted country. His name will reappear at virtually all-important turns in the career of Franz Boas. He was one of the most dedicated and greatest physicians of his time. Jacobi was born in Hartum, a tiny village near Minden. He was the son of Eliezer and Julia Abel Jacobi, a poor Jewish family. They lived in a small, crude "peasant dwelling," a type of building that "had changed very little since the year 1000 . . . they had fireplaces in the center from which the smoke did its best to escape through a hole cut in the roof overhead . . ." Usually without windows, according to Jacobi, "by the time I was born . . . things had improved a little for our home boasted of some small windows with real glass panes"[9,10]

Young Abraham was a sickly child. As a pediatrician, many years later, he concluded that he had suffered from rickets, attributed to poor nutrition and lack of fresh air. Elementary education was not a universal right in Prussia, and deliberately so, to keep the masses ignorant. Although poor, his mother made great sacrifices to assure that he had a proper education. Her neighbors had "warned her . . . not to waste her time on this baby who was far too sickly to live very long."[10] Julia Jacobi "scraped the bottom of the till" to see that her son received an elementary schooling. Abraham responded by working very hard and was able to make his way through the Gymnasium in Minden. His father, Eliezer, was a good friend of Jonas Meyer. While in Minden, Abraham spent much of his time with the Meyer family.[5] It was here that he met Fanny Meyer, later to become his wife. On leaving Minden, he matriculated at the University of Greifswald in Pomerania and in 1851 earned his medical degree at Bonn University. During these years he was exposed to teachers and associates who were intellectually challenging and pro-revolutionary.

It should be noted and emphasized that the discontent in Europe toward the end of the 1840s, touched every soul on the continent, leading to the Revolution of 1848. Although these events happened before Franz Boas was born, the consequences of these uprisings profoundly and permanently affected the lives of millions of Europeans, including the Boas, Meyer, Jacobi families, and many of their friends. The Revolution resulted in a massive exodus of Europeans to America from the mid to late $19^{th}$ century. Included were many of the intelligentsia who sought an escape from the repressive regimes of their countries. It was particularly true of many of the pro-revolutionaries who were forced to escape, and others who sought the freedom that democracy in America offered.[11]

The Revolution of 1848 was, in fact, a multitude of revolutions in the many states and countries of Europe. All it needed to start was a precipitating event. This occurred in 1848 when the French overthrew the monarchy of Louis Philippe. The masses responded, but leadership rested on the intelligentsia. University teachers, students, and some liberal bureaucrats represented them in many instances. Abraham Jacobi was among this group in Prussia that also included Carl Schurz, Karl Marx, Friedrich Engels, and Gottfried Kinkel. Ernst Krackowizer, Franz Boas's future father-in-law, led a student uprising in Vienna; other leaders included Louis Blanc in France, Louis Kossuth in Hungary, and Giuseppe Mazzini in Italy.[12-14]

The lives of the Boas, Meyer, Jacobi, Krackowizer and Schurz families became interwoven as a result of intermarriages and through their mutual experiences during the Revolution of 1848.

Schurz (1829-1906) was born in Liblar, a small town in Prussia. He became a leading scholar, journalist, liberal activist, statesman, soldier and advisor to five presidents of the United States. After Franz Boas arrived in America, he was befriended by Schurz and shared summer vacations with the Schurz family at Lake George, New York. Schurz's parents were Catholic and of modest means. His father was a schoolmaster and his mother was the daughter of a tenant farmer. Carl was raised in a portion of an old castle that his parents rented as a home. After attending the Gymnasium, he matriculated at Bonn University in 1846. He came under the influence of Gottfried Kinkel, professor of rhetoric. At the beginning of the Revolution of 1848, he joined Kinkel in the publication of a liberal newspaper. It became his platform as a leader in the Revolution.[13,14]

The Revolution was short-lived because of the overwhelming odds against its success. It was during the Revolution that Abraham Jacobi first met Carl Schurz. Fearful of capture, Schurz was able to escape the country. Jacobi, Kinkel and Marx were all imprisoned. Jacobi was arrested in Berlin, held without charges and then released. Soon thereafter, he was again apprehended, charged with *lèse majesté* (treason) and imprisoned for two years in Minden. When he was first captured, letters were found in his possession from Fanny Meyer and Sophie Boas. The women were investigated for their political sympathies, but were found innocent of wrong-doing.[5] When Schurz returned to Germany in 1850, he conspired with Jacobi and others to free Kinkel from Spandau Prison. With the help of a prison guard, Kinkel was taken to an attic of the prison where he was lowered by rope to a wagon passing below, and carried away to freedom. Schurz became a folk hero throughout the world for this daring exploit.

After his successful attempt to rescue Kinkel from Spandau prison, Schurz and Kinkel's family escaped to Paris. When the French revolutionary efforts collapsed, their views became an embarrassment to the government. Accordingly, they left for London where Schurz stayed with the Kinkels. While he was there, Johanna Kinkel gave Schurz piano lessons; as a good student, piano playing became a lifelong passion with him. In London he met a young German woman, Margarethe Meyer. They were soon married and sailed to America on a passage said to have been paid for by Sophie Boas.[14,15]

In 1853, the authorities planned to release Jacobi from jail and to "re-arrest him on another charge." Upon his release, a friendly jailer told Jacobi of this plan. To escape recapture, Jacobi sailed to England where he visited Karl Marx and stayed with Friedrich Engels in Manchester, both of whom had also fled Germany. Jacobi attempted to establish a medical practice in Manchester. With little success, he left England and sailed to America on the three-masted schooner *Trimountain.* Once he was settled in New York and had established himself in practice, Fanny Meyer (1833-56), his sweetheart from Minden, joined him. They were married in New York. As a brother-in-law to Sophie Boas, Jacobi came to know the Meier Boas family intimately, established a relationship between the Jacobi, Boas and later, the Krackowizer families, which has continued into the 21th century.

Although he lived in America, Jacobi's life became interwoven with that of his nephew, Franz Boas. He played a significant role in directing the future of this young man. Respecting the aspirations of Franz, Jacobi encouraged Meier not to direct his son into the field of medicine but to permit him to develop his interests in the natural sciences. He later introduced Franz to his future bride.

Jacobi immigrated to America about a year after the arrival of Schurz. They became lifelong friends and each played a major role in helping Franz Boas establish himself in America. After his arrival in New York in 1886, Boas received financial assistance from his uncle who also introduced him to scientific colleagues. Jacobi was a lifelong mentor of Franz and played a profound role as a surrogate father.[8]

Franz Boas was one of six children. His siblings were Helene, Antonie (Toni), Ernst, Hedwig (Hete) and Änne (Aenne) Margaret. Helene died at the age of five before Franz was born and Ernst died in infancy in 1860. Franz wrote,

> I have only very dim recollections of him, but through his death a brother

> was taken from me forever; later to be sure, I got two little sisters, but I never again have had a brother. Through the lack of a brother, my life has become very different than it formerly would have appeared, as I was always thrown more on my own resources than on others . . .[1]

Undoubtedly anticipating the needs of her growing children, Sophie Boas organized the first Froebel Kindergarten in Minden in 1860, based on the principals of Friedrich Froebel who founded the first kindergarten in Blandenburg in 1837. In 1849 he founded a kindergarten training school. It is very likely that Sophie Boas became involved in this movement and founded the first kindergarten in Minden following a course she took under Froebel. The location of her school was in premises provided by a local druggist.[5,6] In reflecting on his years in his mother's kindergarten, Franz wrote,

> We three, my sisters and I, went to the kindergarten together which had been founded shortly before. There we were entertained with little games and tasks, which at the same time were directed toward awakening our minds especially our interest in nature by games, which imitated animal life, and by keeping our own flowerbeds which we had to sow, water, and care for. I do not know whether my love for nature which I possessed very early and still do possess stems from this or whether it was awakened at home where it was my mother who kept us children busy not only as in kindergarten but also made us observe nature . . .[1]

Willy Meyer, the son of Sophie Boas's brother, Abraham Meyer, in addition to being a playmate of Franz Boas at home, spent a summer in Clus with Franz in about 1862. After completing his primary schooling in Minden, Willy obtained his undergraduate and medical education at Bonn University which led to an appointment on the faculty there.[9,10] It was at Bonn that he became an assistant to Professors Busch, Madelung and Trendelenburg. In 1884, Willy's uncle, Abraham Jacobi, convinced him to immigrate to New York where he became an eminent surgeon.[4,10,16] Willy was to share his American experience with his cousin Franz, his uncle Jacobi, and his uncle, Jacob Meyer (Uncle "Kobus") (1834-1906). Jacob Meyer also immigrated to New York, where he became a wealthy importer of fine lace and dry goods from his brother-in-law, Meier Boas, his exporting agent in Germany.

Since both grandparents of Franz were orthodox Jews, his parents, Meier and Sophie, had formal religious schooling. Cole noted that, in spite of their upbringing, his parents' "assimilation into German and secular culture overwhelmed the influence"[5] that his paternal grandparents had in their home. By the time Franz was born, Meier and his family retained only "'an emotional affection for the ceremonial [religion] of his parental home,' and Boas was born free..."[8] Although Franz had formal religious instruction and was confirmed at the age of 13, his attachment to his cultural roots did not encompass a true commitment to a religious faith. In his curriculum vitæ, Franz wrote, "I was spared the struggle against religious dogma that besets the lives of so many young people."[8]

Franz Boas kept his own photograph album and scrapbook, which covered the period from 1863 to 1881. In it are pressed flowers, some of which he collected during his kindergarten years[a]. His curiosity led him to collecting rocks that he brought home from his sojourns on the shores of the North Sea. Franz was a handsome youngster. With the advent of carte de visite photographs in 1859, the Meier Boas family arranged to have a number of family pictures taken while this type of photography was in its

Figures 8 & 9. Carte de visite photographs of Franz Boas. Left: ca.1863. Right: 1868 (American Philosophical Society).

---

[a]Franz Boas's album includes scenes in Minden of the Weser River, an overview of the town, the cathedral, Marketplace, 1875 Gymnasialcapelle, railroad station, post office, the Boas home on Marienstrasse as well as scenes from his trips to Heligoland (1868 & 1871), Jena (1871 & 1872), university scenes at Bonn, Heidelberg and Kiel, a student group, a statue of Beethoven, scenes in Berlin (1881) and other unidentified places (Gertrud Michelson).

infancy (Figures 8 & 9).

There were later photographs of his grammar school class in the school year 1869-70 (Figure 10) and of Franz with his younger sisters in 1871 (Figure 11).

Figure 10. Franz Boas's Minden grammar school class of 1869-70. Franz is standing in the top row on the extreme right (American Philosophical Society).

It was probably his mother, more than anyone else, who encouraged Franz to study the natural sciences. During his years in elementary school and in the Minden gymnasium, Franz Boas had frequent illnesses, which resulted in a number of interruptions to his education. At age six, his doctor sent him to Clus to recuperate from an illness. On other occasions, because of ill health, he was sent to the Heligoland, a rocky British isle in the North Sea, and to Jena. The illnesses, at times, were characterized by recurrent headaches, attributed later to "nervous strain." During these periods he had private tutorial lessons. For these reasons was held back in his Gymnasium years because he was unable to gain all the credits he needed to graduate. Throughout his years in the Gymnasium, his grades suffered from these interruptions.

His athleticism began in the Gymnasium. Although small for his age, he often took 3-4 day hikes in the nearby Porta Mountains with his classmates, an activity he was to enjoy for over 60 years. He also skated and participated in other sporting events.

Figure 11. Carte de visite photograph of Franz Boas and his two youngest sisters. On the left is Hedwig (Hete) and on the right, Änna (Aenna) Margaret. Photographer: Friedrich Haack, Jena, 1871 (American Philosophical Society).

At the age of 15, Franz wrote to his sister, Toni, "If I do not become really famous, I do not know what I will do. It would be terrible if I had to spend my life unknown and unregarded . . . what claim can someone like me have upon fame?"[5] This same theme was repeated while he was on Baffin Island ten years later. As he grew older, it became clear that fame was not a specific goal, but incidental to achieving success and recognition for scientific achievements in his chosen field. Toward the end of his school years, his grades improved considerably. His mother considered his mathematical skills those of a "genius." This observation alone convinced her and some of his teachers that he must go to a university. Throughout the recitation of his early life in his curriculum vitæ, one is impressed with his broad educational experience. His enthusiasm for his subjects is evident throughout this narrative. His early fantasies with fairy tales led to seeking adventure by exploring foreign lands. His interests, from the earliest time, were in botany, zoology, geography, astronomy, mathematics and physics.[1,5,8]

> If I should gather the results of the years up to the Secunda from my present point of view, then I must say that through these years the direction of my life till now and in the future was determined. I had taken a look into most of the branches of natural science and was drawn to all of them equally, so that I already saw that not the descriptive part of natural science but the comparative was really my favorite subject . . . These inclinations claimed so much from me that nothing less could interest me and all other fields of knowledge were almost all painful to me.[1]

During the Franco-Prussian War (1870-1871), Prussian troops were stationed in Minden and marched through the streets of the town. These were exciting days for youngsters. Generally oblivious to politics as a youth, Franz Boas could not help but rally to the support of the troops. Attendant to this excitement was the victory over Napoleon III, which resulted in the consolidation of the German Empire.[5]

> The disturbed times naturally filled us terzianer with enthusiasm and we dreamed about all the possible splendid deeds of war which we would have wanted to perform, if we had been big at that time – but the newly acquired unity of the German Reich also inspired us and increased our love for our fatherland and awoke our pride in it. Still the brilliant success in arms of our soldiers made a very great impression on us. I got my first knowledge of political parties at the Paris revolution, which stirred me no less than the war. I followed this with great interest, yet it died out when the big events were over and I again returned to my old work . . .[1]

In time, Boas "discovered" the classics. He read Greek and Latin literature, ancient history and developed a liking for poetry. He was most excited by the writings of Schiller,

> I could hardly tear myself away from "Wilhelm Tell" and "Die Jungfrau von Orleans..." The stormy fire which swept through them tore me with it so that these plays almost became my daily reading . . .[1]

Boas was a prolific reader with a tremendous capacity of recall, an asset that played no small role in his scientific achievements in the years to come.

> I had begun to learn to play the piano early . . . I found . . . pleasure in the works of the old classical masters. After I grew older I played Haydn, Mozart and Beethoven. Yet besides the piano works of these composers I wanted to become acquainted with their orchestral compositions. For that reason I played the four handed arrangements for which one can at least acquire a concept of things . . . My aim is not to play everything really

> beautifully . . . [but to] be able to play well in order to be able to play a few things nicely for some...[1]

As he faced his university years, he wrote,

> Recently the question has become more and more pressing, what I want to become. From youth on, my favorite desire was to be able to study natural science and when I learned mathematics and physics, both these sciences were what appealed to me most. But I cannot carry out these desires, since my father believes that it would be no sort of study for earning my daily bread. For that reason I have decided, if without preference, on applying myself to the subject lying next to my interest, medicine. The chief reason why I have no desire for medicine is that my favorite sciences are the comparative and medicine has little to do with them. Yet in order to hold open the possibility of later perhaps being able to transfer to another subject I will as far as it is possible study mathematics along with it. If I can still apply myself to another study, it must happen in the next two years, for until then I chiefly listen to general natural science lectures. I hope with my whole heart that this desire which determines my whole life will still be fulfilled by me.[1]

Figure 12. The Boas family in their Marianstrasse home, ca.1881. From left to right: Franz, Sophie, Meier (with cigar), Toni and Hete. Note a copy of the *American* Review on the table. The camel in the picture became familiar sight years later in the Franz Boas house in Grantwood, New Jersey (American Philsophical Society).

Meier Boas felt that, as his only son, Franz should become a businessman, or at least train to become a doctor so that he might earn a reasonable income, not only to support himself, but to render financial aid to his sisters, were it to become necessary after he was gone. Meier believed a career in the natural sciences did not satisfy his criteria. As his son's university days came closer, pressure from Sophie coupled with a letter Meier received from Abraham Jacobi in New York, convinced him that his son should embark on a career in natural science and mathematics. In 1877, Franz Boas left the home that he would never forget. (Figure 12).[5]

**References and Notes**

1. Boas, Franz. *Curriculum Vitæ*, ca.1876, in German. From an English translation by Barbara Boas Crutchley – original in the Library of the American Philosophical Society.
2. Boas, Franz. Letters to family. Boas papers in the Library of American Philosophical Society.
3. Brilling, B. *Die Vorfahren des Professors Franz Boas, in Mitteilungen des Mindener Geschitsund Museumvereins*, Volume 38, 103-112, 1966. An early genealogy of the Boas family. The basis of Brilling's observation that Franz was named after his grandfather Feibes is not clear. Feibes and Franz Boas each had the middle name "Uri," which Franz detested and never used. Perhaps this connection is the basis for Brilling's observation. The name Franz is German for Frank and Francis. Franz Boas named a daughter Franziska. This author was given the middle name Francis after his grandfather. A great-great grandson now bears the name Franz Edward Boas.
4. Boas, Norman F. *Boas Family Genealogy 1650-1985*, 14pp, Stonington. Connecticut. Privately printed 1985. Copy in the Library of the American Philosophical Society.
5. Cole, Douglas. *FRANZ BOAS: The Early Years, 1858-1906,* 360pp, Douglas & McIntyre, Vancouver/Toronto & University of Washington Press, Seattle/London, 1999. The first definitive biography of Franz Boas. Tragically, Douglas Cole died after this volume was completed. He had planned to write the second volume, completing the period from 1906 to 1942. He was very generous with us, sharing his research findings on Franz Boas on a number of occasions.
6. Cole, Douglas. *Kindheit und Jugend von Franz Boas, in Mitteilungen des Mindener Geschicts-verreins*, Volume 60, 111-134, 1988. He narrates the early life of Franz Boas.
7. Kardiner, Abram & Edward Preble. *They Studied Man*, The World Publishing Company, Cleveland and New York, 1961. Biographical material on Franz Boas.
8. *Dictionary of American Biography*, 10 volumes and 8 supplements, American Council of Learned Societies, Charles Scribner & Sons, New York, 1958-88. Brief biographies of Franz Boas, Carl Schurz, Abraham Jacobi.
9. Truax, Rhoda. *The Doctors Jacobi*. Little, Brown and Company, Boston

1952. Biographies of Abraham and Mary Putnam Jacobi.

10. O'Brien, Kathryn E. *The Great and Gracious on Millionaires Row - Lake George in its Glory*. North Country Books, Sylvan Beach, New York, 1978. Includes brief biographies of Carl Schurz, Abraham and Mary Putnam Jacobi as well as other distinguished summer residents at Lake George.
11. Robertson, Priscilla. *Revolutions of 1848: A Social History*, 464pp, Princeton University Press, 1952. An extensive view of the conditions in Europe preceding and following the Revolution of 1848 that had a huge impact on the continent and the relocation of thousands of people.
12. Jacobi, Abraham. *Collectania Jacobi*, 8 volumes, edited by William J. Robinson. The Critic and Guide Company, New York, 1909. A classic on the works and addresses of Jacobi, including a biography of Ernst Krackowizer.
13. Schurz, Carl. *The Reminiscences of Carl Schurz*. In three volumes, the McClure Company, New York, 1908-1909. An autobiography, published after his death.
14. Trefousse, Hans L. *Carl Schurz, A Biography*. Fordham University Press, New York, 1998. A definitive biography and a fine supplement to the Schurz autobiography.
15. Yampolsky, Hedwig ("Hete"). Personal communication. She was the granddaughter of Meier and Sophie Boas. According to a story passed down in the family, Sophie helped pay the Schurz fare on the packet ship that carried Carl and Margarethe to America. Trefousse (supra) states that the cost of the voyage on the *City of London* was paid from an inheritance of Margarethe Schurz.
16. Boas, Norman F. & Barbara L. Meyer. *ALMA FARM – An Adirondack Meeting Place*, Boas & Meyer Publishers, Mystic, CT & Bolton Landing, NY, 1999. A narrative of the summer vacation experiences on Lake George, New York, where the Boas, Meyer, Schurz, Jacobi and Putnam families regularly met.

# CHAPTER II

## UNIVERSITY DAYS - PLANS FOR THE FUTURE

In 1877 Franz Boas left Minden to begin his university studies. As was a custom of the time, he matriculated in more than one university, at Heidelberg, Bonn and Kiel, in that order. This permitted the student to be more selective in the choice of his subjects and teachers. A rather complete picture of his student days can be gleaned from the extensive correspondence with his parents, and particularly that with his older sister Toni (Figure 13).[1] She was four years older than Franz, but they had an extremely close relationship, particularly during his Gymnasium days in Minden. His letters to her were far less inhibited than those to his parents.

Figure 13. Carte de visite photograph of Antonie ("Toni") Boas, oldest sister of Franz Boas. Taken on the trip to America ca.1870s. Photographer: W. Kurtz, New York (Gertrud Michelson).

They were lengthy and revealed much of his day-to-day experiences as a student. Most of this correspondence was saved. His younger sisters, Hete and Aenne, were five and nine years younger than Franz, respectively; too young to share the banter and experiences of a university student.

Scholastically, he applied himself with enthusiasm and diligence, but was buffeted from one scientific discipline to another in an attempt to discover a subject that would satisfy his future goals. Much of this was determined by the strengths and shortcomings of the universities he attended. He had an unrelenting passion for his studies.[2,3]

Franz Boas matriculated at Heidelberg in April 1877. Having come from a large family with many associations in Minden, he found it was difficult to make new friends away from home. Not used to the rowdiness, irresponsible behavior, low morals and drinking of many of the students, he joined a student's association (*Burschenschaft*), a social group that held to higher standards and gave him a sense of belonging. He took fencing lessons, not only as a sport, but to be prepared, should he be confronted with a dueling situation. All of the fraternal groups met regularly and practiced fencing, which was essentially face-to-face dueling with sabers. The specific reasons are not clear, but his first dueling encounter almost certainly resulted from insults, probably anti-Semitic. Although he was cut on his forehead, his opponent's face sustained substantially more wounds and disfigurement than he had received.

On one occasion at Heidelberg, although it was not his typical behavior, Franz got drunk in a beer hall with members of his mathematics club. On his way home, he was arrested for extinguishing some gas lamps on the street – not an uncommon student prank. He was, nevertheless, tried in a student court, convicted and sentenced to three days in the student jail, to be served at a later date.[3]

Academically, Boas spent one semester at Heidelberg before transferring to Bonn University. While he was at Heidelberg his teachers included the illustrious chemists Bunsen and Kekulé, as well as Rudolph Clasius who discovered the second law of thermodynamics. Robert Wilhelm Bunsen is noted for his discovery of the elements cesium and rubidium, the invention of the Bunsen (electric) Cell, the Bunsen Burner, and establishing the science of spectroscopy. Friedrich August Kekulé determined the structure of the benzene ring, one of the most important and basic discoveries in organic chemistry.[5] Other teachers included Moritz Cantor in analytical geometry, Kuno Fischer in philosophy, and Immanuel Fuchs in calculus.[3]

In October 1877 Boas transferred to Bonn University. Only two months earlier his closest friend in Minden, Reinhard Krüer, died in a drowning accident in the Weser River. Despondent over this loss and seeking friendships, Franz joined the *Burschenschaften Alemannia*, one of three such student groups on campus. There were two other *Burschenschaften* but the *Alemannia* catered primarily to Westphalia students. They were liberal in their political beliefs and did not discriminate in their selection of fellow students. It was through Willy Meyer, Franz's cousin, also a student at Bonn, that Franz joined this fraternal organization. It only had only twenty to thirty members who were very close and generally discouraged socializing with other students. Only about ten percent of the student body at Bonn belonged to such groups. Others included the *Korps* and *Landsmannschaften*, which were more conservative, aristocratic, and bigoted.[3] While at Bonn, Boas's arrest papers arrived from Heidelberg. Accordingly, the Bonn authorities jailed him in the student prison one weekend as a penalty for his role in the gas light episode in Heidelberg.

Although dueling was illegal at all universities, the authorities generally ignored it. Hostility existed between the *Korps* and the *Alemannia Burschenschaft* (Figures 14 & 15). Insults, probably anti-Semitic in nature, generated by the *Korps* against the members of the *Burschenschaft*, would not pass Boas without a resolute response. On a number of occasions he challenged his opponents and engaged in a half dozen, or more, duels in his university years – honor was at stake.[3]

Figures 14 & 15. Carte de visite photographs of Franz Boas. Left: As a member of the *Alemannia Burschenschaft* at Bonn, ca.1878-79 (Toni Laufs). Right: As a student at Kiel in 1881 (Schmidt & Wegener) (American Philosophical Society).

At Bonn, Boas initially applied himself toward the study of physics and advanced mathematics. He studied under Theobald Fischer, who had a great impact in gradually shifting his interests into physical and cultural geography. As one of very few students who elected to register in Fischer's courses, Boas came to know him as a friend, often visiting the Fischer home.[3]

In 1878 Toni became quite ill with an acute phase of a rheumatic disorder, which she had suffered for some time. In seeking medical help, she consulted with Dr. Friedrich von Esmarch (1823-1908) in Kiel.[5] He was a renowned surgeon and a professor of surgery at Kiel. He engaged in military service with the Prussian army in the Schleswig-Holstein War and was surgeon general in the Franco-Prussian War. At Christmas break in the same year, Franz visited Toni since she was far from home and family. Her condition worsened to the point that Dr. Esmarch operated on her hip to remove "several pieces of bone." By September 1879 Franz felt that he must transfer to Kiel University to be near his sister. He loved Bonn but he felt he had no alternative. At the same time Docent Theobald Fisher also transferred from Bonn to Kiel where he assumed a professorship in geography. This pleased Boas, for he was now able to continue his studies of geography with his mentor. He studied with Fischer during each of his four semesters at Kiel. The weakness of the physics department and the strength of Fischer's geography influenced Boas toward the latter.[3] Thus these fortuitous conditions and Toni's temporary incapacity each became determinants in his life's career.

In 1881 he wrote his doctoral dissertation on "Contributions to the Understanding of the Color of Water." He did extensive laboratory work but found that most of the equipment available was inadequate for the precise photometric measurements required for this study. His analyses and conclusions were based primarily upon theoretical physics. It was nevertheless an early demonstration of his insistence upon seeking scientific proof before drawing conclusions.[3] This was not long after John Tyndall discovered that the blue of the sky was due to diffusion of light caused by particles in the atmosphere.

While he was working on his dissertation Franz Boas wrote five other theses. One was in theoretical physics. He set out to prove that the force of masses is independent of their speed and acceleration. Another dealt with suspended particles being the cause of diffusion of sunlight. In one thesis he addressed the necessity of geography as a foundation of history. In another theoretical paper, a prophetic one, he determined that Greenland could not extend far north beyond latitude 83°. His final thesis established the fact that Talbot's psychophysical law was in need of mathematical verification, proof of which he published the following year.[4]

As in Heidelberg and Bonn, dueling in Kiel was an "honorable" way of responding to personal insults. During the years 1879 to 1882, a wave of anti-Semitism in Prussia developed. It was less evident at the more liberal Heidelberg and Bonn Universities, but was present to a greater extent at Kiel. The Kiel community was more conservative and bigoted. It joined the hysteria of the times, attacking liberal Jews who were beginning to be disproportionately represented in many professions and businesses. In April 1881 Franz wrote to his family,

> I bring home again – for the last time – a few cuts, even one on the nose. I hope you won't concern yourself too much about it, but with the cursed Jewish situation this winter, one could not come through without quarrel and strife.[3]

Through his university years, Boas's duels resulted in multiple scars of "honor." Ten years later, when he was teaching at Clark University, a journalist described these scars,

> On one side of his forehead, near the temple, are three scars, each over an inch in length. Diagonally across the nose is the scar of what must have been a terrible slash that laid open the member and somewhat altered its elevation. Then from one corner of his mouth reaching back to the ear, is the longest and most conspicuous scar of all. Docent Boas must have got a slash that laid open his mouth open clear to the ear, necessitating the kind of attention of a surgeon.[3,6a]

Years later he no longer considered his scars badges of honor and wrote about his "irresponsible life, which would now sicken me in a day."[3] He would not discuss his duels later in life, and when pressed might attribute his multiple facial scars to bear clawings in Baffinland.[7]

Toward the end of his days at Kiel, Boas came under the influence of the neo-Kantian philosopher Benno Erdmann and developed an intense interest in psychophysics, the study of the physical forces that determine the behavior of the human organism. This experience undoubtedly played a role in directing him toward the field of anthropology. In 1882 Franz Boas graduated magna cum laude from Kiel University.

After completing his studies at Kiel, Franz Boas spent the next two years studying and preparing for his future. During this time he served as a "one-year volunteer" in the German army, in the reserve-officer training program, stationed in Minden. This was an option that he earned as a university graduate, as opposed to serving three years in the ranks. His title was "*Gefreiter* [lance-corporal] Boas of the Third Company, Prince Friedrich of the Netherlands (Second Westphalian No. 15) Infantry

---

[a] My recollections include the scars on his nose and the left side of his face, but I never analyzed the extent or degree of these wounds or paid any real attention to them. We were aware of his duels, but they were never a topic of conversation in the family, at least with the grandchildren.

Regiment." It was a position that he accepted as a learning experience. At this time he grew his first mustache, narrow and neatly trimmed (Figure 16 & 17). As the years progressed, it became bushier and he added a small goatee, possibly to hide the saber scar on his lip. For many years he experimented with and without full whiskers and sideburns, as may be seen in the photographs in this volume. In April 1882 he wrote to his uncle Abraham Jacobi,[1,2]

> I have really become so dull from my military duties that I can not longer think myself into my usual train of thought . . . since I now have military service from 7 in the morning to 7 in the evening, and then of course I am too tired . . .

Figure 16. Carte de visite photograph of Franz Boas as a reserve officer in the German Army, 1881 or 1882. Note the saber scars, particularly on the left cheek, from his mustache to the left ear. Photo by J. Hülsenbeck, Minden (American Philosophical Society).

Figure 17. Photograph of Franz Boas (second from left) with his fellow reserve officers in the German Army. Photograph by Hülsenbeck, Minden, 1881 or 1882 (American Philosophical Society).

With his military duties, he became increasingly frustrated at his inability to spend more time on his studies. When not on duty, he was permitted to go home, where on his off-duty hours, he studied intensely. His mother observed, "I have never seen anyone (except Jacobi) work so much . . ." He became so absorbed with his work that he could focus on nothing else. Following his discharge from the army, Franz wrote a number of very lengthy letters to Jacobi, detailing his academic work, future plans and his contemplated arctic field expedition.[1-3] It was also at this time, with Jacobi as his contact in America, that he attempted, without success, to obtain a fellowship at Johns Hopkins University.[3]

Following his military service, he moved to Berlin to prepare for his future. From childhood Boas dreamed of exploring foreign lands. At the age of twelve, in a letter to his sister Toni, he mentioned plans of traveling to the North or South Polar Regions after completing his university years. With his new orientation toward psychophysics, the two years after Kiel found him preparing for such an expedition. He planned the trip to a part of the world where man's physical environment caused extreme adaptive changes, a fertile area for his studies. Franz Boas, as a geographer, was also intrigued by centuries of speculation as to the existence of a Northwest Passage from the Atlantic Ocean to the Far East. He was not interested in seeking this passage as had Cartier, Frobisher, John Davis, Drake, Sir John Franklin, and others before him. He was attracted to this part of the world, in large part, as a virginal area for geographical studies and for examining the manner in which these northern people had adapted to their hostile environment.[2]

In making preparations for his expedition to the Arctic, Franz Boas studied astronomy, meteorology, and magnetism under W. J. Forster at the Berlin Planetarium. He also met Rudolph Virchow in Berlin, an eminent physician, a founder of cellular pathology and Germany's leading physical anthropologist. Virchow became one of his most important early mentors, particularly in the area of anthropometry (Figure 18). After Boas left Germany, their correspondence continued until the death of Virchow in 1901.[8] Boas also met and studied with Adolf Bastian, Germany's leading ethnologist. Bastian was a prolific writer on ethnology and with Virchow and Hartmann founded the *Zeitschrift für Ethnologie*. Franz studied *Inuktitit* (the language of the Inuit), Danish languages and linguistic techniques; he learned photography; he became familiar with Arctic collections at the Berlin Museum where Adolf Bastian assisted him in his preparations. He studied cartography and topographical mapping. The German Polar Commission offered him transportation to Baffin Island as well as scientific instruments and provisions from their research station on the island. His father and his uncle, Abraham Jacobi, provided some of his funds. The remainder came from the *Berliner Tageblatt*, a newspaper that agreed to help subsidize his expedition, in exchange for fifteen articles on his experiences in the Arctic.[9-11] Meier Boas posted a performance bond to the newspaper. Before the departure of Franz Boas, on May 30, 1883, the editor wrote,

Figure 18. Signed cabinet photograph of Rudolph Virchow by Reichard & Lindner, Berlin, 1881 (N.F.B.)

> A voyage to arctic America by a young German, Dr. Boas, should be seen as a further sign of a resurging interest in polar research . . . Our newspaper takes a warm interest in the revival of German polar research . . . We wish to do our part in furthering the great cause. Therefore, we have contacted Dr. Boas and we have succeeded in securing the right to publish his initial reports . . . In turn, we will help Dr. Boas to carry the material burden of his difficult and courageous undertaking. We hope that we will, by actively contributing to polar research, encourage other people to become interested in this area so that our nation will soon, once again, be permanently and actively involved in the "fight for the pole."[11]

It is doubtful that Boas would have subscribed to this editorial, as he had more esoteric goals. It would not be possible to deliver his reports to the *Berliner Tageblatt* from the Arctic; that would have to wait until his return, at which time the newspaper would serialize them.

In 1881, Dr. Abraham Jacobi arrived from New York to spend the summer resting and hiking in the Harz Mountains (Figure 19). Although he had left Germany in 1853, he returned periodically to attend medical meetings and to visit family and friends. At other times, he corresponded with his family as well as with the Meyer and Boas families regularly. On this occasion he arrived with Emilie Krackowizer and two of her daughters, Alice and Marie, who spent the summer with him. More about them will be related shortly.

Figure 19. Carte de visite photograph of Abraham Jacobi, a very scarce image. Mathew B. Brady, New York (Barbara L. Meyer).

After his arrival in America in October 1853, Jacobi failed in an attempt to start a private practice in Boston, as he had a few months earlier in Manchester, England. With a larger German population in New York, he elected to move there, believing that he might be more successful. He opened a medical office in a tenement-house section of the city in lower Manhattan, and started seeing patients for fees of twenty-five and fifty cents.[4,12]

It was only three years later that his wife, Fanny, died in childbirth at the age of 23. Profoundly saddened, but determined to get on with his life, he married Kate Rosalie Rabbe, a native of Savannah, Georgia. She also died prematurely, following a succession of stillbirths. It was not until 1873 that Abraham Jacobi again considered marriage seriously.[13,14]

During the interval, he became deeply involved in the medical and social affairs of his new country. He found slavery repugnant and became an abolitionist. Undoubtedly saddened by two childless marriages, he developed a growing concern for the welfare of disadvantaged children. Jacobi became dedicated to the care of children as a specialty, knowing of many ways to offer them help. He wrote a book on childcare and many scientific papers on childhood diseases. In 1860, he was appointed the first professor of diseases of children in America at the New York Medical College. In this capacity, he established the first free clinic for diseases of children.

In 1865, he held the chair of diseases of children at the University of the City of New York. In 1870, he was appointed professor of pediatrics at the College of Physicians and Surgeons in New York, where he taught until 1902. In 1873, he married Dr. Mary Corinna Putnam, a brilliant young pioneer physician and daughter of publisher George Palmer Putnam, of whom more will be written below (Figure 20). The doctors Jacobi had two children, Ernst and Marjorie.

Early in his career in New York, Abraham Jacobi met Dr. Ernst Krackowizer who became an intimate friend and medical colleague. They were both scholarly scientists and liberal activists who arrived in America about the same time, having shared similar experiences in Europe during the Revolution of 1848. In New York, both participated in the creation of the German Hospital and both were on the staff of Mt. Sinai Hospital in its formative days. They became inseparable friends. When Krackowizer died prematurely in 1875, Jacobi made every effort to console his widow Emilie (Figure 21). His trip to Germany in 1881 with Emilie Krackowizer and daughters, Marie and Alice, was one way of expressing fondness for their family and respect for his beloved friend, Ernst Krackowizer.

In July they met with Sophie, Aenne and Hete Boas for a visit in the Harz Mountains. A few days later, Franz joined them, but he spent most of his time with Marie. On leaving the Harz Mountains, they all traveled to Minden for a two-day visit and then went their own separate ways. The Krackowizers visited Austria, Emilie's former home, and then settled in

Stuttgart where they remained for two years. Alice and Marie attended a school for girls (Figures 22 & 23).

Figure 20. Dr. Mary Putnam Jacobi (Ernest Jacobi McAneny).

Jacobi returned to America and Franz resumed his studies. From 1881 to 1883, Franz served his time with the German Army and was busy studying and making plans in Berlin for his Arctic expedition. As a result, he corresponded with Marie but saw her infrequently.[3] On May 9, 1883, in expressing his feelings toward Marie, Franz wrote to Jacobi,

> I hope that on my return I can come to America, if only because of Marie. Perhaps I am being very foolish in not telling her what I feel about her, but I have decided that it would be wrong for me, because I have no way of knowing how long it would be before I can establish my own home . . .

Acknowledging the difficulties of a Jew attaining a professorship in a Ger-

Figure 21. Emilie Krackowizer, widow of Dr. Ernst Krackowizer and mother of Marie (Gertrud Michelson)

Figures 22 & 23. Marie (left) and Alice Krackowizer (right) by F. Brandseph, Stuttgart, 1882 (Gertrud Michelson).

man university, he added,

> If I count on a professorship here in Germany I must count on at least 5 years from today – with the best of luck . . . I would not hesitate a moment to accept an offered position wherever it might be, whether in America or even further away . . . you must not think that I want to get any job at the cost of my scientific plans; but I feel a strong working-power within me and know for certain that I will make progress with my studies. Good bye dear uncle . . .[1]

In 1883, having not seen Marie for about 6 weeks, he found an excuse to visit her in Stuttgart in the springtime. This was less than three weeks before his departure for Baffin Land. Knowing that he was leaving on a hazardous journey and with no employment, he left Marie without any further commitments. Unable to bear a separation on this note, he wrote to Marie on May 28, "I cannot leave here without telling you how much I love you...you are the substance of my dreams and desires." Marie promptly shared her love with him – they were secretly engaged.

On June 10, 1883, Marie wrote to her sister Helene Krackowizer Meyer in New York,

> I never dared hope that that somebody wanted me, but he does, actually does and – so I suppose I will have to take him. Can you guess who it is? It can't be but one – there is only one Franz Boas! . . . When you, in writing to mother, pitied the poor family for being obliged to let him go on that dreadful expedition, that a good share of the pity belonged to your sister. I had been so unhappy since 1 of April, for how could I know, that he had only come to Stuttgart to see me again before leaving, when he had never told me. Brave boy! He was going to make us both miserable and not say a word until he came back from his Eskimos. But six weeks was enough for him, and I do not believe I could have stood it much longer – so he told me he loved me and let me tell him how I loved him. And now – it will be easier for both of us . . . to wait until the time comes when he shall have finished the great task that is now before him, and come back to me . . .

In keeping her "secret," she added,

> I must ask you Nell, not to speak to any one about this but of course Theo [Theodore Meyer] if you wish, for there is nobody that knows, but mother, Alice [her sister] & I, Franz and his parents and sisters. Dick [her brother] I can tell sometime, when we get back, and Emil & Bessie [siblings] shall know too in time but not now. Dr. Jacobi may speak to you about it, for Franz told him, even before he told me that he fell for me . . . Wait till you know my Franz, you will like him. I am sure . . . Today he leaves for Hamburg - the 20 for his Eskimos . . .[15]

On the same day, Emilie also wrote to Helene,

> I did like him and what I heard from and about him and his family speaks in favor; also the family is very nice and yet I wish Marie's heart would have

> remained free and she could still look into life without concerns. Already one can see the first emotions in her looks; she's lost some weight and is much more serious, even though she is lovely and attentive, as she always was . . . She will be a helping hand for you and her profession with your girls will give her stability and joy. I'm sure of it! It's the best.[15]

After completing her stay in Stuttgart, it was Marie's plan to make use of her schooling to act as a governess to three nieces and a nephew, the children of Helene and Theodore Meyer, while waiting for Franz to return. On July 1, 1883, Emilie wrote to Helene concerning the loss of Abraham Jacobi's only son,

> Frau Boas again wrote me a cordial letter today to inform me of the death of Ernst Jacobi which really shocked them [On June 10, 1883, only three weeks earlier, Abraham and Mary Jacobi's son Ernst died of diphtheria]. Marie informed Franz of the telegram before boarding to Hamburg, but he didn't tell his mother, which is understandable since bad news always travels very fast, too fast . . . How awful for the poor man who surely had placed all his hopes onto this child which he'd been given this late . . . I still have Mrs. Jacobi's words in my ear which she spoke after a serious illness of the little one upon his recovery: "I think the Doctor could not survive the loss of this child. And yet he will have to bear it like other people do. Yet how, that's the question."

In the same letter she added,

> I wonder now whether he'll [Franz] return happily and whether he'll have a better prospect to find a secure existence in America or at a German university. These are serious concerns which occupy me a lot, of course, my dreams of unifying the whole family probably will never materialize.[15]

On July 18, 1883, Franz wrote a letter to his prospective mother-in-law, Emilie Krackowizer. Cited here is a copy she made of his letter of May 24, 1883,

> Dear Madam, Your daughter probably informed you of what happened, that I told her how much I loved her and will love her. I trust you won't scold me that I declared myself under these circumstances. I feel the obligation to explain to you in detail why I acted the way I did and what my prospects for the future are. Even though I didn't want to leave from here without declaring my love for Marie, I don't think I'd be justified to tie her fate to mine, because the journey ahead of me will be long and not totally without dangers, and I don't yet see a permanent position . . . If there aren't any unforeseen accidents, I shall return near the end of October or the end of November 1884. Should I miss all boats, which only could happen by serious accident, I certainly shall return by a ship from the station there in 1885. If I don't return then, one would have to assume that an accident had befallen me . . . I intend to obtain my habilitation and as I can see conditions

> now I would have a position as professor by 1887-88 at the latest.[b] Conditions for me are unusually positive since there are relatively few candidates compared to the number of universities and since I do have connections in important circles. However, this is but one side. When I return from my journey, I'll come to America under any circumstances. In case it should turn out that there are better professional outlooks there enabling me to get a secure position I would not hesitate to work on it . . .

At the conclusion of Emilie's transcription of Franz's letter, she made a number of notations,

> I answered this letter openly and honestly, that I was not overjoyed by this declaration and that I would have wished that he would have held it back and only revealed it after his return, because his expedition is such an insecure one . . . Of course, Marie now felt obliged by their mutual declaration of love and would never be able to act freely . . . the impending departure and the dangers of the whole enterprise would necessarily cast a shadow on Marie's otherwise serene mind and thus all of our lives would be disturbed for an indefinite period of time . . . Otherwise I couldn't raise any objections against him; his behavior has been impeccable and his family was dear and agreeable to me . . . I was hoping from the bottom of my heart that he'd return soon and healthy, and satisfied with the results of his expedition and then be able to found a secure home for which case I'd be glad to promise him Marie's hand in marriage . . . When his declaration of love followed, the fire was kindled in Marie, even though I attempted to put a damper on it and pointed to all the obstacles and difficulties. His declaration made it into a certainty for her that she hadn't dared to admit to herself and it couldn't be helped any more . . . I can't value his expedition to the Eskimos in Baffin Land and only the scholarly world will have to determine that. If only he's lucky with it and returns home healthy, the rest will follow, because he must be extraordinarily effective and ambitious after all I've heard. He made a good personal impression on me, even though he is not good-looking at all and does look rather Jewish . . . His behavior is quiet, not pushy and one gets the impression that he's acquired a general education and isn't one-sided. Thus nothing speaks against him; his family adores him . . . I liked mother Boas [Sophie] from the very beginning and she didn't seem like a stranger at all; our mutual friendship with Jacobi had leveled the ground there . . . Family life there is exemplary without much ado and luxuries and they all like Marie (but then who doesn't?). She'll be greeted there with open arms, without being able to count on riches. We for our part have to hope that it'll be possible to secure a position for Franz in America in order not to lose her to Europe. Certainly, Marie would find her way also in a German university town, since actually she is rather a German

[b] "Habilitation" here signifies attaining the qualifications to obtain a second doctoral degree to teach in a German University.

character and could lead a rather pleasant if modest life as a professor's wife.[16]

On July 19, 1883, Marie wrote another letter to her sister Helene, after Franz had embarked on his expedition, reviewing the previous two years,

> His two prettiest features are, his black curly head and his dark eyes, which aren't a bit *stechend* [piercing], at least not when looking at me . . . He would be real good looking, if he had not those terrible cuts on his nose and his under lip, which he received in his *Studentenjahre* [student years]. I believe he must have been a real *Hitzkopf* [hothead]. But what does it matter what his outward looks are . . . I don't believe I ever saw so much intellect and sentiment combined in a man, with the exception of father [Ernst Krackowizer]. Then his energy and his will are wonderful. I believe he can do anything he wants to. Now I am not talking as *blinde Verliebte* [blindly in love], but every body that knows him, says the same and that is why great hopes are laid upon this expedition of his. I hope and trust with him that it will be best for his, for our future, not only for the *Wissenschaft* [science]. You see, it is so difficult to get an advanced position in Germany nowadays . . . unless you wait endless years, that a young man must . . .take up some thing Franz is now doing, to get at his end faster . . . on this trip he hopes to collect material enough . . . to keep him busy for <u>twenty</u> years . . . The year before this last, he served in the army, and as he says, that was lost for everything else, as their bodily work is so fatiguing lasting from early morning until evening, that one has not the strength and liking for mental work the rest of the time. This drill may be good discipline for some but on the whole I think it is dreadful to pull a young man out of the midst of his studies. I wish I knew what Dr. Jacobi thinks about it, but this dreadfully sad time, of course he can't bear [to] think of anything else that is all happiness, and I shall probably not know anything of his ideas on the subject before I see him again, although Franz and I have written him several times. I should think it might perhaps be the least little consolation to him, that he has been the cause of all our happiness . . . He [Franz] will probably come home on an American whaleboat, so he will come to me first. Perhaps even if he finds good prospects in America, he will stay there.[15]

Towards the end of this letter, she quotes from an earlier letter to her from Franz,

> The materials I'm about to collect up there, especially with respect to the areas of migration and the routes of the tribes will be the basis for study of the dependence of the areas of migration of these people on natural boundaries...This study in turn shall only be an introduction for a more general discussion of questions relating to the lives of people, which means that the attained results from this expedition shall be of utmost importance...I shall have to do battle with this stuff for the next 20 years or so, and as a consequence there will be some readable, but many more unreadable books about the field. I just wish I wouldn't have to write

unreadable ones! At any rate, I'd be delighted to have you know what I intend to do with my work and where it will lead…

In regard to the family tragedy of the Jacobis, many months later, on February 27, 1884, Mary Jacobi wrote to Sophie and Toni Boas in Minden,

It seemed very hard to go on doing the same things after Ernst was gone. The loss of this darling boy has been so overwhelmingly terrible to the doctor that I have scarcely dared to think of myself. You could imagine what the loss of any son must be to him – after he had waited so long for one . . . how sweet he was with his little sister [Marjorie] and me. I have never seen anything more lovely than the life of these two children together . . . When Marjorie first became a little better [she developed diphtheria at the same time as Ernst], she asked for Ernst to come down to her, and kept constantly talking of him, after he had gone away forever. But when I once said to her, do not ask for him any more, he has left us and will not return – she seemed overawed – and has never spoken of him. Though she said once, when I asked her if she had forgotten him, 'No I have not, mama,' very emphatically.

It must be a great trial to you to have Franz go on an Arctic expedition – the only son. I have read some of his letters, with much interest. I trust he may soon be returned to you, and rendered illustrious by his daring adventures . . .[17]

Before returning to America with Alice and Marie in October 1883, Emilie made some observations on Franz's sister, Toni, in a letter written to Helene on 11th of the month from Minden,

To our great surprise Toni Boas waited us there, who could hardly wait to embrace her future sister-in law. Since all of us had to wait a few hours, we stayed together, had lunch and listened to Toni's talk about Franz. She thinks he's the best, noble and most efficient man on earth and only your father [Ernst Krackowizer] could have surpassed him. It's almost too bad how much she venerated him…They [Meier & Sophie Boas] think a lot of their son but he had a hard fight since both of them were against his venture but when he obtained the means by his own hard work, and then spoke about his love, they also made a requirement of absolute silence and only after many debates did they give their permission since they saw him almost failing. Now they're very nice with Marie and do spoil her awfully; they really seem to love her and they're also very nice to Alice and me. Just now we got word that the *Germania* had been signaled off the Northern coast of Scotland. Of course one doesn't know when a message from Franz will arrive here…It's going to be the only message that can arrive from him.

Before they parted, Marie gave Franz, as a present, a 12"x18" black, white, and red Imperial German flag on which she had embroidered "Marie" in large red letters. Originally intended to be flown from his dinghy, he carried this flag wherever he went on his expeditions (Figure 24).[18]

Figure 24. Copy of Marie's embroidered Imperial German flag made by Doris W. Boas. Original in Library of the American Philosophical Society (N.F.B.).

She also gave him a photograph of herself, probably for his birthday, that was framed with a wooden backboard. He carried it with him on all of

Figure 25. Photograph of Marie Krackowizer given to Franz Boas that he carried on his expedition to Baffinland (Gertrud Michelson).

travels in the Arctic. On the board he wrote a legend, which is barely legible now. It is headed "Marie Krackowizer" and refers to his sloop *Germania* and a *Geburtstag*, probably his twenty-fifth birthday which he expected to, but did not, celebrate in Kikkerton, Baffin Island on July 9, 1883 (Figure 25).

**References and Notes**


1. Boas, Franz. Letters to his family in the Library of the American Philosophical Society. This is a very large archive. During the period before the use of carbon paper, Boas often made manuscript copies of his letters.
2. Cole, Douglas. *Kindheit und Jugend von Franz Boas, in Mitteilungen des Mindener Geschicktvereins*, Volume 60, pages 111-134, 1988. A fine accounting of the youth of Franz Boas.
3. Cole, Douglas. *FRANZ BOAS: The Early Years, 1858-1906*. Douglas & McIntyre, Vancouver / Toronto & University of Washington Press, Seattle & London, 1999. Also personal communications during the time he was preparing the biography of Franz Boas.
4. Stocking, George W. Jr. A biography of Franz Boas in the *Dictionary of American Biography*. 10 volumes and 8 supplements. American Council of Learned Societies, Charles Scribner & Sons, New York, 1958-88.
5. *Encyclopedia Britannica*, www.britannica.com, February 2000.
6. *Worcester Daily Telegraph*, March 6, 1891.
7. Kardiner, Abram & Edward Preble. *They Studied Man*, The World Publishing Company, Cleveland and New York, 1961. Biographical material on Franz Boas.
8. Boas, Franz. Correspondence with Rudolph Virchow in the Library of the American Philosophical Society.
9. Cole, Douglas and Ludger Müller-Wille, *Inuit Studies*, Volume 8, Number 1, 1984. Letters, diaries and notes from the Franz Boas expedition to Baffin Island.
10. Müller-Wille, Ludger. *FRANZ BOAS Among the Inuit of Baffin Island 1883-1884. Journals and Letters*. Edited by Ludger Müller-Wille. Translated by William Barr. University of Toronto Press, Toronto, Buffalo & London, 1998. The most extensive publication on the Boas Arctic expedition.
11. Boas, Franz. *Berliner Tageblatt*. Editorial (May 30, 1883) and articles by Franz Boas, 1884 on his Baffin Island expedition. (Library of the American Philosophical Society).
12. Boas, Norman F. & Barbara L. Meyer. *ALMA FARM, An Adirondack Meeting Place*, Boas & Meyer, publishers, Mystic, Connecticut & Bolton Landing, New York, 1999. Includes a brief biography of Abraham Jacobi.
13. Truax, Rhoda. *The Doctors Jacobi*. Little, Brown & Company, Boston, 1952. Biographies of Abraham and Mary Putnam Jacobi.
14. Jacobi, Abraham. *Collectanea Jacobi*, 8 volumes, edited by William J.

Robinson, The Critic & Guide Company, New York, 1909. Includes biographical material on Ernst Krackowizer.

15. Krackowizer, Marie (Boas). Letters to Helene Meyer (Barbara Meyer collection).
16. Krackowizer, Emilie. Letter of Franz Boas copied and notes on Franz and Marie (Barbara Meyer collection)
17. Jacobi, Abraham and Mary Putnam. Papers in the New York Academy of Medicine Library. Personal letters.
18. Krackowizer, Marie (Boas). German flag embroidered with her name across the white center stripe – the flag carried by Franz Boas wherever he traveled on his Arctic expedition.

# CHAPTER III

## EXPEDITION TO BAFFIN ISLAND 1883-1884

On June 20, 1883, Franz Boas sailed down the Elbe River in Germany on the schooner *Germania* on his way to Baffin Island (Figure 26).[a] She was a small vessel with a crew of six, commanded by Captain A. F. B. Mahlstede. The primary purpose of the voyage of the *Germania* was to pick up a German scientific party in Cumberland Sound on Baffin Island for their return to Germany. Franz Boas left with a heavy heart, knowing that he would be out of contact with his family and Marie for a year without any means of communication. As he sailed north he read Marie's farewell letter that closed, "Onward, I wait for you!"[1]

Die Germania am 20. August. in Kikkerton Harbor

Figure 26. Woodcut of the schooner *Germania* on "August 20" moored in Kekerten (Kikkerton) Harbor, Baffin Island, representing a different voyage of the schooner (American Philosophical Society).

Franz Boas's Baffin Island experiences are recorded in detail in a number of documents. The most intimate chronicle of his experiences is a 500-page letter-diary addressed to Marie that he kept throughout this period. It covered the entire fifteen months that he was on his expedition. Much of it was written in pencil, since ink would coagulate in the cold environs of his tented shelters or snow huts. It was often written under adverse circumstances, in hastily scribbled German script and difficult to

---

[a] Called Baffin Land at the time of the expedition.

read.[b] After Franz Boas died, his daughter, Helene Yampolsky, spent endless hours transcribing large portions of the text, an extraordinarily difficult task and a superb accomplishment.[2] In the diary, on November 5, 1883, by way of apology, he wrote, "Poor Marie, you must study my chicken scratches. My poor handwriting makes me a true criminal and nothing can be done about it…"[1]

The diary contains much of a personal nature, with an outpouring of his affection for Marie. It also records his daily activities, scientific observations, and expeditions. Marie also kept a letter-diary addressed to Franz.[3] Professors Douglas Cole and Ludger Müller-Wille have published extensive excerpts from the diary of Franz.[1,4,5] Müller-Wille, upon the suggestion of the late Douglas Cole, recently edited a complete volume "of all the extant journals and letters Boas wrote in Baffin Island," a huge undertaking and a magnificent accomplishment which took him over ten years. The translations from German were done by William Barr. Müller-Wille included an extensive bibliography of all literature pertinent to the Boas expedition.[4] A number of the brief quotes of Franz Boas used here and some details of his Baffin Island expedition were obtained from Douglas Cole and Ludger Müller-Wille's writings as well as from Müller-Wille's latest volume.[1,4,5]

Some of the photographs taken on his expedition are in the Boas collection in the Library of the American Philosophical Society. Other details of his arctic expedition may be found in the *Berliner Tageblatt*[6] and in the Baffin Island story (incomplete) that he wrote for his children.[7] His scientific reports and cartographic works are detailed in *Baffin-Land, Geographische Ergebnisse . . .*[8] In 1884 and 1885, Boas wrote more than a dozen papers and articles on the Arctic and his experiences in Baffin Island.[9] He also published a glossary of the Inuit language in 1894.

His companion on this expedition was Wilhelm Heinrich Christian Weike (1859-1917). Weike's wife, Mathilde, had been a housekeeper for the Boas family. When she married Wilhelm in 1879, he became their servant and gardener (Figure 27). In preparation for their arctic expedition, Franz and Wilhelm purchased or were given supplies sufficient for a year. Included were guns, ammunition, clothing, food, coffee, tea, rum, a 13-foot dinghy, surveying equipment, a steel sled, trading goods, particularly tobacco, as well as tools, utensils, and knives.

The concept of the expedition was extraordinary for its time – a "virtually one-man expedition," living off the land, "adapting completely

---

b According to Müller-Wille, Franz Boas used the Latin script "with some remnants of Gothic."[2]

the [nomadic] Eskimo mode of life."[1]

Figure 27. Wilhelm Weike and his wife, Mathilde, in photograph taken in Berlin, ca.1884. Weike was Franz Boas's companion on his Arctic expedition (American Philosophical Society).

The *Germania* was a small, two-masted schooner with an auxiliary engine; she probably measured only 40 to 50 feet in length. Aboard were six crewmembers with passengers Boas and Weike. Captain Mahlstede's mate was Wilhelm Wenke. There were two seamen, Anton Andresen and Wilhelm Wincke, a carpenter, F. Carl Johansen, and a cook, Adolph

Lange. There were thus three Wilhelms on board, Wenke, Wincke and Weike.[5]

Their quarters were cramped. Franz had a small cabin with a wooden bunk (Figure 28). In the cabin there were a long table and bench that he used for writing and studying. He ate his meals with Captain Mahlstede.

Figure 28. Franz Boas's cabin on the *Germania*. Note Marie Krackowizer's embroidered German flag, and a coat, rucksacks, and hunting knife on the wall. On the table is the photograph of Marie given to Franz as well as inkwells, and his notebooks. (American Philosophical Society).

After passing through the North Sea, the *Germania* headed northwest toward Baffin Island. As they sailed from the North Sea toward Greenland,

> Here we do not see a single sail on the horizon, there are very few birds around the ship, and a piece of driftwood coming by constitutes an important event in the boring course of each day.[6]

On June 30, 1883, Franz wrote to Marie of his sadness on leaving her but expressed delight to have achieved "one goal of my dreams." He reflects on his dreams of a polar expedition since he was nine or ten years of age. "Now I have attained this; I am on my way so differently from what I had dreamed of. I am not heading out under the orders of a friend, but am dependent on myself."[5]

When they reached the area south of Cape Farewell at the southern tip

tip of Greenland on July 8, 1883, "The wind from the northeast developed into a storm. We experienced high seas and one large wave after another hit the deck of our hard working ship . . ."[6] Although seaworthy, the heavy seas of the North Atlantic were a test of endurance for this small vessel and these recent landlubbers. Franz suffered seasickness, which was especially bad during this severe storm.

The day after the storm, Franz celebrated his 25th birthday. Reflecting on his future, he wrote to Marie,

> It is funny how everybody thinks I am making this trip for fame and glory . . . they do not know me . . . I strive for a higher thing and that this trip is only a means to that goal. I suppose it is true that I want external recognition for my achievements, but only in so far as I wish to be known as a man who will carry out his ideas and act upon them. That is the only kind of recognition I can think of. Empty glory means nothing to me.[1]

Between Greenland and Baffin Island, they encountered many ice floes and huge icebergs. Awed by these sights, he wrote,

> Some floats drifted by the ship, and soon we are surrounded by stacks of ice. They come in the most unexpected shapes. Fish, large gate-like structures, steep cliffs, all washed out of the ice by the water; and everything in the purest sky blue color while under the water appears to be greenish...How weak these descriptions sound, of what we saw; how weak is any painting! Many things combine to give life to it: the moving ship, the ocean alive with birds, the thunder of ice, the thick fog, and the blinding brightness and color which gives a background to the whole picture which cannot be imitated.[6]

In his diary Boas repeatedly recorded his observations on the varying colors of seawater, reflecting the interest expressed in his university thesis on the color of water. He also noted the colors of ice, as with seawater. He sketched some of these huge masses of ice.[5] On July 15th the ship came within sight of Cape Mercy on the tip of Cumberland Peninsula, the southern tip of Baffin Island. His initial excitement of seeing land soon turned into a state of depression, when they ran into a "desert of ice." Because of this, the *Germania* was able to cover only about fifteen miles during the next four weeks (Figure 29). Scanning the horizon became a boring obsession. Living in such cramped quarters for weeks longer than they had anticipated became a great disappointment and drudgery. He wrote, "This trip is really a true test of patience."

On August 10, 1883, in making preparations for their arrival, Boas wrote, "This morning we hoisted it [his dinghy] and now it is also been christened [Marie] . . ." Still despondent and frustrated, he wrote on the same day,

> What will be the outcome when we are still lying around here on 10

August! . . . And if we don't get there at all, what then? . . . What should I do then? I would have to produce a fairly major geographical work very quickly and habilitate myself as a *Privatdocent* and at the same time complete my psychophysical work . . .[5]

Figure 29. Franz Boas aboard the schooner *Germania* en route to Baffin Island. A crew member is seen to the left. Photograph by Wilhelm Weike, 1883 (American Philosophical Society).

One day, stalled along the vast ice floes, they sighted some driftwood. As a diversion from their boredom, the Boas dinghy *Marie* was launched to retrieve it. "We really ought to have hoisted the flag [Marie's], but . . . we had left the mast on board ship . . ."[5]

Finally on August 28th when a fog bank lifted, a passageway in the ice appeared and they were able to proceed to Kekerten, an island in the middle of Cumberland Sound. Thus ended a sixty-nine day journey from Hamburg, a trip that should have taken no more than 30 days. The break-up of ice came very late in the season. On arrival, they were greeted enthusiastically by the Inuit and whalers stationed on the island. The *Germania* was the first boat to arrive that season.

> The gulf is almost never covered with ice to such an extent. And seldom does the wind come as often from a southerly direction, driving the ice from Davis Strait into the sound.[6]

Upon arrival and being greeted by natives of Kekerten Island, he was,

> Appalled by these people . . . Their long black hair, flat faces and watering eyes made a horrible impression on me . . . later I was surprised at seeing many a friendly face as well as many a strong well built body . . . A short time after the anchor had been dropped, we visited the summer tents of the natives . . . made of hides . . . Before we got too close we already knew of them because of their pungent smell, which came from the tanned seal skins used to build the tents . . . If somebody, at that time, had told me that shortly thereafter I would live without disgust in similar circumstances, I would have vehemently rejected such an idea. Yet it wasn't long before conditions and daily routine made me share the beds of the natives . . . How often did I appreciate the friendly fire which warmed the hut comfortably. How often did I appreciate my generous hostess who dried and cleaned my clothes! And how much did I hate to leave a comfortable home to begin another lonely journey from coast to coast or to uninhabited regions![6]

The *Germania's* goal of reaching the German weather station at K'ingua, 100 kilometers to the north, was delayed by ice, impenetrable to this small schooner. Anxious to announce their arrival to the personnel at the weather station, Boas convinced some natives to take him in their small whaleboat to K'ingua. It was a difficult and tortuous trip, sailing through fjords and following narrow watery passages in the ice. They were ultimately successful and joyfully received by the men of the weather station. The *Germania* was finally able to sail to K'ingua on September 16th.[6]

Franz Boas had arrived in a forbidding, desolate part of the world, a place that would challenge him to extremes. Kekerten became his base of operations from late August until early May, from whence he made a number of cross-country surveying and mapping expeditions along the shoreline of Cumberland Sound and into some of the fjords.

Prior to leaving for the Arctic, Franz Boas drew two similar maps in ink on heavy board, coloring the seas in blue. Each measured 13"x13" and encompassed the northern latitudes, with Baffin Island in the center. They also included the territories north of Baffin Island, Labrador, Hudson's Bay and Greenland. On them he drew his proposed expeditionary routes for the years 1883 and 1884. The maps may well have been based partly on the earlier maps prepared by Charles Francis Hall who sought survivors of the lost Franklin expedition members (Figure 30).[a]

Figure 30. Hand drawn map by Franz Boas of his proposed expedition route on Baffin Island. This sketch, one of two, was drawn before sailing on his voyage to the Arctic in 1883 (American Philosophical Society.)

[a] He gave one of the maps to Marie, which is now part of the Boas collection at the American Philosophical Society. The other is in the possession of this author.

Although Boas was specially trained in photography, very few of his Arctic photographs remain. He left Germany with 48 photographic plates. Seventeen were used aboard the *Germania* and the remainder on Baffin Island. Due to poor methodology and in part to Boas's inexperience as a novice photographer, only sixteen plates survived, some with poor images.[5] A few were shipped back home on the *Germania's* return trip to be processed by photographer Hülsenbeck in Minden (Figures 31).[b] The only known photograph of the dingy *Marie* was taken by Franz in October, in Cumberland Sound (Figure 32).

Figure 31. Rest period at Ujarasugdjuling Point in Kangerloaping Bay during a final boat trip of the Fall of 1883. Wilhelm Weike is at the left and three Inuit guides are to the right drinking tea or coffee. They are Ssigna ("Jimmy"), Ütütiak ("Yankee"), and Nachojaschi (sitting order not known). Photograph taken by Franz Boas on October 16, 1883 (American Philosophical Society).

On September 17, 1883, the *Germania,* with the German scientific party, sailed for home (Figure 33). With them they took letters from Boas and Weike for their respective families. Franz Boas wrote, "You can be sure I shall come home healthy and happy. Wilhelm and I are well thus far, and, trust me, I am careful and will return to you in good health . . ."[5] Only once thereafter, in early October 1883, was it possible to send mail home on a supply boat. For a number of weeks Boas was a guest at the home of James Mutch, an agent of a Scottish whaling company. Mutch, and his Inuit friends were of great help by sharing their experiences in the Arctic

[b] Most of the remaining photographs are in the Library of the American Philosophical Society.

with Boas. They helped him with the Inuit language, *Inuktitut*, and assisted him in his overall planning.

Figure 32. The dinghy *Marie* resting on a ice flow in Cumberland Sound, Baffin Island in October 1883. Photo by Franz Boas (American Philosophical Society).

Die Station kurz vor dem Verlassen derselben.

German weather Sta- Cumberland Sound 1883

Figure 33. Woodcut of the German weather station on Cumberland Sound in 1883 (American Philosophical Society).

The primary purpose of the mission of Franz Boas was to map unexplored regions of Baffin Island along Cumberland Sound, its western portion, as well the northern shoreline along Davis Strait. He spent most of his time in Cumberland Sound until mid-winter, during which time he mapped essentially all of the Sound with its fjords. With his maps, he was able to define the hunting routes taken by the Inuit on their migrations from season to season.

The first difficulty that Franz experienced was in hiring guides, since most of the Inuit were hunting in the central regions of the island and had not returned to Cumberland Sound. With the aide of Captain Roach of the local American station, Franz had the good fortune to hire a responsible and dependable native, Ssigna, or Jimmy as the English called him. Ssigna, was a young man of about 35 years of age who was familiar with the topography of the northwest coast and the area of Lake Kennedy. On at least one occasion, on a surveying expedition to Paguistu Fjord on the west coast of Cumberland Sound, Franz, Ssigna, and Wilhelm were accompanied by Ssigna's nephew, Ütütiak and his friend Nachojashi (Figure 34).[5]

> I used this time to chart the islands and to collect knowledge about the land which I intended to visit in the spring. To my great regret, I soon realized that the information which I had received in Europe was altogether undependable and distorted by false information. And since the map of the country was of no use whatsoever, I found myself fenced in from all sides from the very beginning...That I nevertheless found an opportunity for travel in the middle of winter, was entirely to the credit of the director of the Scottish whaling station, Mr. Mutch, who put his dogs at my disposal. Furthermore, since I found a sufficient number of dogs in foreign settlements, I was able to chart the largest part of Cumberland Sound during the winter.[6]

Figure 34. Temporary encampment in Cumberland Sound, Baffin Island at the entrance to Supivisortung Fjord. Left to right are Wilhelm Weike, Nachojaschi, Ssigna, and Ütütiak. Photo by Franz Boas, October 1883 (American Philosophical Society).

By the mid-19th century, Cumberland Sound had become an ideal site for hunting whales. During the early part of the century, many vessels hunted whales in the waters east of Greenland, in Baffin Bay, and in Davis Strait. They included the Basques, ships of the Hanseatic League, Norwegians, Dutch, and Americans. As whales started to become depleted in Baffin Bay and Davis Strait, in the late 1830s, it was discovered that the waters of Cumberland Sound became much more heavily populated.

The Inuit had long known how to catch whales without sophisticated equipment. As the ice floes began to melt and break up in late July and August, the whales would gather at the edge of the ice in the Sound. With harpoons and lines, assisted by dog sleds, kayaks, and small boats, the Inuit would harpoon the whales and drag them onto the ice (Figure 35).

Figure 35. Sketch by Franz Boas drawn on Baffin Island in 1883 of the Inuit "Hauling a whale to shore" (American Philosophical Society).

This led to the establishment of whaling stations on the island of Kekerten in Cumberland Sound by Norwegians and Americans who hailed from New London, Connecticut, along with many other smaller settlements of whaling crews. Although the whale population was already severely depleted by the time Franz Boas arrived, two Kekerten stations were still occupied, serving the few remaining whaling vessels. It is estimated that at the peak of the whaling era,

> . . . approximately 2000 Eskimos lived on the Sound when the whalers first came. Since then their number has gone down with terrifying speed. Today there are no more than 300, divided among seven settlements. Of the 450

> Kikkerton [Kekerten] Eskimos who, at one time were able to furnish crews for 18 boats, only 80 are left![6]

Boas concluded,

> If the catch doesn't improve soon, we may assume that the time will come where the last of the white people will leave this inhospitable land. Then the Eskimos will be forced to leave the Sound also and make their home in the costal areas of Davis Strait where ships come by every year . . . Cumberland Sound will then be even more deserted than long ago. Before, the seemingly never-ending supply of whales attracted whole fleets and created an important place in the economy of the world for this land.[6]

In November 1883, as Boas was embarking on his mapping expedition, he wrote to Marie,

> Daily now I see the little flag you made for me fluttering in the wind. Wilhelm or Ssigna carries it and some others to the places where I make my observations and I always think of you when I see it![1]

Boas describes a brief period of extreme hunger among the natives, and illnesses, including diphtheria, probably introduced by Europeans and whalers. This occurred in October, shortly after his arrival. Some of the children and people who had become his friends died. Boas was looked upon as a "doctor" whose medical help was sought. On one occasion he wrote,

> I always go to them when they call me. And I always feel so unhappy when I am with those people and cannot help them. You do not know how often my heart is heavy . . . maybe that is why I am turning to Marie today to find solace in her love![1]

Never having experienced diphtheria on Cumberland Sound, and due to the recent arrival of Franz Boas, many of the Eskimos blamed him for its appearance. This feeling grew as the disease spread and many Eskimos died. In spite of his ministering to them, deep resentments developed and he was excluded from their homes. It became necessary for him to carefully devise a diplomatic approach to regain their confidence in him. He was able to convince them that he was not at fault and was able to reestablish his friendly relationship with the community.[1]

Boas, Wilhelm and Ssigna were alone for much of the time during their surveying treks, on terrain never seen by Europeans. In addition to getting lost in blinding blizzards, they inevitably experienced periods of hunger, snow-blindness, frostbite and exhaustion.

Boas had to make many adjustments to his new life in Kekerten. Exposed to Scottish and American whalers, many of the Inuit within the vicinity of the whaling stations on Cumberland Sound spoke English, as did Boas at this time. He quickly started to compile a glossary of Inuit words and phrases, so that in time, he was able to converse with the Inuit in *Inuktitut*. He learned to eat raw seal liver and frozen raw seal meat, a staple of the diet. Revolting at first, he adjusted to this diet and, in fact, came to enjoy his meals. Of the seal liver he wrote, "It didn't taste bad once I overcame a certain resistance."

When we were children, all of the grandchildren of Franz Boas called him "Grosspapa [grandfather]." I recently related the story to a youngster – of "Grosspapa" eating raw seal liver. She immediately assumed that this was the reason we called him "Gross-Papa." He often told us of his experiences on this expedition. He also told us of eating raw seal blubber and how the natives would reward their children for good behavior by giving them raw fish eyes, a gastronomic delicacy. On occasion, Boas would shoot a caribou or do his own seal hunting for survival, but he became bored sitting over a seal hole in the ice for endless hours. Wilhelm or Ssigna did most of the hunting and fishing. On December 16, 1883, Franz wrote to Marie, contrasting his life in the Arctic with that at home, recalling that, "a year ago I was in society and observed all the rules of good taste, and tonight I sit in this snow hut with Wilhelm and an Eskimo eating a piece of raw, frozen seal meat which had first to be hacked up with an ax, and greedily gulping my coffee...[5]

He also told us of the games the Inuit played, one of the favorites being *ajarorpaq* or cat's cradle (Figure 36). He taught his children and his

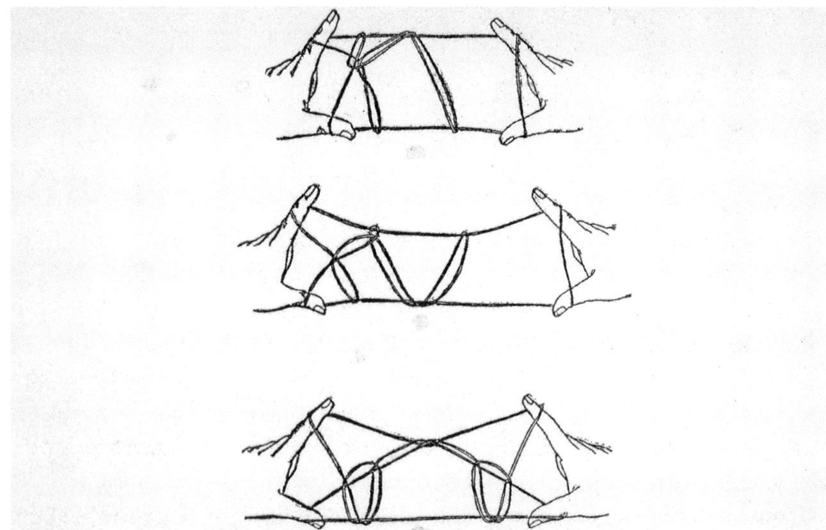

Figure 36. Ajarorpoq or cat's cradle, a game played with thong or string for creating designs and forms. Shown above are, top to bottom, a deer, a hare and ponds. A sketch by Franz Boas (*The Central Eskimo, 6$^{th}$ Annual Report of the Bureau of Ethnology, 1884-85*).

grandchildren to play this game. It is a technique for making figures and designs out of thong with the fingers (we used string), highly developed by the Eskimos as a form of entertainment.

Franz Boas chose to live under adverse conditions for the sake of his scientific curiosity and learning experience. He did not hesitate to face danger, be it dueling or the inherent dangers of Arctic weather. He loved nature in all its extremes, a love affair that remained with him throughout his life. During his university days he took long hikes in the forests and valleys of Germany. He taught his children to love the natural beauties that surrounded them during their summer vacations at Lake George, New York. Even in his old age, he would take hikes with his grandchildren in the foothills of the Berkshire Mountains in Kent and Cornwall Bridge, Connecticut, instilling this same love in them.

The most perilous trek of the Boas expedition began on December 11, 1883. Franz Boas, Wilhelm, and Ssigna left Kekerten for the Foxe Basin, on the west coast; for fourteen days they traversed islands and fjords with temperatures ranging from 40° to 55° below zero. On the 14th,

> The wind had shifted and brought not only warm weather, but also snow . . . Since there was almost no wind, the snow formed a thick cover on the ice and it was almost impossible to get anywhere. The snow continued to fall for nearly two days, but then it cleared and the temperature fell to minus 49 degrees . . .[6]

They built a snow hut and were confined to it because of the weather. Attempts to leave were to no avail.

> On December 19, we had the further misfortune that the spring of one our guns broke . . . so that we couldn't shoot any more seals for oil which we absolutely needed in our lamps . . . But because we couldn't melt any more ice and snow and couldn't heat the snow house any longer, we couldn't remain in this place without running into serious danger . . . I decided to leave everything behind and to walk to the next settlement which was 18 miles away, as the crow flies . . . Early in the morning, at 5 o'clock . . . we were on our way . . . By 11:30 a.m. we were . . . approximately six miles away [from the settlement] . . . At 9 p.m. we heard a dog bark, a sign that we were near a settlement. We changed our direction following the welcome sounds, but soon lost our way again in the rough ice . . . With the dense fog and in the darkness it was impossible to establish our location.[6]

They waited several hours for the "moon to rise again" to re-establish the direction of their trek. Boas wrote in his diary,

> Cold and hungry we walked up and down in one place . . . all night. By 3 o'clock in the morning we set out again. By approximately 4 o'clock we found the tracks of sleds, coming and going. We followed them, but unfortunately in the wrong direction, until we noticed vapors above a water

> hole which indicated where we were. We turned around and, after 26 hours of walking, totally spent...with the thermometer at [minus 45°] so that I could not keep my fingers and nose from freezing, with nothing to eat or drink and no assurance that we would ever find our goal...totally spent, we reached Anarnitung. Poor Wilhelm's feet had become frostbitten . . . and he had to stay with my host in his snow hut for two weeks before I could take him to Kikkerton [Kekerten].[5, 6]

Wilhelm's feet were so severely affected that he had to sit out the next three months at Kekerten. Both Franz and Ssigna ended up with frostbitten noses and fingers.[5,6] In 1964, Henry B. Collins wrote,

> It is probably no exaggeration to say that Boas experienced more real dangers and hardships in his one year of Arctic fieldwork than most anthropologists do in a lifetime.[10]

On December 23, 1883, Franz wrote to Marie comparing the customs of our "good society" with that of the "savages" (Eskimos). Praising their hospitality and learning their customs, he concluded that they should not be censured for their "conventions and superstitions" since "we highly 'educated' people are relatively worse. The fear of traditions and old customs is deeply implanted in mankind...it halts all progress for us." [5]

> I believe that if this trip has been a valuable influence for me (as a thinking person), it lies in the strengthening of the viewpoint of the relativity of creation and that the evil as well as the value of a person lies in the cultivation of the heart, which I find or do not find here just as much as amongst us, and that all service, therefore, which a man can perform for humanity must serve to promote truth. Indeed, if he who promotes truth searches for it and spreads it, it may be said that he has not lived in vain![5]

On Christmas day, as in Minden, Franz celebrated Christmas with the exchange of some presents and a small Christmas tree that he had brought with him from home.

With his future constantly in mind, in January 1884 he wrote to Marie, expressing his desire to settle in America so that he might lead a professional life unfettered by the ever-developing restrictive prejudices in Germany.

> What I want, what I will live and die for, is equal rights for all, equal opportunities to [work] and strive for poor and rich! Don't you think that when one had done even a little towards this, this is more than the whole of science together?[5]

Shortly after the above letter, he wrote, "I do not believe that we, if living under the same conditions, would be so willing to work or be so cheerful and happy! I have to say that as regards character, I am totally contented with the Eskimos...[5]

In making preparations for a geographical expedition, in February

1884 he wrote that, "I am now truly just like an Eskimo," living and hunting according to their ways, rarely eating food except for seal meat and drinking coffee. Although bored with seal hunting and hunting for caribou, he conceded that he had no other options if he were to continue on his exploratory trips.[5]

Early in the winter, many dogs died from a disease. Had it not been for Mutch's dogs, Franz would not have been able go on his mapping expedition. In early February there was another epidemic that killed scores of dogs, leaving none for his contemplated trips inland. By the end of March in 1884, he was able to buy a good dog team from natives living on the northern shoreline of Davis Strait.

In April Franz traveled to Lake Kennedy in lower central Baffin Island, long considered one huge single lake and a favorite place for fishing and hunting caribou. He discovered that Lake Kennedy was, in fact, two enormous inland lakes and assigned them native names, *Amadjuak* and *Nettilling*; names used to this day.[11] He was able to gather sufficient information to draw an approximate outline of these frozen bodies of water. He also surveyed the southwestern coast and was able to conclude that Foxe Channel was a basin. He also made a number of side trips, traveling Inuit hunting trails. Inuit-drawn line-maps contributed greatly to Franz's survey reports.

In May he embarked on his major mapping expedition that carried him across Baffin Island with his dog team and sled to Davis Strait. It was here that he planned to map the north shore of Baffin Island – an extraordinary and difficult project for two young men (Figure 37).

> Traveling becomes tremendously difficult on long distances and with a heavily loaded sled . . . When, in May of this year, I left Cumberland Sound to chart the Davis Strait coastline and to get to know its tribes, I moved in the same way from one settlement to the next and became well familiar with the difficulties of such moves. We had to cross the high plateau of Kignait [Kingnait] and found it nearly without snow. The snow had been blown away by heavy winds. Every Eskimo (and I too) who wanted to cross this piece of land this particular spring had to carry every piece of luggage over large boulders. Since we spent eight days on land, we found it difficult to get enough food for the dogs. Fortunately we met a caribou herd which saved us . . . Heavy storms had caused snowdrifts and within a few days it became obvious that it was impossible to cross the rocky areas with heavy loads. I was forced to leave everything behind which was not absolutely necessary, and I had to hurry on to find some ships as soon as possible.
>
> Our provisions for two men for the following four months consisted of 59 pounds of bread, 36 pounds of meat and much coffee, tea and "Carne-pura" soups, as well as 30 pounds of tobacco and a few thousand powder-caps for

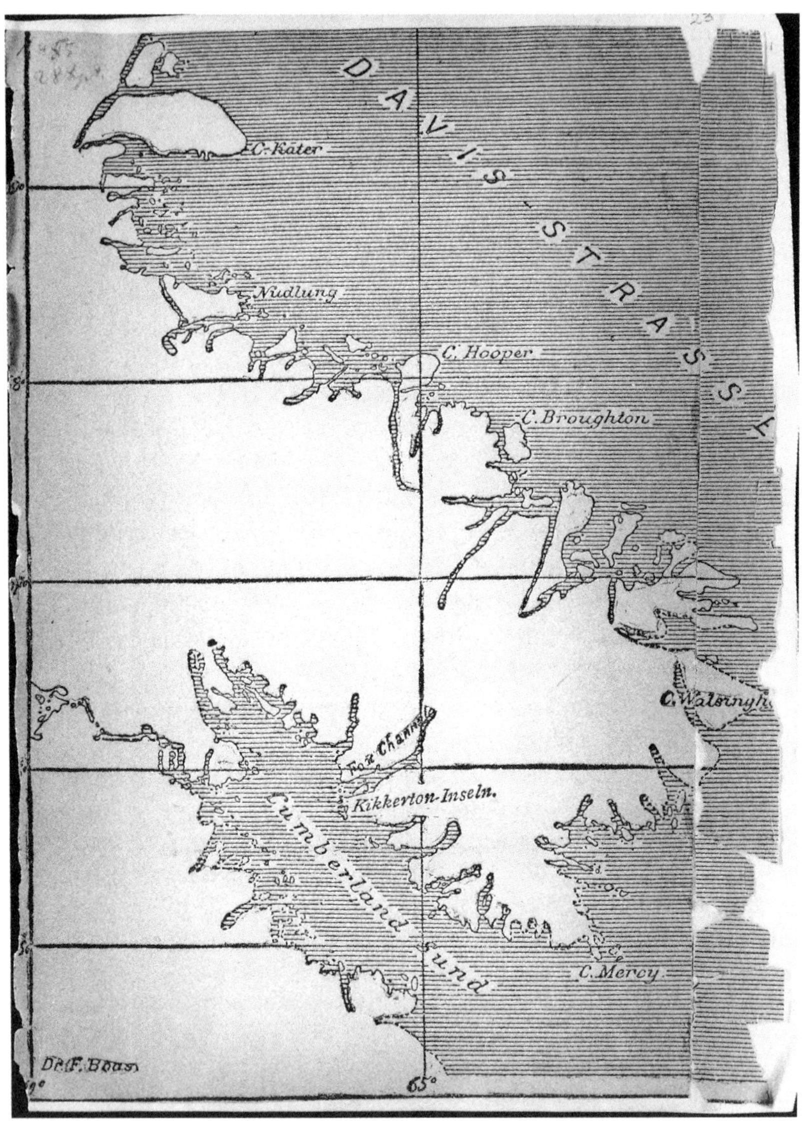


Figure 37. Map of eastern portion of Baffin Island, drawn by Franz Boas for an article in *Berliner Tageblatt*, 1884-85.

barter. The coast of Davis Strait which up to now, was charted as being without indentation, actually has numerous islands behind which there are deep fjords. Since I visited most of them, I had to travel slowly and finally reached Cape Hooper . . . (below 68"3' n. latitude) on June 19. There I left

> most of my load behind and traveled north with a light sled to chart Homes Bay, which was up to then completely unknown . . . even though I lost almost all of my dogs to hunger, when we were stranded in a snow storm for five days, we reached Cape Napor... where I was able to buy a lot of meat from the Eskimos.[6]

He also recorded valuable data on tides, on ice, and on sea currents. During the time he spent in the Arctic, Franz Boas traveled some 2400 miles by dog sled, by foot, in kayaks, and in boats. He corrected major cartographic errors of previous maps of Cumberland Sound and recorded, for the first time, hundreds of miles of the irregular coastline of the northern coastline of Baffin Island.

Before leaving Germany, Boas was interested in studying the migration routes of the Eskimos, which were dictated by seasonal changes in the weather. As nomadic tribes, certain times of the year they would hunt caribou and at other times would remain in the south when whales were abundant in Cumberland Sound. Some of the Inuit were excellent mapmakers, based primarily on visual observations. Boas published a number of their maps in *The Central Eskimo*.[10] With their help and with earlier observations by Frederick Schwatka, Charles Francis Hall, members of the German Polar Station, an old map, and handwritten accounts of whalers, Boas was able to create a map of Baffin Island, recording much valuable information (Figure 38). On it he showed the seasonal migration routes of many Inuit tribes, their manner of transportation (boats, kayaks, sleds or on foot), and their seasonal home sites – a pioneering and invaluable document.

In July 1884 he wrote a nostalgic letter to Marie concerning one of his most cherished forms of enjoyment, "There is one thing that pains me in my soul. My rough, horny fingers will probably never play the piano again, yet I still need music...If only I could just hear a sonata in A-major, or Schumann's Fantasia or the Eroica . . .[5]

Although his mission in Baffin Island was primarily geographical, Boas kept detailed ethnographic notes on the Inuit people. In addition to their migration routes, he also collected an extraordinary amount of data on hunting grounds, old stories, songs, games, customs, religious beliefs, rites of death, special feast days, dietary habits, hunting techniques, types of clothing, dwellings, utensils, ornaments, tools, language, and many other details. Today, over one hundred years later, the vast amount of ethnological data that he amassed serves as a permanent record of another disappearing culture of the world. It is considered a treasure by present day Inuit.

Boas also recorded the Inuit names of over nine hundred geographical

Figure 38. Map prepared by Franz Boas showing the Inuit migration routes, the names of tribes, their manner of transportation and seasonal home sites (*Baffinland, Geographische Ergebnisse einer in den Jahren 1883 und 1884 ausgeführten Forschungriese*, in Dr. S. A. Petermann's *Mitteilungen aus Justus Perthes' Geographischer Anstalt*, Volume 18, No. 80, Gotha: Justes Perthes, 1885).

locations on Baffin Island. He was distressed by many of the names Europeans assigned to these same places. He believed many were frivolous and often used only perpetuate the names of non-deserving men.

He stated,

> I was once in the position to have to give a name and thus committed an act, which should be avoided if possible. In one respect, it can truly be deplored if indigenous names get lost because these are so fitting like the Eskimo ones...one has to raise objections decisively over the Englishmen's and American's usual misuse in giving names.[1]

A number of years later, after a visit to Frobisher Bay, Russell W. Porter named a great ice flow on Baffin Island, "Boas Glacier" (Figure 39).[9] When Boas traveled from Cumberland Sound to the northeast shore of the island, he undoubtedly passed near or over this glacier. There is also a river named in honor of Franz Boas on Southampton Island, "Boas River." Southampton Island is located due west of lower Baffin Island, at the entryway to Hudson Bay and near the Arctic Circle. Boas River is centrally located as the largest river on this island. Southampton Island, about the size of Switzerland, has a shoreline of 1200 miles and encompasses an area of almost 16,000 square miles. The only human habitation is at Coral Harbour on the southeast coast, a small village of about 700 people[11-13] (Figure 40). It is doubtful that Franz Boas would have approved of either of these designations.

Figure 39. Boas Glacier on Baffin Island (From *Bibliography of Franz Boas*, in *American Anthropologist*, N. S., Volume 45, No. 3, Part 2, July-September, 1943).

Isolation in this strange environment permitted Boas to reflect at length on his relationship to society and on his future role in life.

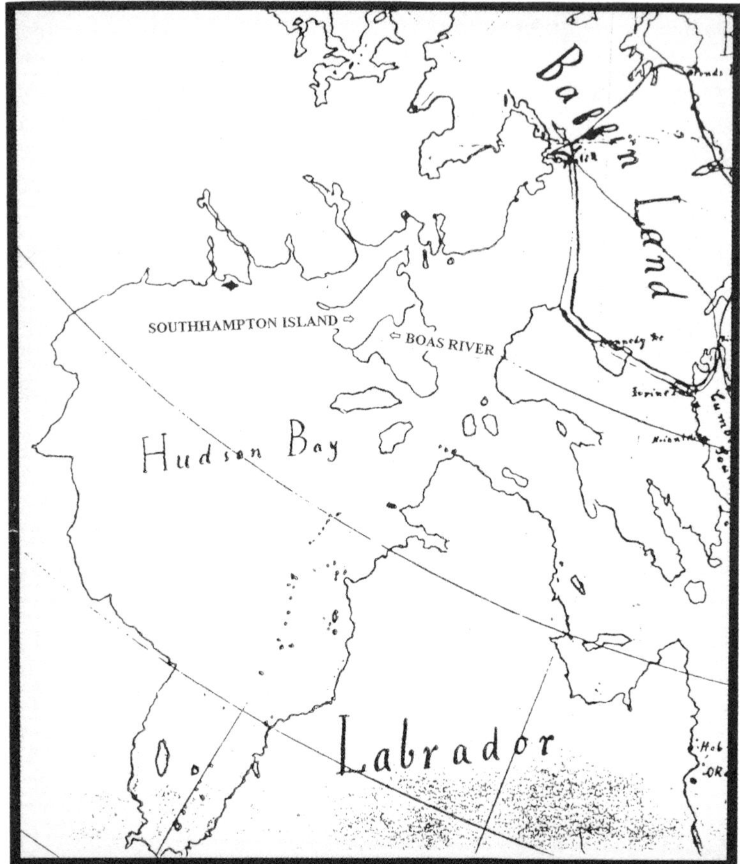


Figure 40. Southampton Island, Nunavut, at the northern extreme of Hudson Bay. This is located on Boas's original map of this area (Figure 30). Boas River is centrally located on the island. Since the island had not been mapped precisely at that time, his was only a rough sketch of the area.. Boas River and the island are identified by later notations (American Philosophical Society).

> I believe that one can be really happy only as a member of humanity as a whole, if one works with all one's energy together with the masses towards his goals. I think if one always felt that way it would be much easier to bear hardships and one would be more thankful for every joy.[5]

His experiences on Baffin Island redirected Boas's energies from geography into anthropology and established a lifetime career from which he did not deviate. His fieldwork in the Arctic helped him create new ethnological and linguistic research techniques, which were invaluable as applied to later studies. This 26 year-old scientist surveyed large portions of the largest island in the Arctic Archipelago. He had identified two enormous lakes, thought to be the single Lake Kennedy, made major corrections of earlier maps of Cumberland Sound, mapped a substantial portion of the coast on Davis Strait, recorded meteorological and tidal data, and collected vast amounts of ethnological material on the Inuit, all in the period of one year.

Delayed because of lack of transportation, Boas and Weike finally left K'ivitung [Kiritung] on Davis Strait on August 26, 1884, on the *Wolf*, captained by John Burnett. She sailed to St. John's, Newfoundland, arriving there on September 7, 1884. On arrival he sent telegrams to his parents, Marie, and the *Berliner Tageblatt*. The following day he wrote to his parents,

> You won't believe how lonely it is, up there in the frozen North, how deeply one feels that only living together with loved and loving people can make one happy. How much I would like to have you all here instead of all the strange faces, to see you and hear your dear voices.[5]

As a returning Arctic explorer, he was "besieged by newspaper reporters, who want to suck me dry." He, nevertheless, refused to give them interviews because of his prior commitment to the *Berliner Tageblatt* . . .[5,6]

On September 10, 1884, Franz and Wilhelm sailed from St. John's to Halifax, Nova Scotia, and then to New York in the steamer *Ardandhu*, arriving on September 21, 1884. Weike returned to Germany shortly thereafter. Boas remained in America until the end of winter.

Franz was met at the boat in New York by his cousin Willy Meyer, who had recently immigrated to America. He briefly visited with Willy, his uncle Jacob Meyer, his aunt Phips, and Abraham Jacobi. Two days later, after buying new clothes, Franz was off to join Marie at Lake George, New York, where he stayed for one week. It was a joyous reunion. Marie was staying with her sister, Helene Meyer, and her family at Alma Farm, their summer home on the lake. This became a favorite summer gathering place for Franz and Marie, and their family for many years, as will be related below.

While in America, Franz Boas improved his English, learned more of life in the States, and looked into job possibilities, should he decide to immigrate. He shared his northern experiences with whalers in New England, and with arctic explorers Frederick Schwatka, Emil Bessels, John Murdoch, and Lucien Turner in Washington, D.C. While in Washington, he met with Major John Wesley Powell at the Bureau of Ethnology, who agreed to publish his ethnological findings on the Inuit. Powell, trained as a geologist, became the leading ethnologist at the Smithsonian Institution. Upon his return to New York, Boas lectured on his travels, wrote his *Berliner Tageblatt* articles, scientific articles, and pieces for the *New*

*Yorker Staats Zeitung*. Unable to find work, coupled with pressure from his family and Professor Theobald Fischer to return home, he faced a dilemma racked with emotion. His parents were distraught. His mother, Sophie, worried that her only son might stay in America, wrote, "I don't know how I could stand it." Franz was beside himself, torn by the thought of leaving Marie again, yet unable to afford marriage. He had exhausted all efforts to find a job and also had a commitment to teach in Berlin. He knew that if he returned home, receiving a professorship might take years, and young professors rarely married before the age of 30. Conservatism was engulfing the German state under Bismarck, with the suppression of liberalism and increased discrimination against Jews. He concluded that to remain in America, wide open with opportunities, was not an option for him at this time. On March 14, 1885, Franz Boas sailed on the ship *Donau* to Bremerhaven.[14]

As reflected in his Arctic expedition, it is clear that Boas was also a good artist. He used it to great advantage when other means of recording artifacts, scenes and events were not possible. As with all of his other scientific techniques, he was meticulous in the detail of his sketches.

Figure 41. Sketch by Franz Boas of his guide Ssigna's igloo. Dated 1887, it was probably drawn from his recollections or from an earlier sketch (American Philosophical Society).

In later years, his artistic ability served as a great advantage when he studied the remarkable art of the Indians of the Pacific Northwest Coast. It is interesting to note that his daughters, Helene and Franziska, were also fine artists. Between thirty and forty of his Baffin Island sketches may be seen in the Library of the American Philosophical Society. Some are on loose leaves, but most are in his sketchbooks (Figures 41).[2] Two examples of his drawings from *The Central Eskimo*[10] are also presented here (Figures 42 & 43). This classic volume, the ethnological report of his expedition, was first published in 1888. The illustrations in this book of arctic sealing were based on photographs of Franz taken in Minden after his return to Germany. Two of the Boas poses in his Arctic attire were reproduced in *The Central Eskimo*, but his face was replaced with that of an Inuit.[15] Wilhelm Weike also posed in his arctic gear (Figures 44-47). The caribou garments were made for Boas and Weike by Inuit women.

Figures 42 & 43. Sketches by Franz Boas. Left: A stone storehouse in Ukiadliving. Right: Qailertetang, a masked figure (*The Central Eskimo, 6th Annual Report of the Bureau of Ethnology, 1884-85*).

While on Baffin Island, Boas collected a few Inuit artifacts, which he took home with him. One such collection included ivory carvings of Eskimos, dogs, sleds, cooking utensils, and an igloo made out of driftwood. For years these became playthings for his children, and later his grandchildren (Figure 48-50).

Long after leaving Baffin-Land, Alfred Kroeber noted, "The Arctic seized him as it had a way of doing. Decades later he confessed being torn by nostalgia whenever there was an opportunity to join an expedition."[16]

Figure 44. Franz Boas, posed in a Inuit caribou hide garment, demonstrates "An Eskimo in the act of striking a seal." Photograph by Hülsenbeck, Minden, winter 1885-86 (American Philosophical Society).

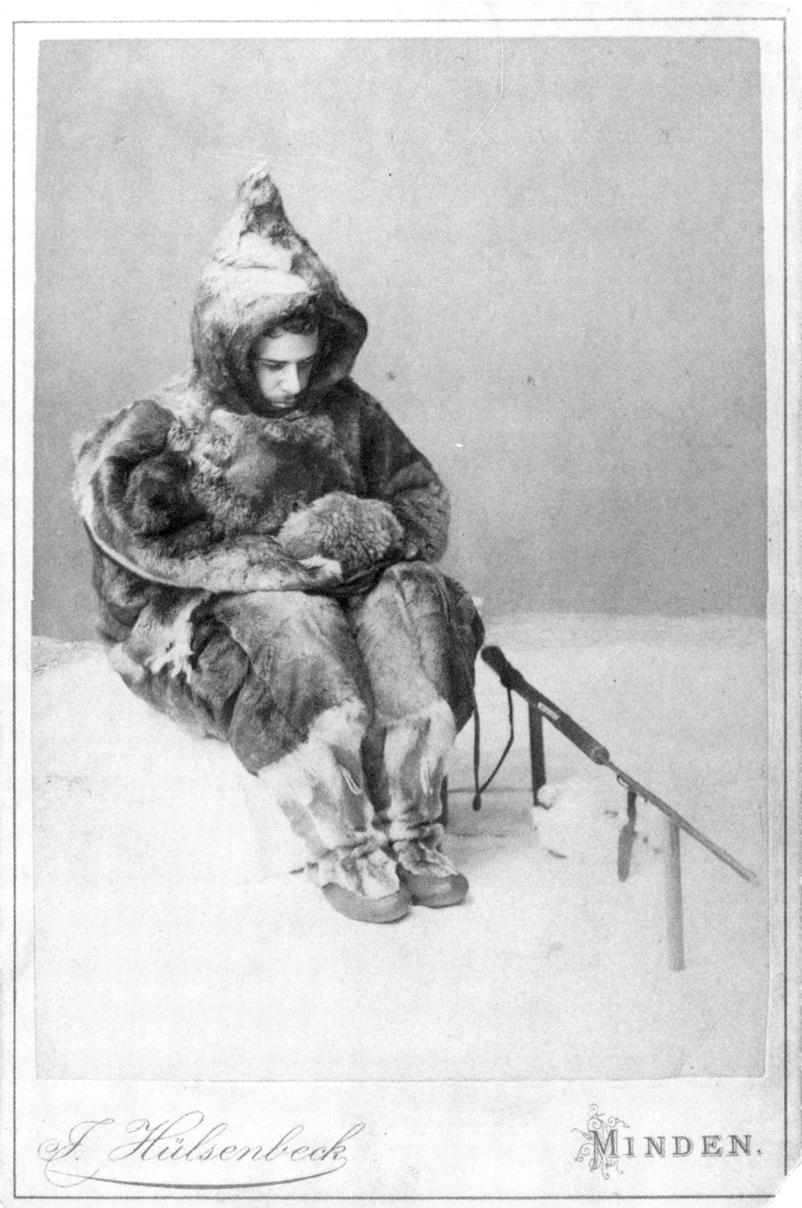


Figure 45. Franz Boas, posed in an Inuit caribou hide garment, demonstrates "An Eskimo awaiting return of seal to blowhole." Photograph by Hülsenbeck, Minden, winter 1885-86 (American Philosophical Society).

Figure 46. Wilhelm Weike, posed in an Inuit caribou hide garment. Photograph by Sweers, Minden, winter 1885-86 (American Philosophical Society).

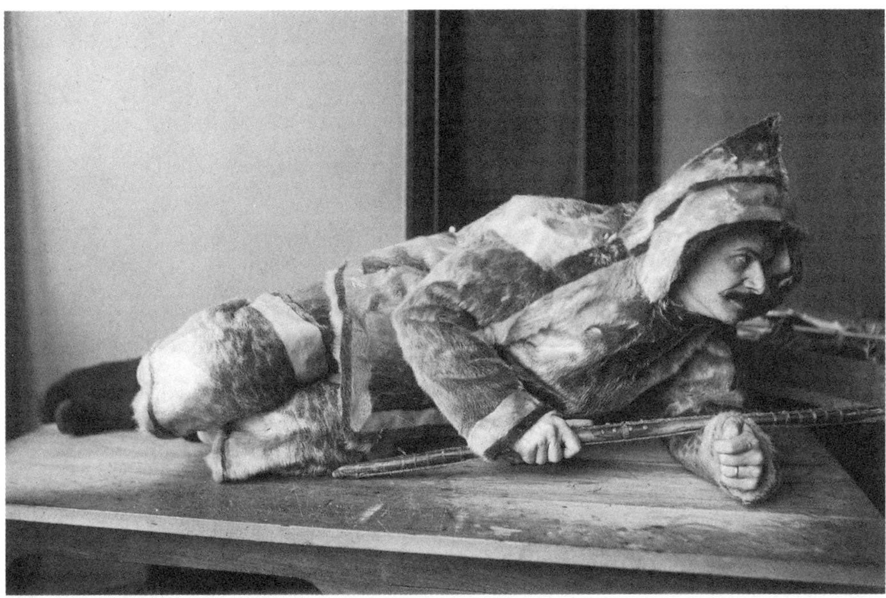

Figure 47. Franz Boas posed in an Inuit caribou hide garment with harpoon used for catching seals (Neg. No 3220. Photo R. Weber, Courtesy Dept. of Library Services, American Museum of Natural History).

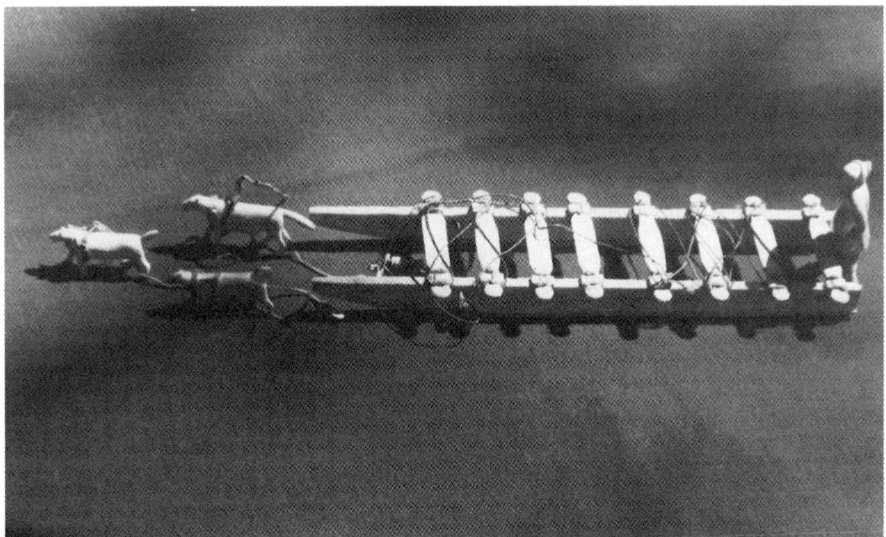

Figure 48. Walrus ivory carvings of an Inuit musher, his sled, and dogs collected by Franz Boas on Baffin Island (Donald P. Boas).

Figure 49. An igloo carved out of a piece of burned driftwood, collected by Franz Boas in Baffin Island. Note the Inuit on the raised sleeping platform with various cooking utensils (Donald P. Boas).

**References and Notes**


1. Cole, Douglas. *"The Value of a Person Lies in His Herzensbildung," Franz Boas's Baffin Island Letter Diary, 1883-1885* in *Observers Observed: Essays on Ethnographic fieldwork (History of Anthropology I),* edited by George W. Stocking, Jr., University of Wisconsin Press, Madison, Wisconsin, 1983.
2. Boas, Franz. Letters to his family and Boas scientific papers from the Library of the American Philosophical Society.
3. Krackowizer, Marie (Boas). Letter-diary to Franz Boas and sketch books of Franz Boas while he was on his Baffin Island expedition – Library of the American Philosophical Society.
4. Cole, Douglas and Ludger Müller-Wille, *Inuit Studies*, Volume 8, Number 1, 1984. Letters, diaries and notes from the Franz Boas expedition to Baffin Island.
5. Müller-Wille, Ludger. *FRANZ BOAS, With the Inuit of Baffin Island 1883-1884. Journals and letters*. Arranged and annotated by Ludger Müller-Wille. Translated by William Barr. University of Toronto Press, Toronto, Buffalo & London, 1998. The most exhaustive record of the Franz Boas Baffin Island expedition, with transcriptions of his letters, diaries and fields notes.

6. Boas, Franz. *Berliner Tageblatt.* Editorial, May 30, 1883, and articles by Franz Boas about his Baffin Island expedition that were printed in 1884 and 1885. Much of the text here derives from these newspaper articles. A complete collection of the original newspaper articles is in the library of the American Philosophical Society. English translations prepared by Professors Rita Terris and Thomas Huber are in the collection of this author.
7. Boas, Franz. Baffin Island story written for his children – an incomplete narrative. Copies are in the library of the American Philosophical Society and in this author's collection.
8. Boas, Franz. *Baffin-Land. Geographische Ergebnisse einer in den Jahren 1883 und 1884 ausgeführten Forschungreise*, in Dr. S. A. Petermann's *Mitteilungen aus Justus Perthes' Geographischer Anstalt*, Volume 18, Number 80. Gotha: Justus Perthes, 1885. The scientific report of the Boas expedition. The sections include a summary of and the story of his expedition, a geographical report, and one on "anthropological geography." This 100-page monograph includes a small map as well as a large fold-out map prepared by Boas, showing Baffin Island. On the large map he has drawn the routes of all of his expeditions. The small map shows the migration routes of the Inuit tribes (Franz Boas's copy in the Norman F. Boas collection).
9. Andrews, H. A. and others. *Bibliography of Franz Boas*, in *American Anthropologist*, New Series, Volume 45, Number 3, Part 2, July-September, 1943. A listing of hundreds of scientific and lay publications of Franz Boas covering 62 years.
10. Boas, Franz. *The Central Eskimo*, University of Nebraska Edition, Lincoln & London, 1964. Introduction by Henry B. Collins of the Bureau of American Ethnology.
11. *Nunavut Handbook*, Edited by Marion Soublière, 413pp, Nortext Multimedia, Inc., Iqaluit, NT, Canada, 1998. An invaluable guide to the new Canadian territory that encompasses Baffin Island and Southampton Island.
12. *BOAS RIVER, District of Keewatin, Northwest Territories*, A map produced by the Army Survey Establishment, R.C.C. Department of Mines and Technical Surveys, Ottawa, 1959-62.
13. Boas River as shown on map of *Western Canada*, National Geographic Society, 1981.
14. Cole, Douglas. *FRANZ BOAS. THE EARLY YEARS, 1858-1906.* Douglas & McIntyre, Vancouver & Toronto and the University of Washington Press, Seattle & London, 1999.
15. Boas, Franz. *The Central Eskimo, 6th Annual Report of the Bureau of Ethnology, 1884-85.* Report on his Baffin Island expedition with many details and illustrations.
16. Kroeber, A. L. *Franz Boas: The Man*, in American Anthropologist, New Series, Volume 45, Number 3, Part 2, July-September, 1943. A student and friend of Franz Boas writes a brief biography, following his death.

# CHAPTER IV

## IMMIGRATION AND EARLY YEARS IN AMERICA

After sailing from New York in March 1885, Franz Boas arrived in Berlin where he spent the next year preparing for an academic career (Figure 50). Soon after arriving, he gave an account of his Baffin Island expedition at a gathering of German geographers. He was received enthusiastically. It was through the recommendations of Theobald Fisher and Gustave Kirschhoff that he decided to seek an appointment in the Geography Department of Berlin University. Professor Heinrich Kiepert, the department chairman, had little interest in Boas, nor in any other younger men who might be a potential threat to his position. He was gruff,

Figure 50. Franz Boas while at the Royal Ethnological Museum, ca. 1885-1886. Photographer: Wilhelm Fechner, Berlin (American Philosophical Society)

uncompromising, unpopular, and primarily motivated to maintaining his position at the university. Franz, nevertheless, persisted with the backing of other members of the faculty. To attain a teaching position at the university as docent in physical geography, he had to submit a thesis to a juried panel of the faculty. He prepared a 100-page monograph detailing his scientific findings, with charts and maps in full color. It was titled *Baffin-Land, Geographische Ergebnisse einer in den Jahren 1883 und 1884 aus geführten Forschungsreise.*[1] Only a handful of these volumes were printed. It took many months to prepare, much of it done while he was at the Royal Ethnological Museum. Kiepert, who had refused to read it, reluctantly accepted his thesis, which was approved late in the spring of 1886. Franz was now considered a *privatdozent* and could now lecture at the university, "but only for student fees."[2,3]

During this time, he was able to visit with his family in Minden. His second youngest sister, Hete, had married one of his friends in Berlin, Rudoph Lehmann. Franz was a witness to the wedding, which was held in a municipal registry office. This created a crisis in the family, for his oldest sister, Toni, had hoped that she might some day win Rudolph's hand.

During the course of his year at the university, Franz gradually drifted away from geography and became more interested in anthropology. According to Stocking, "Boas came finally to reject geographical determinism and to develop his characteristic anthropological viewpoint . . ."[4] He was hired temporarily by Adolph Bastian at the Royal Ethnological Museum in Berlin as his assistant to help prepare exhibits of recently acquired American collections. He also helped catalog the J. Adrian Jacobsen collection of Alaskan and British Columbian Indian artifacts. In the stimulating atmosphere of the museum, he was befriended by and taught by anthropologists Albert Grünwedel, Felix von Luschan, and Wilhelm Grube. He also received instruction from Bastian and pioneer anthropologist and physician, Rudolph Virchow.

While Boas was in Berlin, Norwegian Captain Adrian Jacobsen, who was working for the Berlin Museum, returned from a trip to British Columbia and Alaska with extensive collections of artifacts of Native Americans for the museum. According to Franz Boas,

> My fancy was first struck by the flight of imagination exhibited in the works of art of the British Columbians as compared with the sobriety of the eastern Eskimo. From the fragmentary notes furnished by Captain Jacobsen we divined what a wealth of thought lay hidden behind the grotesque masks and elaborately decorated utensils of these tribes.[5,6]

During the same year, Jacobsen's brother, Fillip, who had also been to the Pacific Northwest, convinced a group of nine Bella Coola Indians to accompany him to Berlin. Here they performed for the public in their native costumes, dancing, re-enacting potlatches, and demonstrating other native rituals (Figure 51). Boas noted, "Opportunity was thus given to cast a brief glance behind the veil that covered the life of those people."[5,6] So fascinated was Boas by this group and their art form that he spent all his free time with them on their two short visits to Berlin. He was so enchanted with them that he referred to them as his "dear Indians." He became determined to visit the Northwest Coast of America to study this extraordinary culture. He also felt that field research with Indians might be more acceptable to academicians in America.[2]

Figure 51. Carte de visite photograph of Bella Coola Indian dancers, Berlin 1885. Note their "grotesque masks" and Chilkat blankets. Photogapher: Carl Günther, Berlin (Gertrud Michelson).

Shortly after his inaugural lecture as a docent, with permission of his superiors, he was again off to America to visit the Pacific Northwest and to investigate job possibilities. He decided to make this journey before his October courses started. He was again torn between remaining in Germany because of family loyalty and leaving for America. After his experiences with the geography department at Berlin University, he was even more certain that his future presented substantial political obstacles.

The paramount and most compelling reason to leave Germany was Marie. His devoted uncle Jacobi was also in New York, two very powerful attractions. He knew that advancement in German institutions might be a slow and frustrating process. Some have written that Boas left Germany because of anti-Semitism. This was undoubtedly a consideration, since those with a Jewish heritage were frequently by-passed for academic positions and promotions. Nevertheless, he had already proven that he could succeed in a very competitive and sometimes bigoted academic environment. His complex arrangements for the expedition to Baffin Island at the age of 25 was a major accomplishment for which he had support of the German government, universities, a major Berlin newspaper, and many of his teachers and friends. He was a very determined man in a hurry, and with his brilliance and persistence, he almost certainly would have succeeded in an academic field in Germany, at least until anti-Semitism became the order of the day, many years later.

Having lived and studied the Inuit on Baffin Island, he felt that his exposure to ethnological fieldwork, to which he became strongly attracted, made him well suited to study the cultures of the Indians of the Pacific Northwest. This, he believed, offered the promise of a more exciting and brighter career in a more democratic environment. His planned expedition to the Pacific Northwest was an opportunity for making the most important career decision of his life.

He sailed to New York with his sister Toni, arriving on July 27, 1886. After he landed in America he had a brief reunion with Marie and his uncles, Abraham Jacobi and Jacob Meyer. He then traveled to Washington, DC to help edit his monograph, the *Central Eskimo,* which the Smithsonian Institution agreed to publish. At the insistence of Jacobi, Franz attended a meeting of the American Association of the Advancement of Science (A.A.A.S.) in Buffalo. He was surprised and delighted to discover that his fame as an Arctic explorer preceded him. He was cordially received and met Horatio Hale and Frederic Ward Putnam. Hale was an ethnologist most noted for his role in the Charles Wilkes Expedition of 1838 to 1842 which sailed to Antarctica, the South Seas, Hawaii, the Pacific Northwest, and around the world. Putnam, about whom much will be related below, was an ethnologist and archeologist at Harvard University, and was to play a significant role in the early career of Boas.[2]

When he was in New York, Boas tried to reach Albert Bickmore, director of the American Museum of Natural History, in the hope of obtaining a position there. Bickmore was away at the time, so Franz had to defer any meeting until later. It had been his hope that Abraham Jacobi and

Carl Schurz might have opened the door for him at the museum through their influence with the trustees.

Anxious to start on his field research, Boas embarked on his first visit to the Pacific Northwest in September 1886 (Figure 52 & 53). The purpose of the trip was to do a reconnaissance of the Indian villages along the coastline of Vancouver Island, to create an ethnographic map of the island, and to collect museum specimens. His reward for this expedition, he hoped, would be that of obtaining a position in an American museum so that he could remain in the United States. His greatest ambition was to become an ethnologist at the American Museum of Natural History in New York. To obtain a job was his overriding goal. Without a source of income, he might have to return to Germany and would be unable to marry Marie.

Figures 52 & 53. Franz Boas ca. 1886. Photographer: A Bogardus, New York (American Philosophical Society). Marie Krackowizer, ca. 1886. Photographer: Wilhelm, New York (Gertrud Michelson)

He left Penn Station on September 11, 1886, on his transcontinental trip to Vancouver to visit the Indians of British Columbia. It was the beginning of a relationship with these Native Americans that was to last for 56 years, the balance of his life; a relationship that has continued to this day through his children, grandchildren, great-grandchildren, and great-

great grandchildren. Franz was essentially without funds for this expedition. Friends made contributions for the trip and Abraham Jacobi offered him a loan of $500.00. Boas reluctantly accepted it upon the urging of Carl Schurz. It was Boas's plan to collect Indian artifacts in British Columbia, sell them to a museum on his return, and repay Jacobi. Schurz arranged for a Northern Pacific railroad pass for travel from Chicago to St. Paul. He was also given a free train ride on the Canadian Pacific Railway on its new route to Vancouver, which had opened the same year. Much of the information on this trip may be found in his letter-diary to his parents.[7,8]

After he established a base in Vancouver, he sailed on the steamer *Barbara Berkowitz* to Victoria, arriving there five days after his departure from New York. According to Boas it was a "steamer with a schooner rigging." Victoria, a frontier city, had been established only forty years earlier. At this time it was a chaotic center of activity with a population of about 13,000, including about 2000 Indians of different tribes. It was the largest city in British Columbia. Many of the inhabitants of Victoria were transients, working on the docks for menial wages. A great confusion in communication existed throughout the community with the mixture of Oriental, European and Native American languages, the latter with several different dialects. The roads were unpaved and many residents lived in barely adequate shanties and hovels. Before attempting to learn these native languages, Boas had to learn to speak Chinook, a rudimentary trade jargon used along the coast. His major goal was to map the locations of the different Vancouver Island tribes and study their linguistic relationships.[2,7]

On leaving Victoria, he sailed north, stopped briefly at Alert Bay, and ended his trip in Newitti, a small Kwakiutl Indian village on the northern tip of Vancouver Island.[a] This was his first substantial field experience with the Northwest Coast Indians. He remained at Newitti for about ten days, sharing potlatches and feasts with this Indian band. At a potlatch on October 7, 1886, he found that the Indian chiefs did not trust him. They thought that he might be a missionary or an Indian agent who had come to stop their potlatch. Uncomfortable in his position, he felt compelled to make a speech. From Rohner's translation of a Franz Boas letter to his parents,

> My country is far from yours; much further even than that of the Queen. The commands of the Queen do not affect me. I am a chief and no one may command me . . . I do not wish to interfere with your celebration. My people live far away and would like to know what people in distant lands

---

[a] This small village no longer exists.

> do, and so I set out . . . And then they said to me "Go and see what the people in this land do," and so I went and I came here and I saw you eat and drink, sing and dance. And I shall go back and say "See, that is how people there live. They were good to me and asked me to live with them."[7]

As an interpreter translated his speech, it was warmly received. Boas had gained their confidence and respect as their friend. Because of abuse that the Indians suffered at the hands of government agents, Boas encountered similar feelings of distrust wherever he traveled. This required repeated and sincere assurances of his well-intentioned motives. He left Newitti accompanied by a native in a small sailboat. They sailed and rowed in Queen Charlotte Straits through a severe storm with treacherous waves. It was a frightening experience reminiscent of a trip he took in Salmon Fjord on Baffin Island in 1883, "All my life long, I think, I shall remember this canoe trip . . . we were able to keep the boat upright by sitting on its edge and bending far over." After hitting a rock and breaking free, they finally arrived at the settlement at Alert Bay.[7] Alert Bay is the home and reserve of the Nimpkish band of the *Kwakwaka'wakw*.[5b] It is a small Indian village on Cormorant Island, lying in Queen Charlotte Straits. Here he stayed for a number of days, recording large amounts of ethnological data. Toward the end of October, the *Barbara Berkowitz* picked him up and he again sailed to Victoria.

Back in Victoria, Boas spend endless hours interviewing many Native Americans who either lived in or were visiting the city. Here he also met merchants, missionaries, clergymen, sailors, and others, all of whom were helpful in answering his unending questions. During the balance of his three-month expedition he took many side trips to Indian villages on Vancouver Island including, among others, Comox, Cowichon, and Nanaimo. He spent many hours interviewing the Bella Coolas living on Vancouver Island. He recorded over one hundred folk stories, took photographs, and collected Indian artifacts and blankets. He also obtained skulls from Indian shell mounds. With his artistic talents, he sketched utensils, totem poles, masks, and other three-dimensional objects. He also prepared maps and recorded linguistic material. He was able to identify "names and ethnological relationships of over 70 [tribal] groups, many previously almost unknown." While in Victoria he met Adrian Jacobsen, who played a significant role in enticing Boas to visit the Pacific Northwest with the artifacts he displayed in Berlin. At this time Jacobsen lived with the Bella

---

[b] The *Kwakwaka'wakw* people are those who speak *Kwak'wala*, a language common to most bands of Indians on Vancouver Island and the lower and western mainland of British Columbia.

Coolas, where he supervised a fishery and an animal breeding station.[2,5,7]

On October 27, 1886, Boas wrote to Carl Schurz, seeking continued help in finding a position in America,

> The kindly interest you have taken in my plans encourages me to write to you about my work here and to remind you of your kind promise to be of help to me in obtaining a position in the museum in New York. I find that my hopes of finding much material of scientific value here have been justified . . . there is so much material that I scarcely know where to begin .

He continued by describing his travels, visiting the Indians, and collecting a large number of native artifacts,

> for museum purposes . . . shall be in a position to arrange the collection . . . If it is impossible to accomplish anything else, perhaps you could succeed in interesting the Trustees and Bickmore sufficiently that they would ask me to arrange the collection after my return. I am convinced the department needs a curator . . . I have also written to Dr. Jacobi not to forget my interests . . .[9]

The many Indian objects he had purchased were shipped to New York before his return. While in British Columbia, as late as November 18, 1886, and while he was preparing his lecture schedule for summer courses in Berlin in 1887, he commented, "If only I shall not have to give the lectures and can stay in New York!"[7]

In December 1886, ready to go east, he wrote to his parents from Vancouver about this new city, barely one year old. It had been built in anticipation of the new terminus of Canadian Pacific Railroad.

> Where there are no houses, even in the middle of the city, there are burned or burning tree stumps. People from all lands . . . swarm about the streets, which are covered with wooden planks. The streets are not yet completely finished, and where there are no wooden side streets . . . there is nothing but impassable swamps . . . The landowners believe the city to be a second San Francisco, but I am afraid they are mistaken . . . The forests can only be conquered in the course of time, and the small amount of gold is insufficient to make the land valuable . . .[7]

Having completed his first fieldtrip to British Columbia, Boas left Vancouver in December 1886, arriving in New York in time for New Year's Day. His final decision, to either remain or return to Berlin, was made a few weeks later.

He kept dreaming of a position at the American Museum of Natural History in New York. He finally contacted Director Albert Bickmore, who was unable to offer him a position. Bickmore felt that other departments at the museum held a higher priority than one in anthropology and was unwilling to consider creating a new opening. Having experienced the free and invigorating life in America, Franz became increasingly disturbed by the direction that politics was taking in Germany – the sacrifice of liberties and the upsurge of nationalism. There was also the threat of war in the Balkans, which might result in being recalled into service were he to return home. Franz persisted in his search for a job by writing to Putnam and others he met, seeking their help to stay in America.

Boas first met Professor Frederic Ward Putnam (1839-1915) at the Buffalo meeting of the American Association for the Advancement of Science (A.A.A.S.), as noted above.[5,10] The scientific careers of these two men became entwined from that time forward. Putnam was a naturalist, archeologist, museum administrator, and teacher. His early training was in comparative zoology at Harvard under Louis Agassiz. After leaving Agassiz, he was placed in charge of the museum of the Essex Institute at Salem (1864) and made superintendent of the museum of the East India Marine Society (1867-69). Under the influence of Putnam and others, philanthropist George Foster Peabody was encouraged to fund the union of the above two museums. As a result, the Peabody Academy of Sciences was established in Salem, Massachusetts, an institution that Putnam directed from 1869 to 1873. In 1874 he was made curator of the Peabody Museum of American Archeology and Ethnology at Harvard College, the product of Peabody's beneficence in 1866. In 1887 Putnam was appointed Peabody Professor of American Archeology and Ethnology at Harvard.[10] It was shortly after this that Boas first met him. Putnam was the permanent secretary of the A.A.A.S. (1873 to 1898). He was elected its president in 1898, a position that Boas was to hold a number of years later.

At the time of their first meeting, young Boas, twenty years Putnam's junior, was bubbling with enthusiasm with plans for anthropological field research in the Pacific Northwest. So impressed was Putnam, they became fast friends. Putnam was a kind, generous, and gracious man, but also academically ambitious and protective of his own soil. The course of Boas's life was profoundly affected by this newly established relationship, one that was to last for well over two decades. Putnam was a descendant of 17th century New England stock, was well placed in society, and had considerable influence among his peers. Boas, anxious to succeed, desperately needed help and good scientific connections if he were to remain in the United States.

In January 1887, the month following his return from the Pacific Northwest, Boas went to the offices of *Science*, the publication of the A.A.A.S., with an article on geography he sought to have published. His arrival was fortuitous, as the editor, N. D. C. Hodges, had been looking for a Berlin correspondent. Although Boas had no such interest, it permitted the two men to have a fruitful exchange of ideas. The visit resulted in the hiring of Boas as an assistant editor, with special attention to geography. Whether Putnam played a role in this decision is not known. On January 24, 1887, Boas signed a two-year contract calling for payment of $150.00 per month.[2]

With his contract in hand, Boas immediately sent a cable home announcing his job offer and plan to file immigration papers. He desperately wanted to marry Marie and in America he foresaw a brighter future with more rapid advancement in his field. His three primary reasons for not returning to Germany included his concern about the inflexibility of university policies on promotions, a fear of the upwelling of anti-Semitism, and the potential for his conscription into the army.[2]

With at least a modest means of support assured and youthful optimism, he elected to stay in America and give up his fatherland permanently. About one month prior to their marriage, Emilie Krackowizer wrote to Sophie Boas,

> Franz loves Marie so much, and she belongs to him with all of her heart that it would have been a serious blow to them if they'd have to separate again and suffer through an uncertain, bitter period of separation! The early engagement, even if it was a bit hasty, now is secure and now both of them shall be rewarded with each other for the sacrifices made...Last week, we were running about almost constantly to find an apartment and to buy Marie's trousseau...It was more difficult to find an apartment since conditions here are tricky and since housing is the major expense...I and Dr. Jacobi advised them not to burden themselves too much...For the time being we plan to have only the closest relatives here for the ceremony which is to be conducted by a judge...there will be a general reception for all friends.[11]

On Thursday, March 10, 1887, Franz Boas married Marie Anna Ernestina Krackowizer in New York in a double ring ceremony, four years after their secret engagement in Germany (Figure 54).[a] The marriage, conducted by a magistrate, took place in the home of Marie's mother, Emilie Krackowizer, in her East 16th Street apartment. In attendance were members of both families, including Franz's sister Toni. Jacobi gave an address at a reception following the wedding. Gifts of money from Franz's father, uncles Jacob and Solomon Meyer, and Jacobi were generous and permitted them to buy furnishings for their first home. With the help of her mother and Toni, Marie found a 3rd floor apartment at 196 Third Avenue, between 17th and 18th Streets. It had two bedrooms, one to be used as a study for Franz. The rent was $35.00 per month.[2] Franz and Marie spent their honeymoon the following weekend at the Krackowizer country estate

---

[a] Franz wore his treasured gold band until his death fifty-five years later.

Figure 54. Marie and Franz Boas at about the time of their marriage. Photographer: Naegeli, New York, 1886 (American Philosophical Society).

in Sing Sing (now Ossining), New York.

Toni Boas was depressed and distraught during the entire year that she spent in New York. Her behavior during this joyous occasion cast a pall over the family. At the age of 32 and still single, she came to believe that she would never marry. Her dear brother was abandoning her by settling in America. She considered it an inopportune decision academically and accordingly, adopted a growing dislike of America. She was a beautiful young woman and a talented musician. Born with perfect pitch, she was an excellent pianist. A portion of her training had been with the Hungarian composer and pianist Franz Liszt. Toni returned to Germany shortly after the wedding.[2]

Marie was born in 1861 in Williamsburg, then a village across the East River from Manhattan, now a part of Brooklyn, New York. She was the third of five children of Ernst Nepomuk (1821-1875) and Emilie Forster Krackowizer (1826-1919).[12] Her parents came from Austria. Emilie was born in Kaiserberg on November 5, 1826, the daughter of the public prosecutor of Wels. Little is known of her ancestors.

Franz Boas never met his father-in-law, who died eight years before he met Marie. The life and achievements Krackowizer, nevertheless, became an inspiration to his son-in-law for the rest of his life. Ernst Nepomuk Krackowizer was born February 3, 1821, in Spital am Pyhrn, a small village on a pass in the Austrian-Italian Alps. His family was Catholic, so according to tradition and church doctrine, one of his given names was chosen in honor of a saint. In his case, he was named after Saint John of Nepomuk, the martyred and patron saint of Bohemia, murdered by King Wenceslaus in 1383.

Earlier ancestors of Krackowizer probably came from Poland. The name "Krackowizer" (Krackowice) means a person from Cracow (Kracow, Krakow), a province and the late medieval capital of Poland on the Vistula River. It is recorded that Krakow was named after the mythical Krak, a Polish prince who is said to have built a stronghold there, ca. 700 A.D. Krak was celebrated for slaying of the dragon that inhabited the nearby mountains by thrusting tar down his throat.

The ancestry of Ernst Krackowizer has been traced to the end of the 16th century.[12] The first known ancestor of Ernst Krackowizer was Paul Krackowizer (1599-1671) who was born in Leopoldschlag, Bohemia, later Czeckslava (Czechoslovakia). He was a butcher and father of six children. Most of his children remained in Leopoldschlag but Ernst's great-great grandfather, Simon Krackowizer, a brewer, moved to Gallenkirchen, a village near Linz, Austria. Most of the next two generations of Krackowizers lived in or near Linz, and many attended St. Peter's Church in Linz, where they were baptized, married, and buried in the churchyard. Ernst Krackowizer's father, Ferdinand Stefan Krackowizer, established the Spitalen line where he served as an overseer of the village. He was also an officeholder under the imperial government but because of his liberal political principles was shunned by those in power. He was a man of intellect and "given to philological and historical studies." Ernst's mother, Therese Richter, was a "modest and cultured woman" who raised a family of seven children.[12]

Inaugurating a long tradition that has, so far, embraced three generations of Krackowizer descendants, Ernst elected to study medicine. He matriculated at the University of Vienna in 1840. He received his undergraduate degree at the University of Vienna and his medical education at the Universities of Vienna and Pavia. He spent his third year at Pavia for exposure to the Italian language and culture. He was a bright and enthusiastic student, quickly absorbing the teachings of his mentors, who had a great respect for him (Figure 55). His sharp wit and humor endeared him to his peers. After graduation, he spent a brief period in the private practice of medicine in Steyer. In 1845 Professor Franz Shuh, chief of surgery at the University of Vienna, invited Krackowizer to join him at the university as his assistant, a choice position for this young physician. As a clinical experiment, it was Krackowizer who was the first person upon whom the anesthetic effects of chloroform were tried in Europe (Vienna), only two weeks after its introduction by Sir James Simpson in his obstetrical practice in England.[13-16]

Figure 55. Photograph of a Portrait of Ernst Krackowizer as a student in Vienna (Gertrud Michelson).

Three years after his university appointment, the Revolution of 1848 broke out throughout the continent of Europe.[17] Austria was a dominant power in Europe at this time, resulting from the Congress of Vienna (1815) that restored its territories. Prince Metternich had ruled Austria with an iron hand for over thirty years. His reactionary regime totally suppressed liberal and revolutionary thought. Finally in 1848, there was a violent response to the years of oppression.

The Revolution of 1848 refers to fifty or more uprisings throughout the European continent, counting the many tiny German (including Prussia) and Italian states, as well as the provinces of the Austrian Empire. Land ruled by the Hapsburgs included Austria, Hungary, Bohemia, northern Italy, and a portion of Poland. The Empire was politically isolated from the rest of Europe, ruled by an oppressive monarchy and the least likely place to expect a revolution. Its capital was Vienna. Poland and Italy were too repressed to even contemplate a revolution, but even this was to be challenged.

The revolutions had been fermenting for some time – many waiting for a dramatic and expected change to take place in France with the death of King Louis Philippe. This was considered a signal for the revolution. Ever since 1789, Europe had looked to France as the natural source of revolutions. It is interesting to note that a revolution did not take place in England, in spite of economic conditions that were in many ways worse than on the continent. England later became a haven for escaped revolutionaries including among others, Karl Marx, Friedrich Engels, Abraham Jacobi, Carl Schurz, and Gottfried Kinkel.

Sixty years of the industrial revolution had created a huge working class "whose miseries were likely to be explosive."[17] Child labor laws were weak to non-existent, labor had poor representation, hours were long, and wages were minimal with barely enough to buy food or afford housing. Following the international financial crisis of 1846, there was massive unemployment in concert with a poor harvest in many places on the continent. Some areas shared the human misery seen in Ireland during the famine years. With the depression of 1847, additional masses were put out of work without compensation, leading to starvation and illness. There was moral degradation, inadequate schooling and loss of hope among the people.

Causes of the revolution were multifaceted. Nationalism was a powerful motivating force for Germans and Italians. Most wanted freedom but did not know how to obtain it. The right to vote was severely restricted in many places, often limited to those paying taxes and to landholders. In France, Prime Minister Guizot stated, "Get rich; then you can vote."[17] Socialism evolved over a 20-30 year period in response to the industrial revolution. Intellectuals developed new social concepts leading to the Communist Manifesto by Marx and Engels. Favoritism at the highest levels of government was rampant. Although the revolutionary response was universal throughout Europe, the rebellions were not coordinated between the various states or between the classes in each state. For this reason and because of the lack of centralized leadership, arms or manpower, the revolutions were destined to fail.

With the rumblings of discontent in 1848, Ernst Krackowizer was one of the first to join the fight for independence against the autocratic powers of the monarchy. As a member of the Student's League and a born leader, he attracted a large contingent of liberal-minded students from the university and led an armed rebellion that included many townsmen. As a lieutenant under the command of General Bem, Krackowizer's contingent occupied an important position on the walls of Vienna.[13,14,17]

Although the revolutionaries took over the government and Metternich fled, their success was brief. General Windisch-Grätz was placed in charge of the imperial forces in Vienna, instituted martial law, and soon overwhelmed the young freedom fighters, brutally slaying many civilians. Emperor Ferdinand I resigned to be succeeded by Emperor Franz Joseph. On July 30, 1849, the police issued a warrant for the arrest of Ernst Krackowizer (Figure 56),

Von der k. k. Polizei = Direktion

Linz den 30. Juli 1849.

Bezd'ek.

Nro. 6223|1002 Steckbrief

wider den Medizinä= und Chirurgiä=Doktor Ernst Krakowitzer, der laut Zuschrift des Wiener Kriminalgerichtes vom 13. d. M. Z. 6492 an die k. k. Stadthauptmannschaft Wien von demselben des Verbrechens des Aufruhrs rechtlich beinzichtigt erkannt worden ist.

Derselbe ist 30 Jahre alt, zu Windischgarsten in Oberösterreich gebürtig, katholisch, ledig, großer ziemlich starker Statur, hat ein längliches blasses Gesicht, hohe Stirn, röthliche Haare, und derlei Augenbraunen, blaue Augen, eine spitzige, ziemlich große Nase, prop. Mund, ein spitziges vorragendes Kinn, röthlichen Backenbart, trägt eine schwarzzeugene Blouse, schwarze Hose, dunkle Weste, einen weißen deutschen Hut, und Stiefeln, spricht deutsch, lateinisch, italienisch, etwas französisch und englisch.

Figure 56. Notice of arrest warrant for Doctor Ernst Krackowizer by the Linz police, in accordance with a communication from the Vienna Criminal Court of Justice (N.F.B.)

It described Krackowizer as follows: "30 years old, born in upper Austria, Catholic, single, large considerably sturdy body, red hair, eyebrows and whiskers, blue eyes, a pointed somewhat large nose, a pointed chin, wearing a black blouse, black trousers, a waistcoat, white German hat and boots. He speaks German, Latin, Italian and some French and English."

He was able to escape, first to Bavaria and thence to Frankfort and

Tübingen, where he remained for nine months and taught at the university. Had he been able to remain in Vienna, he almost certainly would have had a thriving practice. Many years later, Jacobi was to write reminiscences of Krackowizer,

> The revolution was doomed; the thrones were glued together again with the blood of the cultured, self-sacrificing youth of the country . . . He served his country against the absolutistic and reactionary government. He had to flee from Austria to save his life; the venomous persecution followed him all over Germany.[13]

The Revolution of 1848 resulted in a massive exodus of Europeans to America. This included many of the intelligentsia who sought to escape from the repressive regimes of their countries to the freedom offered by the New World. Krackowizer as well as members of the Boas, Jacobi, Meyer, and Schurz families were all powerfully influenced by these events, as were many Germans who immigrated to America. Little did Krackowizer realize at the time that he would meet revolutionaries Abraham Jacobi and Carl Schurz in America. They immigrated to America at about the same time, where their experiences forged close friendships and where they became devoted and inseparable friends for life. They shared and fought for the same democratic ideals in their adopted home.

With the collapse of the revolution, authorities on his trail, the threat of imprisonment, and possible execution for high treason, Ernst Krackowizer left for America in May 1850. He sailed second-class on the packet ship *Henrietta Sloman* from Hamburg to America. It was on this same vessel that Henry Engelhard Steinway [Steinweg], founder of the one of the greatest piano enterprises in the world, sailed to America with his family. They too were "out of favor" politically with the Prussian authorities after the Revolution of 1848.[17,18] Krackowizer, in his humanitarian way, became the representative of his fellow passengers to the captain, repeatedly citing their grievances that included inadequate accommodations, rotten produce, rancid meat and inadequate attention to their health needs.[14,17]

Prior to leaving Vienna, Ernst Krackowizer became engaged to Emilie Forster. During his escape from Austria, travels through Prussia, and voyage to America, he wrote to her frequently in great detail in the form of letter-diaries.[15,16] Emilie joined him in Williamsburg, New York as soon as he became financially secure. They were married there in 1851. Krackowizer established his home and office for the practice of medicine at 105 South 4th Street (Figure 57). He made house calls by horse and buggy, as far away as Coney Island with frequent trips to New York by ferry across the East River. For a time he was on the staff of the Brooklyn

Figure 57. Home and office of Dr. Ernst Krackowizer from ca. 1850 to 1857 at 105 South 4th Street, Williamsburg, New York (Gertrud Michelson).

Hospital.

In 1857, Ernst and Emilie Krackowizer (Figures 58 & 59) moved their family to 49 Amity Street in Manhattan. After this move, he became deeply involved with the medical community. From 1863 until his death, they lived at 16 West 12th Street. It was in New York that he met Jacobi and Schurz for the first time, not having known them in Europe during the Revolution. As humanitarians and social activists, each vigorously pursued their individual goals, participating in and contributing to their new democratic homeland.

Ernst Krackowizer became one of the leading surgeons of New York. Early in his career, in 1857, he created a German dispensary, a small clinic building for outpatients with a few beds for in-patient care. Abraham Jacobi, other prominent German-American physicians, and Carl Schurz joined him in this effort. According to Jacobi,[13] Krackowizer was "the leading spirit" and "was the soul, the brain, the hand of all," as the dispensary evolved to the much larger German Hospital. The German Hospital was eventually renamed the Lenox Hill Hospital, and is located in Manhattan at East 77th Street between Park and Lexington Avenues. William Steinway helped Krackowizer raise over $100,000 for construction of the hospital. They may have first met on the Atlantic crossing they shared in 1850.[15,18] Ernst Krackowizer was memorialized in the Lenox Hill Hospital with an auditorium named in his honor.

Figures 58 & 59. Carte de visite photographs of Dr. Ernst Krackowizer by Mathew Brady, New York (Gertrud Michelson) and Emilie Krackowizer by Bogardus Galleries, New York (Barbara L Meyer).

During the Civil War, Ernst Krackowizer was a member of the Corps of Volunteer Surgeons of the State of New York, under the command of New York Surgeon General S. Oakley Vanderpool. Based on his expertise in developing hospitals, President Abraham Lincoln appointed Krackowizer Special Inspector of Hospitals. According to Abraham Jacobi, Krackowizer "was twice at the seat of war when eminent surgical aid was needed and solicited."[13] On several occasions he was called to the battlefields at Bull Run and Fredericksburg when his special surgical talents were needed. He was a member of the United States Sanitary Commission, a support group for the medical needs of the soldiers during the Civil War. On at least two occasions he traveled to Fortress Monroe in Virginia upon the orders of Secretary of War Edwin Stanton to inspect the facilities there.[15]

Krackowizer was also on the staffs of Mt. Sinai, Brooklyn, New York, and Bellevue Hospitals. Although he published only a few medical case reports, he made some important clinical observations, some of which remain in private unpublished papers. He was the first to introduce the laryngoscope in America.[19] As a political activist, Krackowizer became a member of the "Committee of Seventy," dedicated to municipal reform in New York City.

Figure 60. The summer home of Dr. Ernst Krackowizer on the heights above the town of Sing Sing, New York overlooking the Hudson River (Gertrud Michelson).

For rest and relaxation he bought a luxurious Victorian home, "Greenmont," on a 20-acre tract of land in Sing Sing (now Ossining), New York, high on a hillside overlooking the Hudson River (Figure 60).[b] Krackowizer visited his country home twice a week, an escape from his

[b] Ernst Krackowizer purchased Greenmont from Dr. Horace Green of New York City in 1869. In 1878 the property was sold to the widow of Dr. Green. She, in turn, leased it to Dr. Ralph Parsons who converted the home into a sanitarium. It was subsequently sold to other doctors who maintained it as a sanitarium for 90 years. While it was still a sanitarium, in 1956, Alfred Hitchcock used this former Krackowizer home as a location for the movie, *The Wrong Man*, which he directed and which stared Henry Fonda and Vera Miles. The house and outbuildings were demolished in 1972 to make way for a public housing project of the town of Ossining.[20]

busy practice in New York. It was here that Marie Boas's sister, Helene, married Theodore Meyer in 1875. Ernst and Emilie Krackowizer's five children included Dr. Emil Washington Krackowizer, a physician who married Sarah Elizabeth Partridge; Helene Therese Krackowizer who married Theodore Meyer, an attorney; Marie Anna Ernestina who married Franz Boas; Richard Franz Krackowizer, a bookkeeper; and Adelheid Maria ("Alice"), a schoolteacher (Figure 61).

Figure 61. Children of Ernst and Emilie Krackowizer. Left to right – Alice, Helene, Richard, and Marie (Emil is not present). Photograph ca.1868 (Barbara L Meyer).

Ernst Krackowizer died of typhoid fever in 1875, one month after his daughter Helene's marriage. A non-religious funeral service was held at Greenmont, attended by a large group of physicians from New York. Dr. Abraham Jacobi gave the eulogy. Another medical friend from New York led the graveside services.[13,20] Memorial services were held at Steinway Hall in New York, attended by three thousand people. Carl Schurz gave one of the eulogies. Krackowizer has been referred to as "the William

Osler of surgery." It is interesting to note that years later, the great physician, Sir William Osler, gave eulogies at the funerals of Abraham Jacobi and Mary Putnam Jacobi. While in Sing Sing, New York, the Krackowizer family purchased a burial plot in Dale Cemetery. It was here that Ernst was laid to rest. Many years later Emilie was buried there, as was their daughter Marie and the son-in-law Ernst Krackowizer never knew, Franz Boas. Other members of the Krackowizer and Boas families are also buried in Dale Cemetery.

We return to the new career of Franz Boas. As an assistant editor of *Science*, Boas had the opportunity of expressing his opinions in print. The A.A.A.S. was only four years old when he joined the editorial staff. The journal was more a science newsletter than an academic publication. As such he was able to write many articles, not only on geography, but on other scientific subjects including ethnology. He wrote about fifty short articles and reviews under the titles, *Notes on Exploration* and *Travel and Ethnological Notes*. His aim was to help create a distinguished international science journal, a goal he never achieved. He also wrote a number of editorials attacking the manner in which the United States National Museum and the Bureau of Ethnology exhibited their artifacts, disagreeing with their methodology. The curators of both of these institutions, Otis Mason and John Wesley Powell, respectively, leading ethnologists of their day, disagreed and responded with letters. At times the debate became acrimonious. The Washington scientists assumed that all ethnological artifacts evolved according the Darwinian theory of biological evolution of mankind. Thus the sophisticated artifacts of modern western civilization were positioned at the top of the evolutionary scale, with those of primitive tribes at the bottom of the scale. Artifacts in these museums were exhibited on a comparative basis, from most primitive to most civilized. This completely ignored the often-isolated evolution of different cultures, implying that western civilization was thus superior to primitive tribes. Although it seems trivial now, Boas was right and it established his name as a new intellectual combatant who was not prepared to accept ideas he considered out of date. Although it was early in his career, it started the conceptual thinking of his theory of "Cultural Relativism," to be discussed later.

Because he was well recognized in the scientific community for his Arctic exploits, on June 7, 1887, he received a letter from the pre-eminent physician, Sir William Osler, seeking information on the presence of St. Vitus Dance (chorea) in the Eskimos. Indicating that he was writing a book on this subject, it was Osler's "wish to refer to the Race relations of the disease."[21-23]

Boas joined the American Geographical Society where he tried unsuccessfully to use his influence to improve their substandard journal. He also felt that it was essential to create an ethnology society for the exchange of scientific information. In formulating his plans, he consulted with others, including Carl Schurz, who responded with a letter on December 12, 1887,

> ...I need not assure you that your efforts toward the formation of an ethnological society have my cordial sympathy and I sincerely hope you will succeed. Only let me advise you not to go with the society before the public until you have secured for it sufficient support to ensure it a healthy existence, for some time at least...[24]

In spite of other endorsements from anthropologists Frederic Ward Putnam, Daniel G. Brinton, and J. W. Powell, his efforts at this time failed. America was still in an early scientific developmental stage and not ready to accept new standards. In addition to his duties with *Science*, Boas was busy writing for German journals and began writing articles for the American Folklore Society. The American Museum of Natural History was not interested in the collections of Indian artifacts that he had collected on Vancouver Island, but he was able to sell them to the Berlin Museum for $500.

Boas's social life revolved around the families of Abraham Jacobi, Carl Schurz, the Krackowizers, his uncle Jacob (Kobus) Meyer, his cousins Willy, Theodor and Julius Meyer, and Adele Meyer Smutney. He joined German cultural groups in New York for lectures and concerts. He also established a relationship with Felix Adler (1851-1933), founder of the Ethical Culture Society, a liberal moralistic society. Although born a Jew, Adler rejected the strict dogma of his religion, but "secularized and humanized" its teachings.[2] In addition to holding regular meetings of the society, Adler established a Workingman's School that catered to children at all levels of society, and whose tuition was substantially less than other private schools of the time. Franz Boas served on the board of trustees of the Workingman's School. When his children were of age, some were sent there to be educated.[c]

In February 1888 Meier Boas sold his house in Minden and moved to Berlin. Many personal possessions of Franz were still in the house in Minden. He asked his parents send him the Baffin Island flag that Marie

---

[c] A niece (Alice Elizabeth "Bessie" Krackowizer) and three grandchildren of Franz Boas (Donald, Norman & Barbara Boas) also attended the same school; his son, Dr. Ernst P. Boas, became the physician to Felix Adler during the final years of his life.

embroidered for him, a walrus tusk, personal memorabilia and most of his books, notes and scientific instruments.[2]

About the same time, Franz wrote to his parents announcing the pregnancy of Marie. He and Marie had decided to name the baby either Helene or Ernst, after one of Franz's two siblings who died in childhood.

Boas was asked by the British Association for the Advancement of Science (B.A.A.S.) to conduct research for them. This resulted from his newly acquired expertise in fieldwork with the Indians of the Northwest Coast of America. Horatio Hale, who he first met at the A.A.A.S. meeting in Buffalo, was editor of the Committee of the B.A.A.S. for the Study of the Northwestern Tribes of Canada and was responsible for overseeing this expedition. Boas was charged with doing a "general synopsis of the ethnology of the whole of British Columbia, according to linguistic stocks . . ."[7] Constraints were placed on his research methodology, disturbing to him at first but which were eased in time. He conducted fieldwork for the B.A.A.S during the summer months from 1888 to 1894 and received an annual stipend for salary and expenses. During this time he took six trips to the Northwest, spending over twelve months in the field.

Prior to leaving on his first field trip, he obtained a two-months leave from *Science* and arranged to have Marie stay with her sister, Helene, at Lake George. He left from Montreal on May 25th on a committee's pass on the Canadian Pacific Railroad. During this first trip, he was in the Pacific Northwest from May 31 to July 24, 1888. He arrived in Vancouver, and sailed to Victoria where he spent two weeks. From here he took side trips to local villages where he did anthropometrical studies, interviewed local Indians, and collected specimens. During the next three weeks he sailed to Alert Bay, passed Fort Rupert, and Newitti and entered the inland waterway, sailing to Port Essington on the Skeena River. During this voyage he met with members of many Indian bands including the Haidas, Tsimshians, Tlingits, Bella Bellas, Kwakiutls, and Nimkish. He also spoke with anyone who could contribute ethnological information, including priests, doctors, and local businessmen. He recorded linguistic data, collected artifacts, particularly skulls and skeletons, as was the scientific bent in those days. Toward the end of his travels and after leaving Vancouver, he visited eastern British Columbia, stopping at Lytton on the Fraser River, Golden on the Columbia River, and at Windemere on the Kootenay River, to visit local Indian tribes.

At the time, the collection of skeletal remains and skulls was considered important from the anthropometric standpoint and certainly was an accepted scientific practice. Although trained in anthropometry by Virchow, Boas apparently never used measuring devices with the Inuit nor did he seek buried remains for study during his Arctic expedition. Even in British Columbia, he hesitated to take measurements of Indians and depended more on measuring skeletal remains. He found that removing bones from graves was "repugnant work" which even generated horrid dreams, but "someone had to do it." He purchased 75 skulls, which had been collected for the phrenological market in America after he was assured by the Army Medical Museum that there was a market for them. In spite of his repulsion to collect bones, he concluded that their measurements might be "the most valuable results of my whole trip." He brought back 85 skulls and 14 complete skeletons.[2]

During the remaining trips, Boas continued to record vast amounts of linguistic and ethnological data on the Indians of Vancouver Island and interior of British Columbia. Financial help from the Bureau of American Ethnology supplemented his income on his 1890 fieldtrip.

It was in Victoria in 1886 that Boas first met George Hunt (1854-1933), an Indian on the Kwakiutl Reserve in Fort Rupert and with whom he was to share lifetime experiences. Hunt, bilingual in English and Kwak'wala, was in Victoria at this time as a court interpreter for a number of Indians who were in jail facing trials. His father was an English employee at the trading post of the Hudson's Bay Company in Fort Rupert and his mother, a Tlingit woman. Hunt was an intelligent young man, raised with the Kwakiutl tribe and well informed about the heritage of his friends and neighbors. Before meeting Boas, he assisted other white acquisitors of artifacts and Indian lore. These included Israel Powell in 1881, and Johan Adrian Jacobsen in 1881 and 1885 who collected artifacts for the Berlin Ethnographic Museum. Although Boas and Hunt met only briefly on the B.A.A.S. expedition, Hunt was clearly the man who Boas would select as an interpreter and associate in years to come.

## References and Notes

1. Boas, Franz. *Baffin-Land: Geographische Ergebnisse in den Jahren 1883 und 1884 ausgeführten Forschungsreise*. Ergänzungsheft No. 80 zu *Petermanns Mitteilungen,* 100pp, Justus Perthes, Gotha, 1885 (A detailed scientific monograph of his Arctic expedition with charts and maps including a large fold-out map of his travels on Baffin Island. This thesis was used primarily for his habilitation as a docent at Berlin University – Norman F. Boas collection).

2. Cole, Douglas. *FRANZ BOAS. The Early Years, 1858-1906*, 360pp, Douglas & McIntyre, Vancouver / Toronto and University of Washington Press, Seattle & London, 1999 (The first definitive and an outstanding biography of Franz Boas. Cole had planned a second volume but was unable to complete it because of his untimely death).

3. Kroeber, Alfred L. *Franz Boas: The Man.* In *American Anthropologist, New Series,* Vol. 45, No. 3, Part 2, July-September 1943 (A brief but poignant biography, as a student and long-time friend of Boas).
4. Stocking, George W., Jr. In *Dictionary of American Biography*, 10 volumes and 8 supplements, American Council of Learned Societies, Charles Scribner & Sons, 1955-88 (Brief biography of Franz Boas).
5. Jonaitis, Aldona. *From the Land of the Totem Poles.* American Museum of Natural History, New York and University of Washington Press, Seattle, 1988 (A fine illustrated history of the Northwest Coast collection at the American Museum of Natural History).
6. Cole, Douglas. *Franz Boas and the Bella Coola in Berlin,* in *Northwest Anthropological Research Notes*, Volume 16, No. 2, Fall, 1982 (Detailed description and reaction to Boas's first meeting with the Bella Coola Indians).
7. Rohner, Ronald P. *The Ethnography of Franz Boas*. University of Chicago Press, Chicago and London, 1969 (Compilation and translation of letters and diaries of Franz Boas to family from 1886 to 1931).
8. Boas, Franz. Boas papers in the Library of the American Philosophical Society.
9. Boas, Franz. Letter to Carl Schurz, Victoria, BC, October 27, 1886. Library of the American Philosophical Society.
10. Dixon, Roland B. In *Dictionary of American Biography*, 10 volumes and 8 supplements, American Council of Learned Societies, Charles Scribner & Sons, 1955-88 (Brief biography of Frederic Ward Putnam).
11. Krackowizer, Emilie. Letter to Sophie Boas, February 6, 1887. Library of the American Philosophical Society.
12. Boas, Norman F. *Krackowizer Family Genealogy,* 14pp, Stonington, Connecticut, privately printed, 1984 (Copy in Library of the American Philosophical Society.)
13. Jacobi, Abraham. *Collecteana Jacobi.* 8 volumes, edited by William J. Robinson, the Critic and Guide Company, New York, 1909 (Papers of Jacobi including biographical material on Ernst Krackowizer).
14. Boas, Norman F. & Barbara L. Meyer. *ALMA FARM, An Adirondack Meeting Place*, Boas & Meyer publishers, Mystic, Connecticut and Bolton Landing, New York, 1999 (A chronicle of a 1000-acre farm belonging to Theodore and Helene Krackowizer Meyer, sister of Marie Boas. It is extensively illustrated with photographs, with brief biographies of the Meyer, Krackowizer, Boas, Jacobi, Schurz, and McAneny families, all of whom vacationed in Bolton Landing for many years).
15. Boas, Norman F. Collection of personal papers of Dr. Ernst Krackowizer (Included are his original clinical notes on the first use of chloroform in Europe as an anesthetic).
16. Boas, Ernst P. *A Refugee Doctor of 1850*, in *Journal of the History of Medicine,* Winter, 1948 (A selection from the diaries of Dr. Ernst Krackowizer).
17. Robertson, Priscilla. *REVOLUTIONS OF 1848: A Social history*, Princeton

University Press, Princeton, New Jersey, 1952 (A classic overview of these rebellions).
18. Steinway, Theodore E. *People and Pianos, A Century of Service to Music*, Steinway & Sons, New York, 1953 (100th anniversary of company).
19. Boas, Ernst P. *First Use of the Laryngoscope in the United States* in *Journal of the History of Medicine*, autumn, 1950 (A letter of Krackowizer describing the first use of the laryngoscope in America).
20. *The Republican,* Sing Sing, NY, Sept 25, 1875 (A story on the ownership of the Krackowizer property in Sing Sing).
21. Osler, Sir William. Letter to Franz Boas, June 7, 1887 concerning chorea (Norman F. Boas collection).
22. Osler, Sir William. Letters to Franz Boas (2), n..d. 1887, in the Library of the American Philosophical Society.
23. Osler, Sir William. *On Chorea and Choreiform Affections*, P. Blakiston, Son & Company, Philadelphia, 1894.
24. Schurz, Carl. Letter to Franz Boas, December 12, 1887 in the Library of the American Philosophical Society.

# CHAPTER V

## CLARK UNIVERSITY AND THE MUSEUM YEARS

Upon returning from the Pacific Northwest in July 1888, Franz Boas spent a short time with Marie at Alma Farm on Lake George. When he returned to the offices of *Science* four days later, he received a six-month's notice of dismissal from the editorial staff. It was a budget-saving measure, not the result of dissatisfaction by the organization. A short time later, the editor, N. D. C. Hodges did offer him $50.00 a month to prepare columns on geography and ethnology after his contract ran out.

On August 15th Boas presented his first paper at a meeting of the American Association for the Advancement of Science (A.A.A.S.) in Cleveland. It was an excellent opportunity for him to become better known in America. He was already fairly well recognized in the scientific community and had gained the respect of his colleagues. As a result of the meeting, he was able to extend his contract with the British Association for the Advancement of Science (B.A.A.S.) for another three years.[1]

On September 20, 1888, Marie and Franz had their first child. It was a difficult and prolonged labor. Uncle Abraham Jacobi was in attendance and although it was necessary to anesthetize Marie with chloroform, he was able to complete the delivery with instruments. The little girl was named Helene, after Franz's sister who died at the age of five.[1]

The following January, Boas was elected secretary of the *Gesellig-Wissenschaftlicher Verein* (a socially oriented scientific society) that paid him $400 a year and the Bureau of Ethnology hired him at $150 per month to work on linguistic material. Thus he was able to manage temporarily on this very modest income.[1]

In the spring of the same year, Franz, Marie, Helene, and Alice Krackowizer sailed for Europe on the Hamburg-America Company's steamer *Rugia*. In the mid-Atlantic, a fire broke out in one of the holds. All 182 passengers were ordered on deck. The flames remained out of control for five hours, despite attempts to quench the fire with hoses that flooded the lower deck. In spite of the impending disaster, the captain refused to let his passengers or crew abandon ship, holding them back with a revolver in hand. The fire was eventually extinguished by the use of steam and the ship was able to continue on its way without further incident. On arrival in Germany, they visited with Franz Boas's parents in their new home on *Grossbeerenstrasse* in Berlin, and with other members of the family. Franz spent much of his time studying collections at the museum. During the trip he worked on his B.A A.S. and *Science* reports. Traveling home alone, he stopped in England where he met with E. B. Tylor, chairman of the B.A.A. S. Marie, Helene, and Alice returned to New York about a month later.[1]

Shortly after returning to New York in July, Franz was off again to the Pacific Northwest. He was acutely distressed when he arrived at Victoria upon receiving a letter from Horatio Hale that completely altered his carefully laid plans for fieldwork during the summer. He was told to include surveys of the Tlingit, Tsimshian, and Nootka tribes in his report, visits that had not been on his itinerary. Hale's greatest contribution rested on the ethnological and linguistic observations he recorded on the round-the-world Charles Wilkes Expedition of 1838 to 1842. Since Hale (1817-1896) was forty years his senior and Boas was in no position to protest, he reluctantly complied. Having spent over a year in Arctic fieldwork entirely alone, and having accumulated such a vast amount of material, he too had some justification in asserting his independence in defining his own schedule. After spending over two weeks with the Nootka, he visited Alert Bay for the third time to study the Nimkish band of Indians on Cormorant Island. While there, he stayed with Stephen Spencer, owner of the fish cannery and brother-in-law of George Hunt.[1] He returned home in September to join Marie who was staying with her mother in New York.

The year 1889 was a significant one in the evolution of the career of Franz Boas. He was offered his first academic position in America. It was fortuitous that on his train ride to the A.A.A.S. meeting in Cleveland in 1888, he met G. Stanley Hall, a psychologist. At the time Hall, who trained in Europe and at Johns Hopkins University, was seeking candidates for appointments to the new faculty of Clark University. This institution was chartered in 1887 in Worcester, Massachusetts and was planned as a research university with only graduate students – modeled after some German universities and under the leadership of Hall. Clark University was originated, founded, and heavily subsidized by Jonas Gilman Clark, a wealthy Massachusetts merchant. Hall was very impressed with young Boas after hearing him speak at the A.A.A.S. convention. Since he was seeking candidates for his new faculty, he asked Boas to keep in touch with him. When Franz arrived in Victoria, he found a letter from Hall offering him a position at Clark University for the first school year starting in the fall of 1889.[1,2]

Although he was also offered a position in Washington, Boas did not want to work at the Bureau of American Ethnology. He reasoned that in a bureaucratic environment, he might lose some of his freedom to do scholarly research. In spite of the great influence of Schurz and Jacobi in their respective fields, neither had been successful in helping Franz find a suitable academic appointment. Boas, with only his editorial job at Science, readily accepted Hall's offer and was hired as Docent in Anthropology with a salary of $1500.00 per year, three times that which he had received as an editor. With somewhat over $500.00 a year from the B.A.A.S. and the sale of Indian artifacts and skulls that he had collected, he was able to manage quite well. Hall agreed that Boas would have "unlimited laboratory and library facilities" at his disposal and his summers would be free for research in the Pacific Northwest and elsewhere. At the time, Boas looked upon this appointment as a permanent position.[1-3]

Hall headed the Psychology Department, which he divided into several disciplines, each headed by a docent (Figure 62). For the Neurology Department he appointed Henry Herbert Donaldson who had been a student of Hall at Johns Hopkins University. Donaldson is most famous for his meticulous study on the brain of Laura Bridgman, the famous woman

Figure 62. The "Psychology Group" at Clark University in 1889. Seated from left to right: Thaddeus L. Bolton, Franz Boas, Henry Herbert Donaldson, G. Stanley Hall, Edmund C. Sanford, William H. Burnham and Edward W. Scripture. Standing from left to right: James S. Lemon, Gerald M. West, William O. Krohn, Fletcher B. Dressler, James E. Le Rossignol, William L. Bryan, Alexander Fraser and John A. Bergstrom (Clark University).

who was blind, deaf and mute. Charles Strong, the son-in-law of John D. Rockefeller, was made Docent of Philosophy. William H. Burnham, another Hall student, was appointed Docent of Education, and Arthur MacDonald, Docent of Ethics. Franz Boas's appointment as Docent of Anthropology was the first such university position in America.[2]

Franz was inexperienced at giving lectures. For this reason and because of his German accent, he was somewhat timid. To gain confidence and to obtain a better sense in managing his anxieties, he spent time auditing courses by Donaldson and other faculty members.

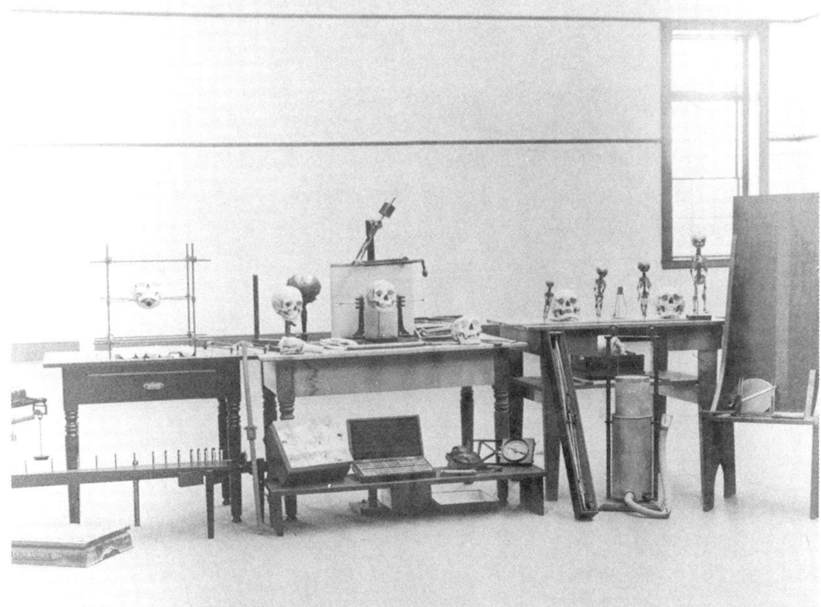

Figure 63. Franz Boas's anthropometric laboratory (Clark University).

The bulk of his research work at Clark was in anthropometrics, for which he had his own laboratory in the main building (Figure 63). His major emphasis in this discipline was to use physical measurements of the human body as a guide to the history and evolution of ethnic groups and in measuring the growth of children.

On one occasion, he proposed doing measurements of public school children in Worcester in order to establish the differential rates of growth and any possible relationship to mental development. Worcester had an exceptional mixture of many groups of families of different national origins, ideal for his purposes. The university and public school authorities approved the project; with matrons assigned to do the measurements on the girls.[2] The plan was viciously attacked by Austin P. Cristy, publisher of the *Worcester Telegram.* In his newspaper he asserted that Boas,

> would never lay a slimy finger on a single Worcester schoolchild...How will these people... enjoy having the hero of German duels feeling their son's and daughter's heads and bodies over, just as he did those of the Eskimaux, ascertaining the altitude of their respective aquillius, Grecian and pug noses, recording the color of their hair and eyes, the distance from the corner of the mouth to the ear, etc...innocent youngsters would be at the mercy of a perverted old lecher who would paw their tender bodies at will...[and further warned parents of]...a hand that fooled around with the topknots of medicine men and toyed with THE WAR PAINT of bloodthirsty Indians will feel of their children's head and bodies... he has scars on his face and head that would make a jail bird turn green with envy...an appearance which is not generally considered au fait, outside the society of criminal classes.[4]

Cristy took a newspaper poll, "Shall Docent Boas and 'his Associates' measure the public school pupils of Worcester – Yes or No?" The final count on May 12, 1891, was "No, 15,116. Yes, 345." The school board and Clark still approved the program. During the measuring process, reporters went to the schools and discovered that the *Telegram* articles had little effect. The students "couldn't wait to be measured." By the time he finished, Boas took over 17,000 measurements. He even checked the eyesight of the children and gave the results to the parents, who were pleased. He weathered this assault and completed his anthropometric studies.[1,2,4]

Being a teacher and surrounded by a scholarly group of scientists led him to formulate and more clearly define his thoughts on anthropology. He placed an ever-growing emphasis on social history as a means of interpreting anthropology. The cultures of diverse racial groups throughout the world evolved to different degrees, primarily as a result of their local historical development, i.e. physical environment, language, inventions, beliefs, customs, and contacts with other racial groups. This was not in accord to strict Darwinian theory when applied to all races evolving as a whole. Boas was not against evolutionary theory but he was concerned with historical misinterpretations. The historical approach would put the burden of proof of existing racial differences on those who subscribed to the evolutionary development of all races as one group. Boas, more than any scientist of his time, was one of the first to debunk racism on an evolutionary basis. In light of this he observed that traditions and beliefs were often not based on scientific truths, "My whole outlook, is determined by the question: how can we recognize the shackles that tradition had laid upon us."[1]

During his summer vacations from the university in 1890 and 1891, he returned to the Pacific Northwest spending most of his time with the Salish and Chinook Indians in Washington and Oregon. His summers were also occupied in writing his reports for the B.A.A.S. and on a special project for the Bureau of American Ethnology. He also published about forty papers on anthropometry, ethnological theory, linguistics, and other subjects.[5]

Worcester, at that time, was an industrial city with a population of about 90,000. It was the home of the American Antiquarian Society and Holy Cross University. Marie had spent time in Worcester as a girl and was somewhat familiar with the city. Franz and Marie rented the lower floor of a house at 210 Beacon Street on a hillside in Worcester. It was located near, but a good walking distance to the university, which was situated about one mile southwest of the center of Worcester (Figure 64). Franz renovated the apartment, created an office for himself, and rented a piano for $12.00 a quarter (3 months). Their new home was well suited for entertaining his new group of associates from the university and their wives. Donaldson and his wife, Julia, became close and lifelong friends.[1]

Figure 64. Marie and Franz Boas standing in front of their rooming house in Worcester, ca.1890-1892 (Gertrud Michelson).

When Franz and Marie's first child, Helene, was three years old (Figure 65), they had their second child, named Ernst Philip. He was born on February 4, 1891, and was named after Franz's brother who died in 1861 at the age of one.[6] Frustrated at being confined to bed for three weeks postpartum, Marie insisted that, "the shrieking Ernst must be the incarnated Raven of Boas's folklore."[1]

Figure 65. Franz, Helene and Marie Boas in a cabinet photograph taken by Rice, Worcester, ca.1890 (American Philosophical Society).

In his third year at Clark University, Boas sought an increase in salary that Hall could not consider. Hall had budgetary constraints placed upon him by Jonas Clark who monitored the budget and all policies of the university very closely and with financial restraint. At the same time, the university was having severe financial difficulties. There was faculty discontent brewing with the loss of their academic freedom imposed by Hall. Both factors presented a clear danger to Boas's future (and the rest of the faculty), with dim hopes for advancement. His position as docent, after all, was a position he had held in Berlin six years earlier. In addition, while in Worcester his family was growing and he again felt the need for a more substantial income.[1,2,5]

The general discontent led to a meeting of the faculty, led by Whitman, Donaldson, and Lombard, with Boas playing a role. Nine members of the faculty, including Boas, agreed to prepare a letter, tendering their resignations as of September 1892. Hall attempted to compromise, but was it too late. Learning of the planned mass exodus of these scholars, president William Rainer Harper of the newly created University of Chicago, traveled to Worcester and invited eight of the nine to join his faculty. They all readily accepted. Boas was the only exception – the university already had an anthropologist and Harper felt that they could not accommodate another one. Fortunately Boas had already committed himself to assist Frederic Ward Putnam in the anthropology department of the World's Columbian Exposition in Chicago. In spite of the unfortunate ending of his tenure at Clark University, he considered it an overall happy experience, with new friends and praiseworthy goals. He had developed his expertise in anthropometrics, bio-statistics, and devoted more time to linguistics and folklore. He was profoundly saddened, however, that Clark University had failed so miserably in attaining its goals as a scholarly graduate institution. Clark, of necessity, became an undergraduate college.[1-3]

About seventy percent of the student body and two thirds of the faculty abandoned the university. The only significant department left was psychology. Alexander F. Chamberlain who had obtained his Ph.D. in anthropology from Boas in March 1892, the first such award in North America, was hired as a lecturer to replace him. By 1911 Chamberlain had attained the position of professor of anthropology.[1,2]

In June 1892, after the completion of his obligations to Clark University, Franz and Marie Boas and their children returned to New York. They then sailed to Germany on the steamer *Darmstadt*, their first trip to Europe since 1889. Franz utilized his spare time on board and in Berlin working on his huge collection of Chinook material. While in Berlin he met Julius Urbach, a Berlin businessman, who had married Franz's sister, Aenne. His oldest sister, Toni, had married Ludwig Wohlauer the previous year. Each couple had a baby in June 1892, Walter Ernst Urbach and Elisbeth Wohlauer. The Boases had to cut their trip short because of an outbreak of cholera in Hamburg and set sail to New York on the ship *Weimar*, arriving on September 2, 1892.[1]

One of the first obligations of Franz, upon returning home to New York, was to consult with Putnam in Cambridge to prepare for his new assignment. The Department of Anthropology at the World's Columbian Exposition in Chicago was to be headed by Putnam. Boas was to become Putnam's Chief Assistant in anthropology at the exposition that was scheduled to open in 1893. Putnam had already conceived of and designed an ethnographical exhibition that would focus on the "past and present peoples of America."[1] An enormous amount of work was required in preparation (Figure 66). Boas had a cadre of Clark and Harvard students, missionaries, army and navy doctors, Indian agents, and teachers measuring Native Americans in the Canadian Arctic, Alaska, Greenland, and throughout the American states. The compilation of the data they gathered was a huge undertaking, with 17,000 bits of information. This vast accumulation of data was to be analyzed and presented at the fair.

Figure 66. Photograph of Franz Boas taken by Smith, Chicago, ca.1892-1893 (American Philosophical Society).

The ethnological material to be featured at the exposition also included massive numbers of artifacts obtained from the Pacific Northwest, an assignment embraced by Boas. Ethnological collections were obtained from the Haidas (by James Dean), the Bella Coolas (by Filip Jacobsen), the Skeenas (by Mrs. O. Morrison), and others. The Northwest Coast exhibits were huge representing three railroad carloads of Haida material, totem poles, masks, and other artifacts. George Hunt was unquestionably Boas's most valued assistant. He had amassed an enormous collection of artifacts from lower British Columbia that included an entire native house. Much of it was Kwakiutl material that constituted the highlight of the exhibits. Hunt helped obtain ethnological data and aided Boas in his linguistic research of the native languages and dialects. Hunt also arranged to have seventeen Canadian Indians come to the fair. They lived on the grounds in their own dwelling, dismantled in British Columbia and re-erected on the fair grounds for their use. The building was decorated with a thunderbird over the door, images of the moon on each side, and was flanked by totem poles (Figure 67). The open area in front of the building was reserved for native dancing, recreated potlatches, other demonstrations, and was surrounded by grandstands for use by the public.[7] According to Kroeber, it was the only exposition "which genuinely instituted broad-scale collecting and research and did result in a great scientific institution [The Field Museum]."[5]

Figure 67. A Northwest Coast Indian "Big House" erected at the World's Columbian Exposition in Chicago in 1892-1893 (Courtesy of the American Museum of Natural History, A. J. Rota copy, No. 322897).

In November Boas moved to Chicago to an apartment near his sister-in-law, Alice Krackowizer, who at this time was teaching in Englewood (near Chicago). She found an apartment for the Boas family. Marie and the two children joined him the following month. The apartment was rather dismal with heating problems, but they could not afford the inflated prices for rentals near the fair. This resulted in a lengthy commute to work.

On March 24, 1893, Marie delivered her third child, named Hedwig (Hete), after Franz's sister. It was not a difficult delivery, but the nurse never arrived, so Franz had to assist the doctor in her delivery at home.

When the fair opened on May 1, 1893, the anthropology building was not ready and required an additional month for completion. Unfortunately it was relegated to one end of the fairgrounds. This was due in part to political considerations, but probably resulted from a greater public interest in competing international exhibits. As a result, the anthropology exhibits were less well attended than had been planned.

Although he had known George Hunt for six years, Franz Boas came to know him intimately during the exposition. Hunt was a key participant in many phases of planning the exhibits at the Columbian Exposition. Personally, Boas spent a great deal of time with the Kwakiutl Indians, learning their cultural and social organization. The *Kwakwaka'wakw* people had no written language. It had been a goal of Boas to create a written language for them. With linguistic data he collected on his fieldtrips and with the help of Hunt, Boas taught Hunt to write in his own language, in a phonetic script, while in Chicago.[1,7]

Shortly after the birth of Hete, she became seriously ill, losing a substantial amount of weight. In the summer, all three children developed fevers; in December they each had influenza, followed by whooping cough. Little Hete developed complications with a pulmonary infection. Her condition deteriorated rapidly with a fever of over 106°. While he attempted to comfort her, she died in her father's arms following a massive hemorrhage.[1] George Bauer, a friend from Clark University who was in Chicago, helped make arrangements for burial in Oak Woods Cemetery. The following day, Franz and Marie rode to the cemetery in a horse-drawn wagon, with Franz holding the tiny coffin on his lap. Bauer and Henry H. Donaldson accompanied them. Another Clark colleague, Oskar Bolza, joined them at the cemetery. On arriving they were distressed to find that, "The cemetery was detestable – a barren, treeless field bordered by swamps and manure fields."[1] The gravesite was so tiny; there was no room for plantings. Following the burial, although they could ill afford it, they purchased a larger plot and later moved the coffin themselves to the new location. In the spring Franz and Marie planted flowers. This cherished site was visited every time Franz passed through Chicago, for the rest of his life.[a] The burial site is marked with a small stone, marked simply "Hedwig."[1,8,9]

The exposition's legacy to Chicago was the new Columbian Museum of Natural History, housed in the Palace of Fine Arts. It had been Putnam's idea to transfer the anthropological collections of the fair to the museum. After having toured the anthropological building, Chicago businessman Marshall Field became sufficiently inspired to donate one million dollars toward the project. The name of this new venue was changed to the Field Museum, in honor of the donor. According to Alfred Kroeber, it was the only exposition that "genuinely instituted broad-scale collecting and research and did result in a great scientific institution."[5,7]

It had been Putnam's goal and dream to become director of the new museum and to retain Boas at the museum as an associate. In spite of the fact that the concept of the museum has been his, Putnam was pushed aside as the result of a polarization of political attitudes against him among the exposition officials, led by the director of the fair, Harlow N. Higginbotham. Upon his rejection, Putnam reported that, "after squeezing the juice out of me they threw me aside as a used up orange."[1,7]

When Putnam returned to Harvard University after the exposition, at the end of 1893, he left Boas in Chicago. He had convinced the museum authorities to use Boas's expertise, since he was one of the very few who could sort out, catalogue, and prepare the exhibits from the vast anthropological collections of the exposition. It had been the hope of both Putnam and Boas that the latter would be appointed curator of ethnology at the museum. Boas worked for a while to help organize the ethnological collections, hoping that this would be his long sought-after academic position. This was not to be,

> Internal tensions, if not dissensions, seem to have been present from the start. All that happened would now be difficult and perhaps fruitless to discover. Boas's personal confidence many years later was to the effect

---

[a] Some years later a memorial stone to Hedwig was placed in the Krackowizer-Boas plot, the family burial site in Dale Cemetery in Ossining, New York. Oak Woods Cemetery, established in 1854, is on a 180-acre site in Chicago, formerly the farm of Illinois Senator Stephen A. Douglas, bordered on the north by 67th street and Cottage Grove Avenue, just few blocks south and west of the site of the World's Columbian Exposition. Buried here are 6000 Confederate soldiers who died in Camp Douglas in Chicago during the Civil War. It has since become one of the finest cemeteries in Chicago. Celebrities buried here include, among many others, mayors of Chicago, William Hale Thompson and Harold Washington, as well as Olympian, Jesse Owens, industrialist George Eastman and physicist Enrico Fermi.[8,9]

> that a joint protest or revolt had been organized by the scientific staff, but when it came to the firing line he alone went forward, and fell. Whatever the antecedent events, there is no doubt that he would not have retreated once he was committed...[5]

With doctor's bills, cemetery costs, and with indebtedness to Putnam, Franz was virtually penniless and had to seek help from his father. This added to his anxieties about his uncertain future in Chicago. Frederick J. V. Skiff was named director of the Field Museum. Although Boas had been considered a logical candidate for curator of the museum, without his knowledge Skiff went to Washington and committed himself to hire William Henry Holmes of the Bureau of American Ethnology for the position. Holmes certainly had excellent qualifications as an ethnologist, but so did Boas who also had special expertise with these collections. Boas's claim to the position was primarily on incumbency rather than on a scholarship superior to that of Holmes. When Boas learned of Skiff's action he was furious, for even Holmes had assumed that Boas would be the choice. Factors that weighed on Skiff's decision were his own attitude and pressures brought on him by William R. Harper, president of the University of Chicago, T. C. Chamberlain of the university, and the scientists in the federal government. Douglas Cole has given an excellent analysis of this contentious episode, which had never been clearly defined by other writers.[1]

Although he had no other job prospects and was distraught by Skiff's rebuff, Boas threatened to quit, fully realizing that he was the only one who could complete the installations for the June opening of the museum. In view of his financial hardships, however, he indicated that he was willing to stay on, but only if Skiff would pay him $1100.00 for the balance of his time in Chicago. Skiff agreed. William Henry Holmes was appointed curator of the museum.[1]

There is little question that the political feelings against Putnam were projected against Boas. There certainly was the typical academic scrambling for the position of curator. There was, however, only handful of men in all of America at this time who had the training or qualifications to be selected as curator of ethnology – probably less than a half a dozen. Ambitious and resolute, Boas probably made his own enemies. Whether there was prejudice based on his German roots or ethnicity, will never be known. Boas's difficulty in finding a job was also compounded by a general depression. It was difficult for institutions to find the financial resources for hiring new employees, not only at the Field Museum but also at the University of Chicago where he had also vainly sought a position.

Upon completing his work at the museum, he visited Hete's grave, determined to revisit this sacred spot whenever he could. He spent a month in New York and then retreated to Bolton Landing where he and Marie stayed in the Emilie Krackowizer cottage. Here he completed his final report on the Chicago Exposition for Putnam and his vice presidential address for the A.A.A.S.[1] His address was one of his earliest attacks on racism. He asserted that there was, as yet, no clear scientific evidence that there were any differences in the mental capacity of different races. Able to relax for a change, he played tennis, probably on the Alma Farm tennis court, hiked in the mountains and fields, and played with his two children, Helene and Ernst.

At about this time, Morris Jesup, president of the American Museum of Natural History in New York City, offered Putnam the position of curator of the Department of Archeology and Ethnology at the museum (Figure 68).

Figure 68. Frederic Ward Putnam at age 70 (Courtesy of the American Museum of Natural History, Neg. No. 2A5220).

In the summer of 1894, with the authorization to hire assistants as needed, Putnam again came to the rescue of one of his favorite young men and offered Franz Boas a temporary position at the museum. Boas's major assignment was to create a group exhibit with life-like manikins in their native costumes engaged in an activity appropriate for their culture. Although dioramas were not a new idea, it was an innovation for the museum. When the Smithsonian Institution learned of this plan, they asked Boas to prepare a group exhibit for it.[1]

Boas now had financial support from the American Museum of Natural History, the Smithsonian Institution, and a grant from the B.A.A.S. With these assignments he was off again to British Columbia to study and obtain materials for these displays. Most of his time was spent at Fort Rupert, the reserve of the Kwakiutl Indians, where his friend George Hunt helped him. The plan for the exhibit in New York was to create manikins demonstrating the "Uses of Cedar." Boas had photographs taken at Fort Rupert of a Kwakiutl woman demonstrating "cedar-spinning." Later, these photographs served as an aid for the sculptor of the manikins and for the design of the exhibit at the museum (Figures 69). The final display unit showed Indians shredding bark, spinning it for making a mat, drying fish over a fire, and placing hot stones in a cedar box to heat water (Figure 70).

This particular exhibit was a favorite of this writer as a youngster over seventy years ago and even drew the attention of J. D. Salinger in *The Catcher in the Rye.*[10] Salinger commented on visits to the museum, passing the huge Haida canoe on the way to view the cedar-spinning exhibit. Although the whole exhibit is no longer intact, portions of it are still present in several different displays at the museum.[7,11]

The Smithsonian exhibit, which Boas designed was quite different and showed the initiation of a Kwakiutl Hamatśa (Figure 71).[a] Since the museum sculptor had no idea of the scene he was to depict, Franz Boas posed as a Hamatśa dancer (Figures 72 & 73). A large number of glass-plate photographs were taken for this purpose. By 1896 Boas had completed his two dioramas of Pacific Northwest Indians, both of which were seen by millions of visitors. The Hamatśa diorama no longer exists.

---

[a] The Hamatśas were members of a cannibal society. The young initiates were selected by members and dispatched to the Cannibal-at-the-North-end-of-the-World for three or four months to absorb the cannibal spirit. In actuality, they stayed in the woods near their own villages. On returning from the "North" they had to be tamed, to be cured of their man-eating urges. This conversion was carried out in the Hamatśa dance, performed by members at the Winter Ceremonials and potlatches.[7]

Figure 69. Kwakiutl Indian woman at Fort Rupert demonstrating the spinning of cedar bark while she is rocking a cradle with her foot. Holding the blanket backdrop are Franz Boas on the left and George Hunt on the right. Photographer: O. C. Hastings (Courtesy of the American Museum of Natural History, No. 11604).

Figure 70. Early group exhibit of Northwest Coast Indians at the American Museum of Natural History, titled "Uses of Cedar," designed by Franz Boas (Courtesy of the American Museum of Natural History, No. 351).

Figure 71. Diorama designed by Franz Boas for the Smithsonian Institution, titled "Hamatśa Coming out of a Secret room" (The Smithsonian Institution, National Museum of Natural History – No. 77-10,037).

Figure 72. Franz Boas posed as a Kwakiutl Hamatśa dancer for the benefit of the sculptor at the Smithsonian Institution in preparing a group exhibit (Smithsonian Institution, National Museum of Natural History – No. 8292)

Figure 73. Franz Boas posed as a Kwakiutl Indian demonstrating the draping of a blanket for the group exhibit at the Smithsonian Institution (Smithsonian Institution, National Museum of Natural History – No. 8302).

In 1894, as a "visiting chief," Boas sponsored a feast for his hosts, the Kwakiutl Indians of Fort Rupert, a very unusual of gesture by a white man (Figure 74). In response, Chief George Hunt bestowed an Indian name on him, *Hi_dzaKwaLal's*, which means "speaking well from the beginning."[12] Giving a Native American name to a white person is a singular honor.

After leaving Fort Rupert, Boas sailed on the steamer *Boskowitz* to Victoria and continued on to the State of Washington to complete his work with Charlie Cultee, a Chinookan Indian. He then traveled to California to do measurements on southern California Indians and ended his trip in San Francisco where he lectured and made himself known to the Stanford University group. Still distraught and depressed without a job prospect, the loss of his little girl, and being away from home for five months, he returned to New York on January 29, 1895.[1] Although in bad financial straits, he still had some income from his temporary assignments from the American Museum of Natural History and the Smithsonian Institution.

While he was away, Marie stayed at Lake George for two months and then moved to a boarding house on East $58^{th}$ Street in New York. In February they moved to a boarding house in Washington for Franz to complete his work for the Smithsonian Institution. They were soon forced to find another boarding house because their landlady was a drunkard.

Figure 74. Kwakiutl Indian Chief Holelide making a speech thanking Franz Boas for his feast held on the shore of Queen Charlotte Straits in 1894. Photo by Franz Boas (Courtesy of the American Museum of Natural History. No. 336118).

His work at the Smithsonian Institution brought him in contact with the Washington anthropologists who were embarrassed and somewhat apologetic about the Chicago episode and the role they played in supporting the Holmes appointment. Nevertheless, Boas was able to re-establish a friendly working relationship with them, even to the point of learning that when the budget allowed, he might have an opportunity to join their staff.[1]

After completing his work in Washington in April 1895, and again without a job, the Boas family sailed to Germany on the steamship *Dania*. Upon arriving, he discovered that his brother-in-law, Julius Urbach, a proprietor of a brewing company was not doing well financially. Toni's child, Elisbeth, had hydrocephalus; she died later in the year. It was also in this year that his cousin Willy Meyer and Lilly lost their eight year-old child from complications of acute appendicitis. Franz spent much of his spare time completing his report for the B.A.A.S. He also started work on his Kathlamet texts (Washington State) and some publications on folklore. Before sailing home, he took a side trip to London where he conferred with Edward Tylor of the B.A.A.S. While there he received a letter from W. J. McGee of the Bureau of American Ethnology offering him an editorial job. Pleased with the offer, but unhappy with such a prospect, he again wrote to Putnam seeking help.[1]

Figure 75. Morris Ketcham Jesup, founder and president of the American Museum of Natural History in New York (Courtesy of the American Museum of Natural History. Copy by Morton Yourow, 2A5200).

When Putnam arrived at the museum in 1894 and became chairman of the department of anthropology, the museum was in financial straits; Morris Jesup had only recently been appointed president of the institution. There had been an anthropology department, created and directed by Albert Bickmore, but it was neglected. In spite of having some exhibit work to complete, Boas was getting frustrated by not having an official title at the museum and being unable to meet regularly with Morris K. Jesup (Figure 75). He asked Putnam to intervene on his behalf with Jesup. By December, Putnam was able to offer Boas an appointment as assistant curator of ethnology and somatology. Boas, however, would not accept it since he would be subservient to Marshall Saville who was already an assistant curator. This was resolved when Putnam appointed Boas his "special assistant," working directly under him. Putnam was ecstatic on January 1, 1896, when Franz Boas assumed his new position.[1] As Putnam was present at the museum only three out of every four weeks, Boas essentially ran the department in his absence (Figure 109).[7]

Morris Jesup (1830-1908) was a very wealthy man who devoted his early career to selling railroad supplies on commission. He made his fortune, however, in later years as a banker, becoming a multimillionaire. With such great success he was able to retire in 1884 at the age of 53. He supported many charitable organizations dedicated to environmental preservation, teaching institutions, the YMCA, and others. His favorite project was the creation of the New York Museum of Natural History in 1869. It was later renamed the American Museum of Natural History. Jesup joined the board of trustees in 1869 and served as its third president from 1881 until his death, visiting the museum virtually every day. During this time he gave the museum $2,000,000 as well as support for Robert Peary's arctic expeditions and the Jesup North Pacific Expedition. During his tenure he restored financial integrity to the museum and generated many large donations from his circle of wealthy friends. From 1899 to 1901 five more wings were added on the 77th Street side of the museum. By 1896 he had created one of the finest museums in America. He sponsored several expeditions to South and Central America that enabled the museum to prepare major exhibits with the many artifacts that were acquired. It was Boas who was to carry the burden of representing North America in the museum, particularly the Pacific Northwest.[13]

The Arctic experiences of Boas, widely reported, particularly among the scientific community, generated a respect among his colleagues and the following of a diverse group, especially whalers and those with tangential interests in the northern climes. Robert E. Peary sought advice on the Arctic region from Boas, based on the latter's experiences on Baffin Island. Peary also corresponded with Boas concerning scientific articles that he wished to have published[14] when Boas was geographical editor of *Science*.

Peary's relationship with the American Museum of Natural History developed through Morris Jesup. Jesup, always a promoter for the museum, helped finance Peary's Arctic expeditions in the hope of gaining valuable publicity and artifacts for the museum. In fact, in 1898 Jesup formed the Peary Arctic Club, an association of wealthy Peary supporters, whose goal was to raise funds from others to help subsidize his Arctic explorations. Jesup was president of this club for the balance of his life.

In 1897, Boas approached Peary and asked him to collect Greenland artifacts for the museum on his planned trip in the same year. He also requested that, if possible,

> It would be of the very greatest value if you should be able to bring a middle-aged Eskimo to stay here over the winter. This would enable us to obtain leisurely certain information, which will be of the greatest scientific importance.[15]

Peary did him one better – he returned with six Greenland Eskimos including two children. Boas hardly needed six Eskimos, much less children, for this task or for any other reason, having spent over one year living with the Inuit on Baffin Island.[1,15] Peary did this without any prior approval by the museum authorities. On September 30, 1897, he returned to New York with his Eskimos, a 37½ ton meteorite, Inuit relics that he had removed from Greenland, as well as tents, sleds, and native clothing for the museum. He also returned with skeletal remains of Eskimos from burial sites in Greenland for the museum's collections. Whether he gathered these latter artifacts at the behest of Jesup, Putnam, Boas or others is not clear. Before permitting the unloading of his ship or the disembarking of his visitors, he generated publicity through the press and opened his ship to the public. As a seasoned self-promoter for his expeditions, he charged the public for viewing the Eskimos and the meteorite he had brought to New York. In two days, 30,000 people paid an admission fee to board the ship.

The Eskimos (Inuit) included three men, one woman, a girl, and a boy. Represented were a father and son, Quisuk and Minik; a husband and wife, Nuktaq and Atangana; a 12 year-old girl, Aviaq; and Uisaakassak, a boy who planned to marry Aviag at some later date. Peary stated, "They will remain with me here this winter, to arrange the ethnological specimens, and will return with me next summer."[15]

The fact was that Peary discharged his responsibility for the Eskimos by delivering them to the American Museum of Natural History on October 21, 1897, for their custodial care and assumed no further accountability for their welfare. Placed in an awkward position, without having been consulted in advance, Morris Jesup assigned William Wallace, the Superintendent of Buildings of the museum, the entire responsibility for their care. Wallace provided the living quarters for them in the basement of the museum.

Two months later, on exposure to infectious diseases to which they were not immune, all six Eskimos developed "pneumonia" and were admitted to Bellevue Hospital. Apparently recovered, they were all returned to their quarters at the museum.

In February of the following year they were all readmitted to the hospital where Quisuk, the father of Minik, died, probably of tuberculosis. Although not well, the remaining group was discharged to stay in a cottage owned by William Wallace in the Highbridge section of New York. Only a month later, Atangana, wife of Nuktaq also died.[b] At this point, Boas agreed that all the survivors should be returned home, but indicated that there would be no ships to Greenland until summertime.[15]

Peary who should have known better than to bring the Eskimos to America, distanced himself from these tragedies, lest his reputation be tarnished. Jesup, as well, could not expose himself to criticism and left it to Boas to "make public statements."[15] By the end of March, Wallace was no longer interested in housing the four remaining Eskimos. After discussing it with Jesup, they agreed that they would be sent to a farm in Lawyersville, New York, owned by Wallace. Minik would remain in the city and stay at the home of Morris Jesup. He was later adopted by Wallace, joined his family and was named Minik Peary Wallace.

In May of the same year Nuktaq and Aviaq died, probably of tuberculosis. Uisaakassak was placed in the hands of Matthew Henson on Peary's ship in New York Harbor. Henson, an African American, was Peary's companion on his Arctic expeditions. This young Eskimo was saddened by the loss of his prospective wife. However, he was happy to be with Henson who could speak his native language and glad that he would be returning home. In July he sailed to Greenland on the ship *Windward*.

It is of some interest to note that in May 1898, Robert Peary completed a two-volume treatise on his Arctic expeditions to that date. He mentioned some of the departed Eskimos as his friends in Greenland, but in the present tense, as though they were still alive.

Upon the death of Quisuq, the authorities at Bellevue Hospital permitted medical students to dissect his body for post-mortem experience. With no acknowledged relative to assume the responsibility of burial, the body was transferred to the American Museum of Natural History for their collection of skeletal remains. Minik, his son, was considered too young to be consulted. Nevertheless, out of respect for the young boy's feelings, a "mock burial' was performed on the grounds of the museum. Alfred Kroeber, a student of Boas, conducted interviews of the Eskimos and was well informed of the burial rituals of the Greenland Eskimos. The "wrapped body of his father" was buried and covered with stones on the grounds of the museum. Minik, who attended and participated in the

---

[b] The diagnosis of "pneumonia" in the Eskimos may well have been initial symptoms of tuberculosis.

burial, had no idea that the interment was a sham.[15]

Following the deaths of the other three Eskimos, as paupers without surviving relatives, their skeletal remains also became the property of the museum authorities. They justified this based on their custodial role including the housing and support of these individuals.

This concluded a sad chapter in the history of the American Museum of Natural History, reflecting on the reputations of Lt. Robert Peary, Morris Jesup, Franz Boas, Alfred Kroeber, William Wallace, and others. Years later when Minik was 17 years old, however, the press reported on the presence of Minik's father's bones on display in the museum, but they were unaware of the sham burial. Nevertheless, the story was published. Minik heard the story through his schoolmates. As a sequel, in January 1907, the New York *World*, ran an "exposé" headlined, "Give Me My Father's Body," dwelling on the misfortune of this young man and the delusion he had lived with over the years.

Kenn Harper has written a book, *Give me My Father's Body,*[15] which is a definitive account of this poignant story, albeit sensationalized. It recounts Peary's Greenland expeditions, his retrieval of Eskimo artifacts, the six Eskimos cited here, and their sad experiences in New York. Also detailed is the intriguing relationship between Jesup and Peary as well as references to Wallace, Boas, Kroeber, and other members of the museum staff. The newspaper exposé in 1907 was a shocking narrative of a young boy discovering his father's bones in the museum – a heartrending story, repeated in the *New York Times* and *Washington Post*[16] in recent years, after the publication of Harper's book. Boas was on vacation leave from the museum when Peary arrived with the Eskimos, thus played no role in receiving them. At the time, Boas was assistant curator of anthropology at the American Museum of Natural History, second in charge to Curator Frederic Ward Putnam. He did concede that following his return, "Although I am not formally responsible, the whole thing falls on my shoulders and I feel a stone around my heart." According to Cole, "it is unclear that anyone was responsible,"[1] but it was nevertheless a most regrettable experience for all concerned.

In a recent article Edmund Carpenter refutes the newspaper and Harper's accounts that Minik's father's remains were on display at the A.M.N.H. Carpenter considers Harper's "a tabloid account of Minik…it provides Harper however with the book's title and the key scene for a potential film."[17] To bring a closure to this story, Carpenter personally arranged to have the skeletal remains of the four Eskimos returned to Greenland for a formal burial.

It should be remembered that, beyond the unhappy Minik episode, ethnologists and anthropologists in the 19th century were trained to utilize anthropometric techniques to study man. It was a standard practice to gather skeletal remains, particularly skulls, to do comparative studies in an attempt to define ethnic groups. As part of his fieldwork, Boas brought many skulls and skeletons to the museum from the Pacific Northwest, with the cooperation of Native Americans. Other American museums had similar collections. Even now, it is estimated that there are over 500,000 museum collections of skulls and skeletal remains. Harper even stated,

> The bones and brains...of the world's great museums were acquired in the spirit of hope and human enlightenment and betterment. Undoubtedly a great deal of valuable knowledge has been derived from their study.[15]

Collecting skulls continued until late in the 19th century, during which time the United States Surgeon General "directed Army personnel to obtain Indian human remains for the Army Medical Museum." Most of the 18,500 body remains held by the Smithsonian Institution came from the Army's acquisitions. Boas wrote in his diary in the 1880s, "It is most unpleasant work to steal bones from graves, but what is the use, someone has to do it." In 1990 Congress passed the Native American Graves and Protection Act, which was a mandate for the return of Indian human remains and artifacts in museums and in private collections, which were not legitimately obtained from Native Americans. The deadline for reporting was November 16, 1995. It remains to be seen how this Act will be implemented with "tens of millions" of artifacts still in institutional and private hands.[18]

Present day criticisms of amassing skeletal remains, as was done in the 19th century, must be interpreted against the mores of that time, when it was accepted as a proper scientific approach toward research; there was little opposition. Even now medical schools, of necessity, must provide human bodies, skulls and skeletons for teaching purposes, most of which are of paupers without known relatives or individuals who have bequeathed their bodies for this purpose.

To return to the career of Boas, in 1895 he still hoped to obtain a teaching appointment at Columbia University. Anxious to help his younger colleague, Curator Frederic Ward Putnam wrote to President Seth Low of Columbia University suggesting that Columbia appoint Boas to a teaching position. He stressed that Boas was the leading physical anthropologist in America and an authority on the linguistics and ethnology of the Indians in the Pacific Northwest. With the help of Abraham Jacobi, Putnam orchestrated a solution for Franz Boas, which was two-pronged.[7] Unbeknownst to Boas, Jacobi wrote to Morris Jesup and offered to donate $1500 toward Boas's salary of $3000 at the museum until Columbia committed itself to hire him. He would then subsidize Columbia in the same amount. This plan was presented to President Low as an inducement to hire Boas. Nicholas Murray Butler also recognized and advised Low that the employment of Boas was an extraordinary opportunity for the university. Low felt that Columbia had to impose limits on spending, for it had recently moved from downtown Manhattan to Morningside Heights and embarked on a new curriculum; the university had many other financial commitments. Low did, however, agree to hire Boas to give a series of five lectures for the year 1896. This arrangement was later continued for year or two. For his lectures Franz received a modest stipend.[1] He was at least progressing toward his academic goals with his museum position and a lectureship. Again Jacobi had come to the financial aid of his nephew. In 1899 Boas was appointed as the first university professor of anthropology in America at Columbia University, a position he was to hold for the next 37 years.[c]

Franz Boas wasted no time in assuming his duties at the university and at the museum. He established his own anthropology club for meetings, which included members of Columbia University and the American Museum of Natural History. He initiated the formation of the New York Academy of Sciences. In 1897 he was appointed chairman of the A.A.A.S committee to consider a new anthropological journal, a successor to *American Anthropologist*. He and W. J. McGee were the actual owners of it and subsidized it for the first three years. When the American Anthropological Association was formed in 1902, it took over the journal. Boas was also instrumental in re-establishing the American Ethnological Society that had been dormant for over fifty years.

Now that he had a formal position at the American Museum of Natural History, Boas had the opportunity to consult with president Morris Jesup in planning research and exhibits – a relationship which led to some extraordinary developments.

The goal of Jesup was to create one of the finest museums in America. To expand the scope of museum activities, Franz Boas conceived of an anthropological expedition to Siberia and the Pacific Northwest to determine the origins of Americans Indians. Although it had long been

---

[c] Daniel Garrison Brinton (1837-1899) was appointed professor of ethnology and archeology in the Academy of Natural Sciences of Philadelphia in 1884 and professor of American linguistics and archeology at the University of Pennsylvania in 1886. Brinton, however, although an excellent teacher, did no field work and confined himself to a much narrower field than did Boas. His writings were based primarily on reports of others.

speculated that they had migrated on the land bridge across the Bering Strait, caused by the lower ocean level during the glaciation period over 10,000 years earlier, there was little scientific evidence to support this theory. It was, however, a subject in which the public and the news media had a continuing curiosity. Morris Jesup had a compelling interest in major noteworthy scientific undertakings and any project that would enhance collections of his museum. With this in mind, and knowing that funding would be forthcoming from Jesup if he were convinced of its value, Boas, with the support of Putnam, proposed this expedition to Jesup, who in turn, quickly endorsed it and made a personal commitment to provide the financial support. Jesup also wanted to use the publicity generated to raise more funds to build another wing on the museum. Putnam and Boas were equally motivated, particularly with the perspective of outdistancing the Field Museum of Chicago that had rejected each of these men. The earlier rejection of Boas by the Chicago group was considered an "unsurpassed insult" by him; Putnam vowed to "show Chicago I can go them one better."[1,19,20] Thus began the Jesup North Pacific Expedition of 1897-1902, a huge scientific undertaking involving many individuals.

Boas was less interested in proving that the forbears of American Indians had crossed the Bering Straits, an almost impossible challenge, than he was in studying the physical and ethnological similarities between the cultures of Northeast Siberia and America's Pacific Northwest. He organized the expedition and selected two scientific groups, one to conduct field studies in Siberia and the other in the northwest coast of America.

There were difficulties in obtaining visas for some members of the Siberian expedition and required political pressure from the United States State Department. Some of the Russian scientists were considered revolutionaries and faced obstacles within their own government.

The Siberian expedition was divided into three groups. One covered the Amur River Valley and Sakhalin Island. A second group covered Northeastern Siberia and the third group studied the natives of Kamchatka Peninsula. Many of the research personnel suffered the hardships of primitive travel over vast distances, forbidding winter weather conditions, and epidemics.[19]

During this five-year period they collected an enormous amount of material on the cultures of the native people of these areas. Some 3000 photographs were taken in Siberia and in the Pacific Northwest. The Siberian expedition accumulated huge amounts ethnological data, skeletal material, plaster casts of faces, physical measurements, phonograph recordings, archeological specimens, and native folklore.

On the American side, Franz Boas personally led and participated with the research team in the Pacific Northwest. He was assisted by profess-sional anthropologists Harlan I. Smith, John R. Swanton, Livingston Farrand, as well as his Indian friend and associate George Hunt and James Teit, a Scotsman who married a Thompson Indian woman. These latter two men were of invaluable assistance in gathering data for the Jesup Expedition. The only field trips Boas made during this expedition were in 1897 and 1900.

On his first trip, he stopped in Chicago to visit old friends from Clark University who were at the University of Chicago, and his sister-in-law, Alice Krackowizer. He also visited Hete's grave and was pleased to see that the grounds were now well maintained. The pansies that he and Marie planted were in bloom. He "picked one to send to Marie." He was saddened to discover that his "best friend in America," Henry H. Donaldson, was ill with osseous tuberculosis.[d] Boas's final visit was to the Field Museum where he met with Skiff. He noted that the museum was in bad condition and was now pleased that he had not been invited to stay there. In addition, he also learned that Holmes had been displeased with his position and status and left, returning to Washington.[1]

Continuing on his trip to the Pacific Northwest, he was accompanied by Harlan Smith, a young archeologist and a protégé of Putnam whom he had met in Chicago, and Livingston Farrand, a young psychologist from Columbia University. Both were untrained in ethnology but suited Boas's needs well.

One of their first stops was in Spences Bridge, British Columbia where they met James Teit (1864-1922). Teit was born in the Shetland Islands and immigrated to Canada in 1882. He settled in Spences Bridges where he married Lucy Artko, a Salish Indian and where he became fluent in native languages. During the Jesup expedition, he worked for Boas during the entire period gathering vast amounts of ethnological data of the natives of the mainland of British Columbia, primarily the Salish Indians. In spite of little formal education, he became an invaluable contributor to

---

[d] The tuberculosis responded to treatment and apparently did not affect his career. Henry Herbert Donaldson (1857-1931) was born in Yonkers, New York. He attended Yale University, received his medical degree at the College of Physicians and Surgeons in New York (1881) and PhD at Johns Hopkins University (1885). After a year at Hopkins as an associate professor of psychology, he joined the faculty of Clark University as an assistant professor of neurology (1889-92). It was here that he met Boas and established a life-long friendship. He next headed the Department of Neurology at the University of Chicago (1892-1906) and completed his medical career as professor of neurology at the Wistar Institute in Philadelphia.

the expedition; some of his ethnological work and observations were published in the final Jesup Expedition reports.[1, 7]

Smith went on to Kamloops and Lytton to do archeological excavations. Boas and Farrand, with Teit as a guide, left on a 38-day expedition on horseback to the Pacific coast, starting up the Fraser River to the northwest. They rode, often slogging through marshland with a ten-horse pack team. They crossed the Coast Mountains to Bella Coola, having traversed over 300 miles. Farrand left the group at Puntzi Lake on Boas's recommendation, to spend one month studying the Chilcotin Indians. George Hunt, well prepared for this visit, greeted them upon their arrival at the Bella Coola reserve. Boas then sailed to Port Essington on the Skeena River, some 250 miles to the north to gather more ethnological material on the Haida Indians.

While in Port Essington, on August 19, 1897, he wrote a somewhat nostalgic letter to Marie on Aenna's birthday about his sisters. Aenna was nine years younger than Franz. He expressed with regrets that she rarely wrote letters to him, a sister whom he hardly knew, having left home when she was a child. "Toni's letters also seem forced. She feels that many, many events have made strangers of us…I wish I could change this; when I think of our earlier relationship, it really depresses me [Toni never forgave Franz for 'deserting' her and going to America]. What can I do to change things? Only with Hete do I feel a real brotherly relationship."[21]

In writing to his parents from Rivers Inlet, British Columbia on September 5th of the same year, he reflected on other ways he could supplement his income, which was always inadequate. He felt that he was "too clumsy to write popular articles" and did not have enough time to do it. He declined an offer from Appleton, a New York publisher, to write a popular book on some of his exploits in the Pacific Northwest. Although wanting to do it, he declined because "it would cost me too much time…I made a rule a long time ago to write nothing that cannot be used as a lecture…"[21]

After spending two weeks with Hunt and the Kwakiutl Indians of Rivers Inlet, he met with Farrand and they left for New York. Smith stayed behind to complete his archeological work.[1,19]

Boas did not join the next two phases of the Jesup Expedition in 1898 and 1899, but his associates, Smith and Farrand did. In the summer of 1898, on leave from the museum, he sailed to Europe. Now, as an experienced museologist, he visited many museums in London, Holland, and Germany – studying exhibits and arranging exchanges and purchases. He, Marie, and the children also paid a nostalgic visit to Minden and visited the Boas family in Berlin – the last time Franz was to see his father.

In 1900 Boas returned to British Columbia, the fourth year of the Jesup Expedition. After a visit to Spence's Bridge, impressed with the valuable data Teit had accumulated, he went to Alert Bay where he stayed for two months before returning home. While there, he stayed at the home of Stephen A. Spencer. Boas spent most of his time interviewing the natives on such subjects as recipes, food preparation and medicines, but particularly on their language, Kwak'wala. He, as always, studied every facet of the culture that was possible to record. He spent some time with Hunt, but had difficulties with the tribe who began to distrust this white man in his collaboration with Hunt. Boas repeatedly reassured them as to his honorable motives and had George Hunt read a letter to them at a feast addressing this issue. His good intentions and diplomacy had beneficial effects on the complainants.[1]

The fieldwork of the expedition was essentially completed in 1900. As was typical of his research methods, Boas and his group accumulated tremendous amounts of ethnological data. Some work with the materials gathered had to be completed, huge quantities of data had to be sorted and studied, and thousands of artifacts had to be described and cataloged. The findings of the Jesup Expedition were edited by Boas and published by the American Museum of Natural History in eleven volumes between 1898 and 1930.

The material collected by the Jesup Expedition gave strong support to the close relationship between the cultures of northwestern America and northeastern Siberia. It did not settle the question of migration during the great ice age, and even suggested that if there had been a west to east migration, reverse migration might also have taken place. Reflecting on the one hundred years that have elapsed from the initiation of the Jesup Expedition, the most enduring heritage is the immense quantity of ethnographic material, photographs and museum artifacts that were amassed. This expedition preserved the history of many cultural groups which would otherwise have been lost.[17,22,23]

In his position at the museum, Boas embarked upon a relentless search for artifacts for its collections. The magnitude of the Jesup Expedition in Siberia and Pacific Northwest motivated him to study other vanishing cultures throughout the world. He became so involved in his museum pursuits that he had to turn down an offer of the Bureau of American Ethnology (B.A.E.) to head their language division. In 1902, however, he was made honorary philologist at the B.A.E., in recognition of his extraordinary grasp of linguistics and his role in developing it as a scientific discipline. Extending his horizons, in 1898 he indicated that there was an urgent need to do field research in eleven western states, encompassing 95 tribes of Indians. He estimated this would cost nearly $300,000.00. It would become a lost opportunity if not implemented. He succeeded only modestly in raising money toward this end, mostly from Henry Villard and Collis P. Huntington.

Boas was able to dispatch Roland Dixon to study and collect artifacts from northern California Indians. His student, Alfred Kroeber left to study the Arapaho's in Indian Territory. In 1901 Boas sent students William Jones to study the Sac and Fox tribes on the Mississippi River, Clark Wissler to the South Dakota Sioux, Livingston Farrand to the Northwest, Constance Goddard DuBois to the Mission Indians in California, and H. H. St. Clair to visit the Shoshone Indians, first described by Meriwether Lewis on the Lewis and Clark Expedition. By now the American Museum of Natural History was in competition with other specimen hunters from the Field Museum and other institutions. Never were there sufficient funds to record the cultures of these diverse tribes in the manner that Boas had done in British Columbia and on the Jesup Expedition.[1]

Although he was against American imperialism, with the advent of the Spanish-American War Boas saw an opportunity to do fieldwork in the Philippines. He suggested that the museum send young researchers to China and Japan to collect artifacts for the museum and attempt to create an Asian Studies Center. Jacob Schiff, the financier, took an interest in Boas's idea and donated $6000.00 per year to this end, making it possible to send some students to the Far East. Boas even pressed for initiating collecting in Africa, the Near East and India. His visions were limitless.

In 1895, with Franz starting to work at the museum in New York, he and Marie found a three-story brownstone building for rent near the museum at 123 West 82nd Street. Emilie Krackowizer occupied the second floor, and thus could share expenses with them. During the next seven years the Boas family grew. Gertrud Marianne (Trudel) was born in April 1897 (Figure 76). Henry (Heine) Herbert Donaldson Boas, named after their close friend, was born in February 1899; Marie Franziska (Fritzi) was the last-born, in January 1902 (Figures 77-80). Marie had her hands full with five children and a husband away from home for long periods of time. When home, Franz was so preoccupied with his work that he was unable to spend much time with the children. In time they were able to afford a sitter who was also an English tutor for the children. This is an odd commentary on the household of one of the greatest linguists of his time. Yet Marie and Franz were raised in families that spoke only German at home. It was easier and important to them that the children learn to speak German well. When possible, Franz read to the children. On one occasion, he read the Ten Commandments from the Bible to them. On reciting,

"Thou shalt have no other Gods but me," seven year-old Ernst responded, "Isn't he greedy!"[1]

Figure 76. Franz Boas and his daughter, Gertrud, ca. 1898 by Rockwood, New York (American Philosophical Society).

Figure 77. Three generations, Meier, Ernst and Franz Boas in Berlin, ca. 1897 (N.F.B.)

It was a comfortable apartment where they were able to entertain friends and museum associates. Members of Franz's mother's family were

Figure 78. The Franz Boas family at home on West 82nd Street, New York. Franz is at the piano; Marie is in the distant chair; Ernst is in the foreground; Helene is next to her father (American Philosophical Society).

Figure 79. Franz and Marie Boas in their West 82nd Street New York home, ca.1899 (American Philosophical Society).

often visitors. This included his cousins Julius, Willy, Theodor Meyer, and Adele (Dele) Meyer Smutney; his in-laws, Helene Meyer and Richard Meyer; his uncle Abraham Jacobi; and Berthe Krüer, a nurse and sister of Franz's close friend in Minden, Reinhard Krüer, who was drowned in 1877.

Figure 80. Photograph of Gertrud (age 3), Helene (age 12), and Ernst (age 9), in 1900 (N.F.B.)

On February 16, 1899, when president Seth Low appointed Franz Boas professor of anthropology at Columbia University at age 41, Boas had attained his cherished goal of obtaining a prestigious academic position in his adopted country. At this point Abraham Jacobi kept his promise. Frustrated by Columbia's procrastination in hiring Boas, he promised Low to pay for Boas's salary of $2500.00 for two years, on the condition that Franz should never be told of it – a poorly kept secret. Although it was no reflection on his ability or qualifications for the position, when Franz learned of it, he was greatly distressed that it had become necessary for his uncle to intervene in this manner. He reluctantly acquiesced for it was too important to him. As usual he was deeply in debt. With both the museum job and his professorship, he now had a salary of $5000.00 a year a sum that would substantially relicve some of his financial problems. As an academician with a large family, he was destined, however, to struggle financially for most of his life.[1]

In 1900 Franz and Marie had two children of school age, Helene and

Ernst. Ernst had been attending the Laura Jacobi School.[e] Laura Jacobi was a niece of Abraham Jacobi and ran this school in Manhattan. In August Franz wrote to his mother, indicating that they wanted to send Ernst to Felix Adler's school. Adler, a friend and educator, was the founder of the Ethical Culture Society and its school. It was less expensive than other schools and "there is not a snobbish atmosphere in this school. About one-half of the students go there free, so that here is a good mixture of the poor and the rich. Even Laura's school is too stuck-up..."[21f]

The true joy of accepting the professorship at Columbia was tempered by tragedies at home. Five days later, Heine Boas, only two weeks of age, suffered from a pulmonary infection and almost died of respiratory arrest. The same day Jacobi brought news that Meier Boas had died. This was a particularly wrenching experience, for his father would never know that Franz had succeeded in his pursuit of an academic position of merit and that he had proved that one could be successful in a commitment to natural science.

With his appointment at Columbia University, Boas was approaching the end of his regularly scheduled field trips. His last one was in 1900, when he went to the Pacific Northwest to help complete the work of the Jesup Expedition. His students would undertake much of his fieldwork. They included Farrand, Teit, Smith, Dixon, Kroeber, Swanton, and others. Summers would now be spent at Lake George or Germany. It was time to become a family man. He had spent seven years separated from Marie and the children for long periods, missing birthdays, family crises, and even a substantial portion of Marie's first pregnancy. He hated being away from them. Alone for much of the time, Marie said, "I often wish there never had been an Indian."[1]

Franz had always thrived physically from his expeditions, maintaining a fit weight of about 160 pounds. He had hiked mountains in Germany, kayaked on frigid seas, and trekked across glaciers and vast barren frozen areas of Baffin Island, sailed the treacherous straits of Queen Charlotte Sound, and ridden horseback hundreds of miles in British Columbia. He would now devote his time to administrative, teaching, and academic

---

[e] Later named the Calhoun School.

[f] Ernst Boas graduated from the Ethical Culture School. Emilie Krackowizer also sent her granddaughters, Elizabeth (Bessie), and Mary (Mollie) Parmelly to the same school. They were the daughters of Emil Krackowizer, brother of Marie Boas. When their mother died in 1899, Bessie and Mollie were raised by their grandmother, who was their legal guardian. After 1907 Bessie was raised by the Boas family in Grantwood, New Jersey.

pursuits at home. In reviewing his accomplishments up until the time of his university appointment, most of his career revolved around museums – all tied in with his field research. He had trained in the Royal Ethnological Museum in Berlin, played a major role in collecting artifacts for the creation of the Field Museum in Chicago, worked with the Smithsonian Institution in Washington and most importantly, played a major role in the great expansion of the American Museum of Natural History in New York. The latter was achieved through the persistence and foresight of Morris Jesup and Boas's role in developing the Department of Anthropology. He had created a critical teaching venue and had acquired a huge number artifacts for the museum.[1]

In 1898 Franz received the Loubat Prize for his monograph the "Social Organization of the Kwakiutl Indians." Aside from field and scientific works, he was pleased and proud to have become an organizational leader at the museum, preparing dioramas, special exhibits on Asia, the southwest and northern Indians, leading the Jesup Expedition, and playing a leadership role in the museum's Department of Anthropology. His organizational expertise was also reflected in his linguistic work at the Bureau of American Ethnology of the Smithsonian Institution. He originated and helped to develop anthropological associations and journals. He published many scientific papers, prepared teaching programs, and defined anthropology as a science. In 1900 he was elected to the National Academy of Science – a great honor. Although very proud of his accomplishments, he wrote to his mother, "Don't think me great. Actually it is very easy to be one of the first among anthropologists over here."[1]

The extensive use of Native Americans in field research was an invaluable innovation by Boas. Had he not met and befriended George Hunt, much of the ethnological history of the Indians of British Columbia would have been lost. George Hunt (1854-1933) deserves special treatment as one of Franz Boas's greatest field researchers and collaborators, a relationship that spanned forty-five years (Figure 81).

During their lifetime, the Boas-Hunt correspondence encompassed over one thousand letters. He was by far Boas's most important correspondent. Hunt's research papers number in the thousands. All are part of the collection of Boas papers in the Library of the American Philosophical Society in Philadelphia.[24] Hunt was the son of an Englishman and a Tlingit woman. He was born and raised in the Native American community of Fort Rupert, where his father worked in the Hudson Bay Trading Post. They lived with the Kwakiutl band of Indians, on the northern end of Vancouver Island, British Columbia. Although he had a limited education, he was very bright and bilingual in English and Kwak'wala.

Figure 81. Photograph of George Hunt taken in 1898 (Courtesy of the American Museum of Natural History. No. 11854).

George Hunt's assistance to Putnam and Boas greatly contributed to the acquisition of enormous numbers of native artifacts for the Chicago Columbian Exposition on 1893. The establishment of the anthropological exhibits, in a great measure, led to the creation of the Field Museum. During the Jesup Expedition and after its conclusion, Hunt's expertise was invaluable. The American Museum of Natural History purchased over 2500 native artifacts through the efforts of George Hunt. This contributed to the establishment of one of the largest collections of Pacific Northwest native artifacts in the world. Franz Boas was an indefatigable worker and often became impatient with Hunt who frequently could not keep pace with him. This was to be expected as Boas had a compulsive drive and could not "afford" to waste his time with distractions. On November 10, 1895, he wrote to Marie from Kinkolith, British Columbia. In commenting on the restlessness of his four-year old son Ernst, he wrote, "I have been impatient as far back as I can remember."[24]

Other ethnologists in the field attempted to lure Hunt away from Boas for their own fieldwork but were unsuccessful. This and the fact that Boas and Hunt had a productive relationship which endured for forty-five years would testify to the unusually close relationship between these two men. Hunt was one of the leading Native American scholars of his time. In addition to gathering vast amounts of material for Boas, he also co-authored major works including *Kwakiutl Texts* and publications of the Jesup North Pacific Expedition in 1905 and 1906.[25]

In March 1900 Hunt wrote to Boas that he was arrested at a winter ceremonial "for going to see...a Hamatśa eating a Daid corps."[7] He was accused of participating in the dance. After Boas came to his rescue, he was released. On many occasions, Hunt wrote to Boas in regard to his large family, their financial difficulties and illnesses, always receiving a compassionate response and often, financial assistance (Figure 82).

Figure 82. Boas with the George Hunt family. Left to right, standing: David, George, Lalaxs'a, Mary (Ebbetts), Jonathan and Franz Boas. Sitting: Marion and Lucy. Front row: Mary and Stanley (American Philosophical Society).

On an occasion when Boas sponsored a feast for the Kwakiutl Indians of Fort Rupert, Boas gave Hunt a letter he composed; Hunt translated it into Kwak'wala and read it to the gathering. After being introduced, he reminded them of his previous visits,

> I always think...it is difficult for you to show the white man in Victoria that your feasts and potlatches[c] are good, and I have tried to show them that they are good...George Hunt...will...read to you what I have told the people in Victoria...I am trying to show them that your ways are not bad ways...the ways of the Indian were made differently from the ways of the white man at the beginning of the world, and it is good that we remember the old ways...Your laws will not be forgotten and the white man will understand that the old ways of the Indians were good... [26]

The mutual respect that Boas and Hunt had for each other bonded them for the rest of their lives. The intensity of Boas-Hunt fieldwork in the Pacific Northwest abated somewhat after the Jesup Expedition and after Boas officially left the American Museum of Natural History. George Hunt, through Boas, however, continued to acquire additional artifacts for the museum for some time. Between 1914 and 1931 Boas visited the Pacific Northwest on at least six occasions, the last being to Alert Bay where he stayed at the home of Daniel and Agnes Cranmer. Agnes was a granddaughter of George Hunt.[27] Totaling all of his trips to British Columbia, Franz Boas spent over two years of his life on his monumental field research with the Native Americans in the Pacific Northwest.

On one occasion in 1903, George Hunt visited Franz Boas in New York to work with him at the American Museum of Natural History on the collections of artifacts they had accumulated for the museum. Hunt kept a diary, which unfortunately ended before he arrived in New York. He was quite despondent and homesick after leaving Fort Rupert, "I was in a world unknown...I feel...like a wounded duck with one wing broken. No friend near me..." Without further entries, it is probable that he adjusted to his trip and enjoyed himself after his arrival.[12,28] George Hunt died in 1933.

---

[c] A potlatch is an ancient Indian ceremony sponsored by a chief or tribal member to fortify his position and power base by displaying his rights to perform special dances, relate legends, wear special masks, and other inherited rights. His guests are served lavish feasts. Following a speech by each visiting chief, praising their host, all those in attendance are given gifts by their host. The size and value of the gift is determined by the importance of the recipient, who in turn becomes beholden to his host. Without a written language, in times past, it was a means of publicly acknowledging the political and tribal power structure.[26]

**References and Notes**

1. Cole, Douglas. *FRANZ BOAS. The Early Years, 1858-1906*, Douglas & McIntyre, Vancouver & Toronto and University of Washington Press, Seattle & London, 1999.

2. Koelsch, William A. *Clark University – 1887-1987 – A Narrative History*, Clark University Press, Worcester, Massachusetts, 1987 (Centennial review including the role of Franz Boas in its early days).

3. Stocking, George W., Jr. In *Dictionary of American Biography*, 10 volumes and 8 supplements, American Council of Learned Societies, Charles Scribner's Sons, New York, 1958-1988 (Brief but concise biography of Franz Boas).

4. *Worcester Daily Telegram*, March 6, 1891 and Albert B. Southwick in *The Telegram*, Worcester, August 31, 1997.

5. Kroeber, Alfred L. *Franz Boas: The Man*, in *American Anthropologist*, New Series, Volume 45, No. 3, Part 2, July-September 1943 (Biographical material on Franz Boas).

6. Boas, Franz. *Curriculum vitae* written as a student in Minden, Germany – in Library of the American Philosophical Society.

7. Jonaitis, Aldona. *From the Land of the Totem Poles*. American Museum of Natural History, New York and the University of Washington Press, Seattle, Washington, 1988 (History of the Northwest Coast collection at the American Museum of Natural History).

8. Moses, John & Maj. Joseph Kirkland. *The History of Chicago, Illinois*, pp604-605, Munsell & Co. Chicago & New York, 1896 (Description of the early days of Oak Woods Cemetery).

9. graveyards.com/oakwoods. 2001 (Detailed history, description and maps of Oak Woods Cemetery in Chicago).

10. Salinger, J. D. *The Catcher in the Rye*, Little, Brown & Co., Boston, 1951 (A visit to the American Museum of Natural History and the Boas diorama).

11. Mathé, Barbara.. Archivist, American Museum of Natural History, New York. Personal communication.

12. Webster, Gloria. Lecture at the American Museum of Natural History, 1997, personal communication (Anthropologist and great granddaughter of George Hunt).

13. Shaw, William B. *Dictionary of American Biography*, The American Council of Learned Societies, 10 volumes with supplements, Charles Scribner Sons, New York, 1961 (A brief biography of Morris Jesup).

14. Peary, Robert E. Letters to Franz Boas October 25, 1887 & December 25, 1887 (Norman F. Boas collection).

15. Harper, Kenn. *Give Me My Father's Body*, Blacklead Books, 2nd printing, Iqualut, Northwest Territories, 1989 (Harper has lived among the Inuit on Baffin Island for many years).

16. *The Washington Post*, Washington, D.C., April 5, 1992.

17. Carpenter, Edmund, *Dead Truth. Live Myth, European Review of Native*

*American Studies*, Volume 11, No. 2, 1997 (Carpenter refutes Harper's report that Minik's fathers remains were on display at the American Museum of Natural History).
18. *The Day*, New London, Connecticut, November 17, 1995.
19. Kendall, Laurel, Barbara Mathé & Thomas Ross Miller, *Drawing Shadows to Stone*, American Museum of Natural History, New York in association with the University of Washington Press, Seattle & London, 1997 (100th anniversary of the Jesup North Pacific Expedition – outstanding history and photograph collection).
20. Dexter, Ralph W. T*he Role of F. W. Putnam in Developing Anthropology at the American Museum of Natural History, Curator*, Volume 19, American Museum of Natural History, 1974.
21. Rohner, Ronald P. *The Ethnography of Franz Boas*, University of Chicago Press, Chicago & London, 1969 (Letters and diaries of Franz Boas to his family from 1886 to 1931).
22. Boas, Franz, editor. *Memoirs of the American Museum of Natural History, Jesup North Pacific Expedition*, 11 volumes, American Museum of Natural History, New York, 1898-1930.
23. Codere, Helen, editor. *Kwakiutl Ethnology*, The University of Chicago Press, Chicago & London, 1966 (Based on writings of Franz Boas on the Indians of the Pacific Northwest).
24. Boas, Franz. Papers of, in the Library of the American Philosophical Society, Philadelphia.
25. Boas, Franz & George Hunt. *Kwakiutl Texts*, 532 pp, 1905 and *Kwakiutl Texts*, Second Series, 1906. Both *Publications of the Jesup North Pacific Expedition*, American Museum of Natural History (In addition to the great achievement in producing these volumes, they are testimony to the tremendous research accomplishments of George Hunt).
26. Jonaitis, Aldona. *Chiefly Feasts. The Enduring Kwakiutl Potlatch*. American Museum of Natural History, New York and the University of Washington Press, Seattle and London, 1991 (A landmark retrospective exhibit of the Boas-Hunt collection at the museum).
27. Cranmer, Agnes. Personal communication (Widow of Daniel Cranmer and granddaughter of George Hunt).
28. Hunt, George. Diary of trip to New York in 1903 to visit Franz Boas. (Collection of Gloria Webster, great granddaughter of George Hunt).

# CHAPTER VI

## VACATIONS AT LAKE GEORGE, NEW YORK

Franz Boas arrived in Bolton, New York on Lake George to join his fiancée, Marie Krackowizer, on September 23, 1884, two days after he first stepped on the shores of America. After his isolation in the Arctic, this joyous occasion and reunion was the beginning of a deep attachment for the Adirondacks. The rugged wilderness of the mountains and forests were particularly appealing to him and were reminiscent of the Harz Mountains where he first met Marie. Bolton was to become a summer vacation site for the entire Boas family for the next thirty years. Spending his vacations for so many years in one place had an enduring effect on the relationships between Franz, his children, family, and close friends.

This chapter will deviate chronologically from the rest of this book since it is a story unto itself. It encompasses the relationship of a closely-knit group of German immigrants who were astute businessmen, lawyers, scholars, and intellectuals, and who shared their experiences with one another at a common meeting place every summer. Included in this group were the Meyer, Krackowizer, and Boas families, as well as the families of Doctors Abraham and Mary Putnam Jacobi, Carl Schurz, Dr. Willy Meyer, and Marjorie McAneny (daughter of the Jacobis).

During the latter half of the 19th century, with the advent of the railroad, vacationing in the Adirondacks and on the upper lakes of New York State became extremely popular. Bolton was no exception. It was a charming small village on the southwestern shore of Lake George. It attracted the families of financiers and industrialists William Bixby, George Foster Peabody, Spencer Trask, and Adolph S. Ochs (*New York Times*); opera singers Marcella Sembrich and Louise Homer; also Alfred Stieglitz, Georgia O'Keeffe, Charles Evans Hughes, Evangeline Booth, Leopold Auer, Efram Zimbalist, scientists Dr. Charles Steinmetz, Nobel Laureate Dr. Irving Langmuir, and many more.[1,2]

Of the group cited in this chapter, it was Louis Henry Meyer (1815-91) who was the first to vacation in Bolton in the 1860s. Other family members and friends followed. This soon led to a summer gathering place for these German immigrants. Meyer's year-round home was on Staten Island, New York, where he developed a sizable estate. His summers were spent with his family in Bolton Landing, a small shoreline section of Bolton on Lake George. "L. H." Meyer was a successful businessman involved in imports and exports with offices in New York and Bremen,

Germany. His company became one of the leading firms that attracted German investment capital into America, much of which related to the rapidly expanding railroad system in the country. At one time he was a partner with Samuel J. Tilden in the firm of Tilden, Sinnott & Meyer. This was a merger of mutual interests, as Tilden's reputation at the time came primarily from his role as a corporate attorney representing scores of railroads undergoing reorganization.[2] Tilden's greatest fame came from his unsuccessful campaign for President of the United States in 1876, an election in which he received the majority of the popular votes but lost on electoral votes. The results in three southern states remained in dispute. After months of controversy over rival sets of returns, Congress established an electoral commission composed of five members of the House of Representatives, five Senators, and five members of the Supreme Court to settle the disputed returns. Their final vote was along party lines. All nineteen electoral votes were awarded to Rutherford B. Hayes, giving him a majority of one electoral vote over Tilden.

In 1875 Theodore Florenz Heinrich Meyer (1844-1929), the son of Louis Henry Meyer, married Helene Mary Theresa Krackowizer at her father's summer home in Sing Sing (now Ossining), New York. Ernst Krackowizer's career has been cited earlier. Although he visited the L. H. Meyers on one or two occasions at Lake George, he never spent summers there. It is significant, however, that one of his daughters, Helene, married Theodore Meyer and another, Marie, married Franz Boas. Ernst Krackowizer's high ideals and generous spirit lived on in the lives of his children and friends. His influence was palpable during the years family members spent in Bolton.[2]

Theodore Meyer was a successful corporate attorney. Early in his career, he formed a partnership with Judge James P. Sinnott, who had earlier been associated with Samuel J. Tilden and his father. Theodore specialized in many of the railroad mergers and reorganizations that had been instigated at the direction of his father. As a young man, he became enchanted with the Adirondacks during his vacations there, primarily because of his love for hunting and fishing. After his marriage, he was determined to share his love for Lake George with Helene and his children and have a place that would become an escape from New York. Between 1875 and 1884, he purchased several contiguous tracts of land in the northern part of Bolton encompassing a huge fertile valley surrounded by the Adirondack Mountains; the entire tract contained over one thousand acres of land. It was here that he created a large gentleman's farm, where he cleared land, built houses, barns and outbuildings, and where he raised

Figure 83. Alma Farm, a view looking south toward Tongue Mountain Range. In the foreground is the horse barn and on the right the farmhouse where the help lived (Barbara L Meyer).

prize-winning Jersey cattle (Figure 83).

The farm, which encompassed Wardboro Valley, had been know as Alma Farm, a name that Theodore Meyer gave to his entire holdings. The family and guests stayed at the "cottage," near the main highway from Bolton to Ticonderoga (Figure 84). Alma Farm became a focal point of the Village of Bolton with over forty employees and their families, most of whom lived in the farmhouse. The farm played a major role in the local economy. Theodore Meyer also built a cottage, referred to as "Rock Rest," within view of the Alma Farm cottage. It was built primarily for Emilie Krackowizer, his widowed mother-in-law (Figure 85).

Theodore and Helene raised six children, Anna Emilie Helene, Louise Wilhelmine Marie, Helene Alice Charlotte, Ernst Louis Henry, Florence Alma, and Theodore Frederick Walter (Figures 86, 87). The farm bustled with activity with these young people and their many visitors. During the time that Franz Boas was on his Baffin Island expedition, his fiancée, Marie, spent much of her time visiting the Meyers in Bolton and helped Helene with her children.[2,4]

Figure 84. Alma Farm "cottage" on the left with the barn on the right. Photographer: Thatcher (Barbara L. Meyer).

Figure 85. "Rock Rest," Emilie Krackowizer's bungalow at Alma Farm, built by Theodore Meyer, where the Boas family often stayed (Barbara L. Meyer).

Prior to 1900, the Boas family stayed at Alma Farm, either in the cottage or in Emilie Krackowizer's small house. On a few occasions they stayed in Carl Schurz's cottage on the lake. Marie and the children spent a great deal more time in Bolton than did Franz. In the 1890s, portions of his summers were committed to frequent trips to the Pacific Northwest, doing work for the British Association for the Advancement of Science (B.A.A.S.), the Smithsonian Institution, and the American Museum of Natural History. He also made some trips to Germany with Marie and the children. He did, however, enjoy resting in Bolton, where he was able to catch up on his writings, analyze, and record the voluminous amount of data that he had accumulated during his field research.

Figures 86 & 87. Cabinet photographs of Theodore and Helene Krackowizer Meyer, in-laws of Franz Boas. Photographer: Wilhelm, New York (Barbara L Meyer).

In about 1900, Franz began renting a farmhouse on Federal Hill in Bolton owned by Abraham Jacobi. It was a spacious two-story building surrounded by open meadows (Figure 88).[b] There was a full-length porch on the east side with a magnificent view of Lake George, an ideal vacation spot for his rapidly growing family. Always generous, Jacobi offered to give the house and farm to Franz. The offer was graciously refused as being too extravagant. Now, as a university professor and free from teaching obligations in the summer, Boas continued to spend part of his summer vacations on anthropological field trips to the Pacific Northwest,

---

[b] The open meadows with the vista of Lake George are all gone. Most of this land is now heavily wooded. The Federal Hill house no longer exists; it burned to the ground in 1993.

the Southwest, Mexico, as well as family trips to Europe. While in Bolton, he continued to spend a great deal of time studying, writing, and preparing

Figure 88. The Abraham Jacobi farmhouse on Federal Hill, used by the Franz Boas family for many years in the summertime (American Philosophical Society).

Figure 89. The shed next to the Federal Hill house used as a study by Franz Boas (Gertrud Michelson).

for his university courses. There was a small shed on the Federal Hill property, which he used as his study (Figure 89). At a professional level, Boas corresponded with other summer residents of Bolton Landing who included, among others, William K. Bixby, Adolph Ochs, and Charles Evans Hughes; the latter he visited at his summer home. For a period of almost twenty years, he also carried out an extensive correspondence with another summer resident, George Foster Peabody.[1,3] Peabody, a banker and philanthropist, was very supportive of Boas, particularly in regard to the civil rights of African Americans. After he retired in 1906, Peabody devoted himself to philanthropy and public service, giving much time and effort to this cause. On February 11, 1907 Boas wrote to him,

> At Atlanta last year...I tried to make the point that racial inferiority of the Negro has never been proved to exist...these facts are hardly understood at all by our people... it is very commonly assumed as proved that the Negroes are destined to remain an inferior race...the point I made should be brought clearly and forcibly to the attention of our people.[3]

Figure 90. Helene and Franz Boas on horseback at Lake George in summer of 1915.(Gertrud Michelson)

For pleasure, Boas went horseback riding (Figure 90), visited his neighbors by horse and buggy (Figures 91), or hiked, a favorite pastime. He enjoyed the lake and the mountains, and thrived with the beautiful scenery. Additional pleasures of the summer included visiting, dining, playing parlor games, and sharing jokes and experiences with his children, neighbors, friends, and family. With five children, the Boas household was a beehive of activity. The children shared their childhood and teenage years with the older children of George and Marjorie McAneny (grandchildren of Abraham and Mary Jacobi), the children of Willy Meyer

(Franz's cousin) and the Theodore and Helene Meyer children at Alma Farm. The young people performed dramatic plays at the Federal Hill site, received piano lessons from their friend Josephine ("Jo") Spring, romped through the fields, and climbed over the stiles on the stonewalls. They went horseback riding, picnicked, played games, and went swimming and boating from the Jacobi dock at Bolton Landing. Franz and Marie thrived with their large family and their young relatives and friends (Figures 92,93).

Figure 91. Probably one of the Maranville carriages with a driver with whip in hand. Seated next to him is Henry Boas. Josephine Spring is in the second row and Gertrud Boas is in the rear seat. Standing are Franz and Franziska Boas . Photograph ca. 1918 (Barbara L. Meyer).

The Boas family also tended to vegetable and flower gardens on their Federal Hill property. On one occasion Franz went to the general store in Bolton Landing to buy some chicken wire to protect their produce from the local fauna. It was a story that he related to us as children. On approaching the storekeeper he asked,

Boas: "Do you have any chicken wire?"

Storekeeper: "Nope."

Boas: "Don't people in town have chickens?"

Storekeeper: "Yup."
Boas: "But surely there must be a demand for it?"
Storekeeper: "Yup."
Boas: "Are you just out of it?"
Storekeeper: "Nope."
Boas: "You don't carry it?"
Storekeeper: "Nope."
Boas: "Why?"
Storekeeper: "Goes too fast."

Figure 92. Franz Boas family and friends at Lake George, ca.1896. From left to right: Ernst Boas,, Walter Meyer, Fanny Barnes, Franz Boas, Bernice Barnes, Gertrud Boas, Marie Boas, Louise Hodge, Molly Krackowizer, Charlotte Hodge, and Helene Boas. Photographer: Thatcher, Lake George, New York (Gertrud Michelson.).

It was Abraham Jacobi who, in many ways, orchestrated the Bolton experience for all of the German families cited above. As noted earlier, Jacobi married into the Meyer family of Minden, Germany and thus became an uncle to both Franz Boas and Dr. Willy Meyer. It was Jacobi who helped convince Franz Boas and Willy Meyer to immigrate to America. As compatriots in the Revolution of 1848, Jacobi's closest personal friends were unquestionably Ernst Krackowizer and Carl Schurz. The intermarriages between the Krackowizer, Boas, and Theodore Meyer families also resulted from Jacobi's friendship with Ernst Krackowizer.

When Marjorie Jacobi married George McAneny, another large family group became committed to summer vacations at Bolton, many of whom still vacation at the McAneny home in Bolton Landing.[1,3,5]

Figure 93. Boas family gathering at Lake George. Left to right - Standing: Ernst, Marie and Franz Boas. Kneeling: Franziska and Helene Boas. Seated: Henry Boas, "Jo" Spring, an unidentified man, and Gertrud Boas (Gertrud Michelson).

In December of 1871, Abraham Jacobi, as president of the New York County Medical Society, welcomed a new member, one whom he had nominated himself, Dr. Mary (Minnie) Corinna Putnam. She was only the second woman to be admitted to the society. Jacobi was twelve years her senior, but they shared many ideals and had a great mutual respect for one another. A professional relationship developed, as did a personal affection. A courtship began and their engagement was announced in the summer of 1872. Abraham and Mary were married in July 1873, an extraordinary union of two of the most distinguished physicians of the 19th century.

Mary Corinna Putnam (1842-1906), a precocious child, was the daughter of publisher George P. Putnam. As a teenager she was determined to become a physician, a goal rarely achieved by women of her time, and an aspiration certainly discouraged by the medical profession. After preliminary training at the New York College of Pharmacy and at the

Female Medical College of Pennsylvania in Philadelphia, she realized that her education was inadequate and incomplete. Her goal was to attend the École de Médicine in Paris, an almost insurmountable challenge. No woman had ever been admitted to this institution. It would have been unthinkable! She nevertheless moved to Paris, where she earned a living by writing and selling articles for publication in American magazines and newspapers. She studied medicine from books that she borrowed from the École and finally applied for admission. Her application was rejected out of hand. After intervention by the Minister of Public Education, she was granted permission to audit one course. She immediately impressed her colleagues with her ability but was unable to take entrance exams without further orders from the Minister. When these came, she easily and impressively passed the exams as the first woman to enter one of the most prestigious medical schools in the world. At graduation in 1871, "She received the highest marks granted by the faculty, together with the second prize for her thesis."[1,5]

On returning to New York in 1871, she opened an office on East 15th Street in New York for the practice of medicine. She was appointed professor at the Women's Medical College of the New York Infirmary, founded by her friend Elizabeth Blackwell. Mary taught *materia medica* and therapeutics here for the next sixteen years. She also joined the dispensary services of Mount Sinai and St. Mark's Hospitals and continued a distinguished practice. She was one of first women to be admitted to the American Medical Association. Her concern with the inferior status of women doctors prompted her to form the Association for the Advancement of the Medical Education of Women in 1872. She wrote over 100 medical articles covering many specialties, including pediatrics, physiology, neurology, pathology, and medical education. As a reformer she also wrote articles on social matters, primary education, and women's suffrage. She gave her support publicly to Native Americans, was an abolitionist, and supported the Consumer's League. The League for Political Education counted her as one of their founders. Mary led the fight for women's suffrage, supported by her husband, in a "masterly address" in Albany in 1894.[6]

In 1878, Dr. Abraham Jacobi founded the Pediatric Service of Mount Sinai Hospital in New York, the first such service in a New York Hospital and one of the first in the United States. The following year he was appointed Hospital Pediatrician and served as chief of the Service until 1883. He remained on the staff of the hospital for the rest of his life and was president of the Mount Sinai Medical Board for many years. Jacobi went on to become the president of the American Pediatric Society (twice), the Association of American Physicians, The New York Academy of Medicine, the New York County Medical Society, and the American Medical Association (1912-13). He is recognized to this day as the founder of American pediatrics.[1,6,7]

Abraham Jacobi's first introduction to Lake George was in 1867 when he purchased Hiawatha Island, a small parcel lying off Bolton Landing. It was on this island that he built a summer cottage of his own design and where he brought his bride for their honeymoon in 1873. Mary had her first child in 1874, which died shortly after birth, devastatingly reminiscent of the experiences of Abraham Jacobi with the loss of his first two wives and their four stillborn infants.[5]

On August 3, 1875, following months of anxiety, Mary delivered a healthy young boy in their home on Hiawatha Island. He was named Ernst after Jacobi's dear friend Dr. Ernst Krackowizer.[8] In 1878 the Jacobis were blessed with the birth of a daughter, Marjorie.

The happy years that followed were filled with the joy of their children and the heavy professional obligations of both Abraham and Mary. Every summer was spent at their home on Lake George. After the arrival of Theodore and Helene Meyer, they became regular visitors to Alma Farm and thus were able to continue the Krackowizer connection.

Tragedy struck again on July 10, 1883, when Ernst Jacobi died of diphtheria. Both children had developed the disease, probably from contact with their German nursemaid who apparently was a carrier of the disease. The Jacobis were devastated. Abraham Jacobi never recovered from the death of their son. He erected a five-ton granite memorial stone in memory of Ernst which is located on the north end of Hiawatha Island.[1,2]

After the death of Ernst, the Jacobis immersed themselves in their work in New York and found it difficult to return to Hiawatha Island. It was not until 1889 when Carl Schurz and his family started spending summers at Lake George that the Jacobis were encouraged to return to Bolton Landing. They stayed with the Schurz family at the Sagamore Hotel and finally decided to build a new home on the mainland. In 1875 Jacobi purchased a heavily forested parcel of land on a hillside about one mile north of Bolton Landing. Here he built a cottage overlooking Lake George. He also built a cottage for Carl Schurz on the same parcel within "shouting distance of each other" (Figure 94). The two men were inseparable. Jacobi later built a large house for his daughter Marjorie and her husband George McAneny on the same parcel. Abraham Jacobi was a frequent visitor to Franz Boas and his family when they stayed in Jacobi's

Figure 94. The cottage built by Abraham Jacobi for Carl Schurz in Bolton Landing, New York. It is no longer standing (Ernest Jacobi McAneny).

house on Federal Hill.

Marjorie Jacobi grew up among her cousins, the four daughters of George Haven Putnam, and was an intimate childhood friend of Anna Meyer, daughter of Theodore and Helene Meyer. When Marjorie was a teenager, Herbert Schurz was one of her beaux.

Towards the turn of the century, Carl Schurz became a founder of the National Civil Service Reform League, dedicated to improving an infirm system plundered by political favoritism. George McAneny (1869-1953) was appointed secretary of this group. As secretary to Schurz, he was invited to Bolton Landing for his first visit. They stayed at the Schurz cottage. It was here that Marjorie Jacobi met George McAneny. They became betrothed and were married on January 4, 1900.[1,3]

McAneny was a self-made man, who at the age of 17 began working for New York City newspapers as a correspondent and reporter. In 1892 he joined Carl Schurz as assistant secretary and later as secretary of the National Civil Service Reform League. He served in this capacity for the next ten years. Although he never attended law school, during the next three years he read law with Edward M. Shepard, an experience that became very useful in his career. When Franz Boas purchased his property in Grantwood, New Jersey, it was McAneny who prepared the land and mortgage deeds and contracts to build his house. While working with

Schurz, his exposure to civil service abuses became a powerful motivation for political reform. McAneny became deeply involved in assignments by the city and state in preparing revisions of civil service rules and laws. He was a co-author of the "Revised New York State Civil Service Law" and drafted and revised Civil Service rules for New York City. Thoroughly immersed in the reform movement, he joined the Fusion Party in 1910 and was elected president of the Borough of Manhattan. During this term he was chairman of the Transit Commission of City Government which developed the dual subway system, and also chairman of the Committee on the City Plan for the Comprehensive Planning and Zoning of New York, the first zoning ordinances adopted in America.

In 1914 he was elected president of the Board of Aldermen. During his tenure in this position he served as Acting Mayor of New York whenever Mayor John Purroy Mitchell, a reserve officer, was called to duty with the United States Air Corps. It was McAneny, as Acting Mayor, who greeted and hosted President Woodrow Wilson on an official visit to New York. Following his term on the Board of Aldermen, he returned to his newspaper interests in 1916, serving as executive manager of *The New York Times* for the next five years. During this time he was also a vice president of the American Newspaper Publisher's Association.

George McAneny received many honorary architectural awards and medals for his city planning, including the Chevalier Legion of Honor from France. He served as chairman of the board of trustees of the City College of New York and continued his public service as chairman of the State Transit Commission, as comptroller of the city, and organized the City Sanitation Department in 1933. In 1936 he was appointed by President Franklin D. Roosevelt to chair the Commission of the United States on Fiscal Relations of the United States Government and the District of Columbia. In addition to all these responsibilities, McAneny was a banker serving as president and later chairman of the board of the Title, Guarantee & Trust Company. He was also a member of the boards of several other banks and insurance companies. It was McAneny who organized the movement to promote New York as the site for the World's Fair of 1939 and was the first president of the Fair Corporation.[9]

George and Marjorie McAneny and their six children were regular summer residents at the Jacobi-McAneny complex in Bolton Landing. The McAneny children played and grew up with the children of the Boas and Willy Meyer families, sharing their experiences at Alma Farm, on Federal Hill and at the Jacobi dock – a favorite place to swim.[10]

Returning to Abraham Jacobi, a huge party was given for him on his seventieth birthday at Delmonico's Restaurant in New York. There were over 400 in attendance, including doctors William H. Welch, John S. Billings, Edward G. Janeway, Willy Meyer, and Stephen Smith. Also included were William Dean Howells, Henry Villard, his son Oswald Garrison Villard, Felix Adler, Franz Boas, and George McAneny. Guest speakers included Sir William Osler, Carl Schurz, and President Seth Low of Columbia University.[5]

Figure 95. Abraham Jacobi in later years (Historical Society of the Town of Bolton).

During his later years, Jacobi spent more time at Lake George with Marjorie and her family and the Boas family (Figure 95). Jacobi's last years were spent organizing, collating, and preparing his personal papers for an autobiography, a monumental task. On a September night in 1918, at the age of 88, he smelled smoke in his house, and recognizing the hopelessness of remaining, escaped by jumping out of a window. Franz Boas from atop Federal Hill saw the fire. He and his daughter Franziska rushed down the hill through the meadows to the blazing structure.[1,2] The

McAnenys arrived from another direction. The loss was total including all of his papers, personal possessions, and the beloved artifacts that had belonged to his son Ernst (Figure 96).

Figure 96. The smoldering remains of the Jacobi house at Lake George, September 18, 1918. Arnold McAneny is hosing the hot embers (Ernest Jacobi McAneny).

The extraordinary odyssey of Carl Schurz continued unabated after immigrating to America. After the Revolution of 1848, in fear for his life, Schurz was unable to return to Germany. As much as he wished to play a role in the abolition of the repressive Prussian regime, his role as a leader of the opposition became impotent. Seeking a new home, along with other revolutionaries from the continent, he immigrated to America where he enthusiastically embraced democracy.

Schurz adopted his new homeland with vigor. His charm and enthusiasm quickly generated friends and a large following, including many outstanding personalities. When he was in Boston he met Longfellow, Emerson, Lowell, Agassiz, Holmes, and others. For three years he lived in Philadelphia and then settled in Watertown, Wisconsin among a large mid-western German community. He gave speeches in his native language supporting the first Republican presidential candidate, John Charles Frémont. The following year he was an unsuccessful candidate for lieutenant governor of Wisconsin.[11,12]

It was in Wisconsin that his remarkable career in the states began; he became known as the leading German American in the United States. His charm, mastery of oratory, not only in German but in English, success as a leader, and spirited adoption of his new country led to an outstanding career, unparalleled in American history. He became Minister to Spain, a major general in the Civil War, a leader in the Republican Party, a confidant of Abraham Lincoln, the second foreign-born cabinet member, Secretary of Interior (preceded by Secretary of the Treasury, Albert Gallatin), United States Senator, publisher, editor and one of the earliest advocates of civil rights of Native Americans and African Americans. He participated in the public sector, an opportunity he was denied in Germany.

During the time of the Lincoln-Douglas debates in 1858, Schurz delivered his first speech in English in Chicago on the question of slavery, which was widely published and established his position in the political field. He first met Abraham Lincoln on a train traveling to a Lincoln-Douglas debate in Quincy, Illinois. In 1859 Schurz passed the bar exam and opened a law office in Milwaukee with an associate, Halbert Eleazer Paine. It is not clear whether Schurz ever seriously practiced law. In 1859-1860 he made a lecture tour in New England, denouncing the policies of Stephen Douglas.

As a strong Lincoln supporter with a powerful voice among mid-western Germans, he became a delegate to the Republican National Convention in Chicago in 1860. After the selection of Lincoln by the convention, Schurz was one of a committee to travel to Springfield to meet with Abraham Lincoln at his home and deliver the news of his nomination. During the presidential campaign, Schurz was one of seven men chosen to direct the campaign, with his efforts aimed toward seeking the German vote for the Republican candidates. His speeches were given eloquently and targeted primarily toward the over one million German Americans who immigrated to America between 1845 and 1854, many of whom had left or escaped Germany following the Revolution of 1848.

Prior to the appearance of Schurz as a Republican advocate, German Americans largely favored the Democrats. Following Lincoln's nomination at the Republican Convention Chicago in 1860, Schurz threw his support toward the election of Lincoln.

Schurz, after initially favoring William Seward as the Republican nominee for president, swung his support and that of his followers to Lincoln during the final roll calls. Although Lincoln was aware of this, on June 18, 1860 he wrote to Schurz,

> I beg you to be assured that your having supported Gov. Seward, in preference to myself in the convention, is not even remembered by me for any practical purpose, or the slightest u[n]pleasant feeling. . . . no

man stands nearer to my heart than yourself . . ."[13]

This was a mutual feeling that these two men retained throughout their lives. With his remarkable gift of oratory, his sincerity, charm, and enthusiasm, Carl Schurz convinced thousands of Germans to switch their allegiance to the Republican Party. In so doing, he, probably more than any other individual, provided the margin for victory for the election of Abraham Lincoln as President of the United States.[11,12]

As a result, Schurz was always welcome at the Executive Mansion. As a reward for his support in the campaign, Lincoln promptly appointed him Minister to Spain. By the end of 1861, bored and restless with the plush and easy life in his new position and disturbed by the war news at home, Schurz pleaded with Lincoln to permit him to return home and join the army. Lincoln agreed and appointed him brigadier general of volunteers a few months later. In June, Schurz took command of a division in the corps of General Franz Sigel at the second battle of Bull Run. The following March, Carl Schurz was promoted to major general in General Oliver O. Howard's corps. Schurz had temporary command of the corps at the battle of Gettysburg, took part in the battle of Chattanooga and finally joined Sherman on his March to the Sea. During the war, he corresponded with and made recommendations to Lincoln on the conduct of the war, at times to the exasperation of the President.

Following the lessons he received from Johanna Kinkel, Carl Schurz developed into an excellent pianist. According to stories passed down in the Jacobi-McAneny family, occasionally, on visits to the White House, Schurz played the piano to entertain President Abraham Lincoln.[10] He also entertained the family of Rutherford B. Hayes by playing at the White House.[12]

After the Civil War, Schurz visited the southern states as special commissioner, appointed by President Andrew Johnson to assess the conditions in the South for the administration. Schurz was an advocate for leniency toward the South and amnesty for southern leaders. His observations were ignored. He subsequently "quarreled with Grant over the harsh treatment meted out to the South."[12]

After the war, as a former editor and writer, Schurz returned to the newspaper business. He became Washington correspondent for the *New York Tribune* in 1865. The following year he moved to Detroit where he founded the *Detroit Post*. The next year he moved to St. Louis where he became editor of the *Westliche Post*, a German newspaper. In the same year he was chosen United States Senator from Missouri for a term ending in 1875.

By the end of Grant's term as president, Schurz had become totally disillusioned with his administration. As the presidential conventions neared, Schurz led an opposition movement and founded the Liberal Republican Party. He gave the keynote address at the convention, following the band's rendition of "Hail to the Chief." Although it was not his choice, Horace Greeley became the nominee for the presidency.

The election of Carl Schurz as Senator from Missouri "electrified" the German American community.[12] Schurz was essentially the voice and pied piper of this group throughout his political life. Although he had the ambition to be president of the United States, born in a foreign country, he did not qualify. He did attain two of the highest positions in the federal government, those of United States Senator and Secretary of the Interior. His political success and following gave him a powerful voice in the administrations of Presidents Lincoln through Cleveland.

The death of Ernst Krackowizer in 1875 was a tragic loss to Schurz. He lost not only a compatriot from the Revolution of 1848, but also a close friend who shared the same exciting ideals in their new lives in America.

The next year, Margarethe, Schurz's wife of twenty-four years died of postpartum complications following the birth of their son, Herbert. Schurz wrote, "For grief like this there is no consolation . . . It is the loss of the best part of one's life."[12]

Unable to run for the office of President, he had to content himself with becoming a president-maker. It was Schurz, more than anyone else, who convinced a reluctant Rutherford B. Hayes to run for the presidency. Following the election of Hayes, Schurz was appointed Secretary of the Interior (1877-81). As a reformer, Schurz introduced competitive examinations for positions in the Department of Interior and adopted measures for the protection of the forests on public lands. He also became an advocate for civil service reform. In addition he took a strong position defending the rights of African Americans and Native Americans.

At the conclusion of Hayes term as President in 1881, Schurz became editor of the New York *Evening Post* and remained in New York for the balance of his life where he had many roots and old friends. He continued to fight for the rights of African Americans and Native Americans, for universal education, and against the political abuses of Tammany Hall (Figure 97). His permanent home in New York was on East 91st Street, next to that of his friend, Andrew Carnegie. His friendship with Abraham Jacobi thrived and they remained the closest of friends. When Franz Boas arrived in New York in 1886, Carl Schurz extended himself to welcome and help this young son of Sophie Boas and nephew of Abraham Jacobi and continued to render aid and advice throughout his remaining years in New York. In 1905 Boas joined Schurz, Jacobi, and Emil Boas in creating the Germanistic Society of America, with Franz Boas as secretary and Schurz as honorary president.

Figure 97. Carl Schurz in later years. Photographer: Falk , New York (N.F.B.).

It was in 1889, through the influence of Jacobi, that Carl Schurz first visited Lake George. After Jacobi built a summer cottage for Schurz, he was asked why he did not own his own place at Bolton Landing. Schurz replied, "Why should I pay taxes when I can walk in Jacobi's woods?"[5] The Schurzes had five children, Agathe, Marianne, Emma (died in childhood), Carl Lincoln, and Herbert, all visitors to Lake George. None had children. All were visitors to Alma Farm at one time or another.

When Carl Schurz died on May 14, 1906, Mary Jacobi said, "The greatest blow has fallen," fully aware "that Jacobi's deep friendship with Schurz surpassed any other existing relationship."[1] Mary Putnam Jacobi died only one month later on June 10, 1906, of a brain tumor, twenty-three years to the day after the death of her son Ernst. Eulogies at her memorial service in New York were given by Sir William Osler and Felix Adler.[5]

When Carl Schurz died, Jacobi was his physician. Schurz's last words, before lapsing into coma were, "Es is enfach zu sterben (It is easy to die)." Addresses at his funeral services "At the House" were given by Felix Adler, founder of the Ethical Culture Society and by Dr. Abraham Jacobi. At the graveside at Sleepy Hollow Cemetery in Sleepy Hollow (formerly North Tarrytown), New York, an address was given by Dr. H. B. Frissell,

> . . . when he came to this country he immediately became a friend of the Indian and the Negro. Not only did he help lead their cause in the great campaign which preceded the Civil War . . . when the struggles were over, he gave up his life largely to helping them into life and liberty. I have been asked to speak here to-day . . . because I represent these two races whom Carl Schurz loved and for whom he labored . . . Never has there been granted to these two races a better friend than this great general . . .[14]

In Bolton Landing, next to the memorial plaque of Abraham Jacobi, is a concrete memorial bench at a spot that Schurz used as a place for meditation. The bench bears the following inscription:

TO THE HAPPY MEMORY OF
1829-1906
**CARL SCHURZ**
SOLDIER – STATESMAN – SCHOLAR – PATRIOT
FOR FOURTEEN SUMMERS 1892-1905 HE ACHIEVED AND RESTED IN THESE PRECINCTS WHOSE BEAUTY WAS HIS NEVER ENDING JOY – ERECTED SEPTEMBER 1925

It is fitting that these two men should be memorialized only a few feet from one another, on a beloved plot of land that had belonged to Abraham Jacobi,

A memorial service was held at Carnegie Hall two days later and included an orchestra conducted by Frank Damrosch and speeches by former President Grover Cleveland, Ambassador Joseph H. Choate, Harvard president Charles W. Eliot, Secretary of the Navy Charles J. Bonaparte, Booker T. Washington, and others.

Franz Boas's first cousin, Willy Meyer, began vacationing at Lake George in about 1900. Willy received his medical degree at Bonn University and later served on the faculty at Bonn as assistant to Professors Busch, Madelung, and Trendelenburg. In 1884 Jacobi encouraged him to immigrate to New York where he married Lilly Ottilie Maass the following year. It was in New York that he became a distinguished and internationally recognized surgeon, specializing in cancer and throat surgery (Figure 98).

Figure 98. Photograph of Doctors Abraham Jacobi and Willy Meyer, ca.1915 (Historical Society of the Town of Bolton).

Willy Meyer was an attending surgeon at the German Hospital (later Lenox Hill Hospital) and professor of clinical surgery at the Women's Medical College of New York City. He operated at the New York Skin and Cancer Hospital and was professor of surgery at the New York Postgraduate Medical School and Hospital. He was also a consultant at the New York Infirmary for Women and Children, Montefiore Hospital, the Hospital for Joint Diseases, and the Glens Falls Hospital. He introduced a number of surgical techniques in America learned from Dr. Trendelenburg and wrote many clinical papers on surgery. He was particularly insistent on prompt surgery for acute appendicitis, having lost a nine year-old daughter from this disorder.

Willy Meyer had two surviving children, a daughter Marjorie, a professional concert singer who married Franz G. Fleming, and a son Dr. Herbert Willy Meyer, a New York physician who married Emmy K. Kaesche. They had two children. Dr. Herbert Willy Meyer became the physician to all the McAneny children.[2]

Soon after his first visit to Bolton Landing, Dr. Willy Meyer purchased some land on Green Island on Lake George where he built a summer home for his family, thus joining the vacationing Boas, Theodore Meyer, Jacobi, Schurz, and McAneny families.

Meyer was described as "a great citizen...loyal, enthusiastic and active in many civic movements...he was prominent in developing a good citizenship and a better community spirit. As a man he was loveable, self-sacrificing...a truly loyal friend, beloved by all."[2] Willy Meyer died suddenly on February 24, 1932, while attending a surgical meeting at the New York Academy of Medicine.

Visits of the Boas family to Lake George became less frequent during and after World War I. Family units drifted apart with the deaths of Schurz in 1906 and Jacobi in 1919. The thousand-acre Alma Farm was sold by the Theodore Meyers to the State of New York in the 1920s to become an addition to the Adirondack State Park. As the Boas children became older and assumed family and work responsibilities, it became more difficult or orchestrate family gatherings in Bolton.

Helene Boas married Cecil Yampolsky, a botanist and a teacher in the New York City Public School system. Ernst went to Columbia University and the College of Physicians and Surgeons where he earned his doctorate in medicine in 1914. He married Helen T. Sisson in 1917. Gertrud became a schoolteacher. Henry attended Storrs Agricultural College and graduated as an agriculturalist. Franziska became an accomplished interpreter and teacher of modern dance. She married Dr. Nicolas Michelson. By 1920 the Boas children in turn started to raise their own families.

**References and Notes**

1. O'Brien, Kathryn E. *The Great and Gracious on Millionaires Row – Lake George in its Glory*, North Country Books, 1978. (Includes biographies of Abraham and Mary Putnam Jacobi and Carl Schurz).

2. Boas, Norman F. & Barbara L. Meyer. *ALMA FARM, An Adirondack Meeting Place,* Boas & Meyer Publishers, Mystic, Connecticut & Bolton Landing, New York, 1999 (The Boas summer vacation place on Lake George including biographical glimpses of the Boas, Theodore Meyer, Krackowizer, Schurz, Jacobi, and Willy Meyer families).

3. Boas, Franz. Boas letter to George Foster Peabody, February 11, 1907 (Many of their letters are located in the Library of the American Philosophical Society, Philadelphia.).

4. Cole, Douglas. *FRANZ BOAS – the Early Years – 1858-1906*. Douglas & McIntyre, Vancouver & Toronto and University of Washington Press, Seattle & London, 1999 (The most definitive biography of Boas, although never completed).

5. Truax, Rhoda. *The Doctors Jacobi*, Little, Brown & Company, Boston, 1952 (Biographies of Abraham and Many Putnam Jacobi).
6. *Dictionary of American Biography*. 10 volumes and 8 supplements, American Council of Learned Societies, Charles Scribner's Sons, New York, 1958-88 (Brief biographies of Franz Boas, Carl Schurz, and the Jacobis).
7. Jacobi, Abraham. *Collectanea Jacobi*. 8 volumes, edited by William Robinson, The Critic and Guide Company, New York, 1909 (Invaluable collection of the writings and speeches of Jacobi).
8. Jacobi, Abraham. *The Most Eminent American Physician of European Birth*, in *American Medicine*, Volume IX, No. 18, May 6, 1905 (A tribute to Dr. Ernst Krackowizer).
9. *WHO'S WHO IN AMERICA*. Volume 26, 1950-51, The A. N. Marquis Company, Chicago, 1950.
10. Personal communication – Ernest Jacobi McAneny.
11. Schurz, Carl. *The Reminiscences of Carl Schurz*. In three volumes, the McClure Company, New York, 1908-09 (An autobiography published after his death in 1906).
12. Trefousse, Hans. *Carl Schurz, A Biography*. Fordham University Press, New York, 1998 (An excellent and valuable biography by Professor Trefousse).
13. *The Collected Works of Abraham Lincoln*, Edited by Roy P. Basler, Volume IV, page 78, Rutgers University Press, New Brunswick New Jersey, 1953.
14. Frissel, H. P. In *Addresses in Memory of Carl Schurz*, May 17, 1906 (Norman F. Boas collection).

# CHAPTER VII

## COLUMBIA UNIVERSITY - THE EARLY YEARS PROFESSOR OF ANTHROPOLOGY

Franz Boas retained his affiliation with the American Museum of Natural History at the time of his professorial appointment at Columbia University in 1899. This dual arrangement was to continue until 1905 when he left the museum to devote his entire energies to teaching and research. For the first few years at Columbia he was still involved in the Jesup Expedition with field trips to British Columbia, his work with the Bureau of American Ethnology of the Smithsonian Institution, the publication of many scientific papers, the founding of the American Anthropological Association, and many other related activities. With all these responsibilities, much of his research time was sacrificed so that he could devote more time to the development of his department.

His primary and overriding goal was to define anthropology precisely in this country. As the primary educator in American anthropology, it was incumbent upon him to define the parameters of this field and create a curriculum that would meet his strict scientific standards and would establish anthropology as an important scientific discipline. Aside from his basic courses in anthropology, his seminars became very important in the education of graduate students. In 1901 the first graduate students with Ph.D.s in anthropology graduated from his classes, presaging a large number to graduate in the ensuing years. Until his own students came into their own as department heads at other universities, virtually all of the graduate students in anthropology in America were attracted to Boas and Columbia University. The Boas school dominated anthropology for many decades.

One of his most trusted and faithful aides was H. A. Andrews, whom he hired in 1897 as his secretary while he was at the American Museum of Natural History. She was a stenographer, typist, editor, and his office manager. She remained with him when he moved to Columbia and continued in this capacity until his death in 1942.

By 1900 Boas was distressed that some projects were not moving forward quickly enough – studies of the vanishing tribes in the Philippines and Asia, publication of the Jesup Expedition findings, and the huge job of labeling and cataloguing museum exhibits. Putnam was inclined to be dilatory in his duties at the museum and was away much of the time.

Without Putnam's presence and authority, Boas could do little but prod him at a distance with his pleas for assistance. President Jesup felt that a full-time anthropologist was needed, but took no action.[1]

In the same year, although not inclined to be active politically in the public sector, Boas accepted a membership in The Civil Service Reform Association in New York. This organization was dedicated to the elimination of favoritism and corruption in the civil service system in the city. Carl Schurz had founded it when he moved to New York. George McAneny, as secretary, tendered the invitation to Boas to join.[2] Schurz, always disturbed by political patronage, had earlier reformed the Civil Service system in his department when he was Secretary of Interior.

Early in the summer of 1900, Marie and the four children, Helene, Ernst, Gertrud, and Henry left for Lake George. When Franz arrived in July, he almost immediately became ill with abdominal pains. Dr. Jacobi diagnosed his condition as acute appendicitis and sent him to the Albany Hospital. His appendix was removed the following day.[a] This appears to have been more than a routine appendectomy. The delay in surgery and his subsequent protracted recovery time suggests that the appendix may well have ruptured. Fearful of his own fate before surgery, he wrote to Marie, "May I say that I love you and our children more than I can say and that life at your side is my happiness."[1]

After he returned to New York in September, he was so weak and tired that he was obliged to return to Lake George to convalesce for a longer period of time. He spent much of his time with Ernst, collecting, classifying, and mounting insects. Improvement came slowly over the balance of the year. As a result, the anthropology department at the museum did not function efficiently, not only because of Boas's protracted period of recovery, but because Putnam was spending a great deal of time in California, nurturing an opportunity to move there. Director Hermon C. Bumpus was unhappy with the backlog of work in the anthropology department and Boas was "disgusted" with Putnam's behavior. Morris Jesup was also disturbed and asked Putnam to make a greater contribution to the museum.[1]

After Putnam returned from Berkeley in January, Jesup again

---

[a] It is interesting to note that his son, Ernst, also had an attack of acute appendicitis at Lake George in the summer of 1903 and that Franz's grandson, this writer, also had acute appendicitis at Lake George in 1932. Ernst was transported to New York where cousin Willy Meyer performed the surgery at the German Hospital (now Lenox Hill Hospital). I had the good fortune of having my surgery at the Glens Falls Hospital, only a few miles away.

confronted him, insisting that he give all his energies to the museum. Jesup finally agreed to a proposal by Putnam that Putnam be made an "advisory curator" with his time and salary halved. Jesup accepted it as a face-saving move so that he could ultimately dismiss Putnam. Unbeknownst to Boas and Bumpus, Putnam and Marshall Saville, museum archeologist, had agreed to rearrange the department of anthropology to suit them, knowing full well that archeologist Savelle had accepted an appointment at Columbia University. Jesup, Bumpus and Boas were furious about these manipulations – Boas was no longer willing to protect his mentor. As a result of Putnam's behavior, Jesup and Bumpus decisively appointed Boas curator of anthropology and Livingston Farrand as assistant curator. Putnam would become an advisor-curator in archeology only. In the meantime, Putnam agreed to serve on the staff of the University of California four to five months a year but did not resign from the museum until 1903. Because of their long and productive, and sometimes difficult relationship, Boas harbored guilt feelings about having taken sides, but commented, "It will be a relief for us when he is gone…I cannot forgive him for the way he betrayed himself in the Saville appointment."[1]

By January, feeling better and with free rein of the anthropology department at the museum, Boas believed that he was long overdue for a raise in salary. After some delays, Jesup granted his request and raised his salary to $3500 a year. He was also given expenses to sail to Europe in the summer of the same year to study collections in museums there, during which time he would visit with his mother and other family members in Berlin.[1]

On returning to New York in October 1901, he discovered that Putnam had left the museum to head the new museum and Department of Anthropology at the University of California at Berkeley. Boas was upset again when he learned that Putnam was sabotaging his plans for fieldwork. California was a major area of Boas's Indian research on "vanishing tribes." He had already received a Collis P. Huntington grant and had sent Kroeber, DuBois and Dixon to do fieldwork in the west with these funds. Putnam had clearly stepped in between Boas and his California supporters, was treading on his carefully cultivated grantors of funds, and appropriated his projects. Putnam even hired Kroeber while Boas was in Berlin and raised funds for Kroeber's Arapaho fieldwork.

From the time of Boas's arrival in America, Putnam had done many favors for him. These included offering him positions on the staff of Science, at the World Columbian Exposition and at the American Museum of Natural History. However, he was undoubtedly jealous of Boas's accomplishments and ambitions and tried to keep him at an academic distance. Putnam's expertise was not primarily in ethnology, but he always protected his own territory from intrusion by others. Even as he accepted his new position in Berkeley, he kept his appointments at Harvard and the American Museum of Natural History.

Boas too, held more than one position at this time, at the museum and at the university. In his case, they complemented one another; the distance between the two institutions was trivial. Serving more than one academic venue at one time was not an uncommon practice in the early 20th century, often done for financial reasons. It was Boas's belief that all of his anthropology students must serve an internship at the museum as part of their university curriculum. He viewed a museum experience as a means of seeing and understanding the differences in the evolution of the varied ethnic groups of the world. This was part of his master plan for anthropology, which necessarily depended upon the cooperation of the museum, university, philanthropy, and the government. This, of course, applied to the Smithsonian Institution as well local government. As late as 1914, Boas wrote to George McAneny, who was then Chairman of the Board of Aldermen of the City of New York. He sought and obtained reassurance that it was perfectly proper for his students to use the American Museum of Natural History as a learning center, although the City of New York subsidized it.[3]

Boas had a profound nostalgia for his experiences in the Arctic. He took advantage of opportunities and the connections he had established to add to the Inuit collections at the museum. His old friend from Baffin Island days, Scotch whaler James Mutch, cited earlier, and Connecticut whaler, George Comer collected artifacts for the museum on their Arctic whaling voyages. Comer, born in Quebec in 1858, moved to Connecticut at the age of ten after the death of his father. As a teenager he joined Captain John Spicer of New London who commanded the whaler *Nile* for his Arctic expeditions. Under Spicer, Comer became master of the schooner *Era* in 1895 which he commanded until she was lost in 1906. He was a cooperative and an enthusiastic collector. On a whaling trip in 1903, he carried three barrels of plaster of Paris with the plan to make casts of native faces and hands for the museum. He also took many glass plate photographs, kept ethnographic records and even recorded Inuit songs on his gramophone. He was later befriended by polar explorers Donald MacMillan and Roald Amundsen and was himself a member of the Explorer's Club. Comer died at the age of 79.[1,4]

In the summer of 1904, Boas again sailed to Europe, to visit home and to attend professional meetings with others in his field. He visited Bonn for the 60th anniversary of the Allemannen and reunions with old fraternity members. He took Marie and Helene to the scene of his first duel in Heidelberg at the Kirshgasse. They visited Stuttgart where he and Marie met in 1883, went to Bavaria to visit his Reichenbach cousins, and to Austria to visit some of Marie's Krackowizer kin. Also included was a visit with his mother in the Harz Mountains. He returned to America on the steamer *Blücher* and arrived in time to attend the St. Louis World's Fair where he presented a paper.[1]

Following his return, the autumn registration at Columbia University recorded an increase in anthropology students from 44 to 186. Anthropology was becoming a very popular subject. With his increasing workload at the university, he found it more difficult to cover both the museum and his teaching responsibilities. He sought and obtained higher salary benefits at the university and some concessions from the museum, but he was beginning to lose interest in the latter. By February 1905 the museum agreed to increase his salary as curator, appoint Saville as associate curator, and appoint an assistant to take charge of ethnology. In spite of Boas's strong position in the anthropology department, his relations with Bumpus deteriorated over disagreements in planning exhibits and interference by Bumpus with the Boas staff. This was followed by criticisms by Jesup. These disagreements culminated in a meeting of the three, Boas, Bumpus and Jesup in Jesup's home.[1]

The controversy was over labeling of the exhibits. Should they be presented and labeled precisely as one might label research material or labeled primarily for educational purposes? Boas considered the former more appropriate and the latter a compromise favoring entertainment. Jesup and Bumpus felt quite the contrary. Boas believed that for scientific accuracy, his system should prevail, yet concluded that it was no longer worthwhile to face these conflicts and interference. An intolerable relationship had evolved between Boas and Bumpus and also led to an irreparable rift between Boas and Jesup. Unresolved, primarily by the animosity of Bumpus, Boas suggested, and it was agreed that he would resign his position. He would continue with the publication of the reports on the Jesup Expedition, the works of the East Asiatic Committee, and complete other works in progress. He would also continue to employ Miss Andrews, and his salary and vacation leaves would remain the same. His resignation as curator of anthropology was tendered in May 1905.[1]

Upon resigning, President Jesup sent him a kind letter of appreciation for his many productive years at the museum. This was followed by a response from Boas who placed the entire blame on Bumpus, when in fact Jesup had appointed Bumpus and essentially backed him versus Boas on this issue.

In early summer, Boas and his family left for Lake George. At about the same time Bumpus approached Clark Wissler (1870-1947), a bright young protégé of Franz Boas, and asked him to become curator of anthropology at the museum. Wissler was born in rural Indiana to a family of migrant "Pennsylvania Dutch" (German). He was a graduate of Indiana University in 1897 and earned his Ph.D. in psychology at Columbia University in 1901. He met Franz Boas the following year and under his influence developed a lifelong interest in anthropology. He soon joined the staff of the American Museum of Natural History as an assistant to Boas and later as assistant curator in ethnology. Upon the resignation of Boas, Wissler remained on the staff as curator from 1905 until 1942. At the same time, he was an assistant and lecturer at Columbia (1903-09) in Boas's department. During this time he carried out fieldwork among the Sioux and Blackfoot Indians.[1]

Wissler's appointment at the museum caused Boas considerable distress. He felt that Wissler had taken on more than he should because of his university obligations, and at most, would only have time for teaching an extension course. Nicholas Murray Butler, Livingston Farrand, and Marshall Saville overruled his stated position in this matter; Wissler was allowed to remain on the regular teaching staff. The circumstances of his appointment to the museum contributed toward a disruption of his friendship with Boas. Nevertheless Wissler's work at the museum was essentially a continuation of the themes Boas had espoused, as was his approach to the numerous Indian field expeditions that he sponsored. From 1924-1940, Wissler was associated with Yale University, first with the new Institute of Psychology (later the Institute of Human Relations) and then as the first professor of anthropology at Yale in 1931. Other positions he held included those as president of the American Anthropological Association in 1919, chairman of the anthropology section of the National Research Council, president of the American Association of Museums (1938-43), and member of the American Philosophical Society.[1,5]

It has been said that with the loss of Boas, Putnam, Farrand, and other younger associates, the American Museum of Natural History suffered a major set-back with a significant decline in its anthropology department that lasted until 1920, when it again be came a center for great scientific advances. During his tenure at the museum, Boas's group amassed huge collections of artifacts, particularly of North America, the Northwest Coast, and the Central Eskimo – an extraordinary achievement. The collections were backed with vast amounts of research and meticulous labeling of artifacts. So ended the active museum career of Franz Boas, which began in the Berlin Ethnographic Museum and continued with his formative role with the Field Museum, contributions to the National Museum of Natural History, and the many productive years at the American Museum of Natural History.

According to his former nemesis and later as a student at Columbia University, George Dorsey wrote in *Science* in 1905,

> As a result of this intelligently directed series of field operations, there grew up in the American Museum of Natural History one of the greatest departments of anthropology to be found in any museum in the world.[1]

The final publications of the Jesup Expedition took until 1930 to complete, thus Boas remained involved in this task for many years. A significant observation of Boas and the Russian groups involved in these studies was that there was a close relationship between the folklore of the Asian Northeast and Pacific Northwest ethnic groups. These observations extended far into Siberia. Waldemar Bogoras concluded, "from the ethnological point of view, the line dividing Asia and America lies far southwestward of the Bering Strait." Boas agreed and concluded, "the tribes of this whole area must be considered as a single race…" There was also evidence of a linguistic as well as physical anthropological relationship of the peoples on both sides of the Bering Strait. The eras of migration were probably not all during the glaciation period. Some may have followed later, since there appear be at least three distinctive ethnic groups that might have migrated at different times. Boas also considered the possibility that there might have been a reverse migration from the Northwest to Siberia – a subject still unsettled.[1]

There is no summary volume of the Jesup Expedition. It was probably not possible to draw any firm conclusions concerning precise migration patterns. The value of the huge collections at the American Museum of Natural History is unquestioned. The photographs, physical measurements, folklore, languages, and artifacts of many ethnic groups on both sides of the Pacific were preserved. These included hundreds of thousands of bits of information on diverse cultures, most of which would be lost forever, were it not for these pioneer anthropologists and their fieldwork.[1,6,7]

By this time Boas had developed and formulated most of his advanced ideas on anthropology. He came to realize that the explanations of ethnic differences and the development of cultures rested greatly on history and all other facets of scientific analysis had to be explained in this light.

Science, truth, and proof were the keystones of his approach. He was intolerant of those who reached conclusions on a speculative level without attempting to prove their conclusions, even though they might be right. Boas had little patience for those who trivialized science and the importance of research. At times he was accused of living in an ivory tower. Even in his own field, he would get angry with those colleagues who sought publicity by publishing findings without proper scientific proof for their claims or sought publicity for their own personal gains. He did, however, appreciate the value of the press and public relations as an adjunct to the support of science. In spite of his dispute with the museum, it remained an important teaching venue for his students, as it has been for many others to this day. He concluded that to develop a master plan for anthropology, it had to be based on cooperative educational efforts of the museum, university, philanthropy, and the government.[1]

In 1904 Boas wrote that there was a fourfold basis to American anthropology,

> Anthropology was the biological history of mankind in all its varieties; linguistics applied to people without written languages; the ethnology of people without historical records; and pre-historical archeology.[1]

Franz Boas had a relationship with the Bureau of Ethnology for virtually all of his professional life in America. The Bureau of Ethnology was formed in 1879 as part of the Smithsonian Institution in Washington and was headed by John Wesley Powell. Shortly thereafter it began issuing publications that focused primarily on archeology, linguistics and ethnology. When Boas first arrived in America in 1884, he visited the Bureau of Ethnology and reported on his Baffin Island expedition. The bureau, under the heading, *The Central Eskimo*, published his experiences. Late in the 19th century, the name of the bureau was changed to the Bureau of American Ethnology (B.A.E.).

Boas initially had acrimonious debates with Otis Mason, curator of ethnology of the United States National Museum and John Wesley Powell, curator of the B.A.E. on their manner of displaying ethnological artifacts. In time, a good symbiotic and productive relationship developed between Boas, Powell, and the B.A.E. It was through the Smithsonian Institution that Boas published many of his major ethnological and linguistic papers. As the result of his major revisions in linguistic concepts and broad knowledge of this subject, Boas was placed in charge of linguistics at the bureau. As the leading linguist in America for so many years, he had a profound effect on this specialized field. This led to his extraordinary project of the cataloging and the editing of *The Handbook of American Indian Languages* (1911).[8]

The American Anthropological Association (A.A.A.) was founded in June 1902, primarily through the efforts of W. J. McGee of the B.A.E. Much of his efforts were made without consulting Boas and his group in New York. McGee favored an open organization that was composed of professionals as well as the laity, whereas Boas, supported by Putnam, Dixon, Farrand, and Smith, favored a strictly professional association. They were disturbed by McGee's plan and clearly did not agree with him. It was McGee and his Washington friends who prevailed, with McGee being elected as the first president of the A.A.A. Boas, Putnam, Holmes, and Powell were elected as vice presidents. In spite of McGee's plan, the A.A.A. became dominated by professionals, among whom Boas played a major role, becoming president from 1907 to 1909.[1,5]

Until their differences evolved in the creation of A.A.A., Boas and McGee had been good friends. McGee had been sympathetic to Boas in the Washington-Field Museum contest with Holmes. Holmes had undercut Boas in seeking the Chicago position and now was undercutting McGee in his aspirations toward directorship of the B.A.E. From 1893 to 1902, McGee had supported Boas in obtaining research funds, was instrumental in appointing Boas honorary philologist at the Smithsonian Institution, and participated financially with him in creating the *American Anthropologist*. He even offered him a position at the B.A.E.[1,5]

For several years, McGee had been acting director of the B.A.E. as the health of John Wesley Powell gradually failed. When Powell died toward the end of 1902, a leadership vacuum was created. The following year, because of distrust and political pressures, Smithsonian Secretary Samuel P. Langley bypassed McGee and appointed William Henry Holmes as curator of the B.A.E. and also permitted him to retain his position at the United States National Museum. In August 1903, McGee, weary from his ordeals, resigned his position at the B.A.E.[1]

Boas took it upon himself to publicly adopt a position against Langley and his appointment of Holmes. In November 1902, he began a lengthy correspondence with Alexander Graham Bell who was a regent of the Smithsonian Institution. He referred to the loss of Powell and the placement of the B.A.E. under the director of the U.S. National Museum. Having found a good ally, Boas continued to correspond with Bell about this and other bureau matters for two years.[9] An open letter Boas published in *Science* on this subject received editorial support. He felt that the appointment of Holmes was a serious blow to the development of ethnological ideas at the institution, a program already weakened by the prolonged illness of Powell. Because of this and the inadequate leadership at the bureau, Boas also wrote to Carl Schurz seeking his help to correct this situation. The B.A.E. had been established in the Department of Interior at the time that Carl Schurz was Secretary of Interior.[a10] Boas expressed his concerns about the future of the B.A.E. without Powell at the helm and with a "non-ethnologist" appointed to head the bureau – a situation not rectified for six years.

The Boas family spent the summer of 1903 at Lake George. Franz decided not to embark on any western expeditions but to spend his time at the Jacobi cottage devoted to writing. His vacation was disrupted when Ernst developed acute appendicitis. He was taken to New York where cousin Willy Meyer at the German Hospital performed an appendectomy. The delay in surgery, predicated on the distance they had to travel, is hard to comprehend in this day and age. In any case the appendix appears not to have ruptured and he recovered without incident.[1]

When Boas returned to New York in the fall, in spite of difficulties associated with the Holmes appointment, he was able to proceed with the *Handbook of Indian Languages*, a monumental project sponsored by the Smithsonian Institution.

For Franz Boas, the three most important institutions in his professional life were Columbia University, the American Museum of Natural History, and the Bureau of American Ethnology. Much of his entire professional career revolved around these centers of research and learning. In 1909 William H. Holmes resigned as chief of the B.A.E., remained as curator of anthropology at the U.S. National Museum, and assumed the position of curator of the National Gallery of Art. Thus a vacancy was created at the B.A.E. with a simultaneous cutback in funds for the bureau. This had an impact on funding for research, which greatly distressed Boas and led to heated disputes between him and the secretary of the Smithsonian Institution. He also felt that he should have been offered the position vacated by Holmes, having made so many contributions to the B.A.E. for a period of over twenty years.[1] It was probably unrealistic for him to consider a position in Washington and to continue with his professorial duties at Columbia University.

In 1905 Berthold Laufer, one of Boas's associates during the Jesup Expedition, sought to sponsor a *Festschrift* (commemorative volume), in honor of the 25th anniversary (1906) of Boas's doctorate, an old German

---

[a] The Bureau of American Ethnology remained in the Department of Interior until it was transferred to the Smithsonian Institution in 1965.

tradition. Included among the committee were Laufer (editor), Nicholas Murray Butler, president of Columbia University (chairman), as a well as Andrew D. White for the Germanistic Society of America, Edward Adams and Jacob Schiff of the West Asiatic Committee, W. J. McGee of the B.A.E., Abraham Jacobi, Carl Schurz, and Eduard Seler from Berlin. Subscribers included, among others, Boas family members, Felix Adler, Isaac N. Seligman, Felix Warburg, and scientific colleagues. There were 46 contributors, including former students, scientific collaborators, George Comer, James Mutch, George Hunt, and James Teit as well as sometimes adversaries William H. Holmes and George Dorsey. Boas's brother-in-law, Rudolph Lehmann, also contributed to the volume.[11]

Sometime after 1903, Boas delegated teaching of the college courses in anthropology to Farrand and other assistants so that he might spend more time in the training of graduate students. The first graduate student at Columbia to receive a Ph.D. in anthropology was Alfred L. Kroeber (1876-1960). Kroeber was born Hoboken, New Jersey and matriculated at Columbia University where he earned his undergraduate and M.A. degrees. He came under the influence of Franz Boas when he was appointed a fellow in anthropology and participated in Columbia expeditions including fieldwork with the Arapaho, Ute, Shoshone, and Bannock Indians (1899-1901). The earning of his Ph.D. in 1901 was probably the third granted in America.[b]

As Boas's first graduate student to earn his Ph.D. at Columbia, it is revealing to note Alfred Kroeber's observations on the Boas teaching style.[12] From the time that Boas was appointed to his position at Columbia, he incorporated two courses, *"Statistical Theory* and *American Indian Languages"* into his teaching program, both of which he taught for his forty years at Columbia.

> His approach to Statistics was wholly theoretical. A grudging minimum of concrete exemplification made the course doubly difficult, and sometimes sterile, to students lacking the necessary mathematical foundation. Boas never conceded them an inch. On the other hand it is not known that he ever reported them as failing…

In describing Kroeber's own doctural examination, sitting around a table with Boas, Farrand, Cattell and Butler, he outlined his doctoral dissertation, answered some questions,

> "avowing ignorance of a series of other fields, and being dismissed…

---

[b] Boas, as noted earlier, awarded the first PhD in America, to Alexander F. Chamberlain in 1892, when he was at Clark University. The second was probably the one received by George Dorsey at Harvard in 1894.

> There was no notification of result, and Boas's only subsequent comment...was that there was a lot that the candidate had not read...

Boas always held that "most Ph.D. candidates do not know enough," but felt that as "good men," with degrees, they would "learn what they need...a refreshing attitude...[12]

For a time Kroeber assisted Boas at the American Museum of Natural History. Upon the recommendation and encouragement of Boas, he received an appointment at the University of California at Berkeley and with the California Academy of Sciences. Thus began a long and distinguished career that led to his appointment as Professor of Anthropology in 1919, a position he held until 1946. He was also curator and then director of the Anthropology Museum at the University of California (1908-46). During his years at Berkeley, he made field expeditions in New Mexico, Mexico, Peru, as well as field trips to study the Indians of California. He was the recipient of many honors and held the positions as president of the American Anthropological Society, American Folk Lore Society, and Linguistic Society of America. "Although it is hard to isolate in his work any lasting theoretical contribution . . . to the general subject to anthropology," Kroeber was a prolific writer (over 700 publications) and was a major player in the development of anthropology in America.[13]

Additional observations by Kroeber on Boas as a teacher are valuable and reflect the long association he had with him. In regard to his graduate students,

> As a teacher, Boas was decidedly one-sided, but his strength also lay in this. Essentially, he would teach nothing but principles, methods, and problems, fortified by only such concrete data as were necessary for his sure and rapid mind to understand the situation. The load was wholly on the student; if he assumed it, Boas was ready to give him intellectual guidance...These attitudes made Boas a supreme teacher for the man who would be a productive scholar in his own right...but on the whole an indifferently successful instructor of average graduates, who are accustomed to a diet of masses of factual content carefully organized for assimilation.[12]

When he first started teaching anthropology at Columbia University, Boas gave courses in general anthropology to undergraduate students. After a few years he discontinued giving these lectures following a disagreement with the college administration. His assistants and associates assumed the burden of teaching these courses. On the other hand, similar undergraduate courses that he gave at Barnard College apparently gave him great pleasure, and thus were continued.

> He may have been less uncompromising toward the girls; they at any rate

> sensed more quickly than their brothers the genius which underlay his unpalatable presentations and gave him a rapport and personal reciprocation which he was human enough to appreciate keenly...[12]

The adherence of Boas to intellectual presentations in his classes or writings sublimated his efforts at "eloquence or aesthetic form."[12] He was always so intent on the content of his deliveries, he was either unaware of this shortcoming, or did not care.

> Platform applause Boas did receive increasingly as he aged...but it is clear that the tribute was to his personality and convictions and courage rather than to his manner of presentation. He was at once too set to his self-imposed tasks, and too proud, to step out of his way to win favor by anything extraneous.[12]

John Reed Swanton (1873-1958) was another anthropologist who was influenced by Boas. He met Boas in 1898 and spent the following two years under his tutelage at Columbia University and at the American Museum of Natural History. This exposure channeled his interests into ethnology. Upon receiving his Ph.D. degree at Harvard, he joined the Bureau of American Ethnology of the Smithsonian Institution where he remained for 44 years, until his retirement. Following Boas's pattern, he did fieldwork with Indians of the Pacific Northwest, as well as with Plains, Southwest, and Southeast Indians. He was a contributor, with Boas, to the *Handbook of American Indian Languages.* Swanton published extensively and also served as president of the American Anthropological Association and American Folklore Society.[14]

Although it is not the intent of this writer to enumerate all the outstanding students who trained under Boas, they were all an integral part of his life. There are a good number, however, who deserve special mention as major contributors to the field of anthropology and who helped define this scientific discipline. Frank G. Speck (1881-1950) was one such individual. He was descended from early Dutch settlers of the Hudson Valley and Mohican[c] peoples of this area. Because of ill health and a "healthier" environment in Connecticut, at age eight, he was placed under the care of Mrs. Fidelia A. Fielding, a Mohegan Indian, at Mohegan[c] (Montville), Connecticut. She was one of the last native speakers of her language. Speck grew up with Indian children during his most formative years. He returned to his family at age fourteen. When he matriculated at Columbia University he was already proficient in French,

---

[c] Although related, the names of the Indian tribes of the Hudson River Valley (Mohican) and Southeastern Connecticut are usually spelt differently (Mohegan).

German, and Algonkian languages, leading to a primary academic interest in the classical languages. While there, he met Franz Boas who encouraged him to enter the field of anthropology. Speck followed his advice and graduated in 1905 with an M.A. in anthropology.[15]

In 1904 he began ethnographic fieldwork among the Yuchi Indians of Oklahoma and continued with graduate work at Columbia until 1908. Speck earned his Ph.D. at the University of Pennsylvania in that year. He remained there the rest of his life doing research and teaching, becoming chairman of the Department of Anthropology in 1925. Speck specialized in linguistics and recorded the Yuchi language and songs. Although a great collector of Indian artifacts, he frequently sold them for the support of his field studies. He became a powerful advocate of rights of Native Americans and published extensively on his fieldwork with the Indians of Oklahoma, Northeast, and Southeast United States as well as on the tribes of Newfoundland and Labrador. He was president of the American Folklore Society (1920-22).[15]

Livingston Farrand (1867-1939) was another outstanding protégé of Franz Boas. He had his early training as a physician, graduating with a medical degree from the College of Physicians and Surgeons in New York in 1891. Never seriously interested in practicing medicine, he gravitated toward the field of psychology. Two years later he joined the faculty of Columbia University in the Department of Psychology under James McKeen Cattell. After Franz Boas arrived at Columbia, Farrand joined him in fieldwork in the Pacific Northwest, assisted him at the American Museum of Natural History, and from 1903 to 1910 served as professor of anthropology at Columbia in the Boas department. The balance of his life was dedicated to public health and education. He spent many years, nationally and internationally, working toward the eradication of tuberculosis. As an educator, he served as president of the University of Colorado (1914-19), chairman of the American Red Cross, and president of Cornell University (1921-37), during which time he was responsible for the creation of Cornell Medical College and the New York Hospital.[16]

Another indefatigable anthropologist was Roland Burrage Dixon (1875-1934). Born in Worcester, Massachusetts, he attended Harvard University earning his A.B. in 1897, and Ph.D. in 1900. Dixon first came in contact with Franz Boas in 1898 at the American Museum of Natural History and was invited to participate in the Jesup North Pacific Expedition. His assignment was to do fieldwork in Alaska and British Columbia. In 1901 he settled in Cambridge where he taught anthropology for thirty-three years and attained the position of professor in 1915. He never married and devoted all his efforts to his chosen profession. During his tenure at Harvard, he conducted extensive fieldwork in Asia, Oceania, North and South America, and published many scientific papers.[17]

Robert Henry Lowie (1883-1957) followed Boasian teachings in many ways. Born in Vienna, his family immigrated to America in 1893. After obtaining his B.A. at the City College of New York, he attended graduate school at Columbia University and earned his Ph.D. under Boas in 1908. While studying at Columbia, he also did fieldwork and collected artifacts under Clark Wissler for the American Museum of Natural History, spending time with the Shoshone and Plains Indians. It was from the latter group that he developed a lifelong interest in the ethnology of the Crow Indians. His initial work at the museum was as a volunteer. In 1901 he was appointed assistant curator and in 1913, associate curator. In 1921 Lowie became assistant professor of anthropology at the University of California at Berkeley, and in 1925 was promoted to full professor and chairman of the department. One of his greatest challenges was against the Boasian concept of "cultural relativism" as opposed to "multilinear evolution." It was within such an area, between Boasian doctrine and evolutionary thought that Lowie was "to concentrate his greatest efforts and find his worst dilemmas."[18]

Another student of Boas was Edward Sapir (1884-1939) who was born in Pomerania (a former province of Prussia) and immigrated with his family to America at the age of five. He took his undergraduate work at Columbia University where he received his Ph.D. under the tutelage of Franz Boas. Boas was particularly influential in steering Sapir's career into linguistics. Sapir was soon sponsored by Boas to do fieldwork in the state of Washington to study the language of the Wishram Indians. Thenceforth, much of his professional life was devoted to the study of the languages and ethnology of American Indians. His first teaching position was as an instructor at the University of Pennsylvania. This was followed by a fifteen-year period as chief of the division of anthropology in the Geological Survey of the Canadian National Museum at Ottawa. In 1925 he taught at the University of Chicago. In 1931 he became Sterling Professor of Anthropology and Linguistics at Yale University, a position he held until his death at the age of 55.[19]

Paul Radin (1883-1859), born in Lodz, Poland, arrived in America with his family when he was an infant. After his undergraduate work at Columbia University, he studied in Munich, but returned to Columbia where he worked under Boas in obtaining his Ph.D. in 1911. He arrived fortuitously at a time when he was also able to meet with a scholarly group of anthropologists including Kroeber, Wissler, Sapir, Lowie, Speck, and Goldenweiser. His career included fieldwork with Sapir on the Geological Survey of Canada as well as many venues for teaching, including Mills College, the University of California at Berkeley, Cambridge University, Black Mountain College in North Carolina, Kenyon College, and four universities in Switzerland. The last two years of his life were spent at Brandeis University. Radin was a prolific writer who focused on the Winnebago Indians, but he also wrote several texts as well as many other scholarly papers.[20]

Another brilliant, but unconventional student of Boas was Alexander Goldenweiser (1880-1940). Born in Kiev, Russia he came to the United States in 1900 with his father and four siblings to seek the freedom of democracy and to escape the authoritarian Russian government with its anti-Semitism. His father returned to Kiev, but Alexander and his brother, Emanuel, remained in the United States. Alexander received his AB at Columbia in 1902, a master's degree in 1904, and a Ph.D. in 1910 (interrupted by year of studying in Berlin and mandatory service in the Russian army in Kiev in 1907-09). Goldenweiser taught at numerous institutions but he was unable to attain a full-time professorship. Although he had a brilliant mind, his standards were unconventional and he demonstrated a lack of responsibility. He was most suited and most successful on the lecture circuit. From 1910 to 1929 he was a lecturer in anthropology at Columbia University, at the Rand School of Social Science and at the New School for Social Research, both in New York. In 1930 he moved to Portland, Oregon as an instructor in sociology at the University of Oregon. From 1932 until his death he was a professor of "thought and culture," holding a part-time position. He did little fieldwork, but was a very stimulating and popular lecturer. He was particularly well versed in theory and methodology in anthropology, with emphasis on psychology, social organization, and religion.[21]

Boas's years from 1902 to 1911 represented a period of "intense scientific activity" that encompassed the teaching and use of his graduate students in many field studies as well as in specialized areas of ethnology and linguistics.[5] Because of his responsibilities as an administrator and teacher, Boas had to depend on others for the gathering of much of the material which he, heretofore, would have done himself. During this period he published three of his most important works. Publication of the *Handbook of American Indian Languages* was a ten-year cooperative effort between Boas, contributors trained by Boas, and the Bureau of

American Ethnology. The plan was revolutionary in the linguistic field and set a pattern for years to come.[8]

In order to comprehend the complexities of world languages and record them in an understandable and pronounceable fashion, one must first understand the physiology of speech.

> In prehistoric times humans probably spoke between 10,000 and 15,000 different languages...This is easy to understand when one understands the physiology of speech. Speech consists of sounds produced by noises made by opening and closing certain portions of the larynx, mouth or nose or by modulating the breathing process [This also includes motions of the soft palate, tongue and cheeks]. As such, the human organism is capable of creating an infinite number of sounds, ergo, an infinite number of languages.[22]

Thus, a printed and pronouncing dictionary of unrecorded and primitive languages poses an extraordinary challenge when one is used to Indo-European language dictionaries. Boas, trained in German, Latin, Greek, and English, had to learn *Inuktitut* during his Baffin Island expedition and was exposed to the unrecorded language of the Indians of lower British Columbia, *Kwak'wala.* He was the first to successfully create an alphabet and record this language, and thus preserve it in perpetuity. He clearly recognized that if native languages were not recorded, they would soon be lost forever. Experts have observed that the current 6000 world languages are dying off rapidly and that half of them will be gone during this century, perhaps sooner with the advent of rapid worldwide electronic communication. Thus was Boas's compulsion to record the languages of Indians, which would almost certainly disappear in a few score years.[22]

> Boas's approach to language was based on the assumption that grammatical categories were unconscious classifications of an infinitely varied human experience, which were historically conditioned and specific to each language. One could not analyze the Eskimo tongue in terms of traditional Indo-European categories...every language was the product of a particular cultural experience and fully adequate to the needs thereof. It was this systematically relativistic viewpoint, which was to serve as charter for the subsequent development of descriptive linguistics in this country.[5]

As a leading scholar in linguistics in America, Boas became the founder of the *International Journal of American Linguistics* and served as a frequent contributor and editor from 1917 to 1939.

Another publication of major significance was his report to the United States Immigration Commission in 1910, published by the United States Senate, *Changes in Bodily Form of Descendants of Immigrants*. It was based on physical measurements of 18,000 immigrants and demonstrated the "interaction of environment and heredity in the growth process." He was able to show that,

> the head forms of children born in the United States differed significantly from those of their parents...thus challenged the dominant tradition in physical anthropology, which based its differentiation of human races on the assumption that head form was relatively impervious to environmental influences.[5,23]

In this, one his most important papers, using anthropometric methods, Boas was able to show that children of immigrants to America were often taller, heavier, had different head shapes (cephalic indices), and were better developed than their parents born in Europe. This introduced a new concept in interpreting physical differences. In this case, ethnicity was the same but the environment, diet, and culture were different and more conducive to the physical development of the human body and changes in the shape of the head.

The observation that the cephalic index could be influenced by environmental factors was a startling new discovery. Boas recognized this and wrote many papers detailing these observations. Lest there be any questions as to his interpretation, he published all of his data leading to this conclusion. In recent years his conclusion has been challenged by some, who reinterpreted Boas's raw data, but since refuted by others. We do not wish to get into this controversy except to emphasize that Boas was meticulous in obtaining and recording his research data. His lifetime was dedicated to the "truth" and when dealing with scientific conclusions he always insisted on "statistical proof" for conclusions reached. He applied this rigid discipline to his own work and was his own greatest critic.

Physical anthropology was an excellent technique for gathering statistical data for comparative studies of various ethnic groups but marriages between different groups introduced difficulties in comparative interpretations. Anthropometry seemed a logical approach originally because of obvious differences in the physical appearance of different cultural groups, but it became hopelessly confusing in attempts to compare measurements of those of nearly similar ethnic features.

In spite of his early training in anthropometry and the use of physical measurements in defining ethnic groups, he became skeptical of these techniques in explaining significant ethnic differences, particularly when applied to mental capacity. At this time, the general tendency was to assume that non-white races were inferior to whites. Boas and others were led to believe that the mental capacities and functions of man are the same all over the world. This was based on the assumption that people everywhere in the world, given the same cultural exposure and opportunities would make the same discoveries and would be on par with those around them. During the years 1894 to 1904, the term "cultural determinism" became the dominant theme in Boas's thinking. This led to the term "cultural relativism." "Man was a captive of his own culture," thus often unable to be objective in assessing other cultures. He stressed that anthropologists had to "free themselves from the bias of their own civilization."[1] We recall well the prejudice that some southern anthropologists had toward African Americans in our lifetime – "Shackles of tradition" that were difficult to cast off.

His third and probably most important publication was, *The Mind of Primitive Man* published in 1911. It was based on many of his previously published papers and written to "confront the widely current stereotype of the mentally inferior and dark-skinned savage." This publication became a keystone to modern anthropological views that culture determines behavior – "cultural relativism" that rejected the Darwinian concept of the evolution of mankind as a whole, "a single human culture."[5,24] *The Mind of Primitive Man* has had some revisions, many printings, and is still in print.

In about 1905 the Germanistic Society of America (G.S.A.) was founded in New York, primarily the inspiration of Franz Boas, but encouraged by Carl Schurz and joined by Emil L. Boas and others in New York. It was a society "Dedicated to promotion of knowledge of German civilization in America and of the American civilization in Germany."[25] The creation of the Germanistic Society was a vehicle for exchanging the views of German Americans with those of their brethren in Germany. It was a forum for sharing their experiences with each other at all levels of society, with particular emphasis on the creation of democratic freedom on both sides of the ocean. German Americans in America as well as many individuals in Germany supported the society with similar feelings. Franz's brother-in-law, Rudolf Lehmann, one of the leading educators in Germany and a professor at the Royal Academy, also joined and was one of the society's important participants in Berlin. In 1909, Rudolph came to the United States, accompanied by his wife Hete, for the express purpose of lecturing at Teachers College and before the Germanistic Society of America.[26]

The first officers included Nicholas Murray Butler, president; Carl Schurz, honorary vice president; Andrew E. White, vice president; Franz Boas, secretary and Emil L. Boas, treasurer. Emil was manager of the Hamburg-American Line and no relative of Franz. The Board of Trustees included W. H. Carpenter, Karl Buenz, Leonard Weber, Everett P. Wheeler, and H.C. Kudlich.

Nicolas Murray Butler (1862-1947) was at that time president of Columbia University. He was appointed in 1902, three years following the appointment of Franz Boas as professor of anthropology. They had a long relationship and shared a voluminous correspondence with each other, particularly as it concerned departmental affairs and grants.[27] In 1912 Butler was on the Republican ticket with William H. Taft as an unsuccessful candidate for Vice President of the United States. He replaced James S. Sherman, Taft's running mate, who died shortly before the election. After World War I, Butler's was a powerful voice for peace. He became president of the Carnegie Endowment for International Peace and was awarded the Nobel Peace Prize with Jane Addams. Boas and Butler had a number of philosophical clashes. Butler, a conservative, and Boas a liberal, did not see eye to eye on a number of contemplated projects and grants of the Anthropology Department.

On May 18, 1906, following the death of Carl Schurz, Franz Boas, as secretary of the G.S.A., wrote to Schurz's son, Carl Lincoln Schurz, on behalf of the G.S.A.

> At a special meeting of the Board of Directors of the Germanistic Society of America, held to give expression to their sorrow at the death of Carl Schurz, Honorary Vice-President of the Society, the following minute was adopted: Through the death of Carl Schurz our nation has lost a revered leader whose unswerving fidelity to truth, whose exalted views of duty, whose splendid courage of conviction have for many years set a shining example that can be ill be spared. The void created by his sudden removal leaves a feeling of universal bereavement. As his fellow-members in the Germanistic Society of America, we wish to express our deep sorrow at our loss. In him we honor one of the founders of the Society, whose warm interest and wise counsel were of inestimable value, and will be sadly missed. Mourning our own loss, we express to the family of the deceased our heartfelt sympathy in their great affliction.[28]

It is not clear how long Franz Boas remained secretary of the G.S.A. He was secretary again from 1919 to 1920, during which time he carried on a lengthy correspondence with Carl Lincoln Schurz, a New York lawyer, in regard to contributions to and the finances of the G.S.A.

By the year 1902, the Franz Boas family was complete – the last child, born in this year, was Marie Franziska. Over the next few years they came to appreciate that, with five children to house in their relatively small New York apartment on West 82nd Street, the time had come to have their own home. Again without the financial resources to take this step, Franz approached Uncle Jacobi seeking help. Jacobi readily complied and had his son-in-law, George McAneny draw up the mortgage and other papers necessary to secure the loan and which would permit Franz to hire an architect and builder. When completed, Jacobi transferred all his interests in the mortgage to his daughter Marjorie McAneny.[29]

The property they selected was in Grantwood, New Jersey, a section of the Borough of Cliffside Park. It was located on a side street, 230 Franklin Avenue, running west of Palisade Avenue. It consisted of four building lots, each 25 feet in width with many large oak trees.[29] It had been the hope of Franz that he would be able to convince some of his colleagues to buy some of his lots, thus creating a small professional residential community. Grantwood is in Bergen County and at the time was relatively wooded with a great deal of open space extending east to the Palisades, a long line of cliffs running parallel to the Hudson River. Columbia University was almost directly across the river. Commuting between the ferry slips at 125th Street in Manhattan and Fort Lee on the New Jersey side became a way of life. Always athletic, Franz used to walk to and from the ferries on both sides. In New York his walk was along 125th Street and on the long hill on Broadway. At the foot of the Palisades in Fort Lee, there was a path and a long wooden staircase up the Palisades to Palisade Avenue, a short distance from his house. It had 180-190 steps.[d] Palisade Avenue was a road that ran north and south, parallel to the Palisades. One always had the option of taking a trolley car up or down the Palisades that he used more often in his later years. Because of the steep ascent, the track had a horseshoe bend (switchback) part of the way to the top. After reaching Palisade Avenue, the tracks continued west about one block to "the Junction," where the rails went east and west and north and south. The Boas home was only two blocks from the junction, thus an easy walk. Franz Boas never owned a car. I cannot recall that he ever drove one, or much less, had a driver's license.

The house was large with wide overhanging eaves on all floors as well as on the dormers of the third floor (Figure 99). The siding had red cedar shingles. There was a front porch on the north side with a high stoop and a porte cochere on the west side of the porch, so that passengers could step directly from a carriage up a single step to the porch. Franz's study was to the left of the entry, as shown with the three double windows. On the east side, off the living room, was a covered porch. The size of the house suggests that it covered at least two of the four building lots. As one of its first subscribers, the phone company assigned him the number of "60." In time, with more subscribers, it was changed to Cliffside 6-0060. This was to be their family home until the death of Franz in 1942.

---

[d] Counted on a number of occasions by Donald P. Boas.

Figure 99. The Boas home in Grantwood, New Jersey, completed in 1908. A photograph taken some years later with Franz Boas standing in the driveway (American Philosophical Society).

Between 1900 and 1930, although much of his fieldwork was left to students and associates, Franz made eight more field trips, including the Pacific Northwest, Mexico, and the Southwest. He also traveled to Germany on a number of occasions, primarily to visit his mother, Toni, and other family members, and to participate in scientific meetings. In about 1910 Franz and Marie had fine formal portraits taken (Figures 100 & 101). In addition, Franz and Marie had a photographer take a rare picture of their five children (Figure 102). On other occasions, photographs were taken with Franz and his colleagues. (Figures 103 & 104).

In 1909 a celebration was held Worcester, Massachusetts on the 20th anniversary of the founding of Clark University. Many distinguished scientists were invited. The thrust of the gathering was to focus on psychology, the primary interest of the founding president of Clark University, G. Stanley Hall. Franz Boas gave the keynote address, titled *Psychological Problems in Anthropology*.[30] Attending from all over the world were psychologists Edward B. Titchener (Cornell University), G. Stanley Hall (Clark University), James M. Cattell (Columbia University), philosopher William James (Harvard University), psychiatrists Sigmund Freud (Vienna), Carl Jung (Switzerland), Adolph Meyer (Cornell and Johns Hopkins Universities), Ernest Jones (London Clinic for Psychoanal-

Figures 100 & 101. Photographs of Franz Boas by Heliotype Company (American Philosophical Society) and Marie Boas by Fechner, Berlin (N.F.B.), both ca.1910.

Figure 102. The children of Franz and Marie Boas, ca.1913. Left to right: Gertrud, Henry, Helene, Ernst and Franziska (N.F.B.).

Figure 103. Franz Boas with zoologist and geneticist Thomas Hunt Morgan at a scientific meeting (American Philosophical Society).

Figure 104. Leo Sternberg, Franz Boas and Waldemar Bogoras (American Philosophical Society).

ysis), and Abraham A. Brill (New York and Columbia Universities). Also present were zoologist Herbert S. Jennings (Johns Hopkins), German chemist Eduard F. Buchner, anthropologist Alexander F. Chamberlain, and many other scientists, totaling forty-three persons (Figure 105). It is interesting to note that Franz Boas was the only one of the nine faculty members who left Clark in 1892 who returned for this event.

Figure 105. Participants in the Clark University 20th anniversary celebration in 1909. Identified, in part, in the front row, left to right: Franz Boas (#1), William James (#3), G. Stanley Hall (#6), Sigmund Freud (#7) and Carl Jung (#8) (Clark University).

Boas was never strongly drawn to archeology. During his early years it was a poorly developed scientific discipline and he had other compelling interests that prevented him from participating. He was "rather contemptuous of most old-style archeologists and their excavations" but "he had a clear and correct idea of the value and importance of archeological work, properly done."[31] In 1910 Franz Boas attended the session of the International Congress of Americanists in Mexico City. As one of its founders, this meeting established the International School of American Archeology and Ethnology. The founding members included the Mexican government, Columbia, Harvard, Pennsylvania and Berlin Universities, and the Hispanic Society of New York. Boas was appointed secretary of the Directive Committee and Director for the year 1911-1912. The school remained active for several years. It finally had to close following the disruptive days of the Mexican revolutions of 1915. While in Mexico Boas did his only significant archeological work where he initiated and directed some archeological digs (Figures 106-110). J. Alden Mason, who was intimately associated with Boas in this work in Mexico and later in Puerto Rico noted that,

> His results and deductions were always good, and in his principal archeological work, that in Mexico, he established the basis for all future work on the sequence of cultures there...Although probably it could never

Figure 106. Franz Boas in a native village in Mexico, 1912 (Gertrud Michelson).

Figure 107. Franz Boas speaking with natives in Teotihuacan, Mexico, 1912 (Gertrud Michelson).

have been his major interest, he might have guided the infant science's feet in the right path a little sooner and have brought it more quickly to its majority.[31]

Figure 108. Franz Boas (in felt hat) at an archeological dig, observed by local natives (Gertrud Michelson).

Figure 109. Franz Boas at site of archeological ruins in Mexico, 1912 (Gertrud Michelson).

Figure 110. Meeting of the anthropological group in Mexico in 1912. Franz Boas is sitting at the head of the table. Photographer: H. J. Gutierez, Mexico City (American Philosophical Society).

On at least one occasion, in 1911, Boas was accompanied to Mexico by Marie and his sister-in-law, Alice Krackowizer. A number of papers, mostly in Spanish, followed from 1910 to 1913. He wrote about his Mexican experiences including reports on the International School of Archeology and Ethnology, Mexican folklore, accounts of archeological findings, and a conference at the National Museum of Archeology in Mexico City. In 1921 he published more extensively on Mexican archeological collections.[32]

In 1913, on one of their many trips to Europe, Franz and Marie Boas traveled to Posen (Prussia) with Franz's sister, Hete, and her husband Rudolf Lehmann (Figure 111). Raised in Berlin, Rudolf graduated from the Friedrich-Wilhelm Gymnasium of Berlin and attended the University of Göttingen in Berlin. For about ten years (1894-1904) he taught at the Victoria-Lyceum, a girls' secondary school or high school in Berlin, probably named after Auguste Victoria, wife of the German Kaiser. At the same time he was a docent at the University of Berlin. Shortly thereafter, Kaiser Wilhelm II appointed him to the Royal Kaiser Wilhelm Academy in Posen, Prussia. He also held a position as Professor of Education at the

State University Breslau. At the Royal Academy he held the position as professor of philosophy and history of German literature and wrote extensively on these subjects. He became one of the leading pedagogical (educational) authorities of Germany. Rudolf and Hete had no children.[26]

Figure 111. Photograph, left to right of Marie Boas, Rudolf Lehmann, Hete Lehmann and Franz Boas, Posen, Prussia, 1913 (Gertrud Michelson).

Abraham Jacobi was one of the few physicians that Franz Boas consulted from the time he arrived in America until Jacobi's death in 1919. Except for sparse references to his health in family correspondence, his only medical history that is available is that recorded by his son, Dr. Ernst P. Boas, in his office records. As a young physician, Ernst made medical notations on his father's health on index cards, the first being, "April 1915 – excision of parotid for parotid tumor – left side." Additional notes referred to the treatment of his father in 1915 and 1917, and again in 1925. When Ernst resigned from his position as superintendent and medical director of Montefiore Hospital in New York in 1928 and entered full-time practice, the Franz Boas medical record became a formal office document "Number 6," which recorded his medical history through April 28, 1941. Correspondence is attached to the record indicating that Franz also consulted with his first cousin, Dr. Willy Meyer in 1921.[33]

In 1915, Franz Boas discovered a firm swelling in front of his left ear, which was enlarging. Although not recorded in these records, it is probable that Willy Meyer was the surgeon who Franz Boas consulted in 1915. Meyer specialized in cancer surgery and was a leader in his field in New York. He quickly determined that this swelling was a tumor of the parotid gland, a large salivary gland, which he successfully removed surgically. Whether it was benign or malignant is not known at this time. In any case, it had not spread nor did it recur. Unfortunately, in the process of removing the tumor, branches of the facial nerve that pass through the parotid gland, were severed – a fairly common and often an expected complication from surgical removal of this gland.

The facial nerve is the seventh cranial nerve and is a sensory and motor nerve. When the motor branches are severed completely, paralysis results of the muscles of the face, including the lower scalp, temple, forehead, lower eyelid, cheek, and lips. This grossly disfiguring deformity often suggests to the viewer that it resulted from a stroke, when in fact the central nervous system is unimpaired. The effect on Franz Boas was devastating, although he faced it with determination. His facial appearance had changed overnight – a condition that he lived with for the rest of his life (27 years). He was never able to escape this fact, nor the chronic symptoms inherent with this disability. Thereafter, rarely would he permit a formal full-face photograph to be taken or one showing the left side of his face. Not only had he lived for 38 years with facial scars from his university dueling years, now he had a greater disfigurement. For those who knew him or came to admire him, it made little or no difference. On the other hand, Boas was a public figure, so he remained sensitive to his appearance before audiences at lectures, at other public appearances, and to those who did not know him personally.

A drooping of his left eyebrow, his left lower eyelid, the entire left cheek, and the left side of his mouth gave evidence of the paralysis affecting the side of his face. As a result, he developed a chronic tearing of his eye requiring the incessant wiping of his face with a handkerchief. He also had some difficulty in his ability to sip or drink fluids. In addition to his German accent, without the full use of his lips and left cheek, his speech lost some clarity and was somewhat more difficult to understand. It is ironic that one of the leading linguists in America had now lost some of his ability in the phonation of certain sounds. During the last twenty years of his life his palsied face was the only one I knew, so I paid little attention to his disfigurement. Nor did I pay any attention to his accent or any speech impediments – I clearly understood everything he said. As children, after our weekly visits to Grantwood, we were always given a kiss by "Grosspapa," usually a wet one from the tearing of his left eye.

In the summer of 1915, Franz Boas embarked on his only other archeological expedition, which was in conjunction with the Insular Survey of Puerto Rico, under the direction of the New York Academy of Science. J Alden Mason was also associated with him on this project. Mason noted, "Although he had suffered a painful facial operation and was not in good health, he immediately plunged into research..." The survey also included Spanish dialectology, folklore, archeology, and physical anthropology. The fieldwork was patterned somewhat after that of the Jesup Expedition. Included in the archeological excavations were Robert Aitken and Hermann Haeberlin.[31]

When Boas returned from his expedition he learned that Frederick Ward Putnam, who had suffered from a protracted illness, had died on August 14, 1915. He promptly wrote a eulogy that was published in *Science,* the journal of the American Association for the Advancement of Science (A.A.A.S.).[34] The publication in this journal was most appropriate, since it was in 1886 that Boas first met Putnam at a meeting of the A.A.A.S. Putnam was the permanent secretary of this organization from 1873 to 1898 and president in 1898, a position Boas was to hold a few years later. Putnam was his supporter and mentor when he arrived in America and played a significant role the career of Boas in the early days in Chicago and at the American Museum of Natural History. In spite of some bitterness and bad feelings toward the end of their relationship at the museum, this presentation gives no hint at rancor but only unrestrained praise.

> With Professor Putnam...the last of the three men has passed away who may well be called founders of modern anthropology in America: Brinton, Powell and Putnam...Professor Putnam's...skill as an organizer, has made him the most potent factor in the development of anthropological institutions all over the country...The Peabody Museum of American Archeology and Ethnology is, perhaps more than anything else, a monument to his life work...In one respect he revolutionized American museum methods...It was he who laid the foundation to the Field Museum of Natural History by organizing the Anthropological Department of the World's Columbian Exposition in Chicago...he was called to New York to organize the anthropological work of the American Museum of Natural History, and here we find him introducing the same methods of development that had been so effective in building up the Peabody Museum...When the development of anthropological work...was planned in the University of California, he was called upon to take a vigorous part in the formulation of plans for a museum and for

> the scientific work of the newly formed department of anthropology...Many others [institutions] were helped by his advice and assistance. Professor Putnam's activities were not by any means confined to the field of his own researches, but he took a lively interest in the advancement of scientific work in the whole country...His influence, that of a sane and sober scientist who values facts higher than fancies will be lasting, and we honor and love one who has helped to lay the foundations on which we are permitted to build.

The outbreak of World War I in 1914 was to have a major impact on the emotions and public posturing of Franz Boas. Although he had been a citizen of the United States for twenty-eight years, he still thought and felt like a German. The onset of the War was the culmination of the forces of imperialism, territorial expansion, and rivalries that had been smoldering and escalating between European and Slavic countries, the Anglo-Saxons, and French for decades. It resulted, in part, from the push by Russia and Serbia for "Pan Slavism" as opposed to continental nationalistic goals. The French sought revenge against the Germans for their loss of Alsace and Lorraine in the Franco-Prussian War of 1870-71 and the German aggression on colonial expansion into Morocco. The British were concerned with the threat of the Germans and their expanding navy. The Serbians were determined to recapture Bosnia and Herzegovina taken from them in 1908 by Austria-Hungary. The assassination of Archduke Ferdinand of Austria-Hungary in 1914 by a Serbian nationalist was sufficient to trigger the onset of World War I. It was a war primarily between the Triple Alliance formed after the Franco-Prussian War in 1871, (German Empire, the Kingdom of Italy, and Austria-Hungary) and Russia, and the Allies to the west.

With the onset of hostilities of the World War and as a former German citizen for twenty-eight years, Franz Boas was profoundly distressed. "His instinctive sympathies were on the German as opposed to the British-French side."[35] His attitude was particularly troublesome, since American sympathies were primarily Anglo-Saxon which was "equally instinctive and inevitable." Now he did not hesitate to voice his opinions publicly on these matters, as he always had done with conviction in the scientific arena. He felt that the war was based on nationalism and unabashed patriotism and that no war should be fought for these reasons. His sentimental ties to Germany did not encompass the imperialistic and territorial goals of the central government.[35]

> He disapproved of the effect the war was having on American democracy and condemned the xenophobia that the war had unleashed in America against the Germans and German culture...He feared that a German defeat

> would unleash a hatred capable of stirring up "her nationalism for centuries to come"...a victory would create an arrogance that would be equally damaging.[35]

This was probably the first time that his public expressions took on a political tone. He maintained his position not only from 1914 to 1917, but even after the United States entered the war. In spite of his anti-war expressions, he was never considered disloyal nor was any action taken against him by those with whom he was associated. Even Columbia University "respected both its own principles and the strong integrity of Boas's personality."[12] Nicholas Murray Butler, nevertheless "retaliated by firing [Alexander] Goldenweiser and refusing to hire another anthropologist."[35] When Margaret Mead arrived at Barnard in 1920, Boas and his anthropology department "occupied cramped and demeaning quarters in the basement of the Journalism Building." This was no happenstance. Butler adopted restrictive admission policies for students that "effectively reduced the College's Jewish population by half."[36] During the war, Butler was strongly in favor of restricted immigration, ordered total military mobilization of the university prior to the entry of the United States in World War I, and fired faculty members who were opposed to his policies. "He took advantage of the state of war to drive out or humiliate every man who held progressive, liberal, or unconventional views on political matters." Boas was against all of these measures. When Butler asked the faculty "what each would do for the war effort," Boas wrote, "Mind my own business."[36]

Franz Boas, in 1870, as a boy of twelve with his friends, saw Prussian troops encamped in his hometown of Minden. Seeing them marching and on their way to France was a very exciting experience for these children – knowing little of the political significance of these events, they even fantasized of going to war themselves. As a university graduate, he served a mandatory term as an officer in the German army. Although he resented the time lost from his studies, he probably was pleased to have been a German soldier. He thrived in his studies during his university days and had excellent relationships with his mentors. His Arctic expedition was subsidized, in part, by the German government; the *Berliner Tagenblatt* that referred to him as a German hero.

He had family in Germany during World War I, including his mother Sophie (died in 1916), sisters Toni, Hete, and Aenna and their husbands, and many cousins including Boas, Reichenbach, Degginer, and Kaufman families. He visited with them on his many trips to Germany. He also attended many scientific meetings in Germany and was awarded numerous scientific honors. With Marie he was able to revisit the beautiful sites of their courting days, his old home, and friends in Minden and again to be in the land where he grew up. It was the place where he was exposed to great German classic literature and music. It was where he came to know and was taught by outstanding German scientists including Rudolph Virchow, Robert W. Bunsen, Friedrich A. Kekulé, Kuno Fischer, Theobald Fischer, Benno Erdmann, and Adolph Bastian.

In 1917, the two Boas sons, Henry (age 18) and Ernst (age 26) were eligible for the draft, a particularly disturbing situation for Franz. He did his best to dissuade them from joining the armed forces. When he had no success convincing them, he commented, "If my father had tried to persuade me in this manner when I was young, I would not have followed his advice."[35]

In spite of his outspoken views on the war, he withheld public expression of his opinions when the United States entered the war in 1917. It was not until after the Armistice that he stepped into a hornet's nest on this issue. He wrote a letter to *The Nation,* published in December 1919, in which he condemned the War Department and the actions of four anthropologists, who had spied for America under the guise of doing legitimate fieldwork in Central America.

> The point which I wish to enter a vigorous protest is that a number of men who follow science as their profession, men whom I refuse to designate any longer as scientists, have prostituted science by using it as a cover for their activities as spies...The very essence of his [scientist's] life is the service of truth...A person...who uses science as a cover for political spying, who demeans himself to pose before a foreign government as an investigator and ask for assistance in alleged researches in order to carry on, under his cloak, his political machinations, prostitutes science in an unpardonable way and forfeits the right to be classed as a scientist.[38]

He was now attacking members of his own profession! John Dewey had advised him not to send the letter, lest it generate attacks on Boas as a German. His colleagues felt that his indiscretion deserved a response. When the American Anthropological Association (A.A.A.) met in Cambridge in 1919 ten days later, a heated discussion was generated by his position and punitive action was taken. He was censured, effectively removed from their governing council and forced to resign as a member of the National Research Council.[12,35] He also suffered reprisals from the Bureau of American Ethnology where he was dropped as their honorary philologist. The incident was soon over and it was not long before he again became a member of the National Research Council and back on the Council of the Anthropological Association.[35,38]

A man so self-reliant in his judgments and so unswerving in adhering to

> them actively was bound to build up a good measure of immediate offences and enmities, perhaps in very proportion to his stature. But it was his stature that the world was interested in, and recognized; and before long again, his colleagues too. It was not the last time that Boas provoked resentment; but it was the last time that resentment found formal or public expression.[12]

Many factors played a role in the reaction of the A.A.A. There were undoubtedly institutional rivalries; many of the members, if not a majority, were archeologists and were thus personally affronted by his position. In the wake of the World War, anti-German sentiment and possibly some anti-Semitism may have encouraged the action.[e]

The same debate continues to this day. During World War II and subsequent military conflicts, the FBI, CIA, and military branches of government have used anthropologists. Even Margaret Mead and Ruth Benedict contributed to the war effort in World War II, but did not do so "under the false pretext of fieldwork."[39]

David Price has written an excellent overview of this whole question. As Boas "prophetically wrote" in his attack on anthropologist spies,

> In consequence of their acts, every nation will look with distrust upon the visiting foreign investigator who wants to do honest work, suspecting sinister designs. Such action has raised a new barrier against the development of international friendly cooperation.[39]

After reviewing extensive files of the FBI and other sources, Price concluded,

> It is time for U.S. anthropologists to examine the political consequences of their history and take a hard, thoughtful look at Boas's complaint and the implications implicit in the association's [American Anthropological Association] refusal to condemn secret research and to re-enact sanctions against anthropologists engaging in espionage.[39]

During the war, in 1917, Boas founded the *International Journal of American Linguistics,* which he sustained and edited until his death. It was the only regular publication in this field and primarily contained material on Native American languages. Although he remained at the helm, from 1930 on it was published under the auspices of the Linguistic Society of America. He also served as editor of the *Journal of the American Folklore*

---

[e] At the time of the vote of the A.A.A., three of the four spies voted to censure Boas. The other, John Mason, who had worked with Boas in Mexico and Puerto Rico, did not join the others and apologized to him for what he had done. He said that he had spied purely out of patriotic duty. Mason was one who gave Boas high praise in the Boas memorial issue of the *American Anthropologist.* Another anthropologist, Samuel Lathrop, spied again in Central America and Peru during World War II.[39]

*Society* from 1908 to 1925.

One of the saddest days that Franz had to face was with the death of Uncle Abraham Jacobi on July 10, 1919. Edward Preble observed,

> His death was doubtless hastened by the burning of his summer home...when he narrowly escaped death and lost his priceless collection of documents...one of the greatest misfortunes the medical profession of the United States has ever sustained.[40]

Aside from his academic and social agenda, Jacobi was the devoted physician to Franz and Marie Boas, their children, members of the Theodore Meyer and Willy Meyer families, Carl Schurz and his family, many friends and neighbors at Lake George and literally thousands of children in New York from all levels of society. So ended a practice that spanned sixty-six years, and the life of a man who for sixty-one years had been an inspiration and enthusiastic supporter of his nephew, Franz Boas. To recapitulate, it was Jacobi who encouraged Meier Boas to permit his son to study the natural sciences and so enter the field of anthropology. It was Jacobi who introduced Marie, the daughter of his closest friend, Dr. Ernst Krackowizer, to Franz Boas. It was Jacobi who encouraged Franz to immigrate to America. He also helped finance a number of field expeditions of Franz and introduced him to Carl Schurz and many in the academic field. Abraham Jacobi was always at hand to advise and help his nephew and was a dedicated and compassionate surrogate father to Franz in America.

In the 1960s New York City memorialized Abraham Jacobi by naming one of its largest hospitals in his honor. The hospital authorities, seeking her permission to name the new institution the Jacobi Hospital after her father, approached his daughter, Marjorie McAneny. She readily agreed and attended the ceremony. Her comment was simply, "That's immortality!"[41,42]

As secretary of the Germanistic Society of America, Franz Boas wrote to Marjorie McAneny,

> At the fifteenth annual meeting...of the Germanistic Society...the following Memorial Resolution upon the lamented decease of your father Dr. A. Jacobi, President since 1915...was unanimously passed: The Germanistic Society records with profound sorrow the death of its beloved President, Dr. Abraham Jacobi, almost the last surviving member of the group of Forty-Eighters who fled from Germany because of their opposition to militarism and autocracy, whose noble and wise aspirations, if achieved, would have rewritten the history of the world and made impossible its bloodiest chapter. To America they brought superb loyalty, absolute devotion and completest faith.
>
> Dr. Abraham Jacobi nobly repaid the debt of gratitude he owed to the

> Republic for its asylum by a life devoted to science and the amelioration of suffering humanity. To the Germanistic Society, of which he was a founder, he brought the clearest understanding of its possibilities for usefulness and wise counsel. His death left a vacancy which cannot be filled, for no one of later generations can supply just that fervent note of high and unselfish devotion to American idealism incorporated in every fibre of such men as Jacobi and Schurz.[43]

A bronze plaque in honor of Dr. Abraham Jacobi is mounted on a large stone in a little park on Route 9N, north of Bolton Landing, New York. The rock is next to a stone bench memorializing Carl Schurz. The park is a portion of the property once owned by Dr. Jacobi. The plaque reads:

IN MEMORY OF
1830 1919
**ABRAHAM JACOBI**
THE PIONEER
OCCUPIED THE FIRST CHAIR OF PEDIATRICS IN AMERICA
A SCHOLARLY AND BROAD-MINDED PHYSICIAN
ONCE PRESIDENT OF THE AMERICAN MEDICAL ASSOCIATION
WHO LOVED THESE WOODS AND WATERS
ABOUT HIS SUMMER HOME
ERECTED BY HIS FRIENDS AND COLLEAGUES
THE ABRAHAM JACOBI MEMORIAL FUND
THE AMERICAN PEDIATRIC SOCIETY
JUNE 13, 1936

**References and Notes**

1. Cole, Douglas. *FRANZ BOAS, The Early Years, 1858-1906*, Douglas & McIntyre, Vancouver & Toronto and University of Washington Press, Seattle & London, 1999.
2. McAneny, George. Letter to Franz Boas, April 4, 1900, American Philosophical Society.
3. Boas, Franz. Correspondence with George McAneny, 1914, American Philosophical Society.
4. Kimball, Carol W. *Capt. George Comer, Last of the Local Whalemen, The Day*, New London, Connecticut, November 11, 1993 (A brief biography of Comer and his exploits).
5. Stocking, George W., Jr. Biography of Franz Boas in *Dictionary of American Biography*, 10 volumes and 8 supplements, American Council of Learned Societies Charles Scribner's Sons, New York, 1961.

6. Kendall, Laurel, Barbara Mathé & Thomas Ross Miller, *Drawing Shadows to Stone*, American Museum of Natural History, New York in association with the University of Washington Press, Seattle & London, 1997.
7. Jonaitis, Aldona. *From the Land of the Totem Poles*, American Museum of Natural History, New York and University of Washington Press, Seattle, Washington, 1988.
8. Boas, Franz. Editor and contributor, *Handbook of American Indian Languages*, Part 1, 1069pp, Bureau of American Ethnology, Bulletin 40, Washington, 1911 (Boas's contributions included the Preface, Introduction and sections on the Tsimshian, Kawkiutl, and Chinook Indians. Also, with Swanton, a section on the Siouan: Dakota and remarks on the Ponca and Winnebago. Three additional volumes of this work appeared in 1922, 1938 and 1941).
9. Bell, Alexander Graham. Correspondence with Franz Boas, 1902-10, American Philosophical Society.
10. Boas, Franz. Correspondence with Carl Schurz, 1902. American Philosophical Society.
11. Laufer, Berthold. *Boas Anniversary Volume: Anthropological Papers Written in Honor of Franz Boas Presented to Him on the Twenty-fifth Anniversary of His Doctorate*, G. E. Stechert, New York, 1906.
12. Kroeber, Alfred L. *Franz Boas: The Man*, in *American Anthropologist,* N.S., Vol. 45, No. 3, Part 2, July-September 1943 (An excellent brief biography of Boas including revealing comments on Boas as a man, teacher and friend).
13. Pitkin, Harvey. Biography of Alfred L. Kroeber in *Dictionary of American Biography*, 10 volumes and 8 supplements, American Council of Learned Societies Charles Scribner's Sons, New York, 1956-60.
14. Dorson, Richard M. Biography of John Reed Swanton in *Dictionary of American Biography*, 10 volumes and 8 supplements, American Council of Learned Societies Charles Scribner's Sons, New York, 1956-60.
15. Witthoft, John. Biography of Frank G. Speck in *Dictionary of American Biography*, 10 volumes and 8 supplements, American Council of Learned Societies Charles Scribner's Sons, New York, 1946-50.
16. Gates, Paul W. Biography of Livingston Farrand in *Dictionary of American Biography*, 10 volumes and 8 supplements, American Council of Learned Societies Charles Scribner's Sons, New York, 1958.
17. Kroeber, Alfred L. Biography of Roland B. Dixon in *Dictionary of American Biography*, 10 volumes and 8 supplements, American Council of Learned Societies Charles Scribner's Sons, New York, 1935.
18. Witthoft, John. Biography of Robert H. Lowie in *Dictionary of American Biography*, 10 volumes and 8 supplements, American Council of Learned Societies Charles Scribner's Sons, New York, 1956-60.
19. Mandelbaum, David G. Biography of Edward Sapir in *Dictionary of American Biography*, 10 volumes and 8 supplements, American Council of Learned Societies Charles Scribner's Sons, New York, 1940.
20. Schusky, Ernest. Biography of Paul Radin in *Dictionary of American*

*Biography*, 10 volumes and 8 supplements, American Council of Learned Societies Charles Scribner's Sons, New York, 1956-60.

21. White, Leslie A. Biography of Alexander A. Goldenweiser in *Dictionary of American Biography*, American Council of Learned Societies Charles Scribner's Sons, New York, Supplement, 1940.

22. Boas, Norman F. *The Creation of a Manuscript Language "Kwak'wala."* Speech given at a seminar sponsored by the Manuscript Society, Victoria, British Columbia May 28, 1995.

23. Boas, Franz. *Changes in Bodily Form of Descendants of Immigrants*, 573pp with 109 tables & 53 graphs. Senate Document 208, 61st Congress, 2nd Session, Government Printing Office, Washington, 1911 (There are other publications on this subject - a preliminary report in 1910 and a reprint in 1912 by the Columbia University Press).

24. Boas, Franz. *The Mind of Primitive Man*, 294pp, Macmillan Company, New York, 1911 (This volume was based on a course of lectures delivered before the Lowell Institute, Boston, Massachusetts and the National University of Mexico. This book was revised, came out in several editions, and is still available).

25. Germanistic Society of America. Papers and correspondence of Franz Boas and others, American Philosophical Society.

26. Victoria-Lyzeum. A letter of thanks from the directors of this school to Rudolf Lehmann for his services as a teacher, Berlin, December 16, 1904. Also newspaper reports of his visit to the United States to lecture at Teachers College and at the Germanistic Society (Norman F. Boas collection).

27. Butler, Nicholas Murray. Correspondence with Franz Boas, American Philosophical Society (This collection encompasses approximately 450 letters).

28. Boas, Franz. Letter to Carl Lincoln Schurz, May 18, 1908. American Philosophical Society.

29. McAneny, George. Correspondence with Franz Boas, February 14 through October 1908, American Philosophical Society (These letters relate primarily to loans and mortgages to acquire property in Grantwood, New Jersey).

30. Boas, Franz. Clark University, a lecture, *Psychological Problems in Anthropology,* 15pp, delivered at the celebration of the 20th anniversary of the opening of Clark University, 1909.

31. Mason, J. Alden. *Franz Boas as an Archeologist*, in *American Anthropologist,* N.S., Vol. 45, No. 3, Part 2, July-September 1943 (This is probably the most definitive report and summary of Franz Boas's thinking and experiences as an archeologist).

32. Andrews, H. A. *Bibliography of Franz Boas*, in *American Anthropologist,* N.S., Vol. 45, No. 3, Part 2, July-September 1943 (This is one of the more complete bibliographies of Boas).

33. Boas, Ernst P. Medical record of Franz Boas dating from 1915 to 1941 (Norman F. Boas collection).

34. Boas, Franz. *Frederic Ward Putnam*, in *Science, N.S.,* Vol. XLII, No. 1080, Sept. 10, 1915 (A reflection on the scientific life of Putnam).

35. Lewis, Herbert S. *The Passion of Franz Boas* in *American Anthropologist*, Vol. 103(2), 447-467, 2001 (An excellent view of Franz Boas as a man and his legacy).
36. Rexer, Lyle. *A Series of Great Teachers Left the Largest Footprints*, in *Columbia College Today*, Volume 22, Number 1, Spring 1996 (An historical review of the anthropology Department at Columbia).
37. Hawkins, Hugh. A biography of Nicholas Murray Butler in *Dictionary of American Biography*, Supplement 4, 1946-1950, Charles Scribner's Sons, New York, 1974.
38. Pinsky, Valerie. *Archaeology, Politics, and Boundary-Formation: The Boas Censure (1919) and the Development of American Archeology During the Inter-War Years.* In *Rediscovering Our Past: Essays in the History of American Archaeology,* edited by Jonathan E. Reyman, Avebury Press, Aldershot, 1992.
39. Price, David. *Anthropologists as Spies,* in *The Nation*, November 20, 2000 (A review and update, eighty-one years later, of the controversy that Boas generated when he condemned anthropologists who spied for the government under the cover of doing fieldwork in foreign countries. It is interesting to note that this article was published in the same journal that published the famous Boas letter in 1919).
40. Preble, Edward. Biography of Abraham Jacobi in *Dictionary of American Biography*, 10 volumes and 8 supplements, American Council of Learned Societies Charles Scribner's Sons, New York, 1960-61.
41. McAnemy, Ernest Jacobi. Personal communication.
42. Boas, Norman F. and Barbara L. Meyer. *Alma Farm. An Adirondack Meeting Place*, Privately printed, Mystic, Connecticut and Bolton, New York, 1999.
43. Boas, Franz. Letter to Marjorie McAneny, November 28, 1919. American Philosophical Society.

# CHAPTER VIII

## COLUMBIA UNIVERSITY – LATER YEARS ORDEALS OF THE 1920s

By 1920 many of Boas's earlier graduate students had become department heads of universities throughout America including Harvard and Yale, the Universities of Pennsylvania, California (Berkeley), Chicago and many smaller colleges. Some of this group held positions at the Bureau of American Ethnology and the American Museum of Natural History. This was probably the most influential period of the Boas school, which was reflected not only by the success of these graduates, but by the impressive group of Boas's newer graduate students.

One of the most dedicated sociologists and anthropologists at this time was Elsie Worthington Clews Parsons (1875-1941). She was the only daughter of Henry Clews and Lucy Madison. Her father was an investment banker; her mother was a grandniece of President James Madison. Elsie graduated from Barnard College in 1896 and received her Ph.D. in sociology at Columbia University in 1899. She married Herbert Parsons, a New York attorney, who was a member of Congress from New York (1905-11). During her early career she was a prolific writer, primarily on women's rights. In 1915 she was stimulated by Franz Boas at Columbia and Pliny Earle Goddard of the American Museum of Natural History to apply herself toward ethnological research. She devoted the rest of her life to fieldwork with Native Americans, especially the Pueblos of the Southwest and also with tribes of Mexico and Ecuador. She made outstanding contributions to her newly chosen field. Her correspondence with Franz Boas numbered over three hundred letters between 1907 and 1941. Acknowledgments of her achievements are evidenced by her election as president of the American Folklore Society (1919-20), president of the American Ethnological Society (1923-25) and president of the American Anthropological Association (1940). In 1919, Parsons was a founder of the New School for Social Research.[1]

Another student of Boas, Melville Jean Herskovits (1895-1963), was a graduate of the University of Chicago and obtained his Ph.D. under Boas at Columbia University in 1923. After receiving his degree, he taught at Columbia and Howard Universities and later became noted for his ethnological research in Suriname, Haiti, Trinidad and Brazil. Most of his fieldwork was done in Africa. He joined the faculty of Northwestern University in 1927, and became professor of anthropology there in

1935. Herskovits wrote many books on African American culture and a brief biography of Franz Boas.[2,3]

Esther Schiff Goldfrank, although not strictly a student of Boas, did fieldwork on American Indian pueblos, under his guidance, in New Mexico in the 1920s. She was born in New York and was a graduate of Barnard College. She later did work with the Blackfoot Indians in Alberta, Canada (1939) and in the same year was an anthropologist on the staff of the University of Washington. During her career she served with the American Ethnological Society as secretary-treasurer, president, and finally as editor. She was also an editor of the American Folklore Society and an author, primarily on the Isleta paintings in Pueblo society. When she died, she left seven linear feet of her scientific and personal papers and photograph albums to the National Anthropological Archives of the National Museum of Natural History of the Smithsonian Institution. This invaluable collection includes a number of photographs taken by Goldfrank of Franz Boas in New Mexico as well as groups of well-known anthropologists who met in the Northeast. Some were taken on a visit to Bolton Landing, Lake George.[4,5]

In 1922 Franz, Marie, and Gertrud Boas traveled to Arizona and New Mexico to join Esther Goldfrank on what appears to have been a sightseeing tour of the Southwest. It was unusual for Marie or his children to join Franz on any of his regular field trips. Marie had joined him on at least two, one to British Columbia and one to Mexico. One of Esther's photographs is of a park ranger with Franz and Marie, taken in the Grand Canyon (Figure 112). On another leg of the trip they visited the Cochiti on the Rio Grande River in Santo Pueblo, about 20 miles west of Santa Fe and 20 miles south of Los Alamos. Photographs were also taken on their departure from this Indian reservation. (Figure 113). On another segment of their trip they visited Valencia County in the western part of New Mexico where they viewed Mount Taylor, an 11,301-foot mountain peak lying between Gallup and Albuquerque (Figure 114).

Some time in the early 1920s, Goldfrank took a number of candid photographs on an outing, titled "Anthropology Pictures" in her album. The location of the outing is not identified, but those who were present included Franz Boas, Gladys Reichard, Ruth Benedict, Edward Sapir, Alfred L. Kroeber, Pliny E. Goddard, and sociologist William Field Ogburn. With the exception of the last two mentioned, the rest have been cited earlier in this text. Pliny Earle Goddard (1869-1928) was an ethnologist who did most of his fieldwork on Indians of the West, with emphasis on the Hupa Indians of California. He taught at the University of California from 1906 to 1914 and thereafter, until his death, was curator of ethnology at the American Museum of Natural History, following in the footsteps of Boas. His publications on West Coast Indians are well known.

Figure 112. Park ranger, Marie, and Franz Boas in the Grand Canyon, ca. 1922 (Smithsonian Institution. Negative 92-1665).

William Fielding Ogburn, born in Georgia in 1896, was a graduate of Mercer University and earned his Ph.D. at Columbia University in 1912. He later taught at Princeton University, Reed College, and at the University of Washington before he took a position at Columbia University as professor of sociology (1917-1927). Upon leaving Columbia, he joined the University of Chicago for the balance of his teaching career as the Sewell L. Avery Distinguished Professor of Sociology.

One of Franz Boas's principal associates during his last fourteen years at Columbia University was Ruth Fulton Benedict (1887-1949).[6] Benedict was born in New York City. When her father died when she was two years old, she and her mother moved to the farm of her mother's parents near Norwich, New York. Ruth had an emotionally tormented childhood with the loss of her father and with a mother who had continuing hysterical outbursts of grief following this tragedy. She came to venerate the memory of her father who she barely remembered. After matri-

Figure 113. Franz Boas in a boat leaving Cochiti, probably on the Rio Grande River, ca.1922 (Smithsonian Institution. Negative 92-1664).

Figure 114. Carl Leon, Franz Boas and Solomon Day at the foot of Mount Taylor, ca.1922 (Smithsonian Institution. Negative 98-41046).

culating and graduating from Vassar College, she embarked on an aimless career. She traveled in Europe, did some charity work and taught at a girl's school in California. In 1914 she married biochemist Stanley R. Benedict, but remained in a quandary, seeking some meaningful career. Attempts at writing poetry and fiction were unsuccessful.

By chance, in 1919 she began attending lectures at the New School for Social Research in New York where she was inspired by two faculty members, Elise Clews Parsons and Alexander Goldenweiser. By 1921 she had decided to pursue anthropology as a career choice and was determined to take graduate work with Franz Boas. Benedict was thirty-two years old and extremely shy.[6] Sensing her anxiety and recognizing her potential, Boas "waived credit requirements to hurry her through to the Ph.D." that was awarded in 1923. She was so touched by his kindness "and grandfatherly resonances" that she started referring to him as "Papa Franz," a soubriquet that all of his subsequent women graduate students used.[6] Boas thoroughly enjoyed teaching young women a Barnard College. On one occasion, Gladys Reichard was provoked at,

> some ludicrous stupidity on the part of some Barnard girls, and he [Boas] said. "Well! They're young!" I answered in a disgusted tone, "They're *young* all right!" Feelingly he said, "*Aber das is kein Fehler* [But that is no shortcoming]."[7]

While Benedict was working on her graduate degree, as Boas's assistant, her first student was Margaret Mead. Although fourteen years older than Mead, a relationship developed between the two, which lasted until the death of Benedict in 1948. As confidantes, both wrote and shared poetry and compositions with one another. From 1923 to 1931, Benedict lectured in anthropology at Columbia University, during which time she did fieldwork with the Serrano Indians in California and the Zuni, Cochiti, and Pima Indians.

In 1931 Boas had Benedict appointed assistant professor of anthropology at Columbia. She assumed much of the burden of teaching and running the Anthropology Department. Upon the retirement of Boas in 1936, she was advanced to associate professor of anthropology and made executive officer of the department. Unhappy with Ralph Linton, Boas's successor, and with World War II imminent, she left Columbia to work in the Office of War Information in Washington. There, Benedict assisted in establishing ethnic profiles of foreign cultures, particularly the Japanese – a valuable service to the war effort.[6]

On returning to Columbia University in 1946, she was the recipient of a large grant from the Office of Naval Research that enabled her to organize and direct a project for Research in Contemporary Cultures. Benedict was a prolific writer. Her book, *Patterns of Culture*, is one of the most important and influential works of the 20th century by an American anthropologist. Benedict was also an editor of the *Journal of American Folklore* for fifteen years and served as president of the American Anthropological Association (1947) as well as president of the American Ethnological Society (1927-29). Ruth Benedict died of a heart attack shortly after she was appointed full professor of anthropology at Columbia, a promotion long deferred because she was a woman.[6]

One of the most independent-minded and controversial students of Boas was Margaret Mead (1901-78). Born in Philadelphia, she was one of four surviving children of Edward Sherwood and Emily Fogg Mead. Her father taught at the Wharton School of Commerce at the University of Pennsylvania. The greatest shortcoming of her upbringing was the nomadic existence of her family. By the time she was a junior in high school, she recalled that she had "lived in sixty houses and eaten food prepared by a hundred and seven cooks...Like a family of refugees."[8] There was ongoing discord between her parents, due in part to some philandering by her father. Edward Mead was very protective of his children, but was unable to show his affection easily. Margaret felt a need for additional emotional support. This she found to some extent in her grandparents; she also sought additional comfort by joining the Episcopal Church at the age of eleven. This was shocking and unsettling to her parents who were agnostics; also an early sign of Margaret's independent nature.

It was with relief that she left her dysfunctional family when the time came to attend college. She began her undergraduate work at DePauw University and later attended Barnard College. In 1924 Mead received her M.A. degree at Columbia University and her Ph.D. under Boas in 1929. For graduate fieldwork, Boas had his own agenda for his students, assigning most to gathering data on American Indians. Mead was no exception. In addition, he suggested that she do comparative cultural studies on adolescent girls. Mead wrote,

> I had a chance to do field work in Samoa, where I wanted to go, instead of working with an American Indian tribe, which was what my professor, Franz Boas, wanted me to do.[9]

She wanted to chart her own future and elected to go to Samoa "out of sheer counter-suggestibility" to the proposal made by Boas. In order to placate him to some degree, she did agree to do adolescent studies on the girls of Somoa. Boas did not want her to go, throwing up all sorts of blocks. He told her that it was too dangerous and "recited a litany of young men who had died or been killed while they were working outside the United States."[9] She insisted that working with Indians would deprive her of her primary goal for the future.

> I knew that there was one thing that mattered more to Boas than the direction taken by anthropological research. It was to behave like a liberal, democratic, modern man, not like a Prussian autocrat...I repeated over and over again that by insisting that I work with American Indians he was preventing me from going where I wanted to work. Unable to bear the implied accusation that he was bullying me, Boas gave in.[9]

With some restrictions as to which island she should conduct her studies, he acquiesced and found funding for her through the National Research Council. Shortly before she left on her expedition, Boas wrote to Ruth Benedict,

> You must know that I myself am not very pleased with this idea of her [Mead] going to the tropics for a long stay...I know that Margaret is high strung and emotional, but I also believe that nothing would depress her more that the inability on account of her physical makeup and her mental characteristics to do the work she wants to do.

While she was in Samoa, her extensive correspondence with Boas demonstrated a heavy dependence on his advice. On returning from her first trip to Oceania, Mead wrote *Coming of Age in Samoa*, prior to the receiving her doctoral degree.[8,10]

Mead was a very bright, ambitious, and productive scientist. She held Boas as her idol in outlining her own approaches to anthropology and tried to emulate him in all of her professional activities. These included memberships in the American Anthropological Society (president), the American Ethnological Society, New York Academy of Sciences, the American Philosophical Society, the American Association for the Advancement of Science (president), a position on the faculty of Columbia University, and one at the American Museum of Natural History (A M.N.H.). Even before she received her graduate degree in anthropology, she was appointed assistant curator of ethnology at the A.M.N.H., a position she held until 1942 when she was appointed associate curator. From 1964 to 1969 she served as curator. She also held a position as adjunct professor of anthropology at Columbia University after 1954 and professor of anthropology at Fordham University (1969-71).

Franz Boas was a stern teacher with a soft heart. His lectures were well organized, but unlike undergraduate lectures, his students were not spoon-fed with facts to memorize and information to be simply recorded on note sheets. He assumed that his graduate students were well grounded in such basics as mathematics (including calculus), languages, basic anthropology, and many subjects on which he was unwilling to spend time. If they did not understand some of these areas, it was up to them to seek the answers. Most of his students were brilliant enough to follow these standards. As difficult as his assignments were, he rarely criticized his students for lack of comprehension or for not doing their homework. In spite of his rigid approach, he was kind, compassionate, and understanding with virtually all of his students, most of whom were motivated to follow his lead. This was particularly true of his women students.

Margaret Mead's arrival coincided with one of the worst decades of his life – the 1920s. During this period he was devastated by the death of a son, a daughter, and the dearest person in the world, Marie. Whether this played any role in the manner in which he dealt with his students is not clear. There is no question that as he approached seventy years of age (1928), Ruth Benedict was already relieving him of some of the burdens of teaching and managing the department of anthropology at the university. With his own tragedies, it seemed that he was even more compassionate with his associates, friends and family.

Franz Boas adhered to a cloistered relationship with the public on scientific information, which is still the ethical standard for most scientists. Until scientific results are published in appropriate scientific literature, it is considered improper to issue press releases or engage in self-promotion. Self-promotion also includes using the public media and lay publications as vehicles to this end. Nevertheless, these were the techniques Mead used to identify herself with the public, with which she was eminently successful.

> Margaret Mead was one of the twentieth century's great adventurers, one of its most accomplished women, certainly its most renowned anthropologist...Mead in every sense of the word was big...She was woman of many contradictions who could be brilliant or naive, enchanting or obstreperous, demanding or forgiving. At times she was in too much of a hurry, and some of the ideas she embraced were silly or unfinished.[8]

Mead's success rested largely on her role with the public in developing her ideas about sex, culture, education and child-rearing "and led some to think, to an era of permissiveness."[8] There is absolutely no question that she did more than any other person in the world to put anthropology "on the map." She wrote thirty-four books, produced ten films and lectured widely all over the world. There was a tremendous response to her publications and lectures that was also reflected by extensive coverage by newspapers and other media. Thousands of young students flocked to university courses in anthropology. It is extremely doubtful that Franz Boas subscribed to her promotional techniques. Alfred L Kroeber commented,

> Margaret loves the marketplace...If you took the best ten percent that [she] has done, you'll find it's more in quantity and better in quality than most other anthropologists.[8]

A cruel assault on the memory of her mentor, Franz Boas, was recorded in her autobiography, one that she hardly needed to secure her position in anthropology. She wrote,

> Boas was a surprising and somewhat frightening teacher. He had a bad side and a good side of his face. On one side there was a long dueling scar from his student days in Germany – an unusual pursuit for a Jewish student – in which his eyelid drooped and teared from a recent stroke. But seen from the other side, his face showed him to be as handsome as he had been as a young man. His lectures were polished and clear.[9]

The Boas family and friends felt compelled to respond to this account. The Mead autobiography, written in 1972 was in error, a fact she must have known. The facial deformity was not "recent" nor was it a "stroke." If Mead knew of his dueling scars of 1877, it is surprising that she did not share the common knowledge that his facial palsy resulted from surgery in 1915. Whether she wrote this deliberately or through carelessness, will never be known with certainty – the effect was the same. This reference was very disturbing to the family.

> If, as you wrote, he had a stroke, it would give adversaries "proof" that his mind was affected by cerebral damage, and that a scientific or sane basis for his work can be held questionable.[11]

If in fact she were correct, it implied that he might have had cerebral impairment for the last twenty-seven years of his life.[11a]

Another remarkable student of Boas was Ella Cara Deloria (1889-1971). She was a Native American, born on the Yankton Sioux Reservation in South Dakota. Bright and anxious to obtain an education, she matriculated at Oberlin College and later attended Columbia Teacher's College in New York. She first met Boas in 1915, when he hired her to do some translations and grammatical work on some unfinished work of James Owen Dorsey of the Smithsonian Institution's Bureau of American Ethnology. Dorsey died in 1895 leaving a large number of unpublished manuscripts on the Siouan languages, as well as a huge collection of Lakota stories, collected by George Bushotter, a Sioux Indian, under Dorsey's supervision. All of these papers were in need of transcription and editing for publication. While Deloria was attending Teachers College, she worked on these papers for Boas, but soon left New York.

Boas and Deloria did not meet again until 1927, when Boas visited her at the Haskell Institute in Lawrence, Kansas. Reestablishing their relationship, he encouraged her to resume her work on the Bushotter papers, and thus began her long commitment to anthropology. She moved

---

[a] Margaret Mead agreed that there should be a correction in the next edition of *Blackberry Winter* as well as a note citing this correction in the *American Anthropologist.*

to New York, worked with Boas until his death in 1942, and with Ruth Benedict until her death in 1948. During this time she completed the work on the Bushotter papers, worked continuously on Sioux grammar and prepared a Sioux-English dictionary as well as many translations of texts in the Dakota and Lakota dialects of Sioux. Deloria did more than any other individual to record linguistics, folklore and the culture of the Sioux, culminating in a fascinating novel, *Waterlily*, a narration of 19th century Sioux life from "the perspectives of women."[12]

Figure 115. Franz Boas on a voyage to Europe, ca. 1922 (Gertrud Michelson).

Franz and Marie took at least two trips to Germany during the 1920s. In 1922 they visited with the family (Figures 115-117) and in June 1929, Franz and Marie took their last European trip together when they sailed on the *S. S. Europa*. They were accompanied by their daughter, Franziska, and went primarily to attend the Americanist Congress in The Hague. A nostalgic visit was also made to Bonn.

After 1920, Bolton Landing on Lake George had lost its attraction as a summer vacation spot for the Boas family. Abraham Jacobi and Emilie Krackowizer had died in 1919. Helene Meyer, now widowed, was barely able to maintain the operation of Alma Farm. Franz and Marie might have continued to visit the Adirondacks, but their children had their own

Figure 116. Marie Boas in the early 1920s (American Philosophical Society)

Figure 117. Franz and Marie Boas on the *S. S. Europa,* 1929 (America Phlosophical Society).

professional lives to lead and families to raise. They did not have the time to travel so far from New York City. Thus ended a thirty-five year relationship with Lake George. With the rapid development of the automobile following World War I, vacation patterns changed significantly and focused more on accessible nearby sites.

In 1924 Ernst and Helen Boas purchased an eighty-acre farm in Wilton, Connecticut, only a one-hour auto trip from New York City. It was somewhat reminiscent of the Adirondacks with densely wooded tracts. Wilton was a rural town of about two thousand people, served primarily by dirt roads and had many active farms. As an abandoned farm, the Boas site still had the main house, two barns and two outdoor privies. The living conditions were similar to those at Lake George; initially there was no electricity, running water, or telephone service.[13] In about 1926, Cecil and Helene Yampolsky also bought a house and an old farm in the foothills of the Berkshire Mountains in Cornwall Bridge, Connecticut. It consisted of fifty acres of woodland and beautiful rolling meadows on a hillside overlooking the Housatonic River valley. Although it was a longer commute from New York, it too was a delightful vacation spot. It was at both of these country homes that Franz and Marie Boas vacationed in their later years.

Franz and Marie spent the summer of 1926 in Wilton. One of the barns, which had been a carriage house, was converted specifically for them as living quarters. Partitioning the loft and covering the walls and ceilings with Celotex accomplished this end. As there were no utilities, it was necessary to draw water from a well, to use outdoor privies, and to cook on a kerosene stove. Nevertheless, it was spacious with bedrooms, a crude kitchen and a large room where they had their meals. Franz spent many hours there writing and working on his papers. Some of the meals and socializing took place in the main house.

All of the grandchildren of Franz and Marie were born in the 1920s. Their first grandchildren were twins, Robert and Philip, born in 1920, the children of Cecil and Helene Yampolsky. Helene and Cecil had met in college. Helene graduated from Barnard College and later obtained her PhD. in botany at Columbia University. It was there that she met Cecil, also a botanist-in-training. They were married and shortly after the birth of the twins, Cecil was assigned to a research project on coconut palms in Java and Sumatra. After returning home, they settled in Grantwood in the home of Franz and Marie.[14]

The next grandchildren born were Donald Philip (1921), Norman Francis (1922) and Barbara Gertrud (1928), the children of Dr. Ernst Philip and Helen Sisson Boas of New York City.

Inspired by his grandfather, Dr. Ernst Krackowizer, and great uncle and aunt, Doctors Abraham and Mary Putnam Jacobi, Ernst Boas had elected to become a physician. He was a graduate of Columbia University and the College of Physicians and Surgeons (first in the class of 1914). It was during his medical training at Mount Sinai Hospital in New York that he met Helen Tuthill Sisson, a student nurse, to whom he became betrothed. Shortly after their marriage in 1917 he joined the army as a captain and sailed to France where he cared for the wounded and ill near the battlefront as an officer in charge of a medical division of a base hospital. Soon after he returned to the states and was discharged from the army, he opened an office for the private practice of medicine. Shortly thereafter, the Board of Trustees of Montefiore Hospital, influenced by his wartime record, appointed Ernst Boas Superintendent and Medical Director of this Bronx institution. It was a position he held until 1928. As a young director of a major New York City Hospital, one is reminded of the roles that his grandfather, Ernst Krackowizer played in creating the German Hospital (now Lenox Hill Hospital) and Abraham and Mary Putnam Jacobi played in the founding the Pediatric Department of Mount Sinai Hospital. It was at Montefiore Hospital that Ernst developed his expertise in the fields of chronic diseases, administrative medicine, cardiology, and gerontology.

> It was here that he and physicist and boyhood friend, Benjamin Liebowitz, invented the first device to continuously record the heartbeat. They named the new instrument, which operated on vacuum tubes, the "cardiotachometer," a technological development which was later incorporated into all heart-monitoring devices.[14,b]

In 1929 Ernst left Montefiore Hospital to return to the private practice of medicine in an office in Manhattan. He joined the staff of Mount Sinai Hospital, and was appointed assistant clinical professor of medicine on the faculty of the College of Physicians and Surgeons. During World War II, he served as chief of a medical division at Mount Sinai Hospital.

He wrote many medical papers and a number of books on cardiology, chronic diseases, and gerontology. Ernst also recorded some of the earliest findings on serum cholesterol levels, establishing their significance in cardiovascular diseases.

He was the founder of and chaired Physician's Forum, a national organization of doctors who were dedicated to establishing a national health insurance program, an approach deplored by the American Medical Association (A.M.A.), which held to the status quo. The Forum rec-

---

[b] The original model is now in the collection of the Smithsonian Institution in Washington, D.C.

ognized "the deplorable state of private health insurance plans and the need for extending health coverage to millions of Americans who were unable to afford basic health care." Ernst testified in Congress on the first attempt to enact a comprehensive national health insurance program, the Wagner-Murray-Dingell Bill, the forerunner to Medicare passed by Congress many years later. Now over fifty years later, the need for a more comprehensive national health program is becoming increasingly apparent. The pioneering of the Physician's Forum established the basis for the gradual evolution of our thinking on this continuing problem.[13,14]

Ernst had many prominent citizens as patients, including former Vice President of the United States, Henry Wallace. It was Wallace who he attended during his campaign for the presidency in 1948 against Harry S. Truman and Thomas E. Dewey. Ernst was also physician to his father, aunts Hedwig (Hete) Lehmann, Alice Krackowizer, and Helene Meyer, his children and other members of his family. Ernst Boas, Abraham Jacobi, Mary Putnam Jacobi, Ernst Krackowizer, and Willy Meyer were all members of the New York Academy of Medicine and all were major contributors to the history and science of medicine. All of the same doctors – including the author of this book, were members of the New York County Medical Society and on the staff of Mount Sinai Hospital.

The last grandchild of Franz and Marie was Gertrud (1929), the daughter of Franziska and Nicolas Michelson. Franziska was also a graduate of Barnard College. She and Nicolai met when he was an intern at Montefiore Hospital attending Gertrud Boas, the daughter of Franz Boas, who had been admitted with poliomyelitis. After Nicolai completed his medical training, he became an assistant his brother-in-law, Ernst Boas, until 1928 when both left their hospital positions. During the Great Depression, Nicolai opened an office for the private practice of medicine and also worked for the Metropolitan Life Insurance Company. However, with the onset of World War II he joined the Armed Forces. Following the war he served in the United States Public Health Service and in Veterans Administration hospitals. He and Franziska were divorced in 1945. Nicolai later remarried and had two children, Ernst and Dina. Nicolai retired in 1976 and died in 1988 at the age of 89.

Franziska had her own career, using her artistic talents and athleticism. While in college she joined a dance group. After studying with Hanya Holm, Mary Wigman and others, she became a teacher and joined in many programs in modern dance. Franziska later established her own dance school in New York City, the Boas Dance Group.

Her curriculum included percussion and dance courses as well as dance analysis, music, and composition. In the 1930s Franziska participated in the famous Bennington College Summer School of Dance. She also taught emotionally disturbed children at Bellevue Hospital – "a ground-breaking effort in dance therapy."[14] In 1941 Franziska led a seminar, "The Function of Dance in Human Society," which "brought together leading anthropologists, including her father, in a series of lectures designed to elucidate the importance of dance in differing cultures."[14]

> Multiculturalism was a prime element in Franziska's own work in the dance field...Her father was especially supportive of her integration efforts and once said to her, with regard to prejudice, "You can do something about this because you are in the arts where everybody is recognized for what he can do." And she did do something about it. She welcomed all ethnic groups into her studio and proved that they could work and live together in harmony.[14]

Later Franziska set up a scholarship program, named for Franz Boas, to enable participation by talented African American students in her summer school at Bolton Landing on Lake George. The summer school, which lasted for four years, was a great success. From 1950 to 1965, she held a position as an instructor in physical education at Shorter College in Rome, Georgia. Her work there was "precedent-breaking." In her department she raised dance to a "new level of distinction."[14]

In addition to her extraordinary talents in the dance field, she was an accomplished artist in sculpturing and drawing, often using sketches to improvise dance movements for her students.

> To sum up Franziska Boas's place in the dance world one must recognize the breadth and depth of her contribution to it. She never achieved the renown of the Bennington "big four" of modern dance – Martha Graham, Hanya Holm, Doris Humphrey and Charles Weidman – but she operated in every way at their high level...her sense of dance, however, was much greater than a studio or stage, for she saw dance, not only as an art form, but as a life-form, and it was within that vision that she lived it.[14]

Visiting *Grosspapa* and *Grossmama* in Grantwood, New Jersey became a weekly ritual for at least nine months of the year, until the oldest grandchildren were late teenagers. Sunday afternoons were always reserved for these occasions. Since the Yampolskys lived with Franz and Marie in the Franklin Avenue house, it was only necessary for the Michelsons and my family to travel from New York for these gatherings. Before the day of Hudson River tunnels and a bridge, in order to get to Grantwood, it was necessary to take a ferry from either Dyckman Street or 125th Street in New York to Fort Lee, New Jersey. After the George Washington Bridge was completed in 1931, it was a simple matter to take this route to the top of the Palisades and Grantwood. Barbara Crutchley noted in her reminiscences,

> We...crossed the Hudson River on the ferry...which cost twenty-five cents. Later when the George Washington Bridge was built, we crossed it on special occasions. The bridge, however, cost fifty cents, so we rarely went that way...My fa-

> ther pointed out the beacon on top of the bridge, which was a warning for airplanes and dedicated to Wiley Post and Will Rogers who had been killed in a crash shortly before...Since then and to this day, every time I have driven by or over the bridge, I think of these two men.[15c]

On entering the Boas house, the first door on the left of the main hallway that had a large stained-glass panel, opened into the office of Franz Boas. On entering this room, one immediately faced his desk, often cluttered with works in progress. To the right, ahead and behind the desk were bookcases occupying all of the available wall space on three sides of the room. Many prints and photographs adorned the shelves and remaining walls, with images primarily of family members and associates (Figure 118). He often met with visiting students and colleagues in

Figure 118. Franz Boas in the study of his home in Grantwood, New Jersey, ca. 1915-1920. Note the stained glass panel in the door.

the office, or if less formal, they would meet in the living room with whoever else might be there. I do not recall spending any time in his study. I do know that it was out-of-bounds when we played hide-and-seek. Directly across the hallway from his office was a small room with rows of stacks, used primarily for storage of reprints, journals, books, and manuscripts. The only telephone in the house was located in this room.

---

[c] We recall the day the bridge opened to the public. By putting 5¢ in a turnstile, one was permitted to walk across the bridge. Our entire family enjoyed this inaugural trip, but only walked half way across and back.

Figure 119. Front hall of the Grantwood house, looking from the living room. The door in the background led to a room with the metal files – later used as a small bedroom for Franz's sister, Hete (Gertrud Michelson).

At the end of the front hallway were stairs to the second floor (Figure 119). At the foot of the stairs was a small room, where Franz had file cabinets for his manuscripts and which was later the bedroom of his sister, Hete. As youngsters, we discovered that by unscrewing knobs on the file drawers, one could pull out the long rods that held the files in place. They made wonderful swords. Only twice in my life can I recall Grosspapa being angry. This was one time, when he caught us dueling. I suspect that he was more concerned about getting the rods back in place than the harm that we would inflict upon one another. The other time was in Cornwall Bridge, Connecticut in about 1930. He was baby-sitting for his four grandsons, presuming we were in bed and asleep. We discovered that one of our beds was much like a trampoline. All four of us began jumping on this sleeping surface, higher and higher with the noise attendant to these gymnastics. Needless to say, Grosspapa was duly upset and subjected us to a verbal lashing. Always a sweet, caring and compassionate person, I would guess we pushed him a bit too far.

The main hall and all the downstairs rooms in the Grantwood house had dark-stained trim around the doors, windows, ceiling, and base boards. This was also true of the boxed-in ceiling beams and the vertical and horizontal decorative wall trim, all shown in the figures presented here.

Figure 120. Living room of the Boas with the hall to the left. (Gertrud Micheson).

Figure 121. The Boas living room facing the tiled fireplace (Gertrud Michelson).

The living room was at the end of the front hall and was entered through a large open arch (Figures 120-122). It was a large room with a tiled fireplace and high mantle. On the east side were large windows and a door that led to a covered porch. On entering the living room, immediately to the right was an upright piano – the only type of piano that Franz ever played. Had there been room for a grand piano, I suspect that it would have been there. Rarely in his life was he without a piano, be it in his student university days or at Clark University when he rented pianos, or in their New York apartment.

Figure 122. The Boas living room facing the east windows. The chair on the left in front of the radiator was the favorite chair of Franz Boas. He always sat here for family gatherings. The round table is the place where the tree was always placed at Christmas time. (Gertrud Michelson).

It was in this room that the family always gathered on Sundays, along with any household guests. Anthropologist Gladys Reichard was frequently present as she rented a room on the second floor during part of this time. The living room was furnished with tasseled upholstered furniture, some of which came from their New York apartment. During these visits, virtually all of the adults smoked cigarettes – Gladys smoked cigars. It is said that Franz never smoked until his women students at Barnard College encouraged him to do so.[16] When he did smoke, it was usually with a cigarette holder. These weekly *Kaffee-klatches* with the adults were animated, spiced with jokes and stories, but of little interest to the grandchildren. We spent most of our time playing in the twin's bedroom on the third floor or playing hide-and-seek, until admonished to stop when our shrieking and yelling became intolerable.

According to my sister, Barbara,

> The whole family would be there – aunts, uncles, cousins, even second cousins – each bringing something for supper...the grownups would sit...and talk, very boring for us children, and my cousin Trudel

> [Gertrud] and I, the two youngest, would go play out in the garden. We would play hide-and-seek in the bushes and generally have a good time, or if it were raining, we would play inside with wooden blocks in Tante Hete's room at the foot of the stairs. Then at supper, the grownups would set out the food and we would all eat together at the large dining room table...I remember loving to watch my Aunt Helene freshly grind the coffee in the Delft coffee mill on the wall in the kitchen...The room to the right of the front door was Grosspapa's library and floor-to-ceiling bookshelves...It was a good place to explore. My favorite room was his study, a bright room...My favorite spot to curl up was on a bearskin rug under his large kneehole desk...I didn't pay much attention to Grosspapa or the other grownups, but I do remember sitting at his feet in the living room and being fascinated with his shoes. He wore black leather ankle-high boots and laces. No one else wore anything like that.[15]

It had been traditional to have a Christmas tree every year with the Boas family in Minden, Germany and with the Franz Boas family in America. In Germany it was almost universally done, even in a secular setting. Franz even carried a small Christmas tree to the Arctic, so that he would not miss this traditional German celebration. It was a time for exchanging gifts. On these occasions the Boas adults and all the grandchildren gathered together in Grantwood on Christmas eve. Barbara records,

> Upon arriving at the house everything was very mysterious. We children were told to go and play in Tante Hete's room...I remember too the splinters we would get in our knees from wood in the floors...dark velvet drapes had been drawn shut [across the opening to the living room]...When all the preparations had been made someone came out and told us it was time to begin. All of us children were to go to the top of the stairs and line up according to size and age... Trudel and I, the youngest, leading the parade. We marched slowly down the stairs, across the hall and into the living room. Around the room on each chair were heaped piles of presents, a separate chair or place for each person. Grosspapa called us all over to the piano where we were joined by the grownups and we all sang together. The two carols I remember were *Stille Nacht, Heilige Nacht* (Silent Night, Holy Night) and *O Tannenbaum* (Oh Christmas Tree). It felt very special singing them in German and we concentrated on doing it well.[15]

A large Christmas tree, adorned with scores of burning candles, was placed near the windows. We were not permitted near the tree for this reason. Nearby were two pails of sand to put out any fire that might result. It is not clear to this day how that would work. In any case, finding our presents was more important than approaching the tree. After the presents were exchanged and supper was served we left Grantwood, ready to celebrate Christmas again the following morning in our own homes.

Next to the living room was a large dining room with a similar fireplace, but with the mantle located just below the ceiling. On it were a number of beer steins, probably from Franz's university days. The dining room table could be expanded to accommodate the large family (Figure 123). The remaining house was spacious. The kitchen was at the back of the building; the coal-fired furnace was in the large basement. On the second floor, at the head of the stairs, was the bedroom of Franz and Marie. Additional bedrooms at the front and rear of the building were used for family or guests. When Emilie Krackowizer gave up her New York apartment, she spent some time here, when not staying with her daughter, Helene Meyer, in Yonkers, New York. The third floor was used entirely by Cecil and Helene Yampolsky and their children.

Figure 123. The Boas dining room with its fireplace and large tiled wall below the mantle. The door to the kitchen is to the right of the fireplace. (Gertrud Michelson).

One of the most memorable family gatherings was in Cornwall Bridge, Connecticut on July 9, 1928, the occasion of the seventieth birthday of Franz Boas. Present to share this occasion were Marie, the Boas children, Helene, Ernst, and Franziska with their spouses, Franz's sister, Hete Lehmann, and the five granchildren (Figures 124).[d]

Figure 124. Franz Boas on his seventieth birthday. Left to right: Standing are Ernst Boas, Helene Yampolsky, and Franziska Boas. Seated are Hete Lehmann, Franz Boas, Marie Boas, and Helen Boas holding her daughter, Barbara. Sitting on the ground are Donald Boas, Robert Yampolsky, Norman Boas, and Philip Yampolsky. Cornwall Bridge, Connecticut, July 9, 1928 (American Philosophical Society).

The Yampolsky property at Cornwall Bridge, lying on the side of a small mountain, included a dense forest with many huge hemlocks. Behind the barn was brook in a deep ravine that flowed into a waterfall, below which was a crystal-clear pool – all wonderful sites for dipping or swimming. At the age of seventy-one, Grosspapa decided that it was time to take his four older grandchildren on a hike through the wilderness. His love for nature was boundless; beginning with hikes in the Porta Mountains near Minden, in the Harz Mountains in Germany, in the fjords of Baffin Island's Cumberland Sound, on arctic glaciers, and his many treks through the Adirondacks and the wilds of British Columbia. He wanted to share his joy with us by hiking over the mountain to Kent Falls State Park, probably four to five miles distant. This, of course, was accompanied with his descriptions of the flora and fauna as we went along. I was the only one who was unable to complete the return trip home under my own power, having developed a blister on a heel. Undaunted, Grosspapa carried me piggy-back the entire distance home – this time along the main highway and up the mountain road.

---

[d] Gertrud (Trudel) was not born until the following year.

With his fame and stature in the scientific community, Franz Boas became an attractive subject for artists. In 1927, Jacob Epstein (1880-1959), a British sculptor, came to New York on the offer of an exhibition in the city. Born on the Lower East Side of Manhattan, at the age of twenty-two he abandoned his family and New York and sailed to Paris to study sculpture, spending some time with Auguste Rodin. He then settled in England where he remained for the rest of his life. Epstein was always unconventional, be it in his social agenda, marital associations or art. "Like his monumental primitive carvings, he stands alone, a colossus bestriding the entire development of Modern Art, always successful, always out of fashion."[17] After virtually all of his creations, Epstein was the object of condemnation for the bizarre renditions of his subjects, yet he was brilliant as a three-dimensional caricaturist. In spite of his rebellious nature and his ambivalent public, his creative abilities were rewarded with a knighthood.

When he returned to New York for the special exhibit of his works, it was his first visit to America in twenty-two years. Although displeased with the arrangements the gallery had made for his show, he was quite successful in selling some of his works. While he was visiting America, he was commissioned to do three portraits, including Paul Robeson, the great African American singer, the educator John Dewey and Franz Boas. The Robeson project remained a sketch until he had more time to create the portrait after he returned home. The Dewey bust was subscribed to by students and admirers of him and presented to Columbia University.[18] The Boas bust was commissioned by some of Boas's friends, but when he asked to see the clay model, Boas was displeased, told his friends not to pay Epstein and have him take it back to England (Figure 125). Always sensitive about the scars on his face and his facial palsy, when Epstein exaggerated these deformities in his model, it is easy to understand Boas's disappointment – an unflattering caricature.[e]

---

[e] The story of the Boas rejection of the Epstein work was told to me by my father and was well known in the family. When my father was in London in about 1953, he visited Sir Jacob Epstein's studio to see the Boas bust. Although not particularly pleased with the image, he planned to purchase a casting. Unfortunately before he had a chance to do so, he became ill and died in 1954. Recalling this story, upon the death of Epstein in 1959, I wrote to Lady Epstein and arranged to have a bronze casting made of the bust. When I received it, I too was disappointed with the ludicrous exaggeration of his facial deformities, but was nevertheless pleased to have this work. According to Lady Epstein, ours was the second casting. In June 1961, Billy Rose, the American impresario, met with Lady Epstein and convinced her to donate all the Epstein plaster casts from his

Figure 125. Bust portrait made by Sir Jacob Epstein, 1927 (American Philosophical Society).

On returning to London, Epstein wrote to Boas, with no apparent ill will, thanking him profusely for a copy of *Primitive Art*, and added,

> I will send you a really decent photograph of the Robeson head & also one of your own bust which has been very well cast in bronze. I recall with pleasure how you sat with such patience & good will during the séances for the bust & am pleased that I've done it.[19]

Another artist who was attracted to Boas was Sergei Konenkov (1876-1971). Konenkov was known as the "patriarch of Russian sculpture." He created huge monuments. Some with "exaggerated forms" but he also created realistic portraits of Russian men of art and science, including Pushkin, Dostoyevsky, Gorky, Pavlov, and Tolstoy, some of which were sculpted when he was in New York. In 1922, after attending an art exhibition in New York, he elected to stay in America and remained until immediately after the end of World War II, when he re-

---

studio to Jerusalem, where he would arrange to have a special museum built to house them.[19]

turned to Russia. While in New York, he sculpted heads of Supreme Court Justices Oliver Wendell Holmes (for the Harvard Law School), Harlan Fiske Stone and Benjamin Cardozo, as well as Albert Einstein, Franz Boas, and some of his Russian works.

Figure 126. Clay bust of Franz Boas made by Sergei Konenkov, ca.1930 (American Philosophical Society).

The Boas bust is realistic and very appealing, bringing poignant memories to those who knew him. Unlike Epstein's bust, none of his features is exaggerated. The original bronze casting was given to Columbia University, but the reproduction rights remained with the family (Figure 126).[f] After Konenkov returned to Russia, he continued to create

---

[f] The Konenkov bust measures 24" in height. Three other copies exist. One is in the Library of the American Philosophical Society; Gertrud Michelson and this writer's family own the other two.

monumental works as well popular wooden sculptures based on Russian fairy tales. In addition to many other honors, he "was declared a Hero of the Socialist Labor, the Soviet Union's highest civilian award."[20]

The 1920s also saw Franz Boas becoming more involved with political and world events. In spite of his unpopular position in opposing a conflict with Germany in World War I, he withheld public expression of his opinions once the United States joined the fight. After the war it became evident, as he had predicted, that the Germans psyche would be badly bruised and nationalism would soon become a motivating force, soon to be led by the repressive regime of the Nazis. It was already clear that intellectual life was being compromised. In order to generate support for the restoration of German intellectual life after the war, Boas continued to be an active member of the Germanistic Society of America. He also played a very active role in the Emergency Society for German and Austrian Science and Art from 1920 to 1928.

In spite of the many physical hardships of an adventurous anthropologist, the pressures of life in academia, the emotional trauma of financial crises, distress over World War I, and the loss of dear little Hete in Chicago, Franz had never been exposed to tragedies such as he had in the 1920s. In 1924, Franz and Marie lost their daughter, Gertrud, to poliomyelitis. She was a Barnard College graduate, a beautiful young woman who had just embarked on a teaching career when she was stricken with this dreadful disease (Figure 127). She died at Montefiore Hospital in the Bronx, where her brother, Ernst, was Medical Director and Superintendent of the hospital. Gertrud was the first of the Franz Boas family to be buried in Dale Cemetery in Ossining, New York, next to the memorial stone of baby Hedwig and Gertrud's Krackowizer grandparents, aunts and uncles.[13]

It was only one year later that tragedy struck again. Franz and Marie's son, Henry and a young woman companion were killed instantly when their car was hit by a train at a railroad crossing in Michigan (Figure 128). Henry attended Storrs Agricultural College (now the University of Connecticut). As a graduate and agriculturalist, he joined his brother-in-law, Cecil Yampolsky, in a vain attempt to save the foundering thousand-acre Alma Farm in Bolton, New York (supra).[14] The only thing that Franz could do to compensate for his sorrow was to initiate a drive to create safer railroad crossings and warning systems in the United States which were rudimentary in those days. Henry was the second member of the Boas family to be interred at the Dale Cemetery.

On December 19, 1929, Marie Boas was crossing Palisade Avenue, a block from her home in Grantwood, New Jersey, when she was suddenly struck by a hit-and-run driver. Taken to a local hospital, she survived just a short time. Although I was only seven years old, it was a day I shall never forget. We were living in Riverdale, New York. Cecil Yampolsky phoned our house. When told of the accident, my father was thunderstruck, turned ashen, and said only, "Mama's dead!" He immediately rushed from the house to Grantwood. Franz was in Chicago at this time. As was his ritual, he almost certainly had visited the grave of his little girl, Hete.

Figures 127 & 128. Photographs of Gertrud M. Boas (N.F.B.) and Henry H. D. Boas (Gertrud Michelson), each taken ca.1922-1923.

The decision as to how to notify their father was left to Ernst and Helene. Franziska, Nicolai and their infant daughter were at sea at that moment, returning from a trip to Europe. It was decided that Helene would immediately take a train to Chicago so that she might break the news directly to Franz and accompany him home. According to Franziska, Franz and Marie had planned to travel together to Chicago, but reconsidered when they realized that they could not afford the cost of another train fare.[g] A greater loss to Franz, losing his beloved Marie, is unimaginable. A year later, on December 14, 1930, while on his last trip to Fort Rupert, British Columbia, he wrote to his children, addressed to Ernst,

[g] This sequence of events was recalled by Gertrud Michelson, as told to her by her mother, Franziska.

> A year ago today I went to Chicago not knowing what fate had in store for me. I said goodbye-goodbye forever - to your mother under the viaduct over 125th Street! You lost a dear mother, and I cannot find myself since then. When my work is done, my thoughts always concentrate on the same thing – Mama, Trudel, Heini, Baby! Oh you all know it! I will find myself eventually and do what has to be done, but the real enjoyment of life is gone. You are all my dear children and grandchildren, and you will not be angry with me when, in addition to you, I think of all our beloved ones who are not with us anymore.[21]

Marie was buried with her two children, parents and siblings in Dale Cemetery. From the instant he met Marie Krackowizer in the Harz Mountains, both knew immediately that they were meant for each other. The letters of Franz and Marie are testimony to the love they shared to the end. They were the parents of a large, adoring family. Marie was a dedicated *Hausfrau*, as was the custom of the times. She was a loving and compassionate mother and grandmother. She was also a bright woman who had no time or opportunity for a career of her own. Little is written of Marie, except for the information available in family correspondence. Nevertheless, she was an integral part and backbone of the career of Franz. Marie was a sounding board for virtually all of the major professional decisions in his life. His unrelenting drive for work and long absences from home on scientific expeditions and meetings were troublesome to both, but accepted as part of his profession. The role that Marie played in support of the work of Franz Boas and in raising their family is a story unto itself.

Not only were there direct losses to the Boas family in the 1920s, but before Marie died, three of her siblings pre-deceased her – Emil Krackowizer (1924), Richard Krackowizer (1926) and Alice Krackowizer (1929), all of whom were buried in the Ossining cemetery.

## References and Notes

1. White, Leslie A. Biography of Elsie Worthington Clews Parsons in *Dictionary of American Biography*, 10 volumes, 8 supplements, American Council of Learned Societies, Charles Scribner's Sons, New York, 1941-45.
2. Herskovits, Melville Jean. *Franz Boas, the Science of Man in the Making*, Charles Scribner's Sons, New York & London, 1953.
3. Herskovits, Melville Jean, in *Who's Who in America*, Volume 26, A. N. Marquis Company, Chicago, 1950-51.
4. Goldfrank, Esther S., in *Who's Who in America*, 37th Edition, A. N. Marquis Company, Chicago, 1972-75.
5. Goldfrank, Esther S. Goldfrank papers in the National Anthropological Archives of the National Museum of Natural History, Smithsonian Institution (Includes all of her anthropological papers and collection of photographs).

6. Stocking, George W., Jr. Biography of Ruth Fulton Benedict in *Dictionary of American Biography*, 10 volumes, 8 supplements, American Council of Learned Societies, Charles Scribner's Sons, New York, 1946-50.
7. Reichard, Gladys. *Franz Boas and Folklore*, in *American Anthropologist*, Volume 45, No. 3, July-September, 1943.
8. Howard, Jane. *Margaret Mead, A Life.* Simon & Schuster, New York, 1984 (A critical biography of a controversial woman).
9. Mead, Margaret. *Blackberry Winter, My Early Years*, William Morrow and Company, Inc., New York, 1972 (Relates primarily to her training, contests with Boas, and her experiences in Oceania).
10. Mead, Margaret. *Coming of Age in Samoa, A Psychological Study of Primitive Youth for Western Civilization*, William Morrow, New York, 1961 (Original publication – 1928).
11. Mead, Margaret. Correspondence with Boas family and friends concerning the subject of Franz Boas's facial palsy (Copies in the Library of the American Philosophical Society).
12. Deloria, Ella Cara. *Waterlily*, Biographical sketch by Agnes Picotte. Afterword by Raymond J. DeMallie, University of Nebraska Press, 1988.
13. Boas, Norman F. *NOD HILL, Wilton, Connecticut, Reminiscences*, Privately printed, Mystic, Connecticut, 1996 (Includes visitations of Franz and Marie Boas to the summer home of Ernst Boas and his family).
14. Boas, Norman F. and Barbara L. Meyer. *Alma Farm, An Adirondack Meeting Place*, privately printed, Mystic, Connecticut and Bolton, New York, 1999.
15. Crutchley, Barbara Boas. Reminiscences. Personal communication, April 4, 2000.
16. Kroeber, Alfred L. *Franz Boas: The Man*, in *American Anthropologist*, Volume 45, No. 3, July-September, 1943 (One of the finest testimonials to Boas as a humanist and disciplined scientist).
17. Stannard, Martin. *Always Successful, always Out of Fashion*, in T*he New York Times Book Review*, August 22, 1993 (Review of a biography of Sir Jacob Epstein).
18. Buckle, Richard. *Jacob Epstein, Sculptor*, The World Publishing Company, Cleveland and New York, 1963 (Biography of Sir Jacob Epstein with hundreds of illustrations of his works).
19. Epstein, Sir Jacob. Letter to Franz Boas, April 29, 192[8]. Boas papers in the Library of the American Philosophical Society.
20. Konenkov, Sergei. Obituary in *The New York Times*, October 12, 1971.
21. Rohner, Ronald P. Compiler and editor of T*he Ethnography of Franz Boas*, The University of Chicago Press, Chicago & London, 1969 (An extensive publication of over 700 pages of letters and diaries of Boas from the Library of the American Philosophical Society, 1886 to 1931).

# CHAPTER IX

## POLITICAL ACTIVISM AND RETIREMENT

As the year 1930 approached, Franz Boas started to face one of his greatest challenges in the political arena (Figures 129). Most of his political life had been confined to the usual infighting done in academia. He studiously avoided involvement in national or international politics until World War I.

Figure 129. Photograph of Franz Boas taken ca.1930 (N.F.B.).

Boas was brought up as a liberal. He was not a radical but his compassion for all mankind guided his emotions and beliefs. How could a person who devoted his entire life to the study of man think otherwise! He was totally dedicated to the belief that racism was a scourge on mankind, and was entirely unjustified based on objective scientific observations. When racism was used as a destructive tool in government, it was time to react. He thoroughly embraced and cherished living in the America but was unable to accept infringements on civil rights guaranteed by the constitution.

Boas was an anti-imperialist, having lived through expansionist policies of France, Great Britain, the Netherlands, Spain, and Germany. On the political scene in America, he voted for William McKinley in 1896, a Republican, running for president. In the wake of the Spanish-American War and American "imperialism," he was disturbed. He had strong feelings against expansionist policies of any country, with the inherent abuses and imposition of one culture upon another. Spain was forced to cede Puerto Rico, Guam, and the Philippines to the United States. In 1916, he voted for Charles Evans Hughes, a Republican, for president in his unsuccessful campaign against Woodrow Wilson. Hughes was born in Glens Falls, New York and summered in Bolton Landing where Boas consulted with him on occasion. In 1924 Boas voted for the liberal, Robert M. La Follette, in his unsuccessful campaign on the Progressive ticket for president against Warren G. Harding. Finally, he voted for Franklin D. Roosevelt in 1940. We do not know how he voted in the other presidential elections.[1,2] As he witnessed more and more abuses of civil rights in America, he assumed a more liberal and public posture. During the last decade of his life, he engaged in passionate and vigorous political activity and railed against racism in all its forms, both in the United States and in Germany.

With the emergence of Nazism, Franz Boas was again torn in his allegiance to Germany and became determined to fight with all his energy against the new regime. In one of his most revealing letters, on March 27, 1933 Boas wrote a passionate plea and appeal for support and understanding to President Hindenburg of Germany. Paul von Hindenburg (1846-1934) was a soldier, field marshal of Germany, and a national hero. He had fought in major German campaigns including the Franco-Prussian War and on the Russian front in World War I. In 1925, at the behest of the Nationalists and Conservatives, he agreed to run for president. Although it was a bitterly contested campaign, he was elected. His presidency was successful primarily because of the veneration the electorate had for him. His nonpartisanship and efforts to promote international accord had a temporary stabilizing influence. Other discordant forces were, nevertheless, at work. In 1932, Adolph Hitler lost in a presidential election bid against Hindenburg. In spite of this, the National Socialist Party gained more strength in the Reichstag, and in January 1933, Hitler was made chancellor. I can recall this day well as evidenced by the anxieties generated in our family – many relatives and friends were still in Germany. In March the Reichstag gave Hitler virtual dictatorial powers. With his power base lost, Hindenburg, although still very popular, became a figurehead with little influence.

The letter Franz Boas wrote to Hindenburg, was undoubtedly written in the wake of the fears generated by Hitler's ascendancy to power and at a time that Hindenburg was unable to be of any help. Whether Boas knew this or considered this a desperate effort to cast his influence is not known.

His Excellency, General Field Marshal Paul von Hindenburg,
President of the *Deutsches Reich,* Berlin, Germany

Your Excellency,

There are periods during which silence would be cowardice and modest reticence be seen as an unworthy weakness. During the World War, the perfidious slander against Germany required leaving a quiet scholar's existence, and I may be so bold as to state that during a period when most German Americans fearfully went into hiding and did not even dare to speak German, I was one of the few who openly, in speaking and writing, opposed the web of lies and as one who did not attempt to deny their German origin. I probably was the only one who raised public protest when the late Dr. Bünz was sentenced to a dishonorable jail sentence because he had provided ships with victuals at a time when British subjects could do so with impunity, raising my voice against measuring Britains and Germans with different yardsticks.

When the war was lost for Germany and frivolous Lloyd George and the vengeful Clemenceau forced a peace treaty, shameful for the victorious powers, by starvation of the German people, the suffering on my Fatherland was very much present in my mind during sleepless nights. I could not be at peace until I was able to do something within my powers to help maintain Germany's inner strength. Thus it came to pass that I donated years of my life to help German Culture and Science. The creation of the Emergency Society and rebirth of the Germanistic Society as instruments to help Germany were due to my efforts, and without me would not have taken place.

At that time, I exhorted young Germans to face the difficulties and to stay at home because Germany was in need of every able person. At that time, I could not have been moved from Germany, even with brute force.

But now? I don't wish to reiterate newspaper reports, which perhaps are guilty of sensational exaggerations. Yet it appears very clear that free expression of opinions is suppressed in an unheard-of way and that even the most modest opposition, i.e. half of the population, is suppressed in the most brutal fashion. No impartial observer will see the latest election as the free expression of a people because it was an election during which only the National Socialists were allowed to have any campaign organization.

My personal opinions are such that I also would become a victim of persecution, like many others. Do I love Germany any less because I consider the currently ruling party aimless and contradictory, since it is a party built upon demagoguery, promising everything without even a hint how these promises might be kept and which, once in a position of power, knows no other political means than suppression of political opponents?

I would be the last person to maintain that no mistakes were made during the past fifteen years. Above all, I regretted the lack of resistance against party influences in the governments. However, they followed the example of the Imperial Governments in which background and properly held opinions, not personal qualities were determining factors. But these inexcusable favors now seem harmless when compared to the ruthless party management of the present to which the best are sacrificed only because their opinions aren't those of the ruling party, or because their family background is considered unacceptable.

Where lies the difference between the extreme left and the extreme right? There probably is no one in Germany, including the Communists, who doesn't feel the painful disenfranchisement that Germany was subjected to. Only those can shed this nightmare who are pushed to the brink of despair by daily suffering, hoping for improvement by any change.

But where then is the path to salvation? One side clamors for a development of patriotism to such an extent that it finally will be victorious against the enemy nations, thus setting Germany free. This is the basic philosophy of the ruling party, but why does it stop with the Germans in South Tyrol who suffer most? Others consider the possibility that the social suffering of our time sets tasks, the solution of which transcends political and national conflicts and thus shall return Germany to its rights. I think it is delusion to think that any one country at this time may isolate herself from the world thus regaining her health. The social needs of the world require cooperation. But when I consider this a necessity, does it mean that I forget my duties towards my Fatherland? The terms national and international do not contradict each other. They have to supplement each other, in spite of all conflicts.

The polarization of German political parties in two extreme groups certainly is due to French politics and British intransigence towards France. Only with this consideration can we explain the intense bitterness, which now burst forth in such an unpleasant manner.

The vulgar, indecent way to wage battle on both sides is repugnant to me, regardless against whom it may be directed. I known it from my own experience, and the denial which pervades our newspapers is pointless. It

> suffices to have seen the posters and the newspapers to know which spirit prevails there now.
>
> Anti-Semitism is yet another issue, and denial doesn't help here, either. Don't I know that honorable men are chased from their office and positions only because they are Jews? Don't I know that defenseless Jews have to fear with every step they take, that they're insulted, the mouths foam with poison and bitterness when the word "Jew" is uttered? Have I not, time and again, with my own ears heard the sentence "Die Jewry, die!?"[a]
>
> I come from a Jewish family, but I feel and think as a German. What do I owe my family? A sense of duty, dedication and the urge to speak the truth without faltering. If these characteristics are unworthy of a German, if filth, vulgarity, intolerance, injustice and lies today are considered German, who wants to be one, then? I've called myself a German time and again and with pride, but things have gotten so far that I'm almost ashamed to be a German. Do you believe that I can respect a flag the symbol of which is a personal insult attempting to defile me and my parents?
>
> And still I can't relinquish hope that these signs of the times are but symptoms of a fever afflicting the body of sick people which, even though deeply wounded, shall recover, and I hope that the Germany which I know and love shall rise again. May this day of recovery come soon![4]

There is no record of a response from President Hindenburg to the Boas plea. When the President died on August 2, 1934, the only stabilizing voice in Germany was lost and the Nazis had complete power.

World War II literally began with Hitler's ascendancy to power with his attacks on human rights and the suppression of those considered to be opponents of the new regime. On May 10, 1933, Josef Goebbels, later Minister of Public Enlightenment and Propaganda, ordered ruffians to confiscate books by Jews and Bolsheviks and all those who posed a threat to the German Reich. Huge numbers of books were taken from the library of the University of Berlin and were thrown into bonfires as a lesson to others whose teachings were a threat to Hitler and his henchmen. Included were works of Albert Einstein, Nobel Laureate Thomas Mann, H. G. Wells, Jack London, Karl Marx, Helen Keller, and others. At the same time, the books of Franz Boas were burned in the square in front of the University of Kiel, where only two years earlier he had been awarded an honorary degree (Figure 130). His books in which he de-

[a] Translated from *Juda verrrecke!* This is the second half of the programmatic Nazi battle cry as penned by Dietrich Eckart, *Deutschland erwache!* (Germany wake up!). It was followed by the quote in the text and based on the German verb *verrecken*, meaning to "croak," a term used for animals.[3]

bunked the racial theories of the Nazis, posed a serious threat.[5,6b] His response was simply, "If people want to be crazy, what can you do about it?"[7]

Copyright 1937, World-Telegram Corporation.

# MAN---- With Variations

Nazis burning books of Dr. Boas in square before University of Kiel, his Alma Mater. He previously was given high honors by the university, but his books demolish Nazi racial theories.

## Anthropologists Smile as Hitler Talks of His "Pure Germany"

*The first of a series of articles on the battle of anthropologists to know man, from the primitive to the modern, before the evidence is lost. The cold answer of science to Hitler.*

By JOSEPH MITCHELL,
*World-Telegram Staff Writer.*

The number of primitives uninfluenced by contact with such products of Western civilization as plug tobacco, the Holy Bible, radio programs, pants, hangovers, pinball games, toothpaste and

acquisitivenes, or the "instinct" of mother love.

The relation of facts about primitive environments to our own steam-heated environment may seem obscure at first, but when one remembers that the anthropologist is preoccupied with the study of races and reflects on the damage done in our time by stress on "racial purity" and "racial characteristics" it is no longer obscure. The insistence on a "pure Germany" by that noble Austrian, Adolf Hitler, and the amazing German racial laws of 1935 are enormously funny and enormously tragic to anthropologists. When Julius Streicher cries that "blood cells of Jews differ greatly from those of Nordics," the anthropologist does not know whether to snicker or to weep.

Faced with these matters Dr. Boas, for example, is forced to reflect that "the world is sick." Dr. Boas knows that the term "race" is vague and

for many thousand years. In Europe, Western Asia and North Africa particularly, no people exist that can derive its ancestry from a single source. The populations of this area are so much alike that the assignment of an individual, on the basis of his bodily appearance, to his proper local group is never quite certain, often impossible.

### Family Strains.

"On account of the diversity of family strains in a population, it is impossible to speak of racial heredity except in regard to such general traits as differentiate whites, Negroes and Mongols, and which are common to all the members of these racial groups. We can study hereditary form and behavior only in family lines.

"No proof has even been given

Figure 130. Newspaper sketch of Franz Boas by Seymour Marcus and the burning of the Boas books by the Nazis in 1933 (The *World-Telegram*, New York, November 1, 1937).

Boas always considered himself a German emotionally and intellectually and was deeply disturbed by the tactics of the evolving regime in Germany. In the same year after the book-burning, on November 20, 1933, he wrote a letter to his three children, Helene, Ernst and Franziska,

> As you know, I had the wish to transfer my library to Germany as a legacy to the *Notgemeinschaft Deutscher Wissenschaft.*[c] For practical reasons I chose the form to sell the library for $1 plus "other considerations" under the condition that I retain user's rights until my death.

---

[b] The Holocaust Museum in Washington, D.C. has an encased exhibit identifying Boas as a victim of the book-burning.

[c] Emergency Committee of German Scholars.

> The limitations imposed on the freedom of scholarly research in Germany, especially the prevention of free use of books in the Social Sciences and questions of race, inasmuch as they don't conform with the partisan views of the current government, have caused me to request the President of the *Notgemainschaft*, Hon. Schmidt-Ott to rescind the contract. As a consequence he returned his copy...
>
> It is my wish that the contract should be adhered to if, at the time of my death, if full scholarly freedom has been re-established, i.e. if full freedom of learning and teaching at the universities has been restored; if the exclusion of Liberals and Jews from the teaching bodies of schools and universities has stopped, and when the reading of works of both popular and academic science no longer is subject to control of a political party.
>
> If this should not be the case, the contract remains rescinded, and you shall inherit the library.
>
> This contract has been cancelled on the part of the *Notgemeinschaft Deutscher Wissenschaft* by Prof. Dr. Jürgens (A manuscript postscript).[8]

This was to be the last academic legacy he could leave to his beloved homeland. In 1939 he received a terse letter from the office of Dr. Jürgens, signed by a secretary.[d9]

> The library activities of the former *Notgemeinschaft Deutscher Wissenschaft,* now *Deutsche Forschungsgemeinschaft*, have been separated so that the *Beschaffungsamt* now officially would be the legal successor of the *Notgemeinschaft* as a partner in the contracts made with you.
>
> The contract with you was initiated at your wish...I regret to inform you that your attitude displayed towards Germany recently has obviated the conditions for acceptance of such a gift and do declare the implementation of the contract entered into with you as null and void.

The final chapter in this correspondence was written by Franz Boas to Doctor Jürgens after receiving the above letter,

> I can't say how sorry I am for you that you were put in a position having to write such a letter. You know me too well from earlier to misconstrue my relationship with Germany.
>
> As matters stand, the letter was totally superfluous. After the major book burnings in 1933, I wrote to the Hon. Schmidt-Ott that my library basically consisted of books on race issues, and that it appeared pointless to send the books over there in order to have them burned. He then returned the contract. The dollar I received had long since been returned to the German consulate. However, at that time I added a codicil to my testament that the contract would reactivate if at the time of my death schol-

---

[d] The closing of the letter, "In *vorzüglicher Hochachtung"* is as impersonal as it can get, short of being a direct insult, according to translator Prof. Thomas Huber.

arship in Germany would be free again…I am now taking notice of the wish of the authority you represent to also ignore this codicil to my testament and shall delete it in the original of my testament.

It strikes me as funny that a government, which does not shy back from blackmail, as I know from my own experience, suddenly wants to be this circumspect.

Things have been strange in my life. When I left Germany as a young man, Germany was so satiated that the presence or absence of an individual did not matter. I remained here because I was offered the opportunity for productive scholarly work. To this was added an idealistic conception of the American institution, which however, was badly shaken in 1898.[e] When the World War broke out, I was incensed about the propaganda that aimed at involving America in the war, and I may claim to have been one of the few German Americans who spoke out for Germany. After the war, I felt the urge to help as much as I could.

You yourself know best how many years I dedicated to this activity and that I refused to accept all thanks, as much as I could, because I thought I was following but a moral obligation.

You may understand that I can't agree with the current German government, and that therefore it is an obvious obligation for me to do anything to get rid of the people who brutalize the people and instill falsehood and lies.

The things I do, I do that the madness which has gripped her people can't last.

What good is power if it corrupts the soul? I wrote this to a friend and told him that Heine's deeply felt strophes go with me always:

Once I had a beautiful homeland.
The oak tree
Grew so tall, and violets nodded gently.
It was a dream.
It kissed me in German, and spoke in German
(One hardly will believe how good this sounded)
    the word: "I love you."
It was a dream.[9]

Throughout this narrative it is clear that Franz Boas, as with many immigrants, was unable to detach himself from his love for his country of birth. It is repeatedly reflected in his letters, political activities, and intellectual pursuits. He had left his family at the age of twenty-five, never to return permanently. Yet, some of the closest members of his family remained in Germany until their death many years later. His love for America, although not expressed as forcefully as that for his homeland, was nevertheless an undercurrent of his whole experience here. As with Jacobi, Schurz, and Krackowizer, he embraced democracy with en-

---

[e] The Spanish-American War.

thusiasm and tried to use it as a disciplinary model not only for Germany but for other autocratic regimes in the world. As a thinking and dedicated American he was also critical of abuses of constitutionally guaranteed rights in our country, often expressing his views publicly.

Boas became chairman of the American Committee for Democracy and Intellectual Freedom and honorary chairman of the National Emergency Conference. He wrote pamphlets, planned and supervised activities of these organizations and prepared petitions of his colleagues in attacking racism and intolerance. His political activities continued relentlessly for the last six years of his life, in spite of failing health. He "committed...his whole soul to the fight for all liberties."[10]

An example of the multitude of avenues he pursued is evidenced by a telegram he sent to Justice Louis Brandeis on June 15, 1936,

> PARISER TAGEBLATT HAS BEEN SOLD TO HITLER / SUBSTITUTE HAS BEEN STARTED BY COLLEAGUES OF EDITOR DR. BERNHARD WHO IS HERE BUT HAS TO SAIL BACK TO FRANCE ON FRIDAY / SO FAR AS KNOWN TO HIM ONE HUNDRED FIFTY THOUSAND FRANCS HAVE BEEN RAISED IN FRANCE / ABOUT FIFTEEN THOUSAND DOLLARS MORE ARE NEEDED / IT IS THE ONLY ANTI HITLER DAILY IN GERMAN LANGUAGE IN EXISTENCE / THE PAPER IS ESSENTIAL IN THE FIGHT AGAINST HITLER / IMMEDIATE HELP IS NECESSARY / CAN YOU HELP THROUGH YOUR FRIENDS IN THE SITUATION / FRANZ BOAS.[11]

Brandeis responded promptly and referred him to Edward J. Kaufman in Washington and, in due course, to others with better contacts.

At home he fought racism wherever he had the opportunity. As a liberal advocate in this cause, others depended heavily on him for leadership in pursuing abuses in human rights, not only in Germany, but also in the United States and the rest of the world. His political activism led him into combat with the Dies Committee in the House of Representatives, a reactionary arm of Congress and later the House Un-American Activities Committee. His unvaried posture was to defend civil rights of Americans that included freedom of speech and association. He championed the ending of the poll tax, which prevented many Negroes from voting. With Paul Robeson, Ralph Bunche, and others, he joined the Council of African Affairs, dedicated to freeing African colonies from imperialistic rule by foreign nations.[13]

Not only was Franz distressed with the atrocities in Germany; he was concerned about the safety of his family. His sister, Toni, remained in Germany where she died in about 1935 (Figure 131). She was a bright and talented musician with perfect pitch. As a young woman she studied the piano with Franz Liszt. On one of her visits to New York in the

1920s, she helped my father select a grand piano. Toni married Ludwig Wohlauer. Their only child died of hydrocephalus as an infant, but they adopted a boy, Hans. When he was of military age, he was conscripted into the German army. He was considered an Ayran, apparently based on his adoption papers. Hans was captured by the Americans and sent to a prisoner-of-war camp in New York State during the war. Following the war he returned to Germany and took a position with a petroleum firm.

Figure 131. Franz Boas's sister, Antoine (Toni) Boas Wohlauer in her Berlin apartment ca.1930s (Gertrud Michelson).

Aenna Urbach, Franz's sister, and her husband, Julius, escaped to Rio de Janiero in the 1930s with three of their six children (Walter, Frida, and Hellmut). A fourth, Hete, had married Cecil Yampolsky's brother, Oskar, and settled in Wisconsin in the 1920s. The remaining two siblings, Franz and Rudolph, with their wives, Ilse and Lotte, were able to immigrate to the United States before World War II with the help of Franz Boas. Franz's sister, Hete, widowed in 1927, also came to the

United States in the 1930s. Thus all of the immediate family of Franz Boas was out of harm's way.[f]

After Boas retired as chairman of the Department of Anthropology in 1936, he retained his office in Schermerhorn Hall at Columbia University as emeritus professor for the balance of his life. He spent many more hours at his desk in Grantwood (Figures 132) to spare himself the long commute to Columbia. He never truly ceased in his relentless drive to write, lecture, and engage in political activism for intellectual freedom and against racial bias.

Figure 132. Franz Boas in his study, Grantwood, New Jersey, 1930s (American Philosophical Society).

---

[f] In spite of efforts to save his immediate family, Jeanne Esther Frank Boas, the widow of his cousin Ernest Felix Gaston Boas, died in Auschwitz in May 1944; their son, Jean Bernard Boas, was deported and died in a concentration camp (Kaunas Reval) in 1942. These were of the family of Salomon Boas, Franz's uncle – the Paris branch of the family.[13,14] Little is known of some of his cousins and more distant relatives who remained in Germany.

At the age of eighty he published his 647-page *Race, Language and Culture.* Were he not living at home with Helene and Cecil, his life without Marie would have been an empty existence. Helene managed the house and took care of her father lovingly. Not only did she handle routine household chores, but also spent many hours helping him with research and writing his manuscripts. Grantwood also had changed. Instead of lovely woodlands surrounding their home, there was now the huge Palisade Amusement Park just east of his house on Palisade Avenue with its noise and large crowds. An apartment house was built across the street from his house on Franklin Avenue. The yard remained beautiful with specimen trees. In the fall of 1939, he wrote to me at the University of Wisconsin,

> You ought to see our sour gum trees; they are red as blood, a beautiful sight. A few days more and all the leaves will be gone.[15]

As the grandchildren grew older, there were fewer Sunday visits to Grantwood (Figure 133).

Figure 133. Family photograph. Left to right: Cecil, Philip and Helene Yampolsky, Franz Boas and Robert Yampolsky, 1930s (Philip Yampolsky).

Always in good health, except for his parotid tumor and other reversible ailments, on December 19, 1931, while attending a dinner meeting, he became acutely ill and was rushed to Mount Sinai Hospital in New York. Cared for by his son, Ernst, it was determined that he had suffered a heart attack (myocardial infarction). After a difficult five days, his subsequent course was uneventful. He remained well until two years later when he developed a transient irregular pulse (atrial fibrillation). Over the next seven years he had additional episodes of fibrillation, mostly of short duration. I recall one episode that occurred while he was having dinner at our home. These attacks were always accompanied with difficulty in breathing. In 1940, his cardiac arrhythmia became permanent and required closer medical management. There is no question that age and his heart ailment took a toll. Never a tall man, as he grew older he seemed small and frail. He even, reluctantly, took brief afternoon naps. He hated to waste time. In spite of his medical handicaps, he remained alert with an unrelenting drive to work in his field and to fight for his principles – an obsessive, compulsive drive which was the hallmark of his life.[16]

During all this time, his immediate family was always nearby and available to help. Helene and Cecil lived with him through most of their married life. Cecil was a botany teacher in a Bronx, New York high school located near Van Cortlandt Park, for most of his professional life. He was a remarkable artist, most of whose works were unpublished. He used a stippling technique to draw botanical specimens in finite detail. Helene, helped her father on many of his projects and participated in the preparation of the Kwakiutl Grammar with him and Daniel Cranmer, who visited Grantwood in 1933.[g] Cranmer was the husband of Agnes Cranmer, a granddaughter of George Hunt

During the 1930s, Franz was a frequent summer visitor at the Yamploskys' Cornwall Bridge home (Figures 134 & 135). Following his death in 1942, Helene translated many of his papers. A major project and perhaps her greatest contribution was the difficult transcription and translation of the Baffin Island letter-diaries that Franz wrote for his fiancée, Marie, while he was in the Arctic. Helene, as were Franz and Franziska, was a talented and skillful artist who started painting in her later years. Helene predeceased Cecil in 1962. During the 1930s, Franz also spent time in Wilton, where the rest of his family would join us (Figures 136 & 137).

Franz Boas alternately visited his families in Wilton and Cornwall Bridge in the summers of the 1930s. It was a simple matter to take the New York, New Haven & Hartford Railway to either place from New York. They both had stations on the Danbury branch line. On one occasion, on his way to Cornwall Bridge, he was sitting with a conductor's musical score in his lap. It was either an orchestral piece or one for a smaller musical ensemble. In any case, as time passed by and he slowly turned the pages, a passenger who had been observing his curious behav-

[g] The text was published in 1947.

ior said, "Sir, please excuse me for interrupting, but what are you doing?" Completely absorbed by the score, and startled by the question, he turned around slowly and said, "Oh – I was just listening to some music." He had the ability to totally detach himself from other diversions, be it with music or when concentrating on his work.

Figure 134. Three generations. Left to right: Ernst P. Boas, Franz Boas, and Norman F. Boas at Cornwall Bridge, Connecticut (N.F.B.).

At Wilton, he often spent time with me, answering a multitude of questions. He helped me in designing models of dodecahedrons (a sym-

Figure 135. Franz Boas and his granddaughter, Gertrud Michelson at Cornwall Bridge, Connecticut, ca.1941 (Gertrud Michelson).

metrical solid with 12 plane faces) and other multifaceted geometric models. When I discussed various theorems in mathematics, he always insisted on proof of their validity – exercises that he probably had not considered since his own children had the same problems. I once asked him if he understood Einstein's General Theory of Relativity. Acknowledging that he did, he proceeded to give me simplified but perfectly clear examples of this four-dimensional concept.

His great love was always linguistics. He made several attempts to teach me Chinook Jargon, a pidgin language based on Chinook and other Indian languages of the Pacific Northwest, flavored with French and English – a useful means of communication. It was derived from the Chinook tribes of Oregon and Washington, which was gradually altered by the contact with traders and white settlers. I asked him one time, how many languages he could speak. With a brief hesitation, he answered "Oh, about seventy." I never doubted it.

To a young boy, he seemed to have answers for everything. One day I found a baby robin on the lawn that was unable to fly. It had broken a

Figure 136. Franz Boas standing next to his grandson, Donald P. Boas and his son Ernst P. Boas at Wilton, Connecticut in the 1930s (N.F.B.).

Figure 137. The spouses of the children of Franz Boas. Left to right: Cecil Yampolsky, Franz Boas, Helen S. Boas and Nicolas Michelson, Wilton (N.F.B.).

wing. After showing it to him, he told me that there was no reasonable hope of saving this unfortunate bird and mercifully euthanatized this small creature for me.

Birthdays were always special for Grosspapa. He always remembered his grandchildren on these days with letters of greeting. Since I had a summer birthday, some of my greetings came from the Pacific Northwest and Germany. We, of course, reciprocated on his birthday, which was on July 9, sometimes with labored attempts to write in German. In 1932 he sent me an RCA Radiogram from Germany, with birthday greetings. My response was "Thank you one hundred times for that telegram. I liked it very much. I am going to keep it for a long time."[h]

The letter he wrote to me on March 26, 1940, is one of many that I cherish. At the time I was a sophomore at the University of Wisconsin. My father kept him informed of my progress.

> [He] tells me about you, how you are getting on and that you are established in your work. I believe you are the only one of my grandsons who is interested in science... Are you interested in politics? I have a lot of that kind of work, particularly in regard to education. I suppose you have heard about the fuss about Bertrand Russell's appointment at Teacher's College.[i] We got a long document out about it. Now our legislature is interfering with the City Schools and so it goes. Well, you have other cares nowadays, but I suppose in times to come you'll follow the way of your daddy, your grandfather & great grandfather Krackowizer.[17]

Of course Franz Boas was famous – I knew it and he knew it. As a young teenager, I was impressed with this fact and used to tease him about it. In fact, I tested his fame by sending him letters with inappropriate addresses. I would leave out the name of the street and even the state. They always reached him. In those days, however, the United States Post Office was more diligent in tracking down addressees. Had they known I was playing a game, it is unlikely that I would have had their cooperation. And of course, my indulgent grandfather always returned the envelopes to me. I have kept them (Figures 138) as I have many other curious collectibles. As a youngster, I collected, among other things, road maps, matchbox covers, animal bones, rattlesnake rattlers, stamps, and autographs. Knowing of my bent in collecting he gave me letters of distinguished scientists and statesmen addressed to him. Included were letters of Albert Einstein, Robert E. Peary, Rudolph Virchow, Louis D.

---

[h] I still have it.

[i] Bertrand Russell (1872-1970) was a renowned philosopher, mathematician, logician, and Nobel Laureate (1950). In 1940 Russell received a teaching appointment at City College, New York, revoked later because of a public protests and a judicial decision that judged him unfit for this position.

Brandeis, Charles Evans Hughes, Sir William Osler, and many more scientists.[i]

Figure 138. Envelope addressed to Franz Boas by his grandson, 1936 (N.F.B.).

One of my prized letters was written by President Franklin Delano Roosevelt to Boas on the occasion of his eighty-first birthday, a story boldly featured in *The New York Times*[18] and *The Herald Tribune.*[19] He wrote,

> July 5, 1939
>
> My Dear Dr. Boas,
>
> It gives me great pleasure to join with others of your friends in extending hearty greetings to you on the happy occasion of your eighty-first birthday. I hope you may long be spared in health and strength to pursue the learned studies, which have made your career so distinguished in the realm of Science.
>
> Very Sincerely yours,
> Franklin D. Roosevelt[20]

In response Boas wrote to the President,

> Allow me to express to you my sincere thanks for your kindly words of congratulations on the occasion of my eighty-first birthday. It is a satisfaction to me to think that I have been able in a small way to repay the opportunities that our country have given to me and to many others...[21]

---

[i] I still have most of these letters. Those which I no longer have, have been donated the Library of the American Philosophical Society. This exposure to the writings of such interesting people inspired me into a lifetime of collecting letters, documents, and manuscripts of many other distinguished Americans.

On this day he also received a round-robin letter from Secretary of Agriculture Henry A. Wallace, Secretary of Interior Harold L. Ickes, Nobel Laureate in Chemistry, Harold C. Urey, Senator Lewis B. Schwellenbach, the Rev. Dr. Henry Sloane Coffin, Bishop Alexander Mann, Philip Randolph, Harlow Shapley, Upton Sinclair, Walter White, A. F. Whitney, Stanley M. Isaacs, Dorothy Kenyon, and many other scientists and statesmen. They wrote,

> Professor Boas, we wish to pay homage to you on your eighty-first birthday. Throughout the years of your long and valuable life we have gratefully honored your contribution to the advancement of science. Such services would seem the utmost to be expected from any one man during the brief span of his years. But you, in these crucial times, have undertaken new duties. Realizing that every decent desire in the heart of man is threatened as it has not been in hundreds of years, you offered to spend the last years of your life in massing your fellow scientists and educators against the lowering forces of reaction.
>
> We, members and supporters of the American Committee for Democracy and Intellectual Freedom, of which you are chairman, are honored by the privilege of assisting you to impress upon American scientists and educators that they – like all men – are not only specialists in occupational fields but also citizens of a country that nourishes those occupations. Because scientists and educators are ranked among the leaders of men, we have rejoiced at the positive program of democracy and intellectual freedom that you have offered us in our struggle to preserve and extend modern civilization. In an hour of need, you have come forward to help the scientist take his rightful place among his fellow citizens in deciding what the future of our society will be – whether it will be aborted by the warmongering barbaric hordes or whether it will expand in peace for the benefit and happiness of all mankind. And we who have enjoyed the fruits of your leadership as honorary chairman of the Council for Pan American Democracy, who have been privileged to be associated with you in the championship of democracy throughout the Western Hemisphere – we sincerely trust that we shall be allowed to profit from your wise advice for many years to come.
>
> All the organizations you lead, inspired by your guidance and devotion, have emerged from the mists of restlessness and uncertainty as veritable towers for the defense of democratic liberties. From them, Professor Boas, we have been able to see with you the campaigns we must wage in school and laboratory. On the public platform – campaigns to instill among men your great devotion to democracy so that they will not falter in the common offensive to preserve and extend those ideals of justice and liberty which have made possible our present blessings.[19]

Many others expressed their feelings on this occasion. Ella Deloria wrote, "I would not trade the privilege of having known you, for anything I can think of." Although many of his students affectionately called him "Papa Franz," Deloria used a more respectful "Father Franz." Franz would respond, "'Ella, you make me feel like a Catholic priest!' and she would reply, 'Next to my own father, you are the most truly Christian man I ever met.'"[22]

Many honors and accolades were bestowed on Franz Boas in the wake of his political activism and during his scientific years. In 1942 George Marshall, chairman of the National Federation for Constitutional Liberties, wrote to Albert Einstein, inviting him to join in a dinner honoring Boas. Unable to attend, Einstein wrote,

> I have the highest admiration for the indefatigable fight of Professor Boas for the protection of freedom and human rights. Unfortunately, however, the state of my health prevents me to attend such occasions. Express my highest satisfaction that the great merits of Professor Boas are finding their deserved appreciation.[23]

Einstein and Boas, two of the most distinguished scientists in America, recognizing the hardships and suffering of some of their colleagues under Nazi rule, did all that was possible to rescue them from impending disaster. Because of their sympathetic and helpful posture in this regard, they received many pleas for help, often daily, all of which were answered personally or through other individuals or organizations formed to expedite these requests. The two corresponded with each other on a number of occasions, primarily in regard to these problems.[24] On February 4, 1934, Einstein wrote to Boas, reciting and lamenting his inadequacy in responding to these pleas,

> I still have some money from my charitable concert…From my earnings it has become almost impossible to give additional financial support for the liberation of those esteemed men from the German Hell…[25]

On another occasion, on March 28, 1937, Einstein wrote to Boas seeking help in obtaining a scholarship for Rudolph Kayser, a German Jewish author who escaped from the Nazis and immigrated to America. It was a letter of introduction to Boas for Kayser's wife. Rudolph Kayser had written books on Spinoza and Kant and had been editor of the noted literary journal, *Die neue Rundshau* (Fisher-Verlag). He was planning to write a book on the intellectual history of the 19th century. Einstein wrote,

> I'm writing to you because it has come to my attention that you have a connection to a scholarship fund. All I can say is that the award of a scholarship in this particular case would be most appropriate, in my opinion, and that I would [be] very much pleased if such an award could be made.[26]

During his professional career, Franz Boas was given many awards and honorary degrees (Figure 139). In addition to the Ph.D. he earned at Kiel in 1881, in 1909 he received an honorary L.L.D at Clark University on the occasion of the twentieth anniversary of the founding of the school, which was also his anniversary of joining their faculty. He also received an honorary D.Sc. at Oxford University, and like degrees at Graz in 1923, and Columbia University in 1929.

Figure 139. Franz Boas in his study, Grantwood, New Jersey, 1930s (America Philosophical Society).

In 1931 his Ph.D., which he had earned at Kiel University in 1881 expired on the 50th anniversary of the award; he was invited to return to have it renewed. This, of course, was an excuse to present him with additional honors. His Ph.D. was renewed and he was also given an honorary M.D. After his return, standing in the dining room in Grantwood, he told me of his visit to Germany and of his M.D. degree. He said that they tried to think of a degree that he did not have and finally settled on the M.D. With a twinkle in his eye, he said "They could have given me a doctorate in theology."

One of his greatest honors was his election to the American Philosophical Society in Philadelphia on April 19, 1935, thus joining other scientists of the 20th century, including, in part, Marie Curie, Thomas A. Edison, Albert Einstein, Gerty T. Cori, Elizabeth Cady Stanton, as well as 123 recipients of the Nobel Prize. Other anthropologist members included Alfred L. Kroeber and Margaret Mead, both students of Boas.

Benjamin Franklin founded the prestigious American Philosophical Society in Philadelphia in 1743. Its earliest members included Franklin, Thomas Jefferson, George Washington, John Adams, Alexander Hamilton, Thomas Paine, Benjamin Rush, James Madison, Charles Wilson Peale, and John Marshall. Fifteen Signers of the Declaration of Independence and sixteen Signers of the United States Constitution were represented. While Thomas Jefferson was president of the Society, General Lafayette and Meriwether Lewis were elected to membership. Since that time, others members have included, in part, John J. Audubon, Charles Darwin, and Ralph Waldo Emerson. It is interesting to note that Franz Boas's voluminous ethnological observations on the Indians of the Pacific Northwest were preceded by those of another Society member, Meriwether Lewis. The latter's diaries on the Lewis and Clark Expedition (1803-1806) included vast amounts of ethnological data on the Indians of the upper Central Plains, the Rocky Mountains, and the present states of Oregon and Washington.[27]

On May 11, 1936, *TIME* magazine wrote an article about Franz Boas, dedicating its cover to him (Figure 140). It was the occasion of his retirement from the Department of Anthropology at Columbia University, an association he had had for forty years and where he had been chairman of Department for thirty-seven years.[28] Boas had many other honors bestowed on him, was a member of "all the national honor societies in science,"[1] as well as an honorary or corresponding member of at least twenty-five foreign scientific societies. The foreign countries represented included Germany (Berlin, Frankfurt, Würzburg, Hamburg, Stuttgart), England, France (Paris), Austria (Vienna), Norway, Sweden (Stockholm), Denmark, Belgium (Brussels), Italy (Florence, Rome), Russia (Moscow), and Mexico.[29]

On April 20, 1940, Franz Boas was honored by receiving the annual award of the Teacher's Union "for outstanding services in the cause of education for democracy." The Teacher's Union awarded same medal to

Figure 140. *TIME* magazine cover photograph by R H. Hoffmann, honoring Franz Boas on his retirement from Columbia University, May 11, 1936 (*TIME* magazine).

Eleanor Roosevelt the previous year. In awarding the medal to Boas, Dr. Jerome Davis,

> declared that the distinguished anthropologist has "blasted" the Nazi theory that the Jews are an inferior race...You have been a distinguished teacher, a citizen who always acts for the public good, a world renowned scholar.[30]

In replying, Boas said,

> We cannot disregard the questions of intellectual and spiritual freedom of the individual. It is only when our children and young people will learn not to regard individuals as a member of a class or race, but to judge them according to their own value, that we will be able to overcome prejudices. Individual freedom and the feeling of social obligation must go hand in hand in order to reach the end that we have in view.[30]

Figure 141. Participants in trans-Atlantic round table radio discussion in 1941. Seated left to right: Harold Urey, Waldemar Kaempffert, Eve Curie and Franz Boas *(Newsweek)*.

Boas also participated in a trans-Atlantic radio discussion on September 27, 1941, in regard to "a world free of war and tyranny." With early radio, this was a very special event. It tied in with the International Conference on Science and World Order in London and was broadcast by the NBC-Red Network and the BBC. Participants in London included biologist Julian S. Huxley, Professor A. V. Hill, Nobel Laureate in physics, and physicist S. Blackett. Those in the New York studio included Franz Boas, Harold Urey, Nobel Prize winner in chemistry, Waldemar Kaempffert, science editor of *The New York Times*, and Eve Curie, author, lecturer, and daughter of Pierre and Marie Curie (Figure 141). Boas emphasized that one of the primary missions of scientists in the future must be,

> To see to it that those who control education are permeated by the conviction that it is one of their prime duties to set free the minds of the youth of our generation so that the young may learn to recognize bias and prejudice, that they will become learners of truth for the sake of truth.[31]

Looking toward the future again, the newspaper *PM Daily* on January 4, 1943, published an interview with Franz Boas on the question, *"What Are We Going to Do With the Germans?"* He had been interviewed a few weeks before his death (Figure 142). The views of foreign correspondent Dorothy Thompson, physicist Albert Einstein, and anthropologist Earnest Hooten accompanied his response. Boas's response to questions was, in part,

> Q: How deeply into the German ruling class will we have to cut to eliminate Fascism in Germany?
>
> A: The whole present ruling clique ought to be eliminated.
>
> Q: In what way? Tried, executed, put in concentration camps?
>
> A: No, in insane asylums
>
> Q: Do you think there is hope for a democratic Germany.
>
> A: I don't see why not.[32]

Figure 142. A newspaper Sketch of Franz Boas (*PM*, New York, January 4, 1943).

Franz Boas wrote a series of revealing letters to his niece, Elizabeth (Bessie) Krackowizer Johnson. Bessie was the daughter of Emil Krackowizer, the brother of Marie Boas. When Bessie was a teenager, she lived in the Boas home in Grantwood and became an integral part of the family. Her mother had died when she was a young girl and her father was unable to care for her at that time. After leaving Grantwood, she married (twice), had five children from both marriages, and lived in California. Between 1935 and 1939, Franz wrote to her unburdening his anxieties and attempting to keep her up-to-date with his family. The following are some of the poignant excerpts of these letters.[33]

> This is always a bad month for me [January]. There are so many sad memories. On the 12th is the birthday of our baby that we lost [Hete], on the 20th it was ten years since Henry was killed...the 7th of Feby. is his birthday – and so it goes. I am probably a foolish old man, but the memories of early times are always freshest on these days. Do you realize that on Dec. 16 it was four years since aunt Marie died?...
>
> My great trouble is my concern about my sisters and their families. On account of the insane policies of the Hitler crowd they have lost their little savings and their incomes and I have to see to it that they get out of Germany and get reestablished somewhere else. Then all the strict regulations against immigration are in the way and make it increasingly difficult to reestablish them. One of my sisters, Tante Toni, is here now. My youngest sister with her youngest son is in Rio de Janiero...I have to support her. Ernst is going to take care of one of his cousins with wife and child [Urbachs]. So there remain three more with their families to take care of and I do not know yet how I can manage it. Besides this there is the endless flood of scientists who are driven out of Germany. There is not a mail in which I do not get frantic appeals for help, but I am absolutely at the end of my resources. I mean we cannot find anything for them. It is the craziest and at the same time most tragic condition you can imagine...I wish I could see you some time again, but I fear my traveling days are over. I have to think all the time of how to preserve my strength, because whenever I overdo it, I get completely played out...Nevertheless, when I compare the amount of work I accomplish with that of many others of my age or even much younger, I pick up courage again...Helene's boys are almost young men now...Helene is doing some work for me and I am enjoying it very much having her help. Ernst has come to be a highly respected member of the medical profession...His eldest boy, Donald...is very tall and interested particularly in mechanics. The second, Norman, is in the age [13] which they are fresh, little imps. He is very intelligent and I have good hopes of him. The youngest, Barbara, is now 7 years old and a darling, lovely...and a good sport...Trudel, I believe, a replica of Tante Marie. She has red hair and the sweetest face...
>
> In July...I stayed in Grantwood. Helene was up here. Frances [Franziska] and her family were with me and the family [Urbachs] of one of

my nephews which I had come here [from Germany] because his life has been made impossible by the swine who are governing Germany nowadays...All this is very hard to bear. I do not mean the help, which I am thankful I can give, but the scandalous persecution that breaks up the lives of innumerable people – and not by any means only of Jews, but of everyone who dares to disagree with the government. I am swamped with letters of Germans of Jewish descent who want to emigrate because they cannot stand the oppression...

We are at present particularly concerned about my sister Hete. She has been with us since December [3 months] and since that time conditions in Germany have come to be so bad that I do not want her to go back. Now the question is how to get her in. She will go to Cuba towards the end of this month to try and get an immigration visa. For that purpose we had to get all her papers from Germany and heaven knows what else. Maybe I'll go along to help her. She is the last one of our family to leave Germany. You cannot imagine how all these things weigh on me...

I am driven so hard with my work and with claims that...I am overwhelmed. I have not the strength I used to have. My eighty years begin to tell. I cannot walk without getting short of breath and my heart troubles me too often. Still, as long as I have the strength I will not give in...

I have to tell you sad news today...aunt Helen [Meyer, sister of Marie Boas] passed away. Ernst, that is my son, was there before and when she died...Now I am the last of our generation in the Krackowizer family and who knows how long I may last. I suppose you know that my heart is not of the best and that I have to avoid all bodily exertion. If I do, I am not troubled, but every now and then there are disagreeable disturbances. I have had this now for eight years, and I am not much worse. So it may go on a few years longer...I was so glad you saw Fritzi [Franziska] and Trudel this summer. Trudel is the image of aunt Marie and she is my idol. Tante Helene [Meyer] died on the date of my Gertrud's death - 15 years ago. I have never felt the same since all that misfortune, Gerturd, Henry, aunt Marie came over me – but I ought not to complain. Helene makes my life happy. I am proud of Ernst's devotion to the ideals of what a physician should be and of the general respect in which he is held and I am glad of the way Frances has developed. I myself must not complain either, for I can still work as a scientist and have the opportunity to make myself useful in matters pertaining to the public need...I was overwhelmed with greetings on my birthday, from the President [F. D. Roosevelt], Senators, Secretaries of the Cabinet, scientists, labor unions, and conservatives – without regard of party. It was more than what I deserved. Let me hear from you, dear child. I always think of you with deep affection...

On December 21, 1942, Franz Boas, invited a few associates to join him at an informal luncheon in the Faculty Room of Columbia University, to honor Professor Paul Rivet. The latter was considered the dean of

French anthropology and was teaching at Columbia University at that time, having escaped from France after the Nazis overran Paris in 1940. According to Claude Lévi-Strauss, a French anthropologist who attended the luncheon, it was the coldest day he had ever experienced. Boas arrived early, as vital and enthusiastic as ever, wearing "A very deplorable stained fur cap – probably from his Eskimo days." While Boas was speaking and having observed, "I have proved a point about race," he suddenly received a "shock," collapsed, and fell back in his chair. Lévi-Strauss, sitting next to him, quickly got up to help but determined that he was already dead. His comment later was that Boas was "One of the last intellectual giants."[34,35k]

The funeral services were held in the living room of his Grantwood home. Present were his three children, Helene, Ernst, and Franziska, with their spouses. Four of his six grandchildren were present, Donald, Norman and Barbara Boas, and Gertrud Michelson. Robert and Philip Yampolsky were in the Armed Forces and unable to attend. A small string ensemble was present with a pianist at Grosspapa's piano. As I recall, they played selections from Beethoven. The open casket was placed on the east side of the room at precisely the spot where the Christmas tree had been placed every year for over thirty years. Standing next to the casket, loving eulogies were given by Helene and Ernst. It was a sad and overwhelming experience, a vision that has revisited me repeatedly for over sixty years. Franz was buried in Dale Cemetery in Ossining, New York with Marie, Gertrud, Henry, and members of Marie's family, near the memorial stone of little Hete.

## References and Notes

1. Stocking, George W., Jr. Biography of Franz Boas in *Dictionary of American Biography*, 10 volumes and 8 supplements, American Council of Learned Societies, Charles Scribner's Sons, New York, 1961.

2. Boas, Franz. *Boas Says He'll Vote for FDR, Because...*, in newspaper *PM*, October 25, 1940 (A lengthy interview with him with an analysis of his position).

3. Huber, Thomas. Translator and interpreter of the Boas-Hindenburg letter, 2002.

4. Boas, Franz. Letter to President Paul von Hindenburg, New York, March 27, 1933. Library of the American Philosophical Society (A very important letter reflecting some of the reasons for his position during World War I).

---

[k] Only six weeks earlier Franz Boas had revised his last will and testament, witnessed by Ruth Benedict, Ruth W. Bryant, and Bertha Edel.[35]

5. Mitchell, Joseph. *MAN – With Variations*, in the *New York World Telegram,* November, 1, 1937 (Franz Boas, his racial theories, and the Nazis).
6. Healey, Barth. *The Burning of Books, the Shattering of Glass, the War*, in the *New York Times*, November 6, 1988.
7. Boas, Franz. In *TIME* magazine, May 11, 1936.
8. Boas, Franz. Letter to his children, Helene, Ernst, and Franziska, Grantwood, New Jersey, November 20, 1933. Norman F. Boas collection.
9. Boas, Franz. Letter from Dr. Jürgens to Franz Boas, March 1, 1939 and a letter from Franz Boas to Dr. Jürgens, March 27, 1939. Norman F. Boas collection.
10. Kroeber, Alfred L. Biography of Franz Boas in *American Anthropologist,* N.S., Volume 45, No. 3, Part 2, July-September, 1943.
11. Boas, Franz. Telegram to Justice Louis Brandeis, June 15, 1936. American Philosophical Society.
12. Lewis, Herbert. *The Passion of Franz Boas*, a lecture. Personal communication, March 20, 2000.
13. Boas family genealogy. Prepared by Norman F. Boas (A copy is in the Library of the American Philosophical Society).
14. Hall of Names, Central Repository of Holocaust Victims at Yad Vashem, Israel (A data base which includes millions of names of those whose who died at the hands of the Nazis during World War II).
15. Boas, Franz. Letter to Norman F. Boas, October 15, 1939.
16. Boas, Ernst P. Medical record of Franz Boas. Norman F. Boas collection.
17. Boas, Franz. Letter to Norman F. Boas, March 26, 1940. Norman F. Boas collection.
18. Boas, Franz. In *The New York Times,* July 10, 1939.
19. Boas, Franz. In *The Herald Tribune*, July 10, 1939 (Round-robin letter to Boas reproduced in its entirely).
20. Roosevelt, Franklin D. Letter to Franz Boas, July 5, 1939. Norman F. Boas collection.
21. Boas, Franz. Retained copy of letter to President Franklin D. Roosevelt, July 1939. American Philosophical Society.
22. Deloria, Ella Cara. *Waterlily*. Biographical sketch by Agnes Picotte. Afterword by Raymond J. DeMallie. University of Nebraska Press, 1988.
23. Marshall, George. Letter to Albert Einstein, February 18, 1941. American Philosophical Society.
24. Boas, Franz. Albert Einstein correspondence. Library of the American Philosophical Society.
25. Einstein, Albert. Letter to Franz Boas, February 4, 1934. Courtesy of Stephen E. Boas.
26. Einstein, Albert. Letter to Franz Boas, March 28, 1937. Norman F. Boas collection.
27. American Philosophical Society, *An Invitation from the American Philosophical Society*, 12pp, Philadelphia, n.d.
28. Boas, Franz. In *TIME* magazine, May 11, 1936 (Cover with photograph of Boas and feature story on his retirement).

29. *American Men of Science*, 5th Edition, The Science Press, New York, 1933.
30. *The New York Times*, story headlined, *DR. BOAS RECEIVES TEACHERS' AWARD,* April 21, 1940.
31. *The New York Times,* story headlined, *SCIENTISTS SEE NEW FREE WORLD*, September 28, 1941.
32. Boas, Franz. Interview in newspaper *PM,* New York, January 4, 1943.
33. Boas, Franz. Letters (7) to Bessie Krackowizer Johnson, January 29, 1935 through October 8, 1939 (Norman F. Boas collection, received through generosity of Bessie's daughter and the author's cousin, Judith Johnson O'Brien).
34. Boas, Franz. Last Will and Testament, November 9, 1942 (Norman F. Boas collection).
35. Boas, Franz. Video documentary film titled *Franz Boas 1858-1942*. A production of Public Broadcasting Associates, Inc., Boston, Massachusetts, Odyssey Series, a PBS presentation, 1980.

# CHAPTER X

## THE LEGACY OF FRANZ BOAS

On the day following the death of Franz Boas, journalist Albert Deutsch wrote the following tribute in the newspaper *PM,*

> In the death of Franz Boas yesterday the world lost one of its greatest men, science one of its outstanding leaders, mankind one of its best friends, democracy one of its staunchest defenders...Boas did prove, by incontestable scientific facts, the essential unity of all races and the fallacy of the myth that any particular race is inherently superior to others. He was the St. George of anthropology who destroyed the race-myth dragon forever, insofar as scientific validity is concerned...He represented the apotheosis of scientific integrity, following truth wherever it led, regardless of personal consequences. He fought fiercely and unceasingly for the cause of academic freedom, and led many causes in behalf of colleagues whose positions were endangered because of their unpopular ideas...Few men of our time have loved truth as passionately as did Boas. Few pursued it with such relentless courage. Few possessed that rare combination of scholarship, scientific achievement and democratic idealism that he represented.[1]

There was a deluge of letters of sympathy following the death of Boas. Some were very special. Daniel Cranmer, the husband of Agnes, (granddaughter of George Hunt), wrote to Helene,

> The sorrowful tidings of our deep affliction reached me today and, oh my dear Helene, if only sympathy were like waves of light, how the rays would pour from my heart to illumine the gloomy veil of grief which wraps you in its somber folds.

It was in 1933 that Dan Cranmer visited the Boas home in Grantwood to work with Franz and Helene on the Kwakiutl Grammar. In the same letter he wrote that "he would sing mourning songs at an upcoming potlatch" and that the Kwakiutl Indians of Fort Rupert (British Columbia) had already sung mourning songs for Boas. Gloria Webster, the daughter of Dan Cranmer, supplied us with a copy of her lecture in which she noted,

> We strengthen what is left of our culture after the white people did their best to destroy it. In that task we are more fortunate than most indigenous groups, because we have a strong foundation to build on and for that we owe much to *Hi_dzaKwal's* (Franz Boas) and *Kixitasu'* (George Hunt)...I wonder how many people whom other anthropologists have studied have the same feeling of respect and affection that our people had and still have for Franz Boas?[2]

With his death, the family no longer needed the Grantwood home. Cecil and Helene, who had lived there virtually all of their married lives, chose to move back to New York City and ultimately retired to their home in Cornwall Bridge. The three surviving children, Helene, Ernst, and Franziska, planned the disposition of the house, its contents, the library, and papers of their father. The house was sold with most of the original furniture for about $3000.00. All of the tools that Franz had used on his Arctic expedition had been stored in the back of the coat closet in the front hall during his entire residence there. Unfortunately they were discarded in haste. The family retained some of the more sentimental pieces. His library, which included thousands of books and pamphlets from his home study, stacks, and his office at Columbia University, was sold to Northwestern University as a special collection. It was done in the midst of World War II; the Germans had defaulted on the contract to receive them as a gift, thus placing the decision in the hands of his children. Anthropologist Melville J. Herskovits, who was on the faculty at Northwestern and who had received his graduate degree from Boas in 1923, made arrangements for the disposition and sale of this collection to Northwestern University. In 1943 four hundred pamphlets, virtually all of Boas's reprints, were donated to the Library of Columbia University.

His huge collection of papers was donated to the Library of the American Philosophical Society (A.P.S.) in Philadelphia. These included thousands of family and professional letters, speeches, manuscripts, diaries, scores of photographs, sketches, and maps. By virtue of having the Franz Boas papers at the A. P. S., with its vast research potential, other anthropologists have since added their papers to the collections at the A.P.S. Included are his students Frank Speck, Elsie Clews Parsons, Edward Sapir, and Ashley Montagu. The papers of his son, Ernst P. Boas, have also been given to the A. P. S. library.[a] For many years the Franz Boas papers have been among the most widely used research collection in the library. According to Robert Cox, Curator, "When the papers of Franz Boas came to Philadelphia…it would have been hard to predict the impact they would have upon the collection of the A.P.S."[3] This collection of anthropological papers is unquestionably the greatest such repository in America. "Among the most frequently used collections are the Benjamin Franklin papers, the papers of artist Charles Wilson Peale and family, and the papers of Franz Boas, founder of American anthropology."[4]

---

[a] In 1981 this author donated the papers of Dr. Ernst P. Boas to the Library of the American Philosophical Society. Ernst, the father of this writer and son of Franz Boas, had a distinguished career in medicine.

Franz Boas was a remarkable individual in many ways. A man of small physical stature, a frail sickly child, he overcame these shortcomings by seeking adventure and enduring hardships that no ordinary person would have faced. His adventures in the Arctic are the prime examples, but he never hesitated to expose himself to danger to pursue his goals, particularly when it came to field research in the Pacific Northwest. He was combative in the academic sphere when he was certain that he was right, in spite of many obstacles. His positions, often controversial at the time, usually turned out to be correct.

A number of observers have called Boas a genius, a word defined as a person with "extraordinary intellectual power especially as manifested in creative activity." This is a term rarely used nowadays. Ernest R. Trattner included Boas in his *Story of the World's Great Thinkers.*[5] All the biographees were credited with theories of the earth and universe, from the Theory of the Solar System by Copernicus to the Theory of Relativity by Einstein. All have altered our thinking of the universe and mankind. He credits Boas with the Theory of Man. Among others he lists are Freud, Pasteur, Marx, Darwin, Malthus, and Lavoisier. Of Boas, Trattner wrote, in reference to *The Mind of Primitive Man,*

> A book which is interwoven by chains of reasoning as strong as they are gripping...Boas accomplishes the gigantic task of putting in order the enormous muddle of provable data, binding them together and interconnecting all parts into a unitary structure. You cannot read him without an innate respect for the scientist who unmistakably displays exceptional penetration, integrity and courage...After a brief introductory paragraph Boas begins at once to pulverize the naive assumption of the superiority of European nations...that the white race represents the highest type of perfection...Boas patiently examined what purports to be evidence and found that there is nothing to warrant the glibly announced biological inferiority of so-called backward peoples...there is no evidence whatsoever to warrant one race's claiming inherent mental superiority over another.[5]

Alfred L. Kroeber, student, associate, and close friend of Boas for almost forty years, has recorded his astute personal observations of the intellect, personality and motivations of Franz Boas[6]

> His intelligence was as massive as it was acute, as wide-ranging as sound. It was fortified by an unquenchable perseverance, an infinite capacity for work...No anthropologist saw as many new problems, opened up so many novel approaches. So far as criticism goes, he was above all self-critical...[He had] an ardent, unsparing drive for understanding, completely controlled by every critical check...In all his enormous output is it difficult to find even minute instances of error of either fact or procedure. On the side of personality, inner integrity of character and rugged self-reliance were perhaps his outstanding qualities...Boas's emotions were as powerful as his intellect, although his control of them was

> so rigorous that he might seem cold...His convictions sprang from so deep down, and manifested themselves so powerfully, that to the run of shallower men, there was something ultra-human or unnatural about him. In consequence he was literally worshipped by some of those that came under his influence, whereas others were dismayed or even repelled...His was a nature that could not fulfill itself without making some enemies, but a larger number of loyal friends and devoted followers...Hunger or thirst, heat or cold, danger or exposure, exertion or luxury, he took in the same stride. Discomfort he disdained to recognize; often perhaps he hardly felt it, so strong were the drives of his energy...Boas would automatically fall into the category of genius as currently rated. That word has however become so ambiguous that further characterization is necessary...Boas was rather a rugged, massive, powerful personality of great caliber, who drove his engine through to the accomplishment of whatever the task in hand seemed to be, rather than following the easier leads of congenital predilections. He was of the Titans – a self-disciplined Titan: a Prometheus rather and an Apollo or Hermes. In many ways the epithet of greatness describes him better that that of genius.

Franz Boas had a remarkable mental facility for storing information. It has already been pointed out that he able to speak scores of different languages – that he could sit for hours "listening" to music by scanning musical scores. One occasion, which I shall never forget, took place when I was in high school. One of my classmates at the Ethical Culture Fieldston School in New York, Hallowell Bowser, was extremely anxious to meet my grandfather. Hal wanted to become a writer when I knew him, and did become distinguished in the field of literature, especially in his association with the *Saturday Review of Literature.* With arrangements made, we went to Grantwood. Hal and my grandfather quickly became engrossed in discussing literature. On mentioning a classic that Hal was currently reading, my grandfather took over, recited the plot and mentioned the characters in the book, to our utter amazement. Hal asked if he were reading the book at present. "Oh no! I read that book about – fifty years ago."

Anthropologist Gladys Reichard, a close collaborator of Boas, recorded some observations on his thought process,

> He could wend his way through a vast morass of notes, however unwieldy or heterogeneous they might be, and see the ultimate conclusion even as a hound can follow a scent. This was true whether the material was his own or someone else's...The strongest rocks in Boas's self-built monument are his texts, his belief that what people record of themselves in their own words will in the last analysis reveal their motivations and ideas most accurately.[7]

Boas had a prodigious drive, physically and mentally. His collection of data and notes from his fieldwork was monumental and his scientific recordings were encyclopedic. This is evidenced by the huge collection of personal and professional letters, scientific notes, papers, and publications that are available to the public for research in the Library of the American Philosophical Society in Philadelphia. His publications, number over 650, including many books that are said to number over 15,000 pages. His professional correspondence encompassed over 35,000 letters, not to mention his personal correspondence, which also numbered in the thousands. It is estimated that there are over 60,000 items in the collection. This in itself is truly remarkable, but even more so when one considers that most of his earlier letters, manuscripts and diaries were handwritten.[6,8]

"We hold these Truths to be self-evident, that all Men are created equal."

On October 18, 1858, Abraham Lincoln wrote,

> I have expressly disclaimed all intention to bring about social and political equality between the white and black races...I have made it equally plain that I think the Negro is included in the word 'men' used in the Declaration of Independence. I believe the declaration that "all men are created equal" is the great fundamental principle upon which our free institutions rest; that Negro slavery is violative of the principle...[9]

The Declaration of Independence was the foremost and primary reference that Lincoln used to address his interpretation of slavery. In his time, however, it would have been inconceivably difficult for him to press for social or political equality. In 1776, African Americans and Native Americans were not looked upon as "men" to be included with their Caucasian brethren who were, "endowed...with certain unalienable rights, that are among these are Life, Liberty, and the Pursuit of Happiness."

The last twenty years of the life Franz Boas were devoted to a relentless political fight against the forces of racism based on his scientific evidence that "All men are created equal." He expanded the meaning of the Declaration of Independence, beyond that which Lincoln was able to do, by further establishing that all men are created with the same universal mental endowment, thus discarding the premise that "primitive man" (African Americans, Native Americans and other non-Caucasian groups) were less endowed than the "highly civilized" white man.

During the latter part of his life, his charges of racism were targeted primarily at Hitler and the Nazis. He, in fact, became the leading voice through the organizations he headed, through lectures, and through the media, and was known throughout the world for his unremitting fight against the forces of bigotry.

When Franz Boas attended school, anthropology as a defined science, barely existed – certainly not in America. The subdivisions of science were in their relative infancy. A scientist, like a general practitioner in medicine, was well versed in many disciplines. There was also a lot less to learn. Boas, for example, had a sound training in chemistry, mathematics, geography, theoretical physics, and the natural sciences. For his final chosen field, he was exposed to physical anthropology, psychology, some ethnology, and psychological anthropology. To meet special needs, he also studied meteorology, navigation, and linguistics. Although there were archeologists, linguists, naturalists and some anthropologists in America when Boas arrived, there was no formal definition of anthropology as a discipline. Even Harvard College, the Smithsonian Institution, and American museums were more oriented toward archeology rather than anthropology.

Boas was the first to truly define anthropology as a scientific discipline. His formulation of anthropology as a science in America met few academic obstacles – there was little challenge in the field. Anthropologists in America had little or no training in the field and majored in other subjects (e.g. archeology, zoology, art, geology). His mentor, Frederic Ward Putnam, primarily an archeologist, did not even attend college. Boas was a pioneer in America in the fields of linguistics, folklore, and native art. He was criticized for not writing about or acknowledging earlier anthropologists in America. This was not true. He clearly gave credit to the contributions of John Wesley Powell at the Smithsonian Institution, Frederic Ward Putnam and to Daniel Garrison Brinton, archeologist and ethnologist at the University of Pennsylvania.[10]

When one reflects on the legacy of Boas, it is hard to conceive that this man was the creator of a scientific discipline that spawned several generations of graduates and has since attracted millions of students nationwide.

Of course, there are often detractors to the accomplishments of those in academia; the ones who have had the greatest impact are often the principal targets. Boas was no exception – but during his lifetime criticism of his specific scientific achievements was minimal. It was primarily after his death that he was attacked at various levels. As is often the case, criticism by others in the same field helps to advance the careers of the critics. Criticism must always be examined in light of changing mores and times and must be examined for the evidence supporting such claims. One of his more belligerent protesters is "alleged to have said that Boas set American anthropology back by 30 years."[11] There was essentially no American anthropology to "set back" when Boas arrived! He was also accused of focusing too much attention on the Native Americans of the Pacific Northwest. Any scientist has his favorite projects with which he may spend an inordinate amount of time. This was true of Boas and the fieldwork he and his students did with Native Americans. More important to him was the fact that all of these cultures were rapidly disappearing; he was impelled by a desperate drive to record all facets of their cultures before they were lost forever. Most important, however, his in-depth studies of the cultures of Native Americans contributed immensely to the understanding of the ethnology of non-Caucasian cultures and contributed to his scientific proof that there were no inherent differences between the diverse cultures of the world – "cultural relativism."

It is not, however, for this author to render a judgment on the analysis the post-Boasian era. A more scholarly analysis is called for by those with more expertise in anthropology. Denigration and disparagement of an individual must be separated from honest well-supported revisionist evidence. Professor Herbert Lewis has done a thorough and admirable analysis of many of the claims alluded to here.[12] After reviewing a multitude of criticisms of Boas's work, Lewis concludes,

> Franz Boas was not an ethical relativist but believed in and spent his life working and fighting for certain values: equal opportunity for all, understanding and mutual appreciation among peoples, freedom of speech and inquiry...he was...an opponent of racism, ethnocentrism, inequality, chauvinism, imperialism, war, censorship, and political cant and mind-fogging sloganeering...there is no way he can be seen as having contributed to "scientific racism"...I maintain that Franz Boas was an outstanding and admirable human being, both in what he attempted and what he achieved; in his values and the way in which he put them into practice; in the costs he was willing to bear for his beliefs, even when these went against his personal and even his scientific interests...The aim of the critical analyst is to tear apart the text in order to reveal its contradictions and hidden assumptions. But we should expect the critics to <u>demonstrate</u> their claims, not just assert them...Franz Boas both professed and acted upon the finest and highest ideals of his (and our) culture and time...concern for the dominated and oppressed, respect for "others" as individuals as well as for other cultures; tolerance and humane dealing; and respect for the eternal quest for knowledge about ourselves and the world...I believe most of us would still want to be judged by how well we served these interests. [12,13]

As stated in the first chapter, Boas frankly acknowledged his Jewishness in the resumé he prepared for applying to Heidelberg University. Franz had formal religious instruction and confirmation, primarily to satisfy his grandparents, but never made a true commitment to a religious faith – and thus was "spared the struggle against religious dogma."[14] Nevertheless, his religious training and family values were sufficient to imbue him with the highest ethical standards that guided his entire life. Although he never practiced a ritualistic religious role as a Jew, others reminded him of his heritage for the rest of his life. He apparently was not faced with this problem to any significant degree in Minden. It was not until he attended Heidelberg, Bonn, and Kiel Universities that he encountered frank anti-Semitism. It was there, as a matter of honor that he responded to anti-Semitic remarks by dueling. Ethnic slurs were totally unacceptable to him and called for a resolute response. His decisive nature was well established by this time. He could not be dissuaded from his Arctic adventure. He relentlessly pursued all goals that he set for himself. He was intolerant of bigots and those who exploited mankind in any form. He was intolerant of those whose scientific contributions deviated from the truth. Although many of his acquaintances were Jews by virtue of family relations and associations, he was not selective of friends based on their religious heritage.

When Franz Boas married Marie Krackowizer, he married into a Catholic family. The Krackowizers had already abandoned their beliefs in Catholicism at the time that Franz and Marie were married. Marie, however, did join the Unitarian Church. Dr. Abraham Jacobi, his uncle by marriage, was a Jew; Carl Schurz was born into a Catholic family. Like the Boas and Krackowizer families, Jacobi, and Schurz had also abandoned formal religious beliefs. Leslie White accused Boas of favoring only Jewish students.[12] It was an unpleasant and uncalled for assault on his integrity. For his entire professional and private life he worked with and befriended individuals of all faiths – Jews included. One only has to look at the roster of some of his better known non-Jewish students and associates, Alfred Kroeber, Ruth Fulton, Elsie Clews Parson, Gladys Reichard, Margaret Mead, Ruth Benedict, Frederic Ward Putnam, Livingston Farrand, Henry Herbert Donaldson, Frank Speck, W. J. McGee, Zora Neale Hurston, and literally hundreds of others. Frank has charged that Boas was not Jewish enough.[15] It is more to the point that Boas's relationship and compatibility with others was on a social and intellectual level, where religious affiliations were of no importance in his relationships with others.

**References and Notes**

1. Deutsch, Albert. Column in the newspaper *PM*, December 22, 1942 (A tribute to Franz Boas).

2. Webster, Gloria. A speech titled, *Consumers, Then and Now, A Centenary Celebration of Franz Boas and the Jesup North Pacific Expedition, 1897-1997*, American Museum of Natural History, New York, November 14, 1997 (A revealing talk with observations on Boas, George Hunt, and the Kwakiutl culture).
3. *News From Library Street*, publication of the American Philosophical Society, Philadelphia, September 2001 (Report on the Montagu collection and other anthropological papers at the A.P.S.).
4. *An Invitation from the American Philosophical Society,"* 12pp, no date.
5. Trattner, Ernest R. T*he Story of the World's Great Thinkers*, The New Home Library, New York, 1938 I (An analysis of the contributions of Franz Boas on the questions of race).
6. Kroeber, Alfred. *FRANZ BOAS: THE MAN*, in Am*erican Anthropologist,* New Series, Vol. 45, No 3, Part 2, July-September, 1943 (Probably one of the best summations of Boas as a man, in all facets).
7. Reichard, Gladys. *Franz Boas and Folklore, American Anthropologist*, Vol. 45, No. 3, July-September, 1943.
8. Boas, Franz. *Guide to the Microfilm Collection of the Professional Paper of Franz Boas*, 1085pp in two volumes, Scholarly Resources, Inc., Wilmington, Delaware, 1972.
9. Boas, Franz. *Frederic Ward Putnam,* in *Science*, Vol. XLII, No. 1080, September 10, 1915 (He cites Frederic Ward Putnam, Daniel Garrison Brinton, and John Wesley Powell as the "founders of modern anthropology in America").
10. Lincoln, Abraham. Letter to James Nicholas Brown, October 18, 1858. In *The Collected Works of Abraham Lincoln*, Rutgers University Press, New Brunswick New Jersey, 1953.
11. Rohner, Ronald P. *The Boas Canon: A Posthumous Addition.* A review of *Kwakiutl Ethnography* by Helen Codere in *Science,* Vol. 158, October 20, 1967.
12. Lewis, Herbert S. *The Passion of Franz Boas* in *American Anthropologist*, Vol. 103 (2), pp 447-67, June 2001.
13. Lewis, Herbert S. *Boas, Darwin, Science, and Anthropology* in *Current Anthropology*, Vol. 42 (3), pp 381-406, June 2001.
14. Boas, Franz. Curriculum vitae in German, ca. 1876. From an English translation by Barbara Boas Crutchely – original in the Library of the American Philosophical Society.
15. Frank, Geyla. *Jews, Multiculturalism, and Boasian Anthropology*, American Anthropologist, Vol. 99 (4), 1997.

# EPILOGUE

Since the death of Franz Boas many scientific papers have been written with critiques and comments concerning Boas's contributions to anthropology. A number of brief biographies have been written of him, each of which covers only a segment of his life. He left a massive record of achievements including publications, manuscripts, and correspondence – so much in fact, that it would be virtually impossible for any single individual to write an all-inclusive biography. This was the experience of Professor Douglas Cole, who had planned to write a complete biography. Although Cole wrote a fine and critically researched memoir, he was only able to cover the first forty-eight years of the life of Boas. He had planned two volumes, but his project was interrupted by his untimely death. Some biographers have focused on his Baffin Island experiences, others on the Pacific Northwest, on his career at the American Museum of Natural History, his ethnography, or on Boas the man.

Some of the books by Franz Boas remain popular and available in reprint form, including *The Mind of Primitive Man, Race, Language and Culture, The Central Eskimo,* and *Primitive Art.* Some others of his out-of-print texts have been reprinted. Many may be found in the antiquarian and used book market.

After World War II, the City of Minden, his birthplace, named a street in his honor called *Franz Boas Strasse.*[1] Several years ago, I had the pleasure of giving reprints of Boas articles and a book from the library of Franz Boas to the Minden Archives. The book had his bookplate that showed the Minden Dom (Cathedral) as seen from inside an arch of the town hall built in ca.1280. It was a good opportunity to give some of his publications to Germany, a goal of Franz that was derailed in his lifetime because of the burning of his books by the Nazis.

Two documentary video films have been produced, highlighting the life of Franz Boas and his role in defining and establishing the disciplines of modern anthropology. One, *The Shackles of Tradition*, was part of a series titled *Strangers Abroad.* Other films in this series included documentaries on Sir Walter B. Spencer, William Rivers, Bronislaw Malinowski, Margaret Mead, and Sir Edward Evans-Pritchard.[2]

The other, *Franz Boas 1858-1942*, was presented on the Public Broadcasting System in the Odyssey Series, hosted by Claude Lévi-Strauss of the College de France. It focused primarily on Boas's fieldwork with the Indians of the Pacific Northwest. Participants included George W. Stocking, Jr., Gene Weltfish, William S. Willis, Jr., Margaret Blackman, Gloria C. Webster, Agnes Cranmer, William D. Sturtevant, Jay Ruby, Bill Holm, and Dell Hymes. Willis focused on the contribution that Boas made in examining the African American culture in the United

States. Boas, after studying the native cultures of the Arctic and the Pacific Northwest, in the twentieth century turned his attention to the ethnography of African Americans in a mixed racial society. He did more than anyone else, on a scientific basis, to dispel the idea that blacks were in any way inferior, physically or intellectually from white men. He persisted for the last half of his life in carrying this message forward with determination and vigor. Unfortunately Boas's racial theories were not well accepted by the public until the brutal practices of Adolph Hitler became known in the 1930s. He, nevertheless, had clearly laid the scientific groundwork establishing that there was no longer any justification for racial bias in any form.[3]

A brief comment must be made on the general pronunciation of our name as "Bo-az." Our family, including Franz and Marie Boas, their descendants, relatives, and close friends has always pronounced it "Bo-as," somewhat like the "as" in Thomas. The section in Webster's Dictionary on Biographical Names lists Franz Boas with his surname pronounced *'bō,az*. Regardless, we do not expect to change people's articulation of the name "Boas." In fact, we no longer correct those who mispronounce our name.

During the forty-five years that Franz Boas traveled to the Pacific Northwest, he literally spent over two years of his life visiting and doing fieldwork with the Native Americans there. On only one occasion with which we are familiar, in the summer of 1922, did Marie accompany him on a trip to British Columbia, the only family member to do so. They stayed in Victoria on Vancouver Island where Franz did research at the museum. In their free time they went mountain climbing together.[4] It was not for another 63 years that a Boas family member was to visit the Indians of British Columbia.[a] In 1985, our daughter, Barbara Johnson Boas, who was living in Portland, Oregon told us of a trip she had taken to Victoria to visit the Royal British Columbia Museum. While there, she went to the office of the anthropology division to seek information on the Hunt family. She introduced herself and, when asked, acknowledged that she was a descendant of Franz Boas. Coincidently, she was told that she had just missed seeing Gloria Webster, a descendant of George Hunt, who almost certainly would have wanted to see her. As we learned later, Gloria is a great granddaughter of George Hunt and the daughter of Daniel Cranmer who had worked with Boas on Kwakiutl texts. I remember meeting Cranmer when he stayed with my grandfather in Grantwood, New Jersey.

---

[a] Since 1985, four generations of Franz Boas's descendants have visited Alert Bay, the youngest being Rachel Johnson, his great-great granddaughter.

We learned that Gloria lives on an Indian reserve in Alert Bay, a village on a small island in Queen Charlotte Straits off the northeast side of Vancouver Island. We subsequently called her and she suggested that we pay her a visit. Unfortunately, the dates of our trip were at a time that she would not be home. Nevertheless, she insisted that we stay at her house. Although we were disappointed to miss her, Doris, Barbara, and I decided to travel to Alert Bay to visit her family and friends. We did stay at her home and were cordially hosted by Hans Amering, a friend of hers who was doing repairs on her house.

The setting is magnificent – a small island in the middle of the Straits and surrounded by high mountains. Gloria's house is located on the waterfront, overlooking the docks and fishing fleet of members of the reserve. We were warmly greeted by all of those who we met. We were the first members of the Boas family, since Franz, to visit one of his favorite places. Alert Bay is on the south side of Cormorant Island. The Indian reserve occupies the western half and the white population occupies the eastern half of the island.

Alert Bay is the home of the Nimpkish (*'Namgis*) band of the *kwakwaka'wakw*.[b] Many residents on the reserve are descendants of George Hunt who lived in Fort Rupert, a Kwakiult (*Kwagu'l*) Indian reserve. He was the son of a British father and Alaskan Indian mother. The Alert Bay reserve covers a large area with private homes and a large school building. There was also a very large "Big House" with beautifully carved cedar logs and a large central area where all communal events were held – dances, feasts, celebrations, and potlatches (Figure 143). Built in 1963, the Big House was truly remarkable in its construction and dimensions. The two post arches were 17 feet high and supported two 70-foot western red cedar logs, each measuring 3 feet in diameter and weighing five tons.[c] In the center of the roof was an opening to permit smoke from the fire on the dirt floor of the arena to escape. Fire is a very important component of many of the dances and meetings held in the Big House. It is also used for cooking.

In front of the Big House is the tallest totem pole in the world, standing 180 feet, so tall that long guy wires must secure it.

The U'mista Cultural Centre is a large building on north end of the reserve that is a combination of a museum and is a teaching center for all

---

[b] The *kwakwaka'wakw* are those who speak *kwak'wala*, a language common to most of the bands of Native Americans who live on Vancouver Island and in the southwestern part of British Columbia. Anthropologists for years have referred to many of these bands as Kwakiutl Indians; that is incorrect. The Kwakiutl band is represented only by those Native Americans who live in Fort Rupert, B.C. and their descendants.

[c] On August 29, 1997, the Alert Bay Big House was burned to the ground by an arsonist, but has been rebuilt in all its splendor.

Figure 143. The Big House in Alert Bay, ca.1970 (U'mista Cultural Centre, Alert Bay, British Columbia).

Figure 144. The U'mista Cultural Centre, as seen from the shoreline, 1985 (N.F.B.).

of its *kwakwaka'wakw* members (Figure 144). The history of the creation of this structure is complex, as related below.

In 1884 the Canadian government outlawed Indian potlatches, but did not strictly enforce this measure for many years. In the 1920s the government began to harass the few remaining tribes that conducted potlatches, primarily those of Alert Bay and Fort Rupert. In December 1921, Daniel Cranmer of Alert Bay sponsored the largest potlatch in memory, called the "Christmas Tree Potlatch" that was held on Village Island and lasted six days. This was a small native village southeast of Alert Bay in the Straits. It was a thriving small community with its own Big House. It is said that over three hundred people attended this great feast. When William Halliday, the Indian agent at Alert Bay, learned of this unlawful gathering, he was furious and threatened Cranmer and other members of the tribe with imprisonment unless they gave up all of their masks and ceremonial paraphernalia used in the potlatch. With little alternative, most cooperated. All of these artifacts were prized possessions, many of which had passed down through generations and had tremendous symbolic significance to their owners.[5]

Halliday sold thirty-three of the artifacts to George Heye for his Museum of the American Indian in New York. The bulk of the confiscated pieces was sent to the National Museum of Man in Ottawa; a portion of this was transferred to the Royal Ontario Museum in Toronto.[6] It took almost sixty years for the government to make amends and return the Ottawa and Toronto pieces. It took even longer to obtain the artifacts that had been in the Heye collection. Most have now been returned. Before releasing the masks and ceremonial paraphernalia from the Museum of Man, the Canadian government insisted that a suitable place be built to house them. Thus, the U'mista Cultural Centre was born. U'mista means the "Return of something important," a term sometimes used in reference to the return of a person after a kidnapping. The Centre has a special room where the masks are now on open display after being held hostage for so many years – a magnificent display of the remarkable artistry and a valuable cultural heritage of these people. In addition, there are museum cases with many fine exhibits of other ceremonial artifacts. The offices contain files dedicated to keeping historical records, doing research, and the housing of resource material for the teachers, who spend a great deal of time teaching the young people dances, tribal folklore, and their language, *kwak'wala.*

On the day after our arrival in Alert Bay, we were invited for luncheon by the board of Directors of the U'mista Cultural Centre at the Centre. It was a memorable event hosted by Bill Cranmer, Gloria's brother and tribal chief. Following a lunch of sockeye salmon, we were treated to a tour of the museum and viewed a showing of a video presentation of *A Box of Treasures*, essentially a history of the Cranmer potlatch and its sequelae.[7] The balance of our brief stay was spent talking with members of the cultural center and it board of directors – primarily in regard to the relationship between George Hunt and Franz Boas. Several of those present were direct descendents of Hunt (Figure 145). Before leaving, we visited a tribal elder, Agnes Cranmer, granddaughter of George Hunt, at her home. Agnes was the wife of Daniel Cranmer and the mother of eight children, including Gloria, Doug, Bill, and Roy. It was in Daniel and Agnes's house that Franz Boas stayed on his last visit to the Pacific Northwest in 1931 (Figure 146).

Figure 145. Shown left to right: Visitors Norman, Doris, and Barbara Boas at the U'mista Cultural Centre with hosts Douglas and William Cranmer. In the background is one of the four carved panels done by Doug, titled, "Bear and Wren," that had been on display at the 1970 Expo in Tokyo (N.F.B.).

Figure 146. Norman F. Boas and Agnes Cranmer on the porch of her house where Franz Boas last stayed in 1931. Photo taken in 1985 (N.F.B.).

Standing on her porch, before leaving, Agnes told me, "If it had not been for your grandfather and my grandfather, we would have no culture left," referring of course to the encyclopedic records that Boas and Hunt created of the *kwakwaka'wakw* – from linguistics, building canoes, erecting totem poles, folklore, potlatches, winter ceremonials to virtually all aspects of their culture. To this day, the Indians, to find out how "things used to be done," refer to Boas's publications. Boas is referred to frequently in the *U'mista News*, a regular publication of the U'mista Cultural Society. The affection held for Franz Boas has been carried forward to succeeding generations of Indians of the Northwest, particularly those of Alert Bay and Fort Rupert where he spent so much time. We left with some sadness with the brevity of our visit, but were determined to return.

It was not long after we arrived home that we again spoke with Gloria. In reconstructing the relationship between Franz Boas and George Hunt, we learned that they first met in 1886. Therefore, the year 1986 would be the one-hundredth anniversary of their first meeting. Gloria suggested that we celebrate this occasion. We quickly seconded this suggestion and both concluded that there should be a family reunion of the descendants of each family, to be held in British Columbia. At that time the descendants of Franz Boas numbered thirty-five individuals covering four generations. With spouses, the number totaled forty-two. Of this number, thirty-two signed up for the double reunion. We all agreed to meet in Vancouver, British Columbia on September 19, 1986. When the time arrived, Boas family members arrived from London, England, Florida, Oregon, Colorado, New York and the New England states. We almost filled a fifty-seat AIR-BC prop plane for the final leg of our trip, from Vancouver to Port Hardy on the northern tip of Vancouver Island. In the meantime over two hundred descendants of George Hunt were preparing for this great occasion.

Upon arriving at the airport in Port Hardy, we were greeted by contingents from Alert Bay and Fort Rupert, including Gloria Webster and Kwakiutl Chief Bill Hunt and were transported by car and ferry to Alert Bay.

On arrival our accommodations were in the private homes of our hosts. We were fully occupied and entertained by four major events – a boat ride to visit historic Village Island, a large gathering in the Big House, visits to the U'mista Cultural Centre, and a similar gathering of families in Fort Rupert.

On the morning after our arrival, our group had the pleasure of visiting the U'mista Cultural Centre and the Nimpkish Burial Grounds where one can see many totem poles. One of particular note was carved by Doug Cranmer as a memorial to his father, Daniel Cranmer. Doug, a very talented artist, had carved other totem poles including one in Stanley Park, Vancouver, masks, other carvings, silk screen paintings, and paintings on the walls of the big House and Cultural Centre.

The entire Boas clan and many of the Hunts gathered later in the morning on the dock where we were to leave on an expedition to Village Island. We sailed on three large fishing boats belonging to fishermen from the reserve, Captains Roy Cranmer (Gloria's brother), Ernie Alfred, and Stan Hunt.

Figure 147. One of the three fishing boats that carried the Boas family from Alert Bay to Village Island, British Columbia, 1986 (N.F.B.).

The one to two-hour trip was inspiring. We passed by the uninhabited mountainous shoreline, with dense growths of conifers and western red cedars (Figure 147). As we approached the island, we sensed what Franz Boas must have felt on his trips to this lovely and lonely spot. In his time it was a thriving small village, now completely abandoned. This happened when all the families left the island, seeking better educational opportunities for their children in Alert Bay. Many of the original houses still stand. The site of the Big House used by Dan Cranmer for his famous potlatch is overgrown with dense vegetation with only the heavy structural beams remaining (Figure 148). Some totem poles remain erect while others lie on the ground, slowly rotting and returning to the earth (Figure 149).[d] Some of our hosts, who had lived on Village Island, recalled the happy days spent there.

The evening was spent in the Big House in Alert Bay, an unforgettable and cherished experience. We continued to exchange stories with our

[d] Most totem poles are carved as memorials to the deceased and are expected to decay with time and slowly vanish from their sites.

Figure 148. The remains of the Big House on Village Island where Daniel Cranmer held his famous potlatch in 1921 as seen in 1986 (N.F.B.).

Figure 149. An old totem pole on Village Island returning to the soil, 1986 (N.F.B.).

new friends. Chief Bill Hunt told me that he still had a bear trap that had belonged to George Hunt. Gloria showed us the diary that George Hunt kept on his trip to New York to visit Franz Boas. Agnes told of Boas's visit to Alert Bay in 1931 when he was a guest of Agnes and Daniel Cranmer in their home. Maggie Frank recalled cooking for Boas when she was a young girl. Other elders also recounted memories of his visits. With almost 250 Boas and Hunt descendants present, Gloria Webster, as representative of the Hunt family, extended her greetings to all, recounting the events which led to this great reunion. Representing the Boas family, I responded and reviewed the forty-five year relationship of Boas and Hunt (Figure 150). At the conclusion of my talk, on behalf of the Boas family, I presented a gift to Gloria for the U'mista Cultural Centre. It consisted of copies of the correspondence between Hunt and Boas numbering over one thousand letters. They were obtained from the American Philosophical Society and kindly prepared by the manuscript librarian, Beth Carroll-Horrocks, for this special occasion.

Figure 150. Norman F. Boas presenting gifts at the reunion from the Boas family to the Hunt family for use in the U'mista Cultural Centre, 1986 (N.B.F.).

Following the formal ceremonies and greetings, we participated in a huge feast that was spread on a row of tables, some forty feet in length. Offered were several kinds of salmon, grilled vertically next to a large fire in the center of the dirt floor, along with a great variety of other foods. At the conclusion of the dinner, a large 100th Anniversary cake was presented. It was cut by Kwakiutl Chief Bill Hunt of Fort Rupert and Franziska, the oldest member of the Boas family, (Figure 151).

Figure 151. Kwakiutl Chief Bill Hunt and Franziska Boas preparing to cut the 100th anniversary reunion cake (N.F.B.).

At the conclusion of the meal, in the evening, tribal members from Fort Rupert and Alert Bay, all in full regalia, performed special dances. As a visiting "tribe," Franziska and the grandchildren of Franz Boas were given button blankets and headdresses to wear so that we might perform the Peace Dance (Figure 152). In spite of her age (84), Franziska, a professional dancer and teacher, participated in the dances. Later, all members of both families danced in a circle around the fire as a climax to a memorable evening.

The following day, we all left Alert Bay with fond memories, to continue our celebration in Fort Rupert, the home of the Kwakiutl band. Again we stayed at the homes of our hosts. Once settled, we took a walking tour of the reserve and waterfront. We visited the art studio of Calvin Hunt and viewed the marvelous prints and carvings by Calvin, Kwakiutl Chief George Hunt, George Hunt, Jr., and Stephen Hunt, all descendants of the original George Hunt. Along the shoreline we witnessed the carving of a totem pole for Emma Hunt to memorialize her husband, Chief Tommy Hunt. We saw the graveyard where George Hunt is buried and the site where a new Big House was under construction (Figure 153).[e]

---

[e] It is now completed.

Figure 152. The Boas family in button blankets for dancing at the Boas-Hunt reunion, 1986. Left to right: Norman F. Boas, Robert & Philip Yampolsky, Franziska & Donald P. Boas, and Gertrud Michelson. Barbara Boas Crutchley, the 6th grandchild of Franz Boas, was ill that night so could not join the group. (N.F.B.).

Figure 153. The skeletal structure of the Big House being erected at Fort Rupert. Note the carved vertical poles, topped with huge logs hewn from western red cedar trees, 1986 (N.F.B.).

Since the building of their Big House was not completed, we all met in the Fort Rupert Community Center. We were treated to a luncheon following which we exchanged greetings again, for most of those present had been in Alert Bay the previous night. After gifts were exchanged, dancing similar to the night before followed, featured by a dance by Calvin Hunt wearing a magnificent carved costume of his design, with an eagle mask, wings, and talons. Another highlight was the dancing of elders of each family, Franziska Boas with Agnes Cranmer (Figure 154). The men of the Boas family were all given button or Chilkat blankets with ermine-trimmed headpieces to wear, so that we could perform the Peace Dance, carefully coached by Emma Hunt on the sidelines. Finally, we all danced in a circle, ending an extraordinary reunion experience.

Figure 154. Agnes Cranmer and Franziska Boas dancing together at the Boas-Hunt Reunion in Fort Rupert, 1986 (Barbara Boas).

The following day we were taken to the Port Hardy airport to return home. We were accompanied by many of our new friends, and had a hearty send-off after our grateful thanks to Gloria for all the hard work she and her family had done to make our trip so pleasant and successful.

In 1990, Doris and I were invited to participate in a potlatch in Alert Bay, sponsored by Roy Cranmer. It also coincided with a celebration of the tenth anniversary of the creation of the U'mista Cultural Centre and the preparation of a Mungo Martin traveling museum exhibit at the Centre. Mungo Martin was a distinguished tribal member and an extraordinary artist. The highlight of the evening for us, was receiving Indian names. This followed the Peace Dance in which we joined visiting Maori chieftains from New Zealand. Doris was given the name *Xwani*, which means "swaying from side to side," symbolizing a motion in dancing.

The name had previously been given to Julia Averkieva when she accompanied Franz Boas on a fieldtrip to Alert Bay in 1931. I was given the name *Hiłdzak̲wal̲al's*, which means "speaking well from the beginning," a name bestowed on Franz Boas by George Hunt almost one hundred years earlier when Boas hosted a feast for the Kwakiutl Indians of Fort Rupert. The selection of these names for us was made by three tribal elders, Agnes Hunt Cranmer, Helen Knox, and Margaret Frank. All were granddaughters of George Hunt.[8]

A major event was held at the American Museum of Natural History (A.M.N.H.) to celebrate the Hunt and Boas collections at the museum. On October 18, 1991, an exhibit opened, titled "CHIEFLY FEASTS. The Enduring Kwakiutl Potlatch." It was conceived and orchestrated by Aldona Jonaitis, historian, anthropologist and vice president of the A.M.N.H and consisted of over 120 artifacts that Franz Boas and George Hunt collected one hundred years earlier. They had never before been displayed at the museum. These scarce and invaluable pieces included facemasks, headpieces, bowls, Hamatśa paraphernalia, art objects, boxes, utensils, and photographs. In order to exhibit them properly, the museum invited Native Americans from British Columbia, including elders and others familiar with these artifacts, to New York to help identify them and recommend the manner in which they should be displayed.[9]

Forty Kwakiutl and other tribal members were invited to New York for the opening day ceremonies and to perform a potlatch at the museum. Symbolic of a traditional potlatch, these Indians arrived by boat (customarily by canoes) to be greeted by Native Americans of New York. The reception was arranged at the 72nd Street pier on the Hudson River. All parties were then transported to the museum to participate in the opening day ceremonies for Chiefly Feasts. The ceremonies for the general public were held in the large two-story room of the museum that was highlighted with marine dioramas and a large whale model suspended from the ceiling. Well over one thousand visitors filled the room, seated in the lower section, with many others sitting on the central stairs and standing on the second floor balcony. Hundreds of school children sat on the floor. The great attraction was a re-enactment of a potlatch by the Indians in their full regalia. After introductory remarks by Aldona Jonaitis and George Langdon, president of the museum, I had the honor of greeting and welcoming the audience with a brief review of the relationship and achievements of Boas and Hunt. George Hunt, chief of the Kwakiutl Band of Fort Rupert, British Columbia, led the potlatch. Following the ceremonies, the exhibits were open to the public. Chiefly Feasts remained on display at the A.M.N.H. for four months. Upon closing, the exhibit went on a tour for the next two and one half years. It was displayed at the Royal British Columbia Museum in Victoria, British Columbia, the Natural History Museum of the California Academy of Sciences in San Francisco, the National Museum of Natural History of the Smithsonian Institution, and the Seattle Art Museum.

In Germany, to honor distinguished departed citizens, celebrations are sometimes held commemorating anniversaries of their death. Such was the case in 1992 when Franz Boas was memorialized both in Minden, Germany and in New York on the 50$^{th}$ anniversary of his death. In Minden, the Minden Historical Society, the Kant Association, and the Minden Museum, in cooperation with the Cultural Office of the City of Minden, sponsored a series of lectures from October 16, 1992 through December 12, 1992. Lectures were given by Professor W. Kummer of the University of Bielefeld, *Franz Boas and the Anti-Evolutionary Turn in Anthropology, Ethnology and Linguistics;* Professor Jürgen Freese of the University of Bielefeld on *Cultural Anthropology of Franz Boas;* Professor Douglas Cole of Simon Fraser University, Burnaby, British Columbia on *Franz Boas – Scientist and Patriot in Two Countries*; Professor Rüdiger Schott of the University of Münster, *Culture and Speech – Franz Boas in Founding Anthropological Linguistics;* and Professor Ludger Müller-Wille, McGill University, Montreal, *Franz Boas and his Researches among the Inuit (1883-84) – the Beginning of an Arctic Ethnology.*[10]

At the same time Professor Paula Rubell, chairman of the Department of Anthropology at Barnard College, arranged a symposium at Barnard College in New York, adopting the tradition of Germany in celebrating a death anniversary. The one-day conference was held in the auditorium of Barnard College on October 10, 1992, titled *Fifty Years Later: The Legacy of Franz Boas*. Participants included Prof. Douglas Cole of Simon Fraser University; Professor Alice B. Kehoe of Marquette University; Professor Regna Darnell, University of Western Ontario; Professor George W. Stocking, Jr., University of Chicago; Dirk Obbink, Barnard College; Professor Barbara Kirshenblatt-Gimblett, New York University; Professor Irving Goldman, Sarah Lawrence College; Ira Jacknis University of California; Aldona Jonaitis, Vice President of the American Museum of Natural History; and William C. Sturtevant, Curator, Smithsonian Institution. Members of the Boas family were invited, as were one or two of his former students. Following the symposium, this writer and his family attended a dinner given for all the participants of the symposium. Invited by Professor Rubell, I was asked to give the after-dinner speech about my grandfather. My reminiscences of Franz Boas highlighted the presentation. It was well received. Aside from the presence of some of his grandchildren, there was not a person in the room, other than family, who had known or had studied under Franz Boas. The talk was a revelation to many on the humanitarian aspects of this distinguished and loving man.[11]

In 1995, the Manuscript Society held its annual meeting in Seattle, during which time a side trip was made to Victoria, British Columbia to visit the Royal British Columbia Museum. The highlight of this trip was a seminar held in the Mungo Martin Big House on the grounds of the museum where the topic, "Creation of a Manuscript Language 'Kwak'wala'" was discussed. I had the pleasure of introducing the subject and our speakers, Gloria Webster of Alert Bay and Professor Jay Powell of the University of British Columbia. I recounted the roles of Boas and Hunt in creating the written language of the Kwak'wala-speaking people. Gloria and Jay were responsible for the orthography used at the U'mista Cultural Centre.[12]

A second exhibit of note at the A.M.N.H celebrated the 100th anniversary of the initiation of the Jesup North Pacific Expedition (1897-1902). It was a special photographic exhibit that ran from November 14, 1997 through March 1, 1998. It presented a remarkable display of photographs taken in Siberia and the Pacific Northwest. Included, from thousands of photographs taken, were images of tribal ceremonies, dancing, potlatches, tribal leaders, totem poles, native villages, native artifacts, and many scenes of activities among various cultures from the two continents. This expedition, planned and led by Boas and subsidized by President Jesup and the museum, was "one of the most important expeditions in the history of American anthropology."[13]

In 1998, Minden, Germany, the birthplace of Franz Boas, celebrated its 1200th Anniversary as a municipality (798-1998). In order to commemorate this occasion, the Minden Kommunalarchiv published a booklet honoring thirty-six celebrities who had been residents or had had some connection with Minden. Commencing with the 13th century storyteller, Gerhard von Minden, it continued with Kings and Queens of Prussia, as well as military men, bishops of Minden, writers, and scientists. Included were Franz Boas and Abraham Jacobi. The year 1998 was also the 140th Anniversary of the birth of Franz Boas, a distinguished son of this small city in western Germany. Each individual was represented in the booklet by a brief biography with a portrait sketch. In addition, two sets of playing cards accompanied this commemorative presentation. Instead of the Jacks, Queens and Kings and Aces, these cards were illustrated with the same portraits as those in the booklet. Abraham Jacobi's appears on the Ace of Hearts and Franz Boas's appears on the Ace of Spades (Figure 155).[14] Minden is currently planning a celebration of the 150th Anniversary of the birth of Franz Boas in the year 2008.[15]

Figure 155. 1200th Anniversary of Minden, Germany with playing cards honoring Abraham Jacobi and Franz Boas, 1988 (Melitta-Kaffee Geniessen, Minden).

## References and Notes


1. Nordsiek, Dr. Hans. Personal communication.
2. Boas, Franz. Video documentary film titled *The Shackles of Tradition*, in a series titled *Strangers Abroad*, produced by Films for the Humanities & Sciences, Inc, Princeton, New Jersey, 1990.
3. Boas, Franz. Video documentary film titled *Franz Boas 1858-1942*. A production of Public Broadcasting Associates, Inc., Boston, Massachusetts, Odyssey Series, a PBS presentation, 1980.
4. Rohner, Ronald P. Compiler and editor of T*he Ethnography of Franz Boas*, the University of Chicago Press, Chicago and London, 1969.
5. Jonaitis, Aldona. *From the Land of the Totem Poles. The Northwest Coast Indian Art Collection at the American Museum of Natural History*, The American Museum of Natural History, New York, and the University of Washington Press, Seattle, 1988.
6. Webster, Gloria. Personal communication.
7. *Box of Treasures*, a video documentary film produced by the U'mista Cultural Centre, Alert Bay, British Columbia, 1985.
8. Webster, Gloria. A speech titled, *Consumers, Then and Now, A Centenary Celebration of Franz Boas and the Jesup North Pacific Expedition, 1897-1997*, American Museum of Natural History, New York, November 14, 1997.
9. Jonaitis, Aldona. Editor of *CHIEFLY FEASTS, The Enduring Kwakiutl Potlatch*, American Museum of Natural History, New York and the University of Washington Press, Seattle & London, 1991.

9. Jonaitis, Aldona. Editor of *CHIEFLY FEASTS, The Enduring Kwakiutl Potlatch*, American Museum of Natural History, New York and the University of Washington Press, Seattle & London, 1991.
10. *Franz Boas (1858-1942), Sein Weg zu den Menschen* (His way to mankind), a program for a series of lectures on the 50th anniversary of his death, Minden, Germany, 1992.
11. *Fifty Years Later: The Legacy of Franz Boas*, Barnard College, New York, Oct. 10, 1992. Program for the symposium.
12. Boas, Norman F. *The Creation of a Manuscript Language* Kwak'wala, lecture at a seminar sponsored by the Manuscript Society, Victoria. British Columbia, May 28, 1995.
13. Kendall, Laurel, Barbara Mathé & Thomas Ross Miller. *Drawing Shadows to Stone: The Photography of the Jesup North Pacific Expedition, 1897-1902*, 112pp, 83 archival photographs, University of Washington Press, Seattle, in association with the American Museum of Natural History, New York, 1997.
14. Nordsiek, Dr. Hans & Marianne. *MINDEN 798-1998. Geschichte von Menschen in 1200 Jahren, Minden*, Kommunalarchiv, Minden 1998 (Text by the Nordsieks, sketches by Prof. Alf Welski and Alexander Ignatius).
15. Schulte, Dr. Monika M. Personal communication, 2004.

# GENEALOGY

## THE BOAS LINE

Helen S. Boas, the daughter-in-law of Franz Boas, prepared the original genealogy of Franz Boas with his help. Additions were made from Brilling's article on the Boas genealogy extracted from the Minden records and from information supplied by Douglas Cole from his research on the family.[1-3] The following is a lineal descent line to Franz Boas from Heineman (b. ca.1650) on his paternal side and Jonas Meyer (b. 1723) on his maternal side. Siblings and their descendants prior to the generation of Franz Boas are excluded from this list but are listed in the complete genealogy.[1] Siblings of Franz Boas and their descendants are listed here through three generations. Marie Krackowizer's genealogy is also presented. In the three genealogical lines presented here, comparable generations have been numbered, with the generation of Franz and Marie Boas being number **VII.**

### I

**Heineman (Chajim)**. First known paternal forebear of Franz Boas. He was born ca.1650 and moved to Werther in the Rhineland sometime between 1700 and 1710. His date of birth and spouse are unknown. They had at least one child.

### II

**Aron Heineman Levi**. Son of Heineman, he was born in the Rhineland ca.1670-90 and died ca.1736 in Werther. His spouse is unknown. They had at least two children.

### III

**Feibes Aron Levi** (1720-1788). Son of Aron and the younger brother of Bendix. In 1807, the Kingdom of Westphalia, which included Minden, Germany, was created by Napoleon I, where he installed his brother, Jerome as King. One of the latter's first actions was to grant Jews full rights of citizenship and require that they assume surnames. In 1808 the descendants of Bendix assumed the surname of Weinberg. Feibes Aron received authorization to settle in Werther in 1746 so that he could marry. His wife's name or date-of-birth are unknown. She died in 1799. In 1771 Feibes received authorization to buy a house. He apparently was well to do, since buying a house required the payment of a high tax. He and his wife had seven children.

## IV

**Bendix Feibes Aron Boas** (1763-1836). Bendix was the fifth of seven children of Feibes Aron Levi and the first to bear the name Boas. In 1793 he received authorization to settle in Lübbecke, Germany, specifically on the basis of the rights of his future wife. According to Prussian law, as the first child of her father, she inherited these rights. In 1793 Bendix married **Schönchen,** the daughter of **Philip Joel.** Bendix became a merchant in Lübbecke selling drapery, cloth, and fabrics. He and his wife had seven children. On August 4, 1808, Bendix Feibes declared that he wanted to take on the surname Boas for himself and his seven children What reasons Bendix Feibes had to choose this biblical name from the Book of Ruth are as little known today, as his relatives' reasons for taking the name Weinberg. Bendix and his wife died in Lübbecke, both in the year 1836.

## V

**Epheibes (Feibes) Boas** (1798-1836). He was the third of seven children of Bendix Boas. Born in Lübbecke, he became a merchant, having worked with his father. In 1821 he moved to Minden where he became an independent businessman in a general store. In 1821 he married **Karoline Frank** (1802-81), the daughter of **Joseph Meyer Frank** (1756-1851). In 1821 Feibes Boas applied for and received citizenship rights from the city manager of Minden. Feibes and Karoline had eight children.

## VI.

**Meier (Meyer) Boas** (1823-1899). Meyer, born in Minden, was the second child of Feibes and Karoline, and became a successful merchant in Minden. He married **Sophie Meyer** (1828-1916) (See GENEALOGY OF THE MEYER LINE below). She was very active socially and founded the first Kröebel Kindergarten in Minden for which she received the Queen Louise Order of Prussia Medal. They later moved to Berlin. Meier and Sophie had six children, all born in Minden (1-6).

## VII

1. **Helene Boas** (1853-1857).
2. **Antonie (Toni) Boas** (1855-1935). Toni, an accomplished pianist, married **Ludwig Wohlauer** and had one child and an adopted son (1-2).
3. **Franz Uri Boas** (1858-1942). He hated his middle name, so never used it. Apparently it had been the middle name of his grandfather Feibes. He married **Marie Anna Ernestina Krackowizer** (1861-1929) in New York on March 10, 1887. (See GENEALOGY OF THE KRACKOWIZER LINE below). Franz and Marie are buried in Dale Cemetery, Ossining, New York (See Figure 239). They had six children (3-8).

Figure 156. Graveyard marker of Franz and Marie Boas, Dale Cemetery, Ossining, New York (N.F.B.).

4. **Ernst Boas** died at the age of one in 1861.
5. **Hedwig (Hete)** (1863-1949). Born in Minden, she died in New York. Hete married **Rudolph Lehmann,** an educator, in Berlin. He died in 1927. They had no children.
6. **Aenna (Anna) Margaret Boas.** Born in 1867 in Minden, she married **Julius Urbach**, a brewer. He died in 1910. Prior to World War II she moved to Rio de Janiero with three of her six children (9-14).

### VIII

**1. Lisbeth Wohlauer** died of hydrocephalus as an infant in 1892.
**2. Hans Wohlauer**. An adopted son who served in the German Army during World War II. Hans and his wife had one daughter, **Gabrielle**.
**3. Helene Boas** (1888-1963). Married **Cecil Yampolsky** (1890-1960s) and lived in New York and Grantwood, New Jersey. They had twin sons, **Robert** (1920-1988) & **Philip** (1920-1997).
**4. Ernst Philip Boas** (1891-1955). A physician, born in Worcester, Massachusetts. He married **Helen Tuthill Sisson** (1894-1962), a nurse. They had three children, **Donald Philip Boas** (1921-2003)**, Norman Francis Boas,** and **Barbara Boas Crutchley.**
**5. Hedwig Boas** (1893-1894). Born and died in Chicago, Illinois.
**6. Gertrud Boas** (1897-1924). A schoolteacher, unmarried.
**7. Henry Herbert Donaldson Boas** (1899-1925). An agriculturalist.
**8. Marie Franziska Boas** (1902-1987). A professional teacher of dance. She married **Dr. Nicolas Michelson** and had one daughter, **Gertrud Michelson Pinsky**. Nicolai and Franziska were divorced.
**9. Walter Ernst Urbach**. He remained in Rio de Janeiro. No children.
**10. Frida Urbach**. Married **?** **Rosenstock**. They remained in Rio de Janeiro and were the parents of two children.
**11. Franz Urbach**. Born in Germany, his wife's name was **Ilse**. They immigrated to the United States in the 1930s to escape Nazi Germany. They had one daughter, **Dorothy (Helga) Urbach.**
**12. Hedwig (Hete) Urbach.** She married **Oskar Yampolsky**, an American, and immigrated to the United States in the 1920s. After the death of her husband, she moved to Mexico City to live with her daughter, **Mariana Yampolsky Van Der Sluis.**
**13. Rudolph Urbach**. Born in Germany, he and his wife, **Lotte,** immigrated to America in the 1930s to escape the Nazis. They had one son, **Peter.**
**14. Hellmut Urbach**. Born in Germany, he immigrated to Rio de Janeiro with his family in the 1930s, married and had one daughter, **Sylvia.**

## THE MEYER LINE

### III

**Jonas Meyer** (1723-1784). He is the first authenticated ancestor of Franz Boas on his mother's side, born in Petershagen. His permission to settle in Petershagen as an ordinary citizen-Jew was dated May 15, 1752; he was appointed director of the Jewish community there. His wife, whose name is not given, died in 1786. She and Jonas had three children.

**IV**

**Meyer Jonas** (1754-before 1821). Meyer Jonas was the first child of Jonas Meyer. In 1777 he married **Jette,** nee **Heine**. He was also appointed director of his community. They had eight children.

**V**

**Jonas Meyer** (1787-1851). Named after his grandfather, he was the fourth born of Meyer and Jette. He married **Jette (Henriette) Menke** sometime after 1808. They moved to Minden later and both died there. They had eleven children.

**VI**

**Sophie Meyer** (1828-1916). The first born of Jonas and Jette Meyer. She married Meier Boas (See GENEALOGY OF THE BOAS LINE above).

## THE KRACKOWIZER LINE

The first major work on the Krackowizer genealogy was done by Ferdinand Krackowizer (1813-93). Franziska Boas transcribed and translated this difficult document. Most of the European members of the Krackowizer family lived in Czechoslovakia and Austria. Additions and corrections have since been received from many members of the family and incorporated in the presentation here.[4]

**I**

**Paul Krackowizer** (1599-1671) was born in Leopoldschlag (Bohemia), later Czeckslava and made his living as a butcher. He married **Judith** <u>?</u> (1608-1668). They had six children.

**II**

**Simon Krackowizer** (1651-1712). The last child of Paul and Judith; he was born in Windhag. Simon was a brewer. In 1679 he married

**Katharina Ursula Strauss** (1660-1722) of Steyr Austria. Her funeral services were held at St. Peters Cathedral in Linz. They had 12 children.

**III**

**Johan Michael Krackowizer** (1682-1767). He was the third child of Simon and Katharina and was christened at St. Peter's Cathedral in Linz. He married **Maria Regina ?** (1691-1776). Johan was a brewer. They had 16 children.

**IV**

**Johan Stefan Krackowizer** (1726-91). He was the 10th child of Johan and Maria and was Overseer of Feyregg. His first marriage was to **Marie Helene Schoiber** (1761-1801). They had 7 children. His second marriage was to **Maria Susanna Neumann** (1725-1773). His third marriage was to **Aloisa Eva Johanna Theria Würsing** (1747-1820). They had 7 children.

**V**

**Ferdinand Stefan Krackowizer** (1777-1828). The son of Johan Stefan by his third wife, Aloisa. He served as a Legal Overseer in Spital am Pyhrn in the Austrian Alps. In 1813 he married **Theresia Sofia Walpürge Richter** (1794-1866), paymaster's daughter. They had 8 children and founded the Spitalen line.

**VI**

**Ernst Nepomuck Krackowizer** (1821-1875). The 4th child of Ferdinand and Theresia. Born in Spital am Pyhrn, he was a physician, revolutionary (1848) and immigrated to America. He married **Emilie Forster** (1828-1919). Ernst and Emilie are buried in Dale Cemetery, Ossining, New York (Figure 240). They had 5 children (1-5).

**VII**

**1. Emilian (Emil) Washington Krackowizer** (1852-1924). A physician, he married **Sarah Elizabeth Partridge** (1854-1898) of Elmira, New York. They had 4 children (1-4).

**2. Helene Maria Therese Krackowizer** (1856-1939). Born in Williamsburg, New York, she married **Theodore Florenz Heinrich Meyer** (1844-1903), an attorney. They had 6 children (5-10).
**3. Marie Anna Ernestina Krackowizer** (1861-1929). Born in New York, she married **Franz Boas** (See GENEALOGY OF THE BOAS LINE above).
**4. Richard Franz Krackowizer** (1864-1926). He was a bookkeeper in New York and later in Birmingham, Alabama. He was unmarried.
**5. Adelheid Maria (Alice) Krackowizer** (1865-1929). Unmarried, she was a teacher who taught in schools in Illinois and Colorado.

## VIII

**1. Krackowizer, Ernst (Nestle)** (1881-1900). Born in Elmira, New York, he died in Pittsburgh, Pennsylvania.
**2. Aimee Lee (Milly) Krackowizer** (1883-1944). She married **Amos G. Torrey** in 1907, but he died two years later. Her second marriage was to **Frederick A. Holmer,** a graduate of the United States Military Academy. She had no children by either husband.
**3. Mary (Molly) Parmalee Krackowizer** (1888-1975). She married **Walter K. Dunn**, a graduate of the United States Military Academy. They had two sons, **Walter & Beverely Dunn**. No further information.
**4. Alice Elizabeth (Bessie) Krackowizer** (1891-1974). She had two children by her first husband, **Robert Hermann Krusi.** They were **Sarah (Sally) Krusi Pollard** who later married **Ian S. Mark,** and **Hermann (Bud) Krusi.** Her second husband was **Rudin Mellin Johnson** (1893-1966). They had three children, **Ernst Krackowizer Martin Johnson, Rudin Mellin Johnson,** and **Judith Alyce Johnson O'Brien.**
**5. Anna Emilie Helene (Nandie) Meyer** (1876-1967). Unmarried and lived in New York.
**6. Louise Wilhelmine Marie (Luli) Meyer** (1877-1957). Unmarried and lived in New York.
**7. Helen Alice Charlotte (Nellie) Meyer** (1879-1962). Unmarried and lived in New York.
**8. Ernst Louis Henry Meyer** (1881-1961). He married **Alyce Gordon Linton**. He was an engineer. They had two children, **Theodore von Lengerke Meyer** (1915-1958), unmarried, and **Barbara Linton Meyer**.
**9. Theodore Frederick Walter Meyer** (1890-1961). He married **Mary Butterfield**. They had two children, **Eric Moffat Meyer** and **Walter Weston Meyer.**

**10. Florence (Flossie) Meyer** (1893-1979). She married late in life to **Frank Waldo**. Flossie and Frank had no children.

### References and Notes

1. Boas, Norman F. *Boas Family Genealogy, 1650-1985, Including the Feibes Boas – Meyer Boas - Franz Boas Line* and *The Jonas Meyer – Sophie Meyer Boas – Meyer Line*, March 1, 1985 (Available in the Library of the American Philosophical Society).
2. Brilling, B. *Die Vorfahren des Professors Franz Boas*, in *Mitteilungen des Mindener Geschichts- und Museumvereins*, Volume 38, 1030-112, 1966 (Translated from German by Barbara Boas Crutchley).
3. Cole, Douglas. Personal communication.
4. Boas, Norman F. *Krackowizer Genealogy*, February 20, 1985 (Available in the Library of the American Philosophical Society).

# INDEX

Relatives of Franz and Marie Boas are cited parenthetically after their names in the Index. Abbreviations used in the Index and in the text are as follows:

| | |
|---|---|
| A.A.A. | American Anthropological Association |
| A.A.A.S. | American Association for the Advancement of Science |
| A.A.P. | Association of American Physicians |
| A.A.M. | American Association of Museums |
| A.E.S. | American Ethnological Society |
| A.F.S. | American Folklore Society |
| A.M.A. | American Medical Association |
| A.M.N.H. | American Museum of Natural History |
| A.N.P.A. | American Newspaper Publisher's Association |
| A.P.S. | American Philosophical Society |
| B.A.E. | Bureau of American Ethnology |
| B.C. | British Columbia |
| B.I. | Baffin Island |
| C.S.R.A. | Civil Service Reform Association |
| C.U. | Columbia University |
| G.S.A. | Germanistic Society of America |
| I.C.A. | International Congress of Americanists |
| I.J.A.L. | International Journal of American Linguistics |
| J.A.F.S. | Journal of American Folklore society |
| M.S.H. | Mount Sinai Hospital |
| N.C.S.R.L. | National Civil Service Reform League |
| N.M.N.H. | National Museum of Natural History |
| N.R.C. | National Research Council |
| N.S.S.R. | New School for Social Research |
| N.Y.A.M. | New York Academy of Medicine |
| N.Y.A.S. | New York Academy of Science |
| N.Y.C.M.S. | New York County Medical Society |
| N.Y.I.W.C. | New York Infirmary for Women and Children |
| N.Y.P.M.S. | New York Postgraduate Medical School |
| N.Y.S.C.H. | New York Skin and Cancer Hospital |
| O.W.I. | Office of War Information |
| R.B.C.M. | Royal British Columbia Museum |
| S.I. | Smithsonian Institution |
| U.S.N.M. | United States National Museum |
| W.M.C. | Women's Medical College |

Adams, Edward, 173
Adams, John, 253
Addams, Jane, 182
Adirondack State Park, 161
Adler, Felix, 93,132,153,159,173
African Americans, 181
Agassiz, Louis, 80,154
Aitken, Robert, 193
Ajaropaq (cat's cradle), 54,55
Alert Bay, B.C., 77,78,94,99,127,136; Indian reserve, 273,274,275,277; fishing boats, 278

Alfred, Ernie, 278
Alma Farm, 63,98,111,141; cottage, 141,142,150,151; 152,159; sold, 161; 212,228
Amadjuk (Lake), 57
American Anthropological Association (A.A.A.), 123,163,168; founding, 171; 174,175,196,197,203,209
*American Anthropologist*, 123,171
American Antiquarian Society, 103
American Association for the Advancement of Science (A.A.A.S), 75,80,98,99,209
American Association of Museums (A.A.M.), 168
American Committee for Democracy & Intellectual Freedom, 250
American Ethnological Society (A.E.S.), 123, 203,204,209
American Folklore Society (A.F.S.), 93,174,203
American Geographical Society, 93
American Medical Association (A.M.A.), 150,215
American Museum of Natural History (A.M.N.H.), x,xi,76,79,93,111-113,115,117,123,127,133,134,136, 143,163,165,166,168,172,174,175-178,193,204-205,209; "Chiefly "Feasts, the Enduring Kwakiutl Potlatch," an exhibit, 284; exhibit on 100th anniversary of Jesup Northwest Pacific Expedition, 286
American Newspaper Publisher's Association (A.N.P.A.), 152
American Philosophical Society (A.P.S.), vi,x,42,133,168,209,253; Boas collection, 263,266; 280
American Red Cross, 176
Amering, Hans, 273
Amundsen, Roald, 166
Amur River Valley (Siberia), 124
Andresen, Anton, 43
Andrews, H.A., 163,167
Anthropology, physical, 180
Anthropometry, 95,180
Anti-Semitism, 21,24,64,75,195,269
Arapaho, Indians, 173
*Ardandhu* (steamer to New York), 63
Aron Heineman Levi (ancestor), 289
Artko, Lucy. See Lucy Artko Teit.
Association for the Advancement of the Medical Education of Women, 149
Association of American Physicians (A.A.P.), 150
Atangana (Inuit), 119; death, 120,121
Audubon, John J., 253
Auer, Leopold, 139
Averkieva, Julia, 284
Aviaq (Inuit), 119, death, 120,121

Baffin Island, 27,31,33,34
Bannock Indians, 173
*Barbara Berkowitz* (steamer in B .C.), 77,78
Barnard College, viii,174,175,203,208, 216,221,228; symposium on 50th Anniversary of the death of Boas, 285
Barnes, Bernice, 147
Barnes, Fanny, 147
Barr, William, 42
Bastian, Adolf, 27,73,196
Bauer, George, 108
Bell, Alexander Graham, 171,172
Bella Bella Indians, 94
Bella Coola Indians, 74,78,79,106,126
Bem, General, 86
Benedict, Ruth, 197,204; early life, 205; education & marriage, 206,207; student of Boas, 207; Margaret Mead, 207; professional career, 207; with O.W.I, 207; author, 207,208; president of A.A.A. & A.E.S., 208; 259; death, 208; 209,210,212,269
Benedict, Stanley R., 207
Bergstrom, John A., 100
Berlin Ethnological Museum, 27,93,95, 169
Berlin University, 187,190
*Berliner Tageblatt*, 27-29,42,58,63,195
Bessels, Emil, 63
Bickmore, Albert, 75,79,117
"Big House" (Alert Bay), 273,274,279
"Big House" (Fort Rupert), 282,283
Billings, Dr. John S., 153
Bixby, William, 129,144
Blackett, S., 255
Blackfoot Indians, 168,204
Blackman, Margaret, 271
Black Mountain College, 178
Blanc, Louis, 10

*Blücher*, steamer, 167
Boas, origin of name, 7; pronunciation, 272
Boas, Änna (Aenna) Margaret (sister). See Änna Margaret Urbach.
Boas, Antonie (Toni) (sister). See Antonie Wohlauer.
Boas, Aron (uncle), 2
Boas, Barbara (granddaughter). See Barbara Crutchley.
Boas, Barbara Johnson (great granddaughter), 272,273,275-277
Boas, Bendix Feibes Aron (great grandfather), 7,290
Boas, Caroline Frank (grandmother), 1,2,6
Boas Dance Group, 216
Boas, Donald Philip (grandson), xi,93, 214,219,224,225,247,257,259,281, 282,292
Boas, Doris Whitehead, xi,273,275-277,283; given Indian name, 283,284
Boas, Emil L., 181
Boas, Ernst (brother – died in infancy), 11,94,104,291
Boas, Dr. Ernst Philip (son), vi, x,93, 104,107,111,129-132,147,148,161, 164,172,185; medical records of F. Boas, 191; 196; marriage and World War I, 215; purchases farm in Wilton, Connecticut, 214; director of Montefiore Hospital, 215; private practice & hospital affiliations, 215; founder of Physician's Forum, 215, 216; Henry Wallace a patient, 216; 224,228,229,245,247,257-259,263, 292
Boas, Emelie. See Emelie Boas Löwenbaum.
Boas, Feibes (grandfather), 1,290
Boas, Franz. American Philosophical Society, vi. x; army duty, 24-26,31 athleticism, 14,15; bookplate, 4; engagement to Marie Krackowizer, 33-37. DAYS OF YOUTH, 1-19; curriculum vitae, 1,4,11-13,15-17; Franco-Prussian War, 16; homes in Minden, 2-4; illnesses as child, 14; Jacobi influence, 11; Jewishness, 1,6,12,13; piano playing, 16; reminiscences, viii; scrapbook, 13. UNIVERSITY DAYS, 20-24; arrested, 21,22; Bonn University, 20,21,24; doctoral dissertations and theses, 23; dueling, 21-25; fraternity life, 21,22; Heidelberg University, 20,21,24; Kiel University, 20,22-24. BAFFIN ISLAND. Planning, 27,31,33,34,42; expedition, 41-71; diary, 42,45-47,51-53,55-57; voyage to Arctic, 41,47; references, 41,42; reflections on goals, plans, future experiences, philosophy, 44-46,61; maps, 48,50, 51,53,54,57-60,62; diphtheria among Eskimos, 53; Inuit glossary, 53,54; hunting and diet, 54,57,66,67,69; perilous trek in blizzard, 55; trek to Davis Strait, 57; Eskimo migration routes, 59,60; ethnology, 59,63; Boas as artist, 64,65; Inuit artifacts, 65,69, 70; to United States in 1884, 63; Baffin Island reports, 72,73,79. IMMIGRATION TO AMERICA 72-81; At Berlin University, 72,74; Bella Coola Indians, 73,74; Pacific Northwest plans & first trip (1886), 75-79; meets Frederick W. Putnam, 80; hired by A.A.A.S, 80,81; decides to immigrate to America, 81; married Marie Krackowizer, 81; on editorial staff of *Science*, 92,94; research for B.A.A.S., 94; B.A.E. support, 95. CLARK UNIVERSITY, 98-105; appointed docent, 99-101; laboratory, 101; measurements of school children, 101; school program attacked by Worcester *Telegram*, 102; racism debunked, 102; home in Worcester, 103; faculty rebellion, 104; resignation 104,105; return to New York, 105. WORLD'S COLUMBIAN EXPOSITION, 105-110; appointed assistant to F.W. Putnam, 105; preparations and collecting artifacts, 105-107; creates written language for Kwakiutl Indians, 108; Marshall Field visits anthropology exhibit – inspired to donate funds to create museum, 109; Boas catalogs anthropology collection for Field Museum, 109; rejected as curator of ethnology, 110; vice presidential

address to A.A.A.S. – attacks racism, 111. AMERICAN MUSEUM OF NATURAL HISTORY & SMITH-SONIAN INSTITUTION. Prepares exhibits for A.M.N.H. & S.I., 112; grant from B.A.A.S., 112; trip to Ft. Rupert, 113; Boas gives feast for Kwakiutls and receives Indian name, 115,116; appointed assistant to Putnam at A.M.N.H., 117,118; Eskimos at A.M.N.H., 119-121; publicity on Eskimo skeletal remains at museum, 121,122. COLUMBIA UNIVERSITY; appointed professor of anthropology, 131; founded New York Academy of Science (N.Y. A.S.), 123. JESUP NORTHWEST PACIFIC EXPEDITION, 123-127; horseback trip across British Colum-bia, 126; museum visits in Europe, 126; appointed honorary philologist at B.A.E., 127; Jacob Schiff grant to Boas, 128; found New York apart-ment, 128,129; Loubat Prize, 133. VACATIONS ON LAKE GEORGE, 139-162; trips to Pacific Northwest, 143; trips to Germany, 143,144; summers on Federal Hill, 143,144; horseback riding, 145; 157,158; founded G.S.A. with Schurz, Jacobi & others, 158; COLUMBIA UNI-VERSITY, EARLY YEARS, defines anthropology, 163; appendicitis, 164; appointed curator of anthropology at A.M.N.H., 165; Putnam interferes with Boas's fieldwork in California, 165; A.M.N.H. as learning center, 165; Inuit collection at A.M.N.H., 166; Lake George (1904), 166,167; increase in anthropology students at C.U., 167; conflicts with Bumpus & Jesup on exhibits, 167; retires from A.M.N.H., 167; fallout with Wissler, 168; vast collection at A.M.N.H by Boas, 168,169; interprets Jesup Expedition findings, 169; defines anthropology, 169,170; relation with B.A.E. and role as linguist, 170; early role in A.A.A., 171; corres-pondence with Alexander G. Bell, 171,172; opposed to Holmes' appointment, 171,172; *Festschrift* for Boas, 172,173; 1st Ph.D. to Kroeber, 173; Boas's teaching style, 173-175; graduate students at C.U., 173-178; most important publica-tions, 178-181; as linguist, 179; cephalic index & anthropometry, 180,181; *Mind of Primitive Man*, 181; Boas role in founding G.S.A., 181; home in Grantwood, N.J.,183; commute to New York, 183; field trips (1900-1930), 184; keynote add-ress at Clark University, 184; 185-187; Boas as archeologist, 187; a founder of I.C.A., 187,188; arch-eological work in Mexico, 188-190; to Europe (1913), 190,191; medical history & surgery for facial tumor, facial palsy, 191-193; archeological expedition to Puerto Rico, 193; eulogy on Frederick W. Putnam, 193; World War I, reaction and expression, 194-196; condemns War Department for using anthropologists as spies, reprisals by A.A.A., N.R.C., & B.A.E. 196,197; exonerated, 196, 197; editor of I.J.A.L. & J.A.F.S., 197,198; review of A. Jacobi's aid to Boas, 98; condolence letter on A. Jacobi, 198,199. COLUMBIA UNIVERSITY & LATER YEARS, graduate student legacy, 202-212; trip to Southwest (1922), 204-206; Margaret Mead as student, 208,209; Correspondence with Mead, 209; Boas's teaching style, 209,210; attitude toward media, 210; Mead falsely charges that Boas had a stroke, 211; work with Ella C. Deloria, 211,212; Germany trips (1920s), 212; end of Lake George summer vacations, 212-214; vacations in Wilton & Cornwall Bridge (Connecticut), 214; grand-children, 214,216; death of Gertrud, 216; weekly family visits to Grant-wood, 217; Grantwood home, rooms, décor, office, 218-223; Christmas in Grantwood, 222,223; 70th birthday celebration, 223,224; Cornwall Bridge hike with grandsons, 224;

subject of artists Jacob Epstein and Sergei Konenkov, 225-228; deaths of Gertrud (1924) & Henry (1925), 228; death of Marie (1929), 228,229; letter on death of Marie, 230; Boas spoke 70 languages, 246; Boas with spouses of his children 247; correspondence with Norman F. Boas & test of his fame, 248; correspondence with President Franklin D. Roosevelt, 249; round-robin letter on 81st birthday, 250; Einstein letter re Boas & Boas-Einstein correspondence, 251; university honors, 251,252; Rieber portrait, 252; election to A.P.S., 253; retires from C.U., 253; honors & member of foreign scientific societies, 253; Teacher's Union award, 253-255; trans-Atlantic round table discussion on war, 255,256; interview with newspaper *PM*, 256; letters to Bessie Krackowizer Johnson re family, Nazi Germany and his health, 257,258; death at C.U. Faculty Room, 259; funeral services at Grantwood, 259; LEGACY OF BOAS, 262-270; condolences, 262; sale of Grantwood home & contents, 263; sale of library, 263; papers given to A.P.S., 263; Boas's intellect and personality, 264-266; "All men are created equal," 266; defines anthropology, 267; religion, 268,269; attacks on Boas's scientific contributions, 267,268. EPILOGUE, 271-288; Biographies of & publications by Boas, 271; film documentaries, 271; last visit to Alert Bay, 276; plan Boas-Hunt reunion, 277; exhibit of Boas-Hunt collections at A.M.N.H., 284; memorials for Boas at 50th anniversary of his death in Minden & at Barnard College, 285,286. GENEALOGY, 289-292

Boas, Franziska (daughter), vi,x,2; born, 128; 146,148,153,161,182, 185,212; career in modern dance, teacher & artist, 216, 217; 224,229, 257-259,263,281; dancing at Boas-Hunt reunion, 283

Boas, Gertrud (daughter), born, 131; 146,147,161,164,185; death, 228,292 229,258,259,292

Boas Glacier, 61

Boas, Hedwig (Hete) (sister). See Hedwig Lehmann.

Boas, Hedwig (Hete) (daughter), 107; death and burial, 108-110; 115,125, 228,229,257,259,292

Boas, Helen S. (daughter-in-law), 161, 214,215,224,247,289,292

Boas, Helene (sister – died age 5), 11,94,98,99,291

Boas, Helene (daughter). See Helene Yampolsky.

Boas, Henry Herbert Donaldson (son), born, 131; 132,146,161,164,185,196; career, 228; death (1924), 228,229, 257,258,292

Boas-Hunt family reunion, 277,280-283; at Alert Bay, 281; Ft. Rupert, dancing and gifting, 281; returning home, 283

Boas, Karoline Frank (grandmother), 290

Boas, Marie (wife), 27,29-34,30,33,36-38,41,44,45,53,54,56,59,62-64,75, 76,81-83,91,92,94,98,99,103-105, 107,108,115,125,126,128,130,132, 134,139-141,143,146-148,164-167, 184,185190,191,195,198,204,205, 212,213,217,223; death (1929), 228,229; 257-259,269,272,291; genealogy, 293-296

Boas, Max (uncle), 2

Boas, Maxwell Norman (great great grandson), cover, frontispiece, xi

Boas, Meier (father), 1,2,7,8,12,17; moves to Berlin, 3,98,103; last visit by Franz, 126;129,131; death, 132; 198

Boas, Dr. Norman Francis (grandson), vi,93,192,193,214,216,219,224,225. 245,247,257,259,263,273,275-277; speech at Alert Bay, 280; Boas-Hunt reunion, 281-283; given Indian name, 283,284; speech at opening of "Chiefly Feasts..." 284; speech at Barnard College symposium on Boas, 285,286; talk at R.B.C.M., 286,292

Boas, Raymond, xi
Boas River, 61,62
Boas, Salomon (uncle), 2
Boas, Schönchen (great grandmother), 290
Boas, Sophie Meyer (mother), 1,2,7,8, 10,11,14,17,30,64; founded Froebel kindergarten, 12; 157,195,290; genealogy, 292,293
Bogoras, Waldemar, 169,186
Bolton, Thaddeus, 100
Bolton & Bolton Landing, New York, 139-162,217
Bolza, Oskar, 108
Bonaparte, Charles J., 159
Bonn University, 10,12,21-24,269
Booth, Eugene, 139
*Boskowitz* (steamer in B.C.), 115
Bowser, Hallowell, 265
*Box of Treasures* (video relating to Cranmer's potlatch), 275
Brandies, Louis D., 248,249
Brandeis University, 178
Bridgman, Laura, 100
Brill, Abraham, 187
Brilling, B., 289
Brinton, Daniel Garrison, 93,123,193, 267
British Association for the Advancement of Science (B.A.A.S.), 94, 95,98-100,103,112,116,143
Bryan, William L., 100
Bryant, Ruth W., 259
Buchner, Herbert, 187
Buenz, Karl, 181
Bull Run, battle of, 156
Bumpus, Hermon C., 164,165,167,168
Bunsen, Robert Wilhelm, 21,196
Bureau of American Ethnology (B.A.E.), 92,95,98,99,103,117,127, 163; formation, 170-172; transfer to Smithsonian Institution, 172; 175,178,179,196,203,211
Bureau of Ethnology, 63
Burlington College Summer School of Dance, 216
Burnett, John, 63
Burnham, William H., 100,101
*Burschenschaften Alemannia*, 21,22
Bushotter, George, 211,212
Butler, Nicholas Murray, 123,168,173, 181; career, 182; 195
California, University of, 165,174,177, 178,203
Cambridge University, 178
Camp Douglas (Chicago), 109
Canadian National Museum, 177
Canadian Pacific Railroad, 77,79
Cantor, Moritz, 21
Cape Hooper, 58
Cape Napor, 59
Cardiotachometer, 215
Cardozo, Benjamin, 227
Carnegie, Andrew, 157
Carpenter, Edmund, 121
Carpenter, W.H., 181
Carroll-Horrocks, Beth, x,280
Catlett, Stephen, x
Cattell, James McKeen, 173,176,184
*Central Eskimo, The*, 75,170
Cephalic Index, 180
Chamberlain, Alexander F.; first Ph.D. in anthropology in America, 105, 173,187
Chamberlain, T.C., 110
*Changes in Bodily form of Descendants of Immigrants*, 179,180
Chattanooga, battle of, 156
Chicago, University of, 105,110,177, 203,205
"Chiefly Feasts, the Enduring Kwakiutl Potlatch," exhibit at A.M.N.H., 284; opening ceremonies, 284,285; two year museum tour, 285
Chilcotin Indians, 126
Chinook Indians, 103,105,246
Choate, Joseph, 159
City College of New York, 177,248
Civil Service Reform Association (C.S.R.A), 164
Clark, Jonas Gilman, 99,104
Clark University, xi,99,103-105; 20th Anniversary, 251,252
Clasius, Robert, 21
Cleveland, Grover, 159
Clews, Henry, 203
Clews, Lucy Madison, 203
Cochiti Indians, 204,206,207
Codere, Prof. Helen, xi
Coffin, Rev. Dr. Henry, 250
Cole, Prof. Douglas, ix,xi,42,271,285, 289

Collins, Henry B., 56
Colorado, University of, 176
Columbia University, 122,123,131-133, 172,175-178,183,187,195,203,205, 206,208,209,214,215,225,227,252, 258,259,263
Columbian Exposition, 105,134,165, 193
Columbian Museum of Natural History. See Field Museum.
Comas, B.C., 78
Comer, George, 166,173
*Coming of Age in Samoa*, 209
Cormorant Island, B.C., 78
Consumer's League, 149
Coral Harbour (Southampton Island), 61
Cori, Gerty, 253
Cormorant, Island, 273
Cornell University, 176
Cornwall Bridge, Connecticut, 245,246
Cowichon, B.C., 78
Cox, Robert, x,263
Cranmer, Agnes, xi,136,271,276,277, 280; dancing, 283; 284
Cranmer, Daniel, 136,262,272, held largest potlatch, 275-277; 278,280
Cranmer, Douglas, 276; artist, 277,278
Cranmer, Gloria. See Gloria C. Webster.
Cranmer, Roy, 276,278,283
Cranmer, William, 275,276
Cristy, Austin P., 102
Crow Indians, 177
Crutchley, Barbara Boas (grand-daughter), xi,93,214,218,221,222, 224,225,257,259,292
Cultee, Charlie, 115
"Cultural Relativism," 92,177,180,181, 268
Curie, Eve, 255
Curie, Marie, 253
Cumberland Sound, 47,48,50,51,53, 59,63

Dakota Indians, 212
Dale Cemetery (Ossining, N.Y.), 92, 228,229,259
Damrosch, Frank, 159
*Dania* (steamer to Germany), 116
*Darmstadt* (steamer to Germany), 105
Darnell, Regina, 285
Darwin, Charles, 253
Davis, Dr. Jerome, 254,255
Davis Strait, 57,58,63
Day, Solomon, 206
Dean, James, 106
Declaration of Independence, "All men are created equal," 266
Degginer family, 195
De Haven, Scott, x
Deloria, Ella Cara, education, 211; career, transcription of Siouian manuscripts, 211,212; creating a Sioux-English dictionary, 212; wrote *Waterlily*, 212; 250,251
De Pauw University, 208
*Detroit Post*, 156
Deutsch, Albert, tribute to Boas, 262
Dewey, John, 196,225
Dewey, Thomas E., 216
Dixon, Roland B., 128,132,165,171; career, 176,177
Dolan, Thomas M., xi
Donaldson, Henry Herbert, 100,101, 103,108; tuberculosis, 125; 269
Donaldson, Julia
*Donau* (ship to Germany), 64
Dorsey, George, 169,173
Dorsey, James Owen 211
Douglas, Stephen A., 109
Dressler, James E., 100
Dunn, Dr. Mary Maples, vi,vii,x
Dunn, Dr. Richard S. vi,vii,x

École de Mediciné, 148
Edel, Bertha, 259
Edison, Thomas, 253
Einstein, Albert, 227,248,251,253,256
Eliot, Charles W., 159
Emergency Society for German and Austrian Science & Art, 228
Emerson, Ralph W., 154,253
Engels, Friedrich, 10,85
Epstein Sir Jacob, career & bust of Boas, 225,226
Epstein, Lady, 225
*Era*, schooner, 166
Erdmann, Benno, 24,196
Eskimos (Inuit), 47,51,52,53; diph-theria, 53; brought to New York, illnesses & deaths, 119,120,122,123

Esmarch, Dr. Friedrich von, 23
Ethical Culture Society, 93,132
*Europa* (steamship), 212,213
Evans-Pritchard, Sir Edward, 271

Farrand, Livingston, 125,126,132,165, 168,171,173; career, 176; 269
Feibes Aron Levi (ancestor) 289
Female Medical College of Pennsylvania, 148
Ferdinand, Archduke, 194
Ferdinand I, Emperor, 86
Ferries, Hudson River, 217,218
Field, Marshall, 109
Field Museum (Chicago), 107; politics of appointments, 109,110; 124,125, 133,134,169,171,193
Fielding, Fidelia A., 175
Fischer, Kuno, 21,196
Fischer, Theobald, 22,23,64,72,196
Flag, German Imperial (Marie's), 37, 38,47,53
Fleming, Franz G., 160
Fleming, Marjorie, 160
Fleming, Paula Richardson, x
Fonda, Henry, 90
Fordham, University, 209
Forster, Emilie. See Emilie Krackowizer.
Forster, W. J., 27
Fort Rupert, B.C., 135,275,281
Foxe Basin, 55,57
Franco-Prussian War, 195
Frank, Caroline. See Caroline Frank Boas.
Frank, Joseph Meyer (great grandfather), 1
Frank, Margaret (Maggie), 280, 284
Franklin, Benjamin, 253,263
Franklin Expedition, 48
*Franz Boas, 1858-1942*, documentary, 271
*Franz Boas Strasse* ( Minden), 271
Franz Joseph, Emperor, 86
Fraser, Alexander, 100
Freese, Jürgen, 285
Frémont, John Charles, 154
Freud, Sigmund, 184,187
Frissell, Dr. H.B., 159
Froebel, Freidrich, 12
Fulton, Ruth, 269
Gallatin, Albert, 155
George Washington Bridge, 217,281
German Hospital (Lenox Hill Hospital), 30,160,172
German nationalism, 80
German Polar Commission, 27
German Weather Station, 47,50
*Germania*, (sloop to B.I.), 41,43-47,49
Germanistic Society of America (G.S.A.), 158; history of, 181,182; 228
Germany, trip to, 164
*Gesellig-Wissenshaftlicher Verein*, 98
Gettysburg, battle of, 156
Glens Falls Hospital, 160
Goddard, Pliny Earle, 203; career, 204
Gold, Irving, 285
Golden, B.C., 94
Goldenweiser, Alexander, 178; fired from C.U., 195; 207
Goldenweiser, Emanuel, 178
Goldfrank, Esther, x; career, photo album, 204
Göttingen, University of, 190
Graham, Martha, 217
Grand Canyon, 204,205
Grant, Ulysses S., 156,157
Grantwood, N.J. 183; home, 183,184, 214,217,218; home sold, 263
Graz University, 252
Greeley, Horace, 157
Green, Dr. Horace, 90
Greenmont, 81,82
Grube, Wilhelm, 73
Grünwedel, Albert, 73
Guizot, Prime Minister, 85

Haeberlin, Herman, 193
Haida Indians, 94,106,126
Hale, Horatio, 75,94; on Wilkes Expedition, 99
Hall, Charles Francis, 48,59
Hall, G. Stanley, 99,100,104,184,187
Halliday, William, confiscated & sold potlatch artifacts, 275
Hamatśas (cannibal society), 112, 114,115
Hamilton, Alexander, 253
*Handbook of American Indian Languages,* 170,172,175,178

Harper, William Rainer, 105,110,121
Harvard University, 176,187,203,267
Hayes, Rutherford, B., 140,156,157
Heidelberg University, 21,23,24,268, 269
Heineman (ancestor), 1,289
*Henrietta Sloman* (steamer to America), 87
Henson, Matthew, 120
Herskovits, Prof. Melville, ix; career, 203,204; 263
Heye, George, 275
Higginbotham, Harlow N., 109
Hill, A.V., 255
Hindenberg, Paul von, 234-236
Hispanic Society of New York, 187
Hitchcock, Alfred, 90
Hitler, Adolph, 234,235,257,266,272
Hodge, Charlotte, 147
Hodge, Louise, 147
Hodges, N.D.C., 80,98
Holelide, Kwakiutl Chief, 116
Holm, Bill, 271
Holm, Hanya, 216,217
Holmes, Oliver Wendell, 154,227
Holmes, William Henry, 110,116,125, 171; resigns from U.S.N.M. & B.A.E., 172,173
Holy Cross University, 103
Homer, Louise, 139
Hooten, Ernest, 256
Hospital for Joint Diseases, 160
Howard, General Oliver O., 156
Howard University, 203
Howells, William Dean, 153
Huber, Thomas, xi
Hudson Bay Trading Post, 133
Hughes, Charles Evans, 139,144,249
Humphrey, Doris, 217
Hunt, Bill, 275-277.279,281
Hunt, Calvin, 281,283
Hunt, Davis, 135
Hunt, Emma (wife of Tommy Hunt), 281
Hunt, George, x; background, 95,99; role at Columbian Exposition, 106-108; 112,113,115,125-127; correspondence with Boas, research papers, contributions, 133-136; visit to New York, 136; death 136; 272, 273,275-277; diary, 278; 279; burial site, 282; 284
Hunt, George (descendant of George Hunt – supra & father of George Hunt,Jr., infra), 281,284
Hunt, George, Jr., 281
Hunt, Jonathan, 135
Hunt, Lalaxs'a, 135
Hunt, Lucy, 135
Hunt, Marion, 135
Hunt, Mary, 135
Hunt, Mary (Ebbetts), 135
Hunt, Stanley, 135,278
Hunt, Stephen, 281
Hunt, Tommy, memorial totem pole, 281,282
Huntington, Collis P., 127,165
Hupa Indians, 204
Hurston, Zora Neale, 269
Huxley, Julian, 255
Hymes, Dell, 271

Ickes, Harold L., 250
International Congress of Americanists (I.C.A.), (Mexico) 187,188; 212 (The Hague)
*International Journal of American Linguisitics* (I.J.A.L.), 179,197
International School of Archeology & Ethnology, 190
Isaacs, Stanley M., 250
Isleta Indians, 204

Jacknis, Ira, 285
Jacobi, Dr. Abraham (uncle by marriage), x,8,12,17,25,27,29, 31, 33,36,63; early years, schooling, medical training, 9; Revolution of 1848, 10; arrested, 10; medical practice, author, teacher, first chair of pediatrics in America, 30; 75,79, 81,85,87,88,91,92,93,98,99; helps in Boas appointment to Columbia, 122, 123; 131,132; rents summer home to Franz Boas, 143,144,146,147; marries Mary Putnam, 148; founded pediatric service M.S.H., 149; president of American Pediatric Society, A.A.P., N.Y.A.M., N.Y.C.M.S., A..M.A., 150; honeymoon & buys Hiawatha Island (Lake George), 150; 70th birthday, 152,153; personal

papers lost in house fire, 153,154; physician to Carl Schurz, 159; 157, 158,160; death, 161; 164,173; home loan to Boas, 183; as Boas's physician, 191; death & memorials, 198, 199; 215,216,269
Jacobi, Eliezer, 9
Jacobi, Ernst, 30,34,37; death, 150; 154 159
Jacobi, Fanny, 8-10; death, 30
Jacobi Hospital, New York, 198
Jacobi, Julia Abel, 9
Jacobi, Kate Rosalie, 30
Jacobi, Laura. See Laura Jacobi School.
Jacobi, Marjorie. See Marjorie McAneny.
Jacobi, Dr. Mary Putnam (aunt by marriage), x,30,31,37,92; medical studies, 148; 1st woman to attend École de Mediciné, practitioner, teacher, author, reformer, hospital affiliations, 149; 158; death, 159; 215,216
Jacobsen, Fillip, 74
Jacobsen, J. Adrian, 73,78,95
James, William, 184,185
Janeway, Dr. Edward G., 153
Jefferson, Thomas, 253
Jennings, Herbert, 187
Jesup, Morris, 111,117; early career, 118; beneficence, 118; founder and president of A.M.N.H., 118; supporter of Peary and Jesup Expeditions, 118; 119-27,132,164,165
Jesup Northwest Pacific Expedition, 123-127,133,163,164,167-169,176, 286
Jews in Minden. Laws and permits, 6,7
Johansen, F. Carl, 43
Johnson, Andrew, 156
Johnson, Barbara Boas (great granddaughter). See Barbara Johnson Boas.
Johnson, Elizabeth (Bessie) (niece), 93, 132; letters from Franz Boas, 257
Jonaitis, Aldona, xi,284,285
Jones, Ernest, 184-187
*Journal of American Folklore Society* (J.A.F.S.), 197,198,207
Jung, Carl, 184,187
Kaempffert, Waldemar, 255
Kaesche, Emma K. See Emmy Meyer.
Kamchatka Peninsula (Siberia), 124
Kamloops (B.C.), 126
Kaufman family, 195
Kayser, Rudolph, 251
Kehoe, Alice B., 285
Kekerten Island, B.I., 47,52,53,55,56
Kékule, Friedrich August, 21,196
Kennedy, Lake, 51,57,62,63
Kent Falls State Park, Connecticut, 224
Kenyon College, 178
Kenyon, Dorothy, 250
Kiel University, 23,24,251-253,269
Kiepert, Heinrich, 72,73
Kignait (plateau), B.I., 57
K'ingua, B.I., 47
Kinkel, Gottfried, 8,10; freed from Spandau Prison, 10,11,85
Kinkel, Johanna, 156
Kinkolith (B.C.), 134
Kirschhoff, Gustave, 72
Kirshenblatt-Gimblett, Barbara, 285
K'ivitung (Kiritung), B.I., 63
Knox, Helen, 284
Koelsch, William A., xi
Konenkov, Sergei, career, 226-228
*Korps* (fraternity), 22
Kossuth, Louis, 10
Krackowizer, Adelheid (Alice) (sister-in-law), 29-32,37,91,98,99,107,125. 191,216; death (1929), 231
Krackowizer, Alice Elizabeth (Bessie) (niece). See Elizabeth (Bessie) Johnson.
Krackowizer, Dr. Emil Washington, 91, 132; death (1924), 231
Krackowizer, Elizabeth Partridge, 91
Krackowizer, Emilie (mother-in law), 29-35,37,81,87-89,99,128,132, 141; death, 212; 223
Krackowizer, Dr. Ernst N. (father-in-law), x,8,10,11,30. EARLY YEARS 83-92; genealogy, 83; education, 83,84; chloroform experiment, 84; revolutionary and arrest warrant, 86; escape from Vienna; diaries, 87; AMERICAN CAREER. married, 87; medical career, 87,88; founder of German Hospital (later Lenox Hill Hospital), 88,89; Civil War Inspector

of Hospitals, 88,89; Committee of Seventy, 90; Greenmont (Summer home), 90,91; death, 91,92; 140,147, 150,157,198,215,216,248
Krackowizer, Ferdinand Stefan, 83
Krackowizer, Helene (sister-in-law). See Helene Meyer.
Krackowizer, Marie (wife), see Marie Boas.
Krackowizer, Mollie, 147
Krackowizer, Paul, 83
Krackowizer, Richard Franz, 91; death (1926), 231
Krackowizer, Simon, 83
Kroeber, Alfred, 109,120,121,128,132, 165; receives 1st Ph.D. in anthropology at C.U., 173,174; Boas as teacher, 173-175; 178,204,253,264, 269
Krohn, William O., 100
Krüer, Bertha, 131
Krüer, Reinhard, 21,131
Kudlich, H.C., 181
Kummer, Prof. E., 285
Kwakiutl Indians, 94,108,113,126,133, 262,273,284
*Kwakiutl Texts*, 135
*Kwak'wala* (language), 127,273,275, 286
*Kwakwa̲wa̲'wakw* people, 78,108

Lafayette, Marquis de, 253
Lake George, New York, 139-162,164, 172,204,213
Lakota Indians, 212
*Landsmannschaften*, 22
Langdon, George, 284
Lange, Adolph, 43,44
Langley, Samuel P., 171
Langmuir, Dr. Irving, 139
Languages, physiology of speech, 178
Lathrop, Samuel, 197
Laufer, Berthold, 172
Laura Jacobi School, 132
League for Political Education, 149
Lehmann, Hedwig (Hete) (sister), 11, 17,20,30,73,126190,191,195,216, 218,222,258,291
Lehmann, Rudolph (brother-in-law), 73,173,181; career, 190,191,291
Lemon, James S., 100
Lenox Hill Hospital 88,89. See also German Hospital.
Leon, Carl, 206
Lévi-Strauss, Claude, 259,271
Lewis & Clark Expedition, 253
Lewis, Prof. Herbert, xi,268
Lewis, Meriwether, 253
Liberal Republican Party, 157
Lincoln, Abraham, 89,155,156; Lincoln-Douglas Debates, 155; "All men are created equal," 266
Linton, Ralph, 207
Liszt, Franz, 82
Lombardo, Warren, 104
Longfellow, Henry W., 154
Low, Seth, 122,123,131,153
Löwenbaum, Emelie Boas (aunt), 6
Lowie, Robert Henry, career, 177
Luschan, Felix von, 73
Lytton, B.C., 94,126

Maass, Lilly Ottilie. See Lilly Meyer.
MacMillan, Donald, 166
Madison, James, 203,253
Mahlstede, A.F.B., 41,44
Malinowski, Bronislaw, 271
Mann, Bishop Alexander, 250
Manuscript Society, meeting in Victoria. B.C., 286
Maori chieftains, 284
*Marie*, dinghy, 45,47,49,50,53
Marshall, George, 251
Marshall, John, 253
Marx, Karl, 10, 85
Mason, J. Alden, 188,189,193,197
Mason, Otis, 92,170
Mathé, Barbara, x
Mazzini, Giuseppe, 10
McAneny, Arnold, 153
McAneny, George, 145,148,150; married, 151; career in New York City government, Acting Mayor of N.Y., N.C.S.R.L., A.N.P.A., honors, banking, Worlds Fair, 151-153; 164, 166
McAneny, Marjorie, 30,37,145,148, 150,151; married, 151; 152,153,198
McGee, W. J., 117,123,171,173,269
Mead, Edward Sherwood, 208
Mead, Emily Fogg, 208
Mead, Margaret, 195,197,207; early

life & education, 208; Somoa, 208, 209; emulates Boas, 209; A.M.N.H., 209; president of A.A.A. & A.A.A.S. & appointments, 209; 269; media, 210; falsely charges that Boas had a stroke, 211; 253,271
Mercer University, 205
Metternich, 84
Meyer, Abraham (uncle), 2,3
Meyer, Adele (cousin). See Adele Meyer Smutney.
Meyer, Alfred, 184
Meyer, Anna Emilie Helene (niece), 141,151
Meyer, Barbara L. (grand niece), xi
Meyer, Bertha (wife of Abraham), 3
Meyer, Emmy, 160
Meyer, Ernst Louis Henry (nephew), 141
Meyer, Fanny (aunt). See Fanny Jacobi.
Meyer, Florence Alma (niece), 141
Meyer, Helene (sister-in-law), 33,34,36 63,91,94,131,140,141,143,145,146, 150,151,212,216,223; death, 258
Meyer, Helene Alice Charlotte, 141
Meyer, Dr. Herbert Willy, 160
Meyer, Jacob (uncle), 8,12,63,81,93
Meyer, Jette (grandmother), 2
Meyer, Jonas (ancestor), 2
Meyer, Jonas (grandfather), 2,9
Meyer, Julius (cousin), 3,93,131
Meyer, Lilly, 116,159
Meyer, Louis Henry, profession, 139-149; partner of Samuel Tilden, 140
Meyer, Louise Wilhelmine Marie (niece), 141
Meyer, Margarethe. See Margarethe Meyer Schurz.
Meyer, Marjorie. See Marjorie Fleming.
Meyer, Richard (cousin), 131
Meyer, Solomon, 81
Meyer, Theodor (cousin), 3
Meyer, Theodore (brother-in-law), x, 91,93,131; profession, 140; purchases land in Bolton, NY, 140,141; created Alma Farm, 140,141; 143, 146,147,150,151,198
Meyer, Walter, 147
Meyer, Dr. Willy (cousin), x, 3,4,12,22, 63,93,116,145,147,152,153; medical training, immigration, surgical career, hospital appointments, 159; family, 160; home on Lake George, 161; death. 161; 164; 172,191,192, 198,216
Michelson, Dina. See Dina Namer.
Michelson, Ernst, 216
Michelson, Franziska. See Franziska Boas.
Michelson, Gertrud (granddaughter), xi,216,221,222,224,246,257-259, 281,282,292
Michelson, Dr. Nicolas (son-in-law), 161; career, 216; death, 216,217;247, 292
Miles, Vera, 90
Mills College, 178
*Mind of Primitive Man*, 181,264
Minden (Germany), history, 1,2; archives, 271; memorial lectures on 50th anniversary of death of Boas, 285; 1200th anniversary of Minden & memorializing of F. Boas & A. Jacobi, 286,287
Minik (Inuit), 119; adopted by William Wallace, 120,121
Mitchell, John Purroy, 152
Mohegan Indians, 175
Mohican Indians, 175
Montague, Ashley, 263
Montefiore Hospital, 160,215,216,228
Morgan, Thomas Hunt, 186
Mosakowski, Dorothy E., xi
Mount Sinai Hospital (M.S.H.), 149, 215
Müller-Wille, Ludger, xi,42,285
Murdoch, John, 63
Museum of the American Indian, (New York), 275
Mutch, James, 166,173

Nachojaschi, 49,51
Namer, Dina, 216
Nanimo, B.C.,78
National Academy of Science, 133
National Civil Service Reform League (N.C.S.R.L.), 151
National Federation for Constitutional Liberties, 251
National health insurance, 216
National Museum of Archeology

(Mexico), 190
National Museum of Man (Ottawa), 275
National Museum of Natural History, (N.M.N.H.), 92,169,172
National Research Council (N.R.C.), 168,196,209
National Socialist Party, 235
Native American Graves and Protection Act, 122
Nazi Germany, 251,259,266
Nettilling (Lake), 57
Newitti, B.C., 77,78
New School for Social Research (N.S.S.R.), 203,207
New York Academy of Medicine (N.Y.A.M.), 150,161
New York Academy of Science (N.Y.A.S.), 209
New York College of Pharmacy, 148
New York County Medical Society (N.Y.C.M.S.), 150
New York *Evening Post*, 157
New York Hospital, 176
New York Infirmary for Women & Children (NY.I.W.C.), 160
New York Postgraduate Medical School (N.Y.P.M.S.), 160
New York Skin & Cancer Hospital (N.Y.S.C.H.), 160
*New Yorker Staats Zeitung,* 63,64
*New York Tribune*, 156
*Nile*, whaler, 166
Nimpkish Indians, 78,94,99,273
Nootka Indians, 99
Nordsieck, Dr. Hans, xi
Northwestern University, x,203,204, 263
Nuktaq (Inuit), 119; death, 120,121

Oakley, Surgeon General S. Vanderpool, 89
Oak Woods Cemetery (Chicago), 109
Obbink, Dirk, 285
Oberlin College, 211
O'Brien, Judith (grandniece), xi
Ochs, Adolph S., 139,144
Ogburn, William Field, 204; career, 205
O'Keefe, Georgia, 139
Oregon, University of, 178
Osler, Sir William, 92,153,159,249
Quisuk (Inuit), 119; death & mock burial, 120,121
Oxford University, 252

Pacific Northwest field trips, 163
Paine, Halbert E., 155
Paine, Thomas, 253
Pantzi Lake, B.C., 126
Parsons, Elsie Worthington Clews, career, 204,207,263,269
Parsons, Herbert, 203
Parsons, Dr. Ralph, 90
Partridge, Elizabeth. See Elizabeth Partridge Krackowizer.
Pavia, University of, 84
Peabody, George Foster, 80,139,145
Peabody Museum of American Archeology & Ethnology, 193
Peale, Charles Wilson, 253,263
Peary Arctic Club, 118
Peary, Robert; expeditions promoted by Morris Jesup, 118,119; brings six Greenland Eskimos to A.M.N.H., 119-121; 248
Pennsylvania, University of, 177,187, 203
Philippe, King Louis, 85
Physician's Forum, 215,216
Pima Indians, 207
Pinsky, Dr. Valerie (great granddaughter), xi
Porter, Russell W., 61
Port Essington, B.C. 94,126
Post, Wiley, 218
Potlatches, 136; outlawed, 274,275; of Roy Cranmer, 283; at A.M.N.H., 284
Powell, Israel, 95
Powell, Prof. Jay., 286
Powell, John Wesley, 63,92,93,170, 171,193,267
Preble, Edward, 198
Price, David, 197
*Primitive Art*, 226
Princeton, University, 205
Putnam, Prof. Frederick Ward, x,75; early career, 80; 93,105,105; Field Museum is his idea but rejected as director, 109; returns to Harvard, 109,111; appointed as a curator at A.M.N.H., 112; 117-119,121-

124,134,163-165; joined University of California, 165-166; death, 193; 267,269
Putnam, George Haven, 151
Putnam, George Palmer, 30
Putnam, Mary Corinna. See Dr. Mary Putnam Jacobi.

Rabbe, Kate Rosalie. See Kate Rosalie Jacobi.
Racism, debunked, 102,111; 266, 267, 272
Radin, Paul, career, 177
Rand School of Social Research, 178
Randolph, Philip, 250
Reed College, 205
Reichard, Gladys, 204,207,221,265,269
Reichenbach family, 195
Republican National Convention (1860), 155
Revolution of 1848, 84-87; massive immigration to America, 87
Richter, Therese, 84
Rivers Inlet, B.C., 126
Rivers, William, 271
Rivet, Paul, 258,259
Roach, John, 51
Robeson, Paul, 225,226
"Rock Rest," 141-143
Rodin, Auguste, 225
Rogers, Will, 218
Roosevelt, Eleanor, 254
Roosevelt, Franklin D., 152,249,258
Rossignol, James E., 100
Royal British Columbia Museum (Victoria, B.C.), 272,286
Royal Ethnological Museum (Berlin), 72,73,133
Royal Ontario Museum, 275
Rubell, Prof. Paula, xi,285
Ruby, Jay, 271
*Rugia* (steamer to Germany). Fire on board, 98
Rush, Benjamin, 253
Russell, Bertrand, 248

St. Louis World's Fair, 167
St. Mark's Hospital, 149
Sakhalin Island (Siberia), 124
Salinger, J.D., 112
Salish Indians, 103,125
Samoa, 208
Sanford, Edmund C. 100
Sapir, Edward, career, 177; 178,204, 263
Saville, Marshall, 165,167,168
Schiff, Jacob, 128,173
Schott, Rüdiger, 285
Schulte,Dr. Monika, xi
Schurz, Carl, x,8; early years, 10; Revolution of 1848, 10,11; to America, 11; 76,79,85,87,88,91,93 99,143,147; cottage, 150,151, 153, 158; settles in Wisconsin, 154; political career, Minister to Spain, major general in Civil War, Secretary of Interior, U.S. Senator, editor, 154-159; Lincoln presidential campaign, 155; helped Franz Boas, 157, 158; death, 158,159,161; 164, 172,173,181,182,198,199,269
Schurz, Carl Lincoln, 158,182
Schurz, Emma, died as child, 158
Schurz, Herbert, 151,157,158
Schurz, Margarethe Meyer (wife of Carl), 11; death, 157
Schurz, Marianne, 158
Schwatka, Frederick, 59,63
Schwellenbach, Lewis B., 250
*Science*, 80,92,94,98-100
Scripture, Edward W., 100
Seler, Edward, 173
Seligman, Isaac, 173
Sembrich, Marcella, 139
Serrano Indians, 207
Seward, William, 155
*Shackles of Tradition, The*, Boas documentary, 271
Shapley, Harlow, 250
Shepard, Edward, 151
Sherman, James S., 182
Sherman, General William T., 156
Shorter College, 217
Shoshone Indians, 173
Shuh, Dr. Franz, 84
Sigel, General Franz, 156
Simpson, Sir James, 84
Sinclair, Upton, 250
Sinnott, Judge James P., 140
Sioux Indians, 168,211
Sisson, Helen T. See Helen S. Boas.
Skeena Indians, 106

Skeena River, B.C., 126
Skeletal remains; for teaching and anthropology, 122
Skiff, Frederick V., 110,125
Smith, Harlan I., 125,126,132,171
Smith, Murphy, x
Smith, Dr. Stephen, 153
Smithsonian Institution, x, xi,112; diorama, 114-116; 133,143,163,166, 170,204,267
Smutney, Adele Meyer 3,93,131
Southampton Island, 61,62
Spanish-American War, 128
Speck, Frank, career, 175,176,178,263; 269
Spencer, Stephen, 99,127
Spencer, Sir Walter B., 271
Spence's Bridge, B.C., 125,127
Spicer, John, 166
Spring, Josephine ("Jo"), 146,148
Ssigna (Jimmy), 49,51,53-56,64
Stanton, Edwin, 89
Stanton, Elizabeth Cady, 253
Steinmetz, Dr. Charles, 139
Steinway, Henry Engelhard, 87
Steinway, William, 88
Sternberg, Leo, 186
Stieglitz, Alfred, 139
Stocking, George W, Jr., ix,271,285
Stone, Harlan Fiske, 227
Storrs Agricultural College, 228
Strathman, 6
Strong, Charles, 101
Sturtevant, William, 271,285
Swanton, John R., 125,132; career, 175

Taft, William Howard, 182
Tammany Hall, 157
Teachers College (New York), 181,211
Teit, James, 125-127,132,173
Teit, Lucy Artko (wife of James), 125
Terris, Rita, xi
Thompson, Dorothy, 256
Tilden Samuel J. 140; presidential candidate, 140
TIME magazine, 254
Titchener, Edward B., 184
Tlingit Indians, 99
Totem poles, tallest, 273
Trask, Spencer, 139
Trattner, Ernest, R, 264
Truman, Harry S., 216
Tsimshian Indians, 94,99
Turner, Lucien, 63
Tylor, Edward Burnett, 99,117
Tyndall, John, 23

Uisaakassak (Inuit), 119,121
U'mista Cultural Centre (Alert Bay), 274; artifacts returned, 275-277; reunion gifts to, 280; 10th Anniversary, 283; 286
*U'mista News*, 277
United States National Museum (U.S.N.M.). See National Museum of Natural History (N.M.N.H.).
Urbach, Änna (Aenna) Margaret (sister), 11,17,20,30,105,126,195, 257,291
Urbach, Dorothy (Helga) (grandniece), 292
Urbach, Franz (nephew), 292
Urbach, Frida (nephew), 292
Urbach, Hedwig (Hete). See Hete Yampolsky.
Urbach, Helmut, (nephew), 292
Urbach, Ilse, 292
Urbach, Julius (brother-in-law), 105, 116,291
Urbach, Peter (grandnephew), 292
Urbach, Rudolph (nephew), 292
Urbach, Sylvia, 292
Urbach, Walter Ernst (nephew), 105,292
Urey, Harold C., 250,255
Ute Indians, 173
Ütütiak (Yankee), 51

Vancouver, B.C., 77,79,94,95
Vancouver Island, B.C., 77,78
Van der Sluis, Mariana Yampolsky (grandniece), 292
Vassar College, 207
Victoria, B.C., 77,78,94,95
Vienna, University of, 83,84
Village Island, B.C., 275,277,278; totem pole and "Big House" remains, 278,279
Villard, Henry, 128,153
Villard, Oswald Garrison, 153
Virchow, Dr. Rudolph, x,27,28,73,94,

196,248
Wagner-Murray-Dingell Bill, 216
Wallace, Henry A., 216,250
Wallace, William, 119-121
Warburg, Felix, 173
Wardboro Valley, 141
Washington, Booker T., 159
Washington, George, 253
Washington, University of, 204,205
Weber, Leonard, 181
Webster, Gloria C., xi; testimonial to Boas, 262; 271-273,276,277,279, 280,283,286
Weidman, Charles, 217
Weike, Matilda, 42
Weike, Wilhelm Heinrich Christian, 42-45,53-56,63,68
*Weimar* (steamer to New York), 105
Welch, Dr. William H., 153
Wenke, Wilhelm, 43,44,49,51
West, Gerald M., 100
*Westliche Post*, 156
Whaling, 51-53
Wheeler, Everett P., 181
White, Andrew D., 173,181
White, Walter, 250
Whitman, Charles O., 104
Whitney, A.F., 250
Wigman, Mary, 216
Wilhelm, Kaiser II, 190
Wilkes, Charles, expedition, 75
Williamsburg, New York, 83
Willis, William S., 271,272
Wilson, Woodrow, 152
Wilton, Connecticut, 214,245,246
Wincke, Wilhelm, 43,44
Windemere, B.C., 94
Windisch-Grätz, General, 86
*Windward* (ship to Greenland), 120
Winnebago Indians, 178
Wisconsin, University of, 248
Wishram Indians, 177
Wissler, Clark, background, 168; appointed curator of A.M.N.H., 168; professor of anthropology at Yale University, 168; 177,178
Wohlauer, Antoine (Toni) (sister), 20, 37; illness 23; 73,75,81,82,105,126, 195,240,241,257,291
Wohlauer, Elisbeth, 105; death, 116; 292
Wohlauer, Hans, 292
Wohlauer, Ludwig, 105,241,291
*Wolf* (ship to Newfoundland), 63
Women's Medical College (W.M.C.), 160
Worcester, Massachusetts, 99,101,103
Worcester *Telegram*, attacks Franz Boas, 102
Workingman's School, 93
World's Columbian Exposition. See Columbian Exposition.
World War I, causes, 194

Yale University, 177,203
Yampolsky, Cecil (son-in-law), 161; purchased farm in Cornwall Bridge, Connecticut, 214,224; 217,223,224, 228,229,247,263,292
Yampolsky, Helene Boas (daughter), vi,xi,42,98,104,107,111,130,131, 147,148,161,164,166,167,185,214, 217,221,223,224,229,257-259,262, 292
Yampolsky, Hete (niece), 292
Yampolsky, Mariana. See Mariana Van de Sluis.
Yampolsky, Oskar, 292
Yampolsky, Philip (grandson), xi,214, 219,223,224,257,259,281,282,292
Yampolsky (grandson), Robert, 214, 219,223,224,257,259,281,282,292
Yuchi Indians, 175

Zimbalist, Efram, 139
Zuni Indians, 207

## The Author

Norman Francis Boas, M.D., born in New York in 1922, is the son of the renowned cardiologist, Ernst Philip Boas, M.D. and is the grandson of anthropologist Franz Boas. After attending the University of Wisconsin, he earned his medical degree at Harvard Medical School. His medical career spanned a period of forty years during which time he did research in endocrinology and rheumatology at Mount Sinai Hospital in New York and served as an established investigator in biochemical and clinical research at the National Institutes of Heath. He was also a senior surgeon in the United States Public Health Service during the Korean War, an assistant clinic professor of medicine of Yale University, and practiced medicine in both Wilton and New London, Connecticut.

He was a senior attending physician at the Norwalk Hospital in Connecticut, director of the Research Department and chief of the Rheumatology Section and Clinic. In later years he served as a consultant in rheumatology on the staff of the Lawrence and Memorial Hospital in New London.

In addition to writing many scientific papers, he is also an historian and collector of manuscripts. He has published and edited many other papers and books on historical events and on individuals from the American Revolution to Abraham Lincoln. As president of the Stonington (Connecticut) Historical Society, he led a drive by the society to acquire the Captain Nathaniel B. Palmer House in Stonington. It was Palmer who discovered the Antarctic Continent in 1820 and was the leading designer of clipper ships in the 19th century. The house is now designated by the National Park Service as a National Historic Landmark and is open to the public as an interpreted site.

**Books by the Author**

*Coronary Artery Disease*, (with Ernst P. Boas), 1949.

*JANE M. PIERCE (1806-1863). THE PIERCE-AIKEN PAPERS*, 1983.

*JANE M. PIERCE (1806-1863) THE PIERCE AIKEN PAPERS. SUPPLEMENT*, 1989.

*Stonington During the American Revolution*, 1991.

*Colonel Jonathan Palmer's War Diary, Stonington, Connecticut 1774-1775*, 1992.

*NOD HILL, WILTON, CONNECTICUT, Reminiscences*, 1996.

*ALMA FARM – AN ADIRONDACK MEETING PLACE,* (with Barbara L. Meyer), 1999.

*SEAPORT AUTOGRAPHS*, 96 catalogues with brief biographies and descriptions of over 15,000 letters, documents and manuscripts of distinguished Americans, 1975-2004.